C0-ARR-806

Foreign Multinationals in the United States

Why do so many foreign firms in the United States experience disappointing performances?

The United States is the world's largest host economy for foreign multinationals. Although the growth and impact of these firms in the United States has been the subject of extensive studies, their management and performance has been largely neglected.

In this volume, leading scholars in international business and business history in the United States, Europe and Japan examine the experiences of a range of firms in the US. They look at British, Canadian, French, German, Spanish and Japanese firms, and span sectors including automobiles, banking, electrical goods, petroleum and steel. Together, their contribution presents a unique evolutionary and comparative perspective on the management and performance of foreign companies in the United States over the past 50 years.

This book will be of essential interest to all those with a professional or academic interest in international business, management, business history, or business in the United States.

Geoffrey Jones teaches at the University of Reading, UK, and at Harvard Business School, US. He has published widely on the history of international business, including *The Evolution of International Business* (1996) and *Merchants to Multinationals* (2000). He is currently completing a history of Unilever since 1965. Professor Jones is a former President of the European Business History Association, and currently President of the Business History Conference in the United States.

Lina Gálvez-Muñoz teaches at the University of Reading, UK, and the University of Seville, Spain. She was a member of the Unilever History Project from 1998 to 2001. She is the author of *La Compañia Arrendataria de Tabacos: Cambio Tecnológico y empleo femenino* (2000), a history of the Spanish Tobacco Industry based on her PhD thesis completed at the European University Institute in Florence in 1998. She has published various articles about the tobacco industry, gender and business, regulation and state-owned enterprises. Her current research is on the nationalization of foreign companies by Franco.

Routledge International Studies in Business History
Series editor: Geoffrey Jones

1 Management, Education and Competitiveness
Europe, Japan and the United States
Edited by Rolv Petter Amdam

2 The Development of Accounting in an International Context
A festschrift in honour of R.H. Parker
T.E. Cooke and C.W. Nobes

3 The Dynamics of the International Brewing Industry since 1800
Edited by R.G. Wilson and T.R. Gourvish

4 Religion, Business and Wealth in Modern Britain
Edited by David Jeremy

5 The Multinational Traders
Geoffrey Jones

6 The Americanization of European Business
Edited by Matthias Kipping and Ove Bjarnar

7 Region and Strategy
Business in Lancashire and Kansai 1890–1990
Douglas A. Farnie, David J. Jeremy, John F. Wilson, Nakaoka Tetsuro and Abe Takeshi

8 Foreign Multinationals in the United States
Management and performance
Edited by Geoffrey Jones and Lina Gálvez-Muñoz

9 Co-operative Structures in Global Business
A new approach to networks, technology transfer agreements, strategic alliances and agency relationships
Gordon H. Boyce

Foreign Multinationals in the United States

Management and performance

Edited by Geoffrey Jones and Lina Gálvez-Muñoz

London and New York

First published 2002 by Routledge
11 New Fetter Lane, London EC4P 4EE

Simultaneously published in the US and Canada
by Routledge
29 West 35th Street, New York, NY 10001

Routledge is an imprint of the Taylor & Francis Group

Typeset in Baskerville by Wearset, Boldon, Tyne and Wear
Printed and bound in Great Britain by MPG Books Ltd, Bodmin

British Library Cataloguing in Publication Data
A catalogue record for this book is available from the British Library

Library of Congress Cataloging in Publication Data
A catalogue record for this book has been requested

ISBN 0-415-25055-2

Contents

Figures

Tables

Contributors

James Bamberg took his PhD at Cambridge University. He is based at the University of Cambridge as Group Historian of the global oil company, BP. He has written two volumes of BP's official history, including most recently *British Petroleum and Global Oil 1950–1975: The Challenge of Nationalism* (Cambridge University Press, 2000). He is also a Visiting Fellow at the Centre for International Business History, University of Reading.

Ludovic Cailluet wrote a doctoral thesis on the structure of management at Pechiney between 1880 and 1970 at the University of Lyon which was awarded in 1996 the best European business history dissertation award of the European Business History Association. He has taught at the University of Reading and is currently Associate Professor at the Graduate School of Management (ESUG-IAE) of the University of Toulouse. He is also a Visiting Fellow of the Centre for International Business History, University of Reading. He has published articles about the history of the European aluminium industry and the international transfer of management models in *Accounting, Business and Financial History*, the *European Yearbook of Business History* and *Entreprises et Histoire*. He serves on the Council of the European Business History Association and is the secretary of the journal *Entreprises et Histoire*. His current research project deals with French foreign direct investment in the US since 1945 and the mutual transfer of knowledge between parent and affiliates.

John H. Dunning has been researching into the economics of international direct investment and the multinational enterprise since the 1950s. He has authored, co-authored, or edited 40 books on this subject and on industrial and regional economics. His latest monographs are an updated edition of *American Investment in British Manufacturing Industry*, first published in 1958, a new book of essays, *Globalisation at Bay*, and a newly edited volume, *Regions, Globalisation and the Knowledge Based Economy*. John Dunning is Emeritus Professor of International Business at the University of Reading, UK, and state of New Jersey Emeritus Professor of International Business at Rutgers University, New Jersey, US. In addition, he has been Visiting Professor at several universities in North America, Europe and Asia. He is also Chairman of the Graduate Centre of International Business at the University of Reading. He is currently Senior Economic Adviser to the Director of the Division on Transnational Corporations and Investment of UNCTAD in Geneva, and Chairman of a London-based economic and management consultancy, Economists Advisory Group Ltd.

Juan José Durán is Professor of Business Economics. He has written extensively on the internationalization of Spanish companies, multinational firms and international finance. He is the director of the Carlos V International Centre and former Dean of the Faculty of Economics and Business Administration in the Universidad Autónoma de Madrid. His work on Spanish multinationals is well known.

Wilfried Feldenkirchen studied economics and history and received his PhD in 1974, and his Habilitation in 1980. In 1982 he won the Maier-Leibnitz-Prize, and the Newcomen Prize in 1987. From 1980 to 1990 he was professor at the universities in Bonn and Saarbrücken. Since 1990 he has held the chair for economic and business history at the University of Erlangen-Nürnberg.

Lina Gálvez-Muñoz is Lecturer in International Business History at the University of Reading, UK, and in Economic History at the University of Seville, Spain. She was a member of the Unilever History Project based in London from June 1998 to January 2001. She is the author of *La Compañía Arrendataria de Tabacos: Cambio tecnológico y empleo femenino* (2000), a history of the Spanish Tobacco Industry based on her PhD thesis completed at the European University Institute in Florence in 1998. She has published various articles about the tobacco industry, gender and business and state-owned enterprises. She is currently editing a special issue on Spanish Business History on *Cuadernos de Economía y Dirección de Empresas*, and with Matthias Kipping a special issue of *Business History* on *Regulating Dependency: Government and the Business of Addiction.* Her current research is about the nationalization of foreign companies by Franco's regime in the 1940s and 1950s.

Geoffrey Jones is Professor of International Business History at the University of Reading, UK and Thomas Henry Carroll Ford Foundation Visiting Professor of Business Administration at the Harvard Business School in the United States. He is also Visiting Professor at Erasmus University, Rotterdam, Netherlands. He is the author of numerous books and articles on the history of international business, including *British Multinational Banking 1830–1990* (1993), *The Evolution of International Business* (1996) and *Merchants to Multinationals* (2000). He is currently President of the Business History Conference of the United

States and the Association of Business Historians in Britain, and is a former President of the European Business History Association. Professor Jones is currently completing a history of Unilever between 1965 and 1990.

Jean-François Hennart is Professor of International Management at Tilburg University, The Netherlands. He taught previously at the University of Illinois at Urbana-Champaign and at the Wharton School of the University of Pennsylvania. His research focuses on the transaction costs approach to international private economic institutions, such as the multinational firm and its contractual alternatives. He serves on the board of editors of the *Journal of International Business Studies*, the *Strategic Management Journal*, *Management International Review* and the *Journal of World Business*. He is the author of *A Theory of Multinational Enterprise* and has published extensively in international business, strategy, organization and business history journals on the theory of the multinational firm, types of market entry, joint ventures, international financial institutions, free-standing firms, and countertrade. He is currently involved in a study of exits of Japanese-owned affiliates in the United States.

Tyler Priest is a Visiting Assistant Professor of History at the University of Houston-Clear Lake. He holds a PhD in history from the University of Wisconsin-Madison. He is co-author of *Offshore Pioneers: Brown & Root and the History of Offshore Oil and Gas* (1997) and author of a forthcoming history of the Shell Oil Company. He is also completing a manuscript on the history of the US steel industry and its quest for strategic minerals.

Thomas Roehl is Assistant Professor of International Business at Western Washington University. He received his PhD from the University of Washington in Economics in 1983. He has taught at University of Washington, University of Michigan and University of Illinois. He is teaching courses on the international business environment, global strategy and Asian business. Professor Roehl's research interests include Japanese business relationships, alliances and foreign investment. He has done research about Japan in several industries, including aerospace, pharmaceuticals and trading companies. Recent papers include 'Trojan Horse or Work Horse', a study of the effect of Japanese investments in the US, and a study comparing the management styles of Korean and Japanese multinationals. He is a co-author with Hiroyuki Itami of a major work in *The resource based theory in the strategy literature: Mobilizing invisible assets.*

Graham D. Taylor is currently Professor of History and Vice President (Academic) at Trent University in Peterborough, Ontario. He received his PhD in History from the University of Pennsylvania and has taught at Dalhousie University in Halifax, Nova Scotia where he was also Dean of Arts and Science. He has a number of publications in the field of Canadian and international business history, including *DuPont and the International Chemical Industry* (with Patricia Sudnik) (Boston: Twayne 1984) and *A Concise History of Business in Canada* (with Peter Baskerville) (Toronto: Oxford University Press 1994).

Adrian E. Tschoegl has a PhD in International Business from the Sloan School at MIT, and a Masters in Public Administration and a BA in Political Science, both from UCLA, and is now professor at the Wharton School of the University of Pennsylvania. His research interests centre on international banks – who they are, where they go, when they go there, what they do there, how they go, and why they go. Adrian Tschoegl has published numerous monographs and articles in scholarly journals on international banking, Japanese finance, gold prices, and international trade and business. Prior to coming to Wharton, he worked for the Tokyo branch of SBCI Securities, a subsidiary of Swiss Bank, as a macro-economist following the Japanese economy. Adrian Tschoegl has also been a Visiting Scholar at the Bank of Japan's Institute for Monetary and Economic Studies and has taught at the University of Michigan's business school.

Fernando Úbeda is Associate Professor of Finance. He is a graduate in Business Administration from the Universidad Autónoma de Madrid, gained his PhD in the same university and is Master in International Business from the Centro Internacional Carlos V-UAM. Fernando Úbeda has a particular research interest in international finance and strategic management of multinational firms.

Mira Wilkins, Professor of Economics, Florida International University, Miami, Florida, has long specialized on the history of multinational enterprise and has published extensively on this subject. In the course of her research, Mira Wilkins has visited some sixty-three countries on six continents. Her two-volumes, *The Emergence of Multinational Enterprise: American Business Abroad from the Colonial Era to 1914* and *The Maturing of Multinational Enterprise: American Business Abroad from 1914 to 1970*, were published by Harvard University Press in 1970 and 1974. Earlier (in 1964) she wrote a history of Ford Motor Company's international operations. Her attention over the last quarter century has focused on the history of foreign investment in the United States. In 1989, Harvard University Press published her *The History of Foreign Investment in the United States to 1914*. A second volume, covering the years 1914–45, is forthcoming in the near future, while a third volume that is in process will span the years from 1945 to the present. The article in this volume previews some of the findings that will appear in far greater detail in the third volume of her history of foreign investment in the United States.

Kenichi Yasumuro took his PhD at the Kobe University of Commerce. He is now Professor of International Business, at Kobe University of Commerce. He specializes on theory, history and management of global business. He has published extensively about the subject, including Kenichi Yasumuro and D. Eleanor Westney 'Knowledge creation and the internationalization of Japanese companies', in Ikujiro Nonaka and Toshihiro Nisiguchi (eds) *Knowledge Emergence* (2001); Kenichi Yasumuro 'Japanese general trading companies and "free-standing" FDI after 1960', in Geoffrey Jones (ed.) *The Multinational Traders* (1998); and numerous articles and books in Japanese.

Ming Zeng is Assistant Professor of Asian Business at INSEAD. His research is focused on partner dynamics in strategic alliances and evolution of foreign direct investment. He has published in *Organization Science* and *Journal of International Business Studies.* Professor Zeng obtained his PhD in International Business from University of Illinois at Urbana-Champaign.

Preface

The idea of this book originated in a conference on *Management and performance of foreign companies in the United States*, held in Unilever House in Rotterdam in August 2000, and sponsored by Unilever within the Unilever History Project directed by Geoffrey Jones. During the research on the history of Unilever it emerged that that company, although one of the world's largest multinationals, accustomed to operating in diverse political and economic environments, had experienced acute difficulties managing in the United States. It seemed appropriate to establish whether this experience was unique, or part of a wider trend. It turned out that it was not easy to establish such a comparative picture. The United States is by far the world's largest host economy for multinationals, yet there is considerable anecdotal evidence about the managerial problems experienced by foreign companies investing in that country. Yet the number of well-documented case studies of such problems is remarkably small. We started to be as interested in the uniqueness of the United States as a host economy as the companies treated in this volume. Like them, we also had our 'American Dreams' and the conference and this volume is the outcome. We were lucky to attract an international team of scholars, drawn from the United States, Japan and Europe to participate in the project. Although each of the chapters in this book began their lives at the Rotterdam conference, they have all been rewritten extensively for publication.

We would like to thank Unilever for both sponsoring the project and allowing the editors absolute autonomy. Several individuals made important contributions to the successful completion of the project. We would like to thank Jaap Winter and Ton Bannink from Unilever for their helpful assistance and many kindnesses when organizing the conference. In addition to the team of contributors, who rewrote their original conference papers with remarkable thoroughness and speed, we would like to thank Ferry de Goey, Peter Miskell, Keetie Sluyterman, Barry Supple, Rob von Tulder and Joop Visser for their help as chairmen and commentators during the conference. We hope that the following pages will demonstrate the contribution business history can make to the study of major issues in contemporary business.

Geoffrey Jones
Lina Gálvez-Muñoz
Boston and Reading, January 2001

1 American dreams

Geoffrey Jones and Lina Gálvez-Muñoz

This volume is concerned with foreign-owned companies in the United States. During the postwar decades academic and media attention was focused on the enormous size and impact of US multinationals on foreign countries. They were variously lauded for transferring superior US management and organizational skills to the recipient countries (Dunning 1958) and condemned for their threat to national sovereignty (Servan Schreiber 1968). Multinationals were often treated as synonymous with American firms, and the reverse story – of foreign companies in the United States – was barely considered an issue. An article in the leading journal for the study of multinationals, *Journal of International Business Studies*, published in 1974, observed that 'almost nothing is known about foreign manufacturing investments in the United States' (Arpan and Ricks 1974). By then, however, foreign multinational investment in the United States was mounting. Twenty years later foreign investment in the United States was almost equal to American investment overseas. There has over this period emerged an extensive literature on the growth and impact of foreign business, written both by scholars and by others concerned especially to warn of its alleged dangers and threats.

The wide-ranging literature on foreign multinationals in the United States is reviewed below, but the purpose of this study is to focus on one major issue – the management and performance of foreign firms – and to examine it at the micro-level. While there is considerable anecdotal evidence about the managerial problems experienced in the United States by foreign companies, the number of well documented case studies is minimal, and the issue has never been addressed in a book-length study. This volume is distinguished by its attention to the experience of individual firms examined over substantial time periods since 1945. The studies include some of the largest inward investors in the United States, but also cover examples of smaller companies and non-traditional investors in the United States. The following chapters are written by some of the world's leading scholars on the multinational enterprise and business history. They are distinguished by their range of expertise and by the variety of national experience. The remainder of this chapter will provide some context for their studies and highlight the most important issues arising from their work.

The United States as a host economy

It is now widely acknowledged that worldwide foreign direct investment (FDI) grew to a substantial size during the nineteenth century, and that by 1914 its size relative to the world economy could be compared to that of the 1990s (Dunning 1983, Jones 1996). The United States was a very early pioneer of outward multinational investment (Wilkins 1974), but it was also a recipient of FDI from the colonial period, as foreign firms – like millions of immigrants – sought to benefit from the rapidly expanding market and rich resources of the country. As Wilkins has described, foreign companies from numerous countries and in numerous industries had invested in the United States by 1914 (Wilkins 1989). Although firms from the large European capital exporting economies such as the United Kingdom and Germany were pre-eminent, the range of inward investors extended from Japanese soy sauce manufacturers through to Bulgarian insurance companies. Given the great uncertainties of historical estimates of FDI, the relative importance of the United States as a host economy before World War II is somewhat unclear, but existing research suggests that it was the world's first or second largest host economy. Dunning's historical estimates suggest that the United States held 10 per cent of inward FDI in 1914 – almost certainly the largest single host economy – and 7 per cent in 1938, probably in second place to Canada which accounted for 10 per cent (Dunning 1983). In her rankings of individual host economies, Wilkins places the United States first in 1914 – followed by Russia and Canada – and second in 1929 – preceded by Canada and followed by India (Wilkins 1994).

Multiple factors lead foreign firms to invest in the United States. Following Dunning's eclectic paradigm, foreign companies can be seen seeking to exploit their 'ownership' or competitive advantages in technology, management, capital or ethnic links in the United States. However, it was really the locational advantages of the United States that led so many foreign firms to locate there. The United States was characterized by its large and dynamic market. The population of the United States grew from 40 million in 1870 to almost 100 million in 1913, and had reached 150 million in 1950. By the beginning of the twentieth century it was already the largest market in the world. Moreover, from the 1860s until after World War II it was protected from foreign imports by ever higher levels of tariffs. The United States not only had large markets, however, but also extensive natural resources of oil and land which attracted foreign firms.

The scale of the US market and its resources were not only huge, they were also accessible. While both the Federal and state governments restricted foreign ownership of firms in industries regarded as strategic or otherwise sensitive, such as banking and coastal shipping, and later air travel, overall the United States was and remained an open economy for foreign investors (Wilkins 1989: 607). The business system was also open: foreign firms were able to purchase US firms easily, if they had the money and if their American owners wished to sell. These locational factors continued to drive foreign investment into the United States after 1945, in the period covered by this study.

Although between 1945 and the mid-1960s the United States may have accounted for an astonishing 85 per cent of all new flows of FDI, as Wilkins shows in Chapter 2 the United States continued to be an important host for foreign companies. An estimate in 1960 identified the world's three largest host economies as Canada (24 per cent), the United States (14 per cent), and the United Kingdom (9 per cent) (Stopford and Dunning 1983). Subsequently the growth of FDI into the United States became a torrent. By 1980 the United States held 16 per cent of total world inward FDI and was clearly the single largest host economy. By 1998 the proportion was over 21 per cent. As in previous eras, the extraordinary size of the United States drew foreign firms to the United States. As tariff barriers fell, protectionism became a less important factor, but the growth of non-tariff barriers such as Voluntary Export Restraints (VER)s from the 1970s stimulated a new wave of import-substituting FDI, notably from Japanese automobile and electronics companies.

While the size of FDI in the United States had reached awesome proportions by 2001, it remained modest in proportion to the equally awesome size of the American economy. This had always been the case. Wilkins has documented the considerable impact of foreign firms on the US before 1914 in a range of industries, from pharmaceuticals such as aspirin through to artificial silk, cotton thread, brewing and chocolate (Wilkins 1989: 621–2). However, in the really critical and dynamic US industries of that era, such as steel, automobiles or petroleum, foreign participation varied from modest to non-existent. This remained true over the subsequent half century, though there were very important foreign-owned firms in particular industries. These included Shell's oil and chemicals business, whose post-1945 story is discussed by Priest in Chapter 10. In consumer goods, there was the remarkable growth of Lever Brothers – a subsidiary of Anglo-Dutch Unilever – whose sales of soap and, from the 1930s, edible fats rose from $1 million in 1913 to $200 million in 1946. Lever basked as one of the great consumer goods companies in the United States, alongside Procter & Gamble and Colgate. However, foreign-owned firms remained of relatively modest importance in the US economy, and in the major growth industries of the postwar years, such as computers, and in all the service sectors including banking, they were conspicuous by their absence.

As Wilkins notes in Chapter 2, there has been a radical shift in the relative importance of foreign-owned business in the United States since the

Table 1.1 Inward FDI as a percentage of GDP for US and selected countries 1980–97 (%)

	1980	*1985*	*1990*	*1997*
United States	3.1	4.6	7.2	8.4
EU	5.5	8.6	11.0	15.2
UK	11.7	14.0	22.4	21.5
Germany	4.5	6.0	6.8	9.9
Japan	0.3	0.4	0.3	0.6
All developed	4.8	6.1	8.4	10.5

Source: World Investment Report (1999).

1970s. While foreign firms have little presence in computers and in the entire IT industry, they have built a large and sometimes leading presence in chemicals, pharmaceuticals, petroleum, automobiles, electronics and banking, among other industries. The chapters in this book include studies of many of these industries. However, as Table 1.1 shows, foreign-owned companies remain significantly less important in the United States than in developed economies generally, though vastly more important than in Japan, as measured by the criterion of inward FDI as a percentage of gross domestic product (GDP).

A more sophisticated measure of the extent to which a particular host country is involved in international production is an index of 'transnationality'. This is based on the average of four ratios: FDI inflows as a percentage of gross fixed capital formation for the past 3 years; inward FDI stock as a percentage of GDP; value added of foreign affiliates as a percentage of GDP; and employment of foreign affiliates as a percentage of total employment. A calculation of such an index for 1996 shows the United States with a notably low transnationality index compared to most developed economies, marginally ahead of Germany and Italy and quite a way ahead of Japan, but significantly less than almost every other Western European economy (World Investment Report 1999: 17).

These overall measures of the importance of FDI in the United States need to be qualified insofar as the investments of foreign companies are unevenly spread over the country. Foreign firms invest in particular clusters, and the firms of different countries have different geographical distribution patterns (Coughlin 1993; Shannon, Zeile and Johnson 1999). There were some notable nationality clusters, such as the extensive concentration of businesses from Spanish-speaking Latin American countries in Miami, south Florida. There was a wide difference between states in the share of private sector employment accounted for by affiliates of foreign companies. In 1996 they were highest in Hawaii (11 per cent), South Carolina (8 per cent) and North Carolina (7 per cent). Japanese-owned affiliates contributed about 70 per cent to affiliate employment in Hawaii, whereas European-owned affiliates accounted for about three-quarters of affiliate employment in the Carolinas. In contrast, the employment share of foreign affiliates was below 2 per cent in Montana and the Dakotas, and apart from Hawaii the employment impact of foreign multinationals was concentrated on the East Coast of the United States. Yasumuro in Chapter 12 addresses, from a new perspective, the issue of geographical location and its consequences for the knowledge acquisition of foreign firms in the United States.

Although the firms of many countries invested in the United States after 1945, as previously, in quantitative terms there was an extraordinary concentration of inward FDI from Canada, a handful of Western European economies and – from the 1970s – Japan. The United Kingdom never lost its position as the largest single inward investor. Given that the United States was also the largest direct investor in the United Kingdom throughout the twentieth century – the UK hosted the largest single share of US FDI in 1998 (over 18 per cent of the total) – the image of multinational investment in the twentieth century as one essentially of cross-Atlantic investment flows between English-speaking economies is not too far-fetched. The United Kingdom, The Netherlands, which shared with the UK the ownership of two of the largest foreign firms in the United States (Shell and Unilever), and Canada formed a trio of persistent large investors in the country. In 1950 these three countries accounted for 54 per cent of total inward FDI in the United States. In 1998 they still accounted for 40 per cent. The other large investors were Switzerland, together with France and Germany. In contrast, some European countries were strikingly insignificant as inward investors in the United States. These included Italy with 0.47 per cent of total inward FDI in 1998 and Spain with 0.28 per cent (Survey of Current Business: July 1999). Durán and Úbeda in Chapter 7 provide an insightful account of the activities of non-traditional investors from Spain in the United States.

Table 1.2 gives the 20 largest foreign multinationals in the United States – defined as firms whose US operations have sales greater than or equal to $550 million and 3000 or more employees – at the benchmark date of 1997 according to the recent study at Wharton. It confirms the concentration of large inward investment in the hands of firms from a few countries, with the petroleum industry as the most obvious outlier to this generalization.

Table 1.2 has already in part been overtaken by major corporate restructuring, as firms continue to expand and rationalize their businesses in the United States. Major developments have included the merger of Daimler and Chrysler in 1998 to create the German-registered Daimler-Chrysler, which now employs over 120,000 people in the United States, and BP's acquisition of Amoco in 1998 and Atlantic Richmond in 2000, which resulted in nearly one half of BP's capital employed being in North America. Other major developments include Unilever's divestment of its US speciality chemical business in 1997, followed 3 years later by the

Table 1.2 The top 20 foreign multinationals ranked by sales of US operations, 1997

Parent firm	*Nationality*	*Industry*	*US sales ($000)*	*US employees*
Sony	Japan	Electronics	19,200,000	42,000
BP	UK	Petroleum	18,719,370	12,700
Seagram	Canada	Films/alcohol	17,250,000	31,500
Petroleum de Venezeula	Venezeula	Petroleum	12,969,363	4,900
Unilever	UK/Neths	Consumer	12,504,495	31,446
Shell	UK/Neths	Petroleum	12,404,700	20,467
Honda	Japan	Automobiles	10,351,805	12,887
Bayer	Germany	Chemicals	9,019,599	24,300
Aramco	Saudi Arabia	Petroleum	8,006,000	3,500
News Ltd	Australia	Media	7,752,322	13,084
Nestlé	Switzerland	Foods	7,646,300	35,500
Toyota	Japan	Automobiles	7,525,582	36,981
Philips	Neths	Electronics	7,159,195	22,800
Siemens	Germany	Electronics	7,159,195	45,140
Pechiney	France	Fabricated metals	6,976,512	33,619
Pharmacia	Sweden	Chemicals	6,932,700	30,891
Daimler-Benz	Germany	Automobiles	6,679,100	23,000
SmithKline Beecham	UK	Chemicals	6,649,537	19,900
ABBAsea Brown Boveri	Switzerland	Electronics	6,600,000	26,000
Bridgestone	Japan	Rubber	6,500,000	45,000

Source: Gittelman, Kogu and Barrett.

$24 billion acquisition of the foods company Bestfoods in 2000, and Nestlé's $10 billion acquisition of the US petfoods business Ralston Purina in 2001. Seagram left the list altogether following its acquisition by France's Vivendi in 2000.

In the following chapters, several of the very large investors seen in Table 1.2 will be examined in depth, while the experiences of others will be noted at least tangentially.

The performance of foreign firms in the United States

Before the recent past there is no systematic evidence on the performance of foreign firms in the United States. Given that the theory of multinational enterprise argues that foreign firms possess an 'advantage' when they invest in a foreign market, it might be anticipated that they would earn higher returns than their domestic competitors. It is therefore curious that from the time of Dunning's early postwar study – reported in Chapter 3 – onwards there have been repeated suggestions that, in aggregate, foreign firms may have underperformed their domestic competitors in the United States. As Wilkins notes in Chapter 2, 'case studies of foreign direct investors in the United States are strewn with stories of difficulties and lack of appropriate returns'.

Certainly, since the 1970s many foreign companies have experienced serious problems with US investment. These problems had a range of causes, including the sheer scale of the US market, its often ferociously competitive nature – a greater shock to European than Japanese companies – the difficulties of acquiring good US companies at a reasonable price, and many problems in the area of post-entry management (Rosenzweig 1994). Many British companies, by far the largest investors, encountered serious problems (Stopford and Turner 1985: 104); but the difficulties appear common to all foreign investors. 'To judge from the cases of Volvo and Ericsson', a major study of Swedish direct investment in the United States concluded in 1990, 'even large and internationally experienced Swedish multinationals seem to underestimate the difficulties presented by the US market' (Agren 1990: 213).

It is hard to provide generalizations from the case study evidence, except to say that the experience of foreign firms in the United States spans a wide spectrum from triumphs to catastrophes. Among the great triumphs before 1914 were the German firm Bayer's investments in dyestuffs and aspirin (Wilkins 1989: 389–90), though this venture was sequestrated as a result of World War I. It seems quite common for great success in one generation to be followed by subsequent failure or even withdrawal. This appears to have been the fate of almost all of the numerous British free-standing companies which invested in the United States before 1914 (Wilkins 1988). There are many other examples. Before 1914 the British merchant house Balfour Williamson constructed a large business empire on the West Coast, spanning shipping, wheat, land, financial services and large-scale oil production in California. But the oil was sold to Shell in 1911 and during the interwar years most of the other US business was divested (Jones 2000: 60, 101–2). The US affiliate of Courtaulds, the British rayon company, was highly profitable and successful in the interwar years, only to be sold to US investors during the crisis of World War II (Coleman 1969). However, there are also well documented cases of chronic failure, such as the British tyre company Dunlop's large-scale business in the interwar United States (Jones 1986).

The case study evidence on success and failure continues in the postwar years. Renault, among other European automobile manufacturers, floundered in the United States with the acquisition of American Motors. Renault's travails in the US automobile industry are rehearsed by Cailluet in Chapter 6. As Tschoegl describes in Chapter 8, British banks – with the conspicuous exception of HSBC – made large and spectacularly unsuccessful investments in the United States in the 1970s and 1980s, culminating in divestment on a large scale. The forays of the Japanese electronics giants Sony and Matsushita into Hollywood similarly became oft-cited classics of business failure. On the other hand, there were also many successful new foreign businesses built, sometimes in surprising sectors. For example, the British family-owned trading company John Swire & Co., which owned large transportation and other interests in Asia Pacific, became a US Coca-Cola bottler in 1978 and by the 1990s was counted among the leading US Coca-Cola bottlers (Jones 2000: 323).

During the postwar decades the same pattern of once successful inward investors losing their positions was repeated. A classic example was Lever Brothers, whose remarkable performance in the interwar years was observed previously. In the immediate postwar period the US share of Unilever's total sales and pre-tax profits was around 20 per cent. By 1977 the proportions were 6 and 2 per cent; this understated the scale of the problems at Lever, which was loss-making by that period, because the figures included the profitable tea and soup business of T J Lipton. During the late 1940s Lever was overtaken by its chief US competitor Procter & Gamble which introduced synthetic detergents. Lever's market share of detergents had fallen to 24 per cent in 1955, and 15 per cent by 1980. Its smaller toothpaste business, which originated through the acquisition of Pepsodent in 1944, was overtaken by Colgate, while its margarine business – also through an acquisition – only held a small market share. After the postwar loss of momentum, Lever went into a spiral of decline with insufficient investment in new products and brands and in manufacturing plant. The lack of strong brands left Lever with higher marketing costs than its US competitors, while cost-cutting at factories gave it higher manufacturing costs ('Unilever Fights Back in US' 1986; Jones forthcoming).

During the 1990s a number of studies attempted to investigate the issue of performance on a more quantitative basis. A study in 1991 using a sample of foreign-owned firms active in the United States between 1978 and 1988 suggested that the US subsidiaries of foreign-owned firms failed less than domestically-owned firms (Li and Guisinger 1991). In Chapter 11, Hennart, Roehl and Zeng pursue the issue of exits in a new study. However, most attention has focused on financial performance, where the overwhelming thrust of studies has been to suggest that foreign-owned firms earned lower financial returns than their domestic equivalents in the United States. These studies adopted several approaches. A major study in 1993 using tax data for the year 1987 showed the remarkably low returns of foreign-controlled companies, even when the data was broken down into non-financial, manufacturing and wholesaling industries, and when the ratios were recomputed using sales rather than assets as the scaling factor in the denominator. The key data from this study is given in Table 1.3.

Table 1.4 presents some of the conclusions from a new data set on estimates of the rate of return for foreign-owned US non-financial companies desegregated by industry and valued in current period prices for the period 1988–97. These estimates showed that the average return on assets (ROA) for the period 1988–97 was 5.1 per cent. The ROA for manufactur-

Table 1.3 Taxable income as a percentage of total assets and sales in foreign- and US-controlled companies in 1987 (%)

	Taxable income	*Assets*	*Taxable income*	*Sales*
	Foreign	*US*	*Foreign*	*US*
All industries	0.58	2.14	0.89	4.37
Non-financial	1.01	3.79	1.00	3.51
Manufacturing	1.60	4.94	2.39	4.21
Wholesale	0.68	3.24	0.29	1.41

Source: Grubert, Goodspeed and Swenson (1993).

ing was 5.8 per cent and for services 3.5 per cent. The ROAs in different manufacturing sectors varied widely, including 7.9 per cent in instruments and 7.6 per cent in chemicals, down to 2.3 per cent in electronic and other equipment and 0.5 per cent in motor vehicles and equipment. Most striking was the ROA Gap: the ROA of foreign-owned companies less the ROA of US-owned companies which is shown in Table 1.4.

The table shows that the ROA of all foreign-owned non-financial companies was consistently below that of US-owned companies between 1988 and 1997, though the gap narrowed over time. The ROA gap was negative in most industries, but in petroleum and chemicals it was positive, while the gap was especially large and persistent in services.

As Wilkins notes in Chapter 2, a variety of explanations have been explored for the apparent underperformance of foreign firms in the United States. A favourite explanation centred on the possibility of transfer pricing and the suggestion that foreign firms were actually doing better than it seemed, but this has proven hard to verify empirically. The 1993 study by Grubert, Goodspeed and Senson suggested that as much as 50 per cent of

Table 1.4 ROA gap of foreign-owned US non-financial companies, 1988–97

	1988	*1989*	*1990*	*1991*	*1992*	*1993*	*1994*	*1995*	*1996*	*1997*	*Aver-age*
All industries	−1.8	−2.1	−3.1	−3.1	−2.9	−2.6	−2.2	−1.9	−1.3	−1.0	−2.2
Manufacturing	−0.8	−1.3	−2.5	−2.6	−1.8	−1.4	−0.6	−1.1	0.1	0.9	−1.1
Food	−5.2	−9.2	−9.7	−8.0	−6.8	−5.2	−5.7	−6.8	−2.0	−0.6	−5.9
Chemicals	1.3	2.6	0.9	−0.1	0.3	1.8	1.7	−1.0	1.0	0.2	0.9
Petroleum/coal	2.4	4.2	3.9	1.8	3.1	2.7	3.6	3.4	4.8	5.1	3.5
Electronic	−6.4	−7.8	−9.1	−6.3	−5.9	−6.7	−5.2	−3.8	−3.8	−1.7	−5.7
Motor vehicles	−11.0	−13.0	−6.1	−4.8	−8.2	−3.7	0.7	1.3	−3.5	2.3	−4.6
Transportation	5.3	1.4	−7.8	−2.1	−0.6	2.3	0.6	3.8	5.3	4.4	1.3
Communication	−6.7	−5.1	−0.3	−3.3	0.5	−1.9	1.1	3.8	6.7	0.4	−0.6
Services	−5.6	−5.4	−6.2	−8.3	−7.7	−7.8	−9.3	−9.3	−7.7	−5.0	−7.2

Source: Mataloni (2000).

the difference in reported profits might be due to transfer pricing, but equally that none of the difference could be due to transfer pricing. Mataloni explored a number of different factors. On the whole, industry mix – or the concentration of foreign firms in low profit industries – was not seen as a problem. There was a significant influence of market share, and in general as a foreign-owned company's market share increased, the gap between its ROA and the average ROA for US-owned companies decreased. There was also a significant age effect. The negative ROA gap of foreign-owned companies tended to rise or fall with their degree of newness. One reason was that a large proportion of US companies acquired by foreigners had below average profitability (Laster and McCauley 1994). It can also be argued that a significant learning experience effect was evident. In general, Mataloni concluded that age effect and market share were the two most satisfactory explanatory variables (Mataloni 2000).

The most difficult variable to test, which is only partially captured by the age effect variable, is the issue of management failure or, more exactly, the question whether foreign managers found the United States a peculiarly difficult market in which to operate. It would certainly not be implausible to argue that managers from smaller countries, whether in Europe or Japan, found the large and diverse US market a complex one. The idiosyncratic US legal system added a further dimension of distinctiveness about the US. As noted above, there consists considerable case study evidence that foreign firms did experience such problems. The next section explores this issue in more detail.

A final consideration, although an important one, concerns the appropriateness or otherwise of using financial performance as a measure of success and failure. It is evident from the following studies that the United States was such a large and strategic market that many foreign companies felt they had to be represented there, almost regardless of the cost. Cailluet shows in Chapter 6 that this view was not confined to firms: the French government regarded it as strategically vital for Renault to be in the United States. This was very apparent in oligopolistic industries in which US, European and Japanese-based firms encountered one another. In the case of Unilever given above, Unilever's problem was not only that its returns from the US were small, but that its weakness in the United States enabled its global competitor Procter & Gamble to use profits made in that country to attack Unilever's heartland in Europe (Jones forthcoming). More generally, as Dunning notes, already in the 1960s British firms can be seen as engaging in what became known as 'asset augmenting FDI'. This issue is also discussed below.

Management control

Many of the chapters in this volume refer to the management problems experienced by foreign companies in the United States. It is the norm rather than the exception for foreign companies to experience cross-cultural problems in foreign countries, but what made the United States special was the size and strategic importance of that market, and perhaps the scale of the problems.

It is evident from many chapters that the issue of control lay at the heart of many of these management problems. Foreign companies made large investments in the United States which they then had difficulty 'controlling' in a purposeful way, especially but not only in the period between the 1940s and the 1970s. As Cailluet notes in Chapter 6, it took Renault a quarter of a century to get its managers into the US affiliate in which it first invested in 1977. Chapters 9 and 10 explore this issue in an exceptionally lucid way. Shell and BP, after its acquisition of Sohio, had majority control of US affiliates, but neither were able to exercise 'control' over these affiliates for sustained periods, until accumulated frustration led to radical intervention, the despatch of executives from Europe and the progressive integration of the US operations into the rest of the business.

The problem of exercising control over the US business seems to have been a general one. This issue lay at the heart of Unilever's problems in the United States, even though its two affiliates Lever and Lipton were wholly-owned. The strongly established tradition at Unilever was that local autonomy was best, and this was believed to be specially the case for the United States, where the outstanding successes of the interwar years had been under American management. The US affiliates were not part of the product group management system which developed from the 1950s, known as Co-ordinations (Bartlett and Ghoshal 1989). Lipton and Lever reported directly to Unilever's collective chief executive, the Special Committee, and had their own reporting systems. There was no transfer of personnel over the Atlantic, while even visits by European executives to the United States were strictly regulated (Jones forthcoming). As the performance of Lever in the United States deteriorated, Unilever in Europe began to consider ways to integrate the business more closely, and consequently to allow a flow of resource and knowledge from Europe to America, but the US management worked assiduously to preserve their autonomy. As a retrospective article described in 1986, 'while Unilever typically spreads the corporate gospel by circulating a cadre of expatriate managers through its subsidiaries around the world, it left Lever largely untouched, lurching from crisis to crisis under a succession of local managers'. Periodic initiatives to 'control' their US business made little progress until 1978 when, as part of a major policy shift – which also included a large acquisition – a main board director was sent to reside in the United States, who in 1980 became chief executive of the Lever affiliate ('Unilever Fights Back in the US' 1986).

Why was it so difficult to control American affiliates, even wholly-owned ones? At least three major reasons are evident. The first was anti-trust. Between the 1940s and the Reagan administration's relaxation of anti-trust in the early 1980s, foreign companies lived in fear of the mysterious but obviously potent power of US anti-trust laws. It was the unpredictability of US anti-trust laws that made them especially disturbing to foreign executives. Unilever became enmeshed in anti-trust following its acquisition of a synthetic detergent from Monsanto in the late 1950s; all through the 1960s and 1970s it received legal advice that it should not be seen to exercise too tight control over its US affiliates, in case its whole world-wide business was investigated, a fate which had earlier befallen the UK chemicals company ICI.

A second problem was that the US market appeared so unique in the postwar years that it was regarded as a special case. It was not simply its size and the high income levels which marked it out. A number of industries, such as banking, were extraordinarily isolated from the rest of the world. Brands, products and standards differed between the United States, Europe and other markets. Tea provided one example. Tea was largely drunk iced in the United States from at least the early twentieth century, a habit unknown elsewhere until the 1980s.

Over the last two decades the United States market has been partially integrated into the world economy, and this process underlay the series of interventions by foreign parents over the recent past designed to integrate American affiliates more closely with the rest of the firm. Yet the distinctiveness of the United States persists. One proxy measure is the information given on corporate websites. While in 2001 the websites of European and Japanese parent companies proudly stress their US affiliates, the websites of most US affiliates often barely mention any foreign participation in their business. This is the case of Mack Trucks, discussed by Cailluet in Chapter 6, and also many other firms. The website of Burger King hardly refers to its ownership by Britain's Diageo; nor does the website of Citizens Financial, New England's largest bank, refer more than very tangentially to its ownership by Britain's Royal Bank of Scotland. Shell's campaign to be seen as an American company, discussed in the chapter by Priest, fits here.

A third problem concerned the culture of US management and foreign perception of that management. In the wake of World War II, both Americans and foreigners had a general belief that US management was superior to, and more advanced in a range of techniques, to European, Japanese or any other management. This was an extremely widely held conviction in postwar Europe, where the US victory in the War was generally perceived to have been based on a superior business and political system (Zeitlin and Herrigel 2000). During the 1960s, the prestige of US blue chip companies such as IBM, Ford and Procter & Gamble was enormous, and the United States that could put a man on the Moon was also seen as the exemplar of best management practice. This situation had a number of consequences. It made little apparent sense for foreign managers to seek to control superior US managers, nor did it make sense for American managers to accept guidance from foreign managers. This situation changed, more especially with the growing competitiveness problems of the US economy from the 1970s, and by the following decade US firms were emerging as rather successful in learning from Japanese and other foreign firms.

Nonetheless, management problems for foreign firms in the United States have not gone away. Foreign firms continue to find it hard to attract and retain high quality American managers. In part this is because such managers are accustomed to being at the centre of decision-making and to have a career path open to the highest levels of a company. Given that the top echelons of European and Japanese firms remain dominated by home country nationals – as do those of US firms – this route to the top is seen as not available, especially as few Americans would wish to live outside the country for a prolonged period while working their way up corporate hierarchies. A further problem is that American managers have a strong emphasis on 'autonomy' and 'independence' which makes them resistant to control from elsewhere, especially if it is by foreigners. Relatively few Americans have knowledge or interest in foreign countries: currently only some 20 million Americans hold passports (Handy 2001). Many American managers experience difficulties conceptualizing a world outside the United States and corporate interests which could be separate from those of the firm in the United States (Rosenzweig 1994).

Foreign companies investing in the United States have to make choices between transferring or imposing their own management systems on American affiliates, or seeking to adapt to the local culture. As Yasumuro notes in Chapter 12, one group of Japanese inward investors, most notably the automobile assemblers, explicitly sought to transfer their management systems to the United States, choosing to locate their plants in regions with weak industrial heritages in order to facilitate this. These Japanese investors were not alone. Sweden's Volvo, following the acquisition of the White Motor Corporation in the 1980s, forcefully introduced a relatively paternalistic variety of the Swedish management style (Agren 1980: 149–73). However, the cost of not adapting to American management culture may be that learning about the US market is stunted, and that the foreign firm fails to capture the very entrepreneurship and innovatory spirit that makes investing in the United States so attractive.

The evidence presented here raises a whole number of conceptual issues regarding the definition of 'control' in a multinational enterprise. Evidently the ownership of all or most of the equity of a US affiliate did not bring automatic 'control' over affiliates during the postwar decades, beyond the receipt of dividends, and even then the payment of dividends was often a matter of negotiation between parents and affiliates. Beyond that, the amount of control exercised by a foreign parent – among them the largest multinationals in the world – was often fragile. From the late 1970s, company after company has intervened to exercise greater control over American affiliates.

Exploiting and acquiring knowledge

Although Dunning found only four companies which explicitly stated that their objectives in the United States were to exploit knowledge, it is probable that many companies, even in the immediate postwar decades and indeed earlier, invested in the United States to acquire 'knowledge' of various kinds, from marketing skills to technology. Feldenkirchen in Chapter 5 explores how Siemens sought to acquire knowledge through strategic alliances. Certainly from the 1970s a series of studies stressed knowledge acquisition as a major determinant of FDI in the United States (Daniels 1970; Ajami and Ricks 1981; Kim and Lyn 1987). From 1982 to 1992, the share of foreign-owned affiliate spending on total US private sector R&D increased from 9.3 per cent to 14.5 per cent. By 1992, US affiliates of foreign-owned firms performed $13.7 billion worth of R&D, employed over 100,000 people in US-based R&D activity, and accounted for 12 per cent of US jobs in high technology manufacturing activities. There were considerable industry-specific differences in this respect. Affiliate shares of US industrial R&D were particularly large in three manufacturing industries: industrial chemicals (47.5 per cent); pharmaceuticals (42.7 per cent); and audio, video and communications equipment (33 per cent) (Reid and Schriesheim 1996). Studies showed that these foreign firms were motivated by explicit strategies to acquire technology and to keep abreast of technological developments in the United States (Dalton and Serapio 1998).

While in theory the transfer of knowledge within firms should be considerably easier than through markets, many of the chapters in this volume show that this was not the case. This historical evidence certainly supports recent research suggesting that intra-firm knowledge flows are neither easy nor costless. Attempts to quantify intra-firm knowledge transfers historically are handicapped by the lack of convincing measures of what constitutes knowledge, but nonetheless the point comes through clearly from the evidence (Zander and Kogut 1995, Gupta and Govindarajan 2000). In the oil industry, Shell Oil in the United States developed a wonderful technological capability, the use of which was not fully accessible elsewhere within the Shell Group until 1984. In the reverse instance, the 'Chinese wall' separating BP and Sohio meant that the British parent's depth of organizational and technological resources could not be deployed in the United States.

Similar obstacles to internalization appear to have existed in other companies. The reasons lay especially in particular institutional arrangements within firms, and often in the unwillingness of US executives to compromise their autonomy. In the case of Unilever, the firm was the world's largest margarine manufacturer, but its Lever subsidiary in the United States ran an unsuccessful and low productivity margarine manufacturing plant. Similarly Unilever emerged by the 1980s as the world's largest ice cream company, but as late as 1989 Unilever held only 1 per cent of the United States' ice cream market. In both products, Unilever encountered through the postwar decades major problems transferring knowledge from Europe to the United States inside its own organization. On the other hand, the case of Unilever shows that even within the same company there were significant differences to knowledge transfer in different products. In the case of tea, Unilever's interests were more or less confined to the United States and Canada before the mid-1960s. In the United States, T J Lipton was the only national marketer of tea and supplied a large part of the national tea market. From the mid-1960s Unilever began to develop its tea business elsewhere, a process which led to its growth as the world's largest tea company through the acquisition of the Lipton tea business outside the United States in 1972 and Brooke Bond in 1984. Unilever was able through the 1970s and 1980s to achieve important transfers of knowledge from T J Lipton about the production and marketing of iced tea, specialty teas and instant teas, all developed in the United States. It often seems that US managers were more willing to transfer abroad superior knowledge than to receive it (Jones forthcoming).

In many cases foreign multinationals sought access to US knowledge through acquiring a US firm. Many of the firms discussed in this chapter grew mainly or entirely through acquisitions in the United States. Unilever's business was rebuilt through acquisitions, beginning with the acquisition of the specialty starch and chemicals company National Starch in 1978. This was acquired less because Unilever wanted a chemicals company than because it wanted a well managed company with strong management. Subsequently Unilever built a large new personal care business though acquiring a series of US firms such as Chesebrough Ponds (1986), Calvin Klein (1989) and Faberge Elizabeth Arden (1989), while its margarine (and later ice cream) businesses were rebuilt in the United States through the device of closing down their own plant and acquiring other firms. In the case of margarine, Unilever rejected a recommendation by McKinsey to close down its US margarine business in 1980, but it did close down its manufacturing plant and have its margarines largely made by co-packers, especially the Shedd division of Beatrice Foods. Then in 1984 Unilever acquired Shedd, which had just begun selling its own proprietary brands, and emerged as the largest and most efficient margarine manufacturer in the United States (Jones forthcoming).

It is evident that acquisitions represented an attractive but potentially hazardous way to acquire American knowledge. There was a noteworthy tendency for foreign firms to pay too much for poorly performing US firms, while the retention of senior management often seems to have been problematic. A recent study by Krug and Nigh showed that turnover of senior executives rose at about the same rate through the third year following a US acquisition – itself noteworthy given that foreign firms were often seeking access to US technology or know-how. Moreover, turnover in foreign acquisitions persisted through the sixth year after the acquisition, while turnover returned to a 'normal' rate in purely domestic acquisitions (Krug and Nigh 1998). This study raises the possibility that senior US executives were not comfortable working with foreign firms, perhaps because their own career prospects were not deemed satisfactory, or because of cross-cultural problems.

The most successful acquisition strategies seem to have included arrangements to retain local expertise. This became a key element in Unilever's strategy in the United States. In the case of the National Starch acquisition in 1978, the company's management was given assurances of autonomy, including that for 10 years National Starch would keep its own report and accounts, that no one from Unilever would sit on its board, and that Unilever and National Starch research would be kept separate, or rather that the Americans would have access to Unilever research and not vice versa. This remarkable agreement took place in the context of Unilever's arch-competitor Procter being an important customer of National Starch, so an arms-length arrangement of some kind was important. This was sufficient to keep National Starch's management in place, and to facilitate the desired knowledge transfer to the rest of Unilever, where chemicals had been a weak product area. By the mid-1980s, National Starch executives had assumed responsibility for Unilever's worldwide chemical business (Jones forthcoming).

The following chapters explore these and other issues related to the management and performance of foreign multinationals in the United States using a wealth of new empirical data and employing a strong evolutionary perspective which permits a clear understanding of the changing dynamics of relationships and situations over time.

References

Agren, L. (1990) *Swedish Direct Investment in the US*, Stockholm: Institute of International Business, Stockholm School of Economics.

Ajami, R.A. and Ricks, D.A. (1981) 'Motives of non-American firms investing in the United States', *Journal of International Business* 12: 25–34.

Arpan, J.S. and Ricks, D.A. (1974) 'Foreign direct investments in the US and some attendant research problems', *Journal of International Business Studies* 5, 1: 1–7.

Bartlett, C.A. and Ghoshal, S. (1989) *Managing Across Borders*, Boston, Mass: Harvard Business School Press.

Coleman, D.C (1969) *Courtaulds*, vol. 2, Oxford: Clarendon Press.

Coughlin, C.C. (1993) 'Cross-country locational differences of foreign manufacturers in the United States', in D. Woodward and D. Nigh (eds) *Foreign Ownership and the Consequences of Direct Investment in the United States*, Westport, Conn: Quorum.

Dalton, D.H. and Serapio, M.G. (1998) 'Foreign R&D facilities in the United States', in D. Woodward and D. Nigh (eds) *Foreign Ownership and the Consequences of Direct Investment in the United States*, Westport, Conn: Quorum.

Daniels, J.D. (1970) 'Recent foreign direct manufacturing investment in the United States', *Journal of International Business Studies* 1, 1: 125–32.

Dunning, J.H. (1958) *American Investment in British Manufacturing Industry*, London: Allen & Unwin.

—— (1983) 'Changes in the level and structure of international production; the last one hundred years', in M.C. Casson (ed.) *The Growth of International Business*, London: Allen & Unwin.

Gittelman, M., Kogut, B. and Barrett, R. (2000) *The Continuing Impact of Foreign Multinationals on the United States Economy*, Philadelphia: The Wharton School.
Grubert, H., Goodspeed, T. and Swenson, D. (1993) 'Explaining the low taxable income of foreign-controlled companies in the United States', in A. Giovannini, R. Glenn Hubbard and J. Slemrod (eds) *Studies in International Taxation*, Chicago: University of Chicago Press.
Gupta, A.K. and Govindarajan, V. (2000) 'Knowledge flows within multinational corporations', *Strategic Management Journal* 21: 473–96.
Handy, C. (2001) 'Tocqueville revisited. The meaning of American prosperity', *Harvard Business Review* January: 57–63.
Jones, G.G. (ed.) (1986) *British Multinationals: Management, Ownership and Performance*, Aldershot: Gower.
—— (1996) *The Evolution of International Business*, London: Routledge.
—— (2000) *Merchants to Multinationals*, Oxford: Oxford University Press.
—— (forthcoming) *A History of Unilever since 1965*.
Kim, W.S. and Lyn, E.O. (1987) 'Foreign direct investment theories, entry barriers, and reverse investment in US manufacturing industries', *Journal of International Business Studies* 118, 2: 53–67.
Krug, J.A. and Nigh, D. (1998) 'Top management turnover: comparing foreign and domestic acquisitions of US firms', in D. Woodward and D. Nigh (eds) *Foreign Ownership and the Consequences of Foreign Direct Investment in the United States*, Westport, Conn: Quorum.
Laster, D.S. and McCauley, R.N. (1994) 'Making sense of the profits of foreign firms in the United States', *Federal Reserve Bank of New York Quarterly Review* 19, 2: 44–75.
Li, J. and Guisinger, S. (1991) 'Comparative business failures of foreign-controlled firms in the United States', *Journal of International Business Studies*, 22, 2: 209–24.
Mataloni, R.J. (2000) 'An examination of the low rates of return of foreign-owned US companies', *Survey of Current Business*: 55–73.
Reid, P.P. and Schriesheim, A. (eds) (1996) *Foreign Participation in US Research and Development. Asset or Liability?* Washington, DC: National Academy Press.
Rosenzweig, P.M. (1994) 'The new "American challenge": Foreign multinationals in the United States', *California Management Review* 36, 3: 107–23.
Servan-Schreiber, J.J. (1968) *The American Challenge*, New York: Atheneum.
Shannon, D.P., Zeile, W.J. and Johnson, K.P. (1999) 'Regional patterns in the location of foreign-owned US manufacturing establishments', *Survey of Current Business* 79, 5: 8–25.
Stopford, J. and Dunning, J.H. (1983) *Multinationals: Company Performance and Global Trends*, London: Macmillan.
Stopford, J. and Turner, L. (1985) *Britain and the Multinationals*, Chichester: John Wiley.
Survey of Current Business (July 1999), Washington D.C.: US Department of Commerce.
'Unilever fights back in the US' (1986) *Business Week* 26 May.
Wilkins, M. (1970) *The Making of Multinational Enterprise*, Cambridge, Mass: Harvard University Press.
—— (1974) *The Maturing of Multinational Enterprise*, Cambridge, Mass: Harvard University Press.
—— (1988), 'The free-standing company, 1870–1914', *Economic History Review* 15, 3: 483–510.
—— (1989) *The History of Foreign Investment in the United States to 1914*, Cambridge, Mass: Harvard University Press.
—— (1994) 'Comparative hosts', *Business History* 36, 1: 18–50.
World Investment Report (1999), New York: United Nations.
Zander, U. and Kogut, B. (1995) 'Knowledge and the speed of the transfer and imitation of organizational capabilities: An empirical test', *Organisation Science* 6, 1: 76–92.
Zeitlin, J. and Herrigel, G. (eds) (2000) *Americanisation and its Limits*, Oxford: Oxford University Press.

2 An overview of foreign companies in the United States, 1945–2000[1]

Mira Wilkins

When I started to write this chapter in the summer of 2000, I read on-line: 'Terra buys Lycos in $12.5 billion deal'. The Spanish acquirer, Terra Networks, was an Internet provider, an affiliate of the Spanish Cia. Telefónica (which in recent years had become a major multinational enterprise).[2] Telefónica was Spain's largest business (Carreras and Tafunell 1997: 284). In 1997, the state-owned Telefónica had been privatized. It lost its 'monopoly' in Spain, and thus Telefónica had diversified its product lines and moved internationally. Terra Networks reflected the new order. Its American target, Lycos, was also an Internet provider, one of the numerous Internet firms that had emerged in the United States in the late 1990s. Headquartered in Waltham, Mass., Lycos had in 1999 sales of $137 million and a loss of $52 million. Its initial public offering had been in April 1996. By the time of the foreign take-over, it was America's fourth largest Internet portal. Of the three companies participating in this transaction – Telefónica, its affiliate Terra Networks, and Lycos – only Telefónica pre-dated the 1990s. When the merger was consummated in October 2000, the value of the 'deal' had been reduced to $4.5 billion (*Financial Times* 2000c). What was remarkable about the Terra-Lycos merger was how it reflected the huge sums offered and spent on US acquisitions in 2000 ($12.5 billion and then $4.5 billion – both huge sums – for a firm with $137 million in sales and no profits!). Second, how rapidly values fluctuated. And, third, how indicative the transaction was of the novelties of the new century – the telecommunications revolution, the newly privatized Spanish giant's expanding into the United States and using its core competence to seek to reach the Spanish-speaking population in the United States through the take-over of a newly formed company in a new industry (Telefónica 2000). In a sense this acquisition captured so much of the contemporary story line – not only in its size, but in its symbolism: new business actors in an increasingly globalized economy, where the United States (albeit internationalized) is central. All participants in the world economy had to be in the United States, whether through new establishments or acquisitions.

Another merger of 2000 told a similar tale. The French Vivendi (the old Générale des Eaux, transformed from a supplier of water into a media conglomerate) announced the purchase of Seagrams, a Canadian enterprise whose US business had for two generations – that is since the 1930s – exceeded its Canadian operations (*Financial Times* 2000a). The merger of the French and Canadian companies had major US spill-over effects. This was not atypical. Mergers of large foreign companies usually have had ramifications in the United States.

Today's businesses, no matter where they are headquartered, (if they are to be important) have to have a US presence; interestingly, this notion characterized not only the start of the new millennium, but also almost all of the twentieth century. That century has been legitimately labeled 'the American Century', for what happened in the United States has had consequences everywhere. Throughout the past 100 years, the United States has been the leading economic power, a position ratified after World War I and unambiguously reconfirmed after World War II. By the end of World War II, with European economies in disarray, with the Russian economy struggling to recover from the damages of war, with Japan a defeated power, with China poised for its transformation into a communist state, the United States stood tall as a strong, mighty economic and political force.

The decades after World War II saw the internationalization of American economic life, increasing, not evenly, not steadily, but nonetheless occurring in an unprecedented manner (Wilkins in process). At the start of the twenty-first century, an American might wake up and brush his/her teeth with a plastic toothbrush; the crude oil that went into making that plastic might be from Nigeria, imported by a foreign-owned multinational enterprise (MNE). The plastic itself might be made by a German MNE in the United States. The American might wash his/her face with Lux soap, produced in the United States, by a British-Dutch MNE. He/she would likely turn on a TV set, which might carry a familiar, well-known American brand, but be sold by a French MNE that 'owned' the brand name. The American might drive to work in a Honda, built in a factory in Maryville, Ohio. The car might be insured by Kemper Corp., owned by a Swiss MNE (Zurich Insurance). Perhaps, the driver was worried about catching cold; he/she might take an aspirin, made in the United States by the German Bayer.[3] At the office, the Internet servers would be likely to be American (but with Lycos Spanish-owned this was beginning to change).[4] Lunch might be at Burger King, owned by a British MNE (Diageo). We could go on.

By 2000 the internationalization of US daily life was far from intrusive, yet it was deep not superficial. At the start of the new millennium, Americans had come to take for granted (to accept) US-made Japanese cars; that Zurich Insurance owned one of the largest American insurance groups made little difference to the latter's long time customers; few Americans knew (or cared) that Burger King was British-owned (ask most Burger King consumers if they had heard of Diageo or its predecessor

Grand Metropolitan and no doubt there would be a blank stare). In 2000 the computer industry was overwhelmingly American (although barely a decade earlier, there had been worries lest the Japanese come to dominate this post-World War II industry). Nonetheless, anti-foreign, nationalist sentiments were not 'dead'. When it appeared that the big domestic merger with international implications, the WorldCom take-over of Sprint, would falter (and soon did), rumours circulated that Deutsche Telekom would acquire Sprint, one of America's leaders in long-distance service. The rumours sparked opposition in the US Senate to a 'foreign government-owned' acquirer (*Miami Herald*, 4 July 2000).

In 1945, some aspects of this internationalization were not only in place, they were of long-standing: Shell and Unilever were important enough for their products to have been incorporated in Americans' routine existence. Seagrams had larger operations in the United States than in Canada, where it was headquartered, and its alcoholic beverages were familiar fare. Other 'foreign-owned' companies and their brands were well known to the average American, and not because of imports but because of foreign direct investments (FDI). The difference between 1945 and 2000 lies in the extent and depth of the internationalization of the US economy. And what is particularly awesome is the size of some of the recent take-overs of US companies by investors from overseas, along with the linkage effects of mergers abroad on the US domestic economy. Over the years there had always been both new entries and take-overs, but the extent of the 1998–2000 foreign acquisitions had no precedent.

Because the United States has been over many years so great a host to FDI, there has been during 1945–2000 a formidable set of writings that cover all aspects of this subject: there are abundant books, journal articles, dissertations, unpublished papers, as well as government surveys, reports, and hearings, to say nothing of the newspaper and magazine commentaries. The post-World War II published materials came in waves, with the first set beginning in the late 1940s (mainly an academic collection of books and papers) and documenting the pre-1914 British role in the development of the American West (assuming the British firms' activities in the United States to be part of an age gone by that required recording) (for example, Brayer 1949; Clements 1953; Spence 1958; Jackson 1968). A popular and large group of writings emerged in the 1970s, with titles such as *The Infiltrators* (1971) and *America for Sale* (1978). Although some of these studies considered historical data, most of this second wave of publications dealt with the newly accelerating foreign inward investments of the 1970s (for example, Faith 1971; Crowe 1978; most important, US Department of Commerce 1976; historical writings, still on the American frontier, included Kerr 1976). This set of publications came as inward FDI expanded rapidly in the 1970s and as economic growth in the American economy seemed somewhat eclipsed (US growth rates were substantially lower than in the 1960s). A third wave of writings on inward FDI arrived in the late 1980s, reflecting the even greater influx of FDI and Americans' worries over the nation's economic position in the world economy. There were 1988–9 titles such as *Buying into America: How Foreign Money is Changing the Face of Our Nation*, *The New Competitors*, and *Selling Out* (Tolchin and Tolchin 1988; Glickman and Woodward 1989; Frantz and Collins 1989) along with ones on history, seeing its relevance to the contemporary scene (Wilkins 1989). Edward M. Graham and Paul Krugman's excellent 1989 book *Foreign Direct Investment in the United States* soon appeared in a second and then a third edition, each with revisions (Graham and Krugman 1989, 1991, 1995). The *Annals*, always up-to-date, had a 1991 issue devoted to all facets of FDI in the United States (Ulan 1991). Robert Lipsey (in 1993) published an article entitled 'Foreign Direct Investment in the United States: Changes over Three Decades' (Lipsey 1993). The stream of publications flowed on in the 1990s, even as the FDI in the United States for a while grew more slowly and for the most part no longer shocked Americans (see, for example, Woodward and Nigh (eds.) 1998). The 1998–2000 surge in take-overs is already provoking a flood of new publications.

Over the decades, the great quantity of commentaries (and the above is merely a tiny sample) has ranged from passionate pieces expressing outrage to quiet serious analyses. Detailed academic research came from business school professors, and from experts in economics, political science, law, geography, sociology, history, et cetera (the et cetera included works of accountants to regional specialists). Government hearings and government-sponsored reports evaluated how inward foreign investors affected and were affected by public policies on anti-trust, discrimination in hiring, tax revenues, trade, and bank safety. There were studies on how to attract to the United States additional foreign MNEs, and also many others on the costs as well as the benefits of these investors. Published and unpublished research was narrow and broad, general or source-country, industry-, or US-region specific; some studies dealt with particular foreign companies' investment decisions in a single locale. Numerous directories tabulated the various participants in inward FDI.

After this 'glut', is there anything new to be said about foreign business, its management, and its performance in the United States in the post-World War II years? I think so. The perspective of five and a half decades supplies us with an opportunity to consider significant trends. Thus, I do not want to repeat what is widely available. Rather, I seek to offer a broad-brush interpretation of the way I personally see the paths of foreign MNEs in the United States since World War II. Unless otherwise indicated, much of what follows is based on material prepared in connection with my history of foreign investment in the United States (Wilkins in process).

As a start, before I explore the post-World War II patterns, three 'contextual perspectives' are essential. First, a view of the nation itself: by all measures the United States is immense – in physical size, in population size, in gross national product size. It abuts Canada to the North (which covers slightly more space but is much smaller in population and GNP) and Mexico to the South. Some statistics from 1998: geographical size ('surface area' in square kilometres): US 9.36 million, Canada 9.97 million, Mexico 1.96 million; population size: US 270 million, Canada 31 million, Mexico 96 million; GNP: US $7.9 trillion, Canada $612.2 billion, Mexico $380.9 billion) (*World Development Report* 1999–2000: 230–1). The United States is not only large by every criterion, but it is diverse, both geographically (physically) and ethnically. Its various states, however, from 1789 onward, were in a 'common market', not permitted under the Constitution to erect tariff barriers; the Federal government alone had this right. From 1945 to the early 1960s, this common market was a highly protected one, separated from the rest of world by long-standing tariffs, and also from Europe and Asia by the wide Atlantic and Pacific Oceans. From 1962 onwards, US Federal governmental-imposed barriers to trade fell rapidly. Transportation costs went down sharply, and when in the 1960s jet travel became the norm, America moved closer to the rest of the world, linked through unprecedented movements of individuals, including those associated with business activities. Communications further improved and became cheaper, as telex, international telephone, fax and, in the late 1990s, Internet reduced distances. While, historically, many foreign MNEs had invested in the United States to get behind (within the confines of) the tariff wall, while many continued to invest to avoid actual or potential barriers to trade (in time, mainly non-tariff barriers), what was always most attractive to foreign companies about the United States as a locale for investment was the sheer size of economic opportunities, the importance of the United States relative to other nations. There persisted a 'geographic distance' from Europe and Asia and a need by businesses to be near customers. Awareness of the opportunities (information and knowledge) rose as the costs of transportation and communication dropped. Since 1994, Canada, Mexico, and the United States have been joined in the North American Free Trade Agreement (NAFTA), which has altered the economic relationships among the three countries, even though many of the close continental trade and investment connections preceded NAFTA. Throughout, the *national* identity of each country in this trade agreement has remained vigorous. NAFTA does not carry with it any loss of political sovereignty, although there is considerable evidence that it has affected the investment configurations of some foreign enterprises within the United States.

The second contextual point is that throughout the period under consideration, the years after World War II to the present, using historical cost as a measure, the level of US direct investment abroad has exceeded that of FDI in the United States; in the 1970s and 1980s the ratio moved toward 1:1 and by the end of the 1980s, some observers assumed that FDI in the United States would soon surpass US business abroad. The path was not straight, however, and in the 1990s, US business at home and abroad renewed its strength; while FDI in the United States continued to mount (particularly at the end of the 1990s), the ratio of American business abroad to foreign business in the United States grew and then stayed steady, rather than contracted. Contrary to the predictions, measured by historical cost, the level of FDI in the United States never outstripped that of US business abroad (Lipsey 1993: 117; *Survey of Current Business* 1950–2000, 1999b: 50, 2000b: 59).[5] The point needs to be made, however, that in the postwar period, just as in prior times, FDI was always a two-way street and the lanes were always of different widths.[6] Thus, both American companies' building on the advantage of the opportunities (and knowledge generated) at home expanded abroad, while foreign companies' recognizing some of those same opportunities in the United States entered and developed new business with alacrity. The process was synergistic.

The third contextual commentary deals with the dramatic changes in the world economy since 1945. It has not only been the 'pull' of the United States that has brought the rise in inward FDI, but economic expansion around the world has meant the growth of enterprises (particularly in Europe and Japan) able to take advantage of those opportunities available in America. In addition, decolonization and the anti-MNE views that often accompanied decolonization resulted in the need for European firms to shift their perspective; at the same time, a communist China for several decades diverted Japanese MNEs away from their nearby market toward the United States. In western Europe and Japan corporate structures evolved differently in different nations (Group of Thirty 1999), but the attraction of the United States as a locale for MNE expansion was shared.

Let us turn now to explaining the inward FDI in the United States in more detail. What were the trends related to this inward FDI from 1945 to 2000? What was important about it? What distinguished the inward FDI of 1945–70 (when US business abroad was in the spotlight) from the FDI after the 1970s when the numerators and the denominators in the cross-investment ratios – based on historical costs – became very close and then separated? How do the changes in the world economy affect the rise of FDI in the United States? Let us look at these matters from five separate vantage points: (1) the nationality of investors in the United States (composition and experience); (2) the industries transformed within the United States; (3) the regions within the United States affected; (4) the performance of foreign MNEs; and (5) the changing public policies toward the inward FDI.

Nationality

In 1945 (and in 1950; I will use the 1950 figures since they are available), in 2000 (I will use 1999 figures as the latest available at the time of writing), as in 1900 and in 1914 (and in the interwar years), British direct investment in the United States exceeded that by any other single foreign nationality (Wilkins (ed.) 1977; *Survey of Current Business* 2000b; Wilkins 1989, forthcoming). This transatlantic association, this 'special relationship' between the UK and the US, was not a source of conflict in the period after World War II, although there had been a long history of ambivalence on the part of Americans and a strong strain of populist anti-British feeling that had periodically surfaced in various assertions of US sovereignty (Wilkins 1989, forthcoming, in process; Moser 1999).

While, in the 1950s, scholars were documenting the end to the era of British cattle ranches and British contributions to the making of the American West, the British (actually British-Dutch) Lever Brothers were constructing a New York office building that was an architectural icon, symbolic of the 'new America' (Wilkins in process). In the early 1960s, there was a fair number of British companies in the United States that had been in business in this country for much of the twentieth century and some that extended back to the nineteenth century (Dunning 1960–1; Wilkins 1989, forthcoming; on these, see Dunning, Chapter 3 of this volume). In the 1960s, 1970s, 1980s, and 1990s, British firms expanded in the United States, encountering the repeated experience that although Americans spoke English and had a British heritage, there was something unique about the country, something unfamiliar and not to be taken for granted. British companies faced the constant dilemma of either trusting to American managers, or installing men from the home office. In any case, British companies felt it imperative to be present in the United States.

In 1950, in terms of FDI in the United States, Canadians ranked a very close second to their transatlantic mother country ($1,029 million compared with $1,168 million). Canadian importance in the United States was because of language, proximity, and the particular conditions arising from World War II. Like British FDI, Canadian FDI had a lengthy history in the United States. In the first year that the Commerce Department published figures on inward FDI by nationality (1934), UK direct investments were 45 per cent of the total, while the Canadians were already in second place with about 24 per cent of the total (US Department of Commerce 1937: 32–3). With the inward Canadian direct investments, there was rarely friction between Americans and their northern neighbours (an exceptional case of conflict arose when the Canadian government-owned Canada Development Corporation took over Texasgulf in 1973) (Lamont 1979: 20–3).[7] US direct investments in Canada were always larger than vice versa; while Canadians expressed great concern about inward US investments, Americans were generally complacent about the counterpart relationship. Indeed, when the US Department of Commerce began collecting systematic information on US business abroad, it had to specify

Table 2.1 Foreign direct investment in the US (in US$ millions) by nationality, 1999, 1950

Rank and nationality – 1999		*Rank and nationality – 1950*	
1. United Kingdom	183,145	1. United Kingdom	1,168
2. Japan	148,947	Japan[b]	
3. Netherlands	130,703	4. Netherlands	334
4. Germany	111,138	Germany[b]	
5. Canada	79,716	2. Canada	1,029
6. France	77,622	France[b]	
7. Switzerland	55,280	3. Switzerland	348
Other countries[a]	200,177	Other countries[b]	512
Total	986,668	**Total**	3,391

Sources: 1999: *Survey of Current Business* (2000b: 68); 1950: US Department of Commerce (1962: 34).

Notes

a Each less then $55,000 million and included in other countries.

b Not specified in source; each probably less than $300 million and included in other countries.

that Canada was 'foreign' (most American companies administered their Canadian business separately from their 'international' business and thought about Canada in a rather different manner from the rest-of-the-world) (Wilkins 1970, 1974).

In the postwar decades, as continental European and then Japanese FDI in the United States mounted, Canadian stakes in the United States became *relatively* less important. In 1999, as Table 2.1 shows, in terms of FDI in the United States, while the Canadian interests had grown dramatically and in absolute terms were very large, Canada now ranked in fifth place, surpassed by Japanese, Dutch, and German FDI, as well as by the UK leader. (UK FDI in the United States was far more than double that of the Canadian FDI.) Graham Taylor in Chapter 4 has much to say on Canadian multinationals in the United States.

Dutch FDI in the United States was in third place in 1934, in fourth place in 1950, and back in third place in 1999. A significant portion of the Dutch stake in each of these years was the Dutch interest in British-Dutch Shell Oil (Shell Union Oil before the name change in 1949). German direct investment in the United States had been sequestered during World War I and then again during World War II. For all practical purposes, no German FDI existed in the United States in 1950. Slowly the FDI had climbed reaching sizeable proportions by 1999 (see Table 2.1). French direct investors in the United States have also played a role, in particular sectors, while the trade marks of Swiss firms, such as Nestlé, and the pharmaceutical products of Swiss participants have had a lengthy history in America (Wilkins 1993, 1999a).

The rise of continental European direct investments in the United States was far less conspicuous than the soaring Japanese FDI. The Japanese FDI in the United States that had existed before World War II had been taken over by the Office of Alien Property Custodian after the Japanese attack on Pearl Harbor. In the postwar period there was a resumption of Japanese FDI, at first in the same sectors that earlier existed (principally trading companies and banking) and then in a wide range of new activities. Gradually in the 1970s and then by the 1980s Japanese FDI had become conspicuous and, to American observers, 'threatening' (Wilkins 1990; Graham 1998: 43–4). This rapid rise and the scale were very new, as were the characteristics of the investments. Even though both Germany and Japan had been enemies of the United States in World War II, many Americans had German heritage (German immigration to the United States in past years had been very large). American 'heterogeneity' prior to World War II had been mainly based on continental European backgrounds. In the West, in California in particular, there had long been the presence of Japanese and anti-Japanese sentiments; California passed its first 'anti-Japanese' legislation in 1913 (McGovney 1947).[8] Pearl Harbor had been an attack on American soil. The formidable 1980s expansion of Japanese companies in the United States evoked a 'clash of cultures'. It took time, along with the economic problems in Japan in the 1990s, for an adjustment in sentiments to occur. By 2000 the Japanese car had become 'familiar' and most Americans who drove such cars were born after 7 December 1941 (the date of Pearl Harbor).[9]

In the 1970s, much of the nervousness over 'foreign investments' in the United States had been over those by 'Arabs', which were based on the rise in oil prices and new oil exporting countries' surpluses. Table 2.1 has no Arab nation as key in FDI. Yet, many Americans' worries over 'foreign' take-overs and over the unfamiliar arose in this context and in the early 1980s, the expansion of Kuwait Petroleum Co. in the United States was the occasion for the temporary revival of applications of the Mineral Lands Leasing Act of 1920 and a vigorous debate about state-owned companies and their role in inward foreign investments (US Congress 1982).[10]

Table 2.1 reveals that in 1999 80 per cent of FDI in the United States came from seven nations. The concentration of investment emanating from western Europe and Canada was historically in keeping with America's past; the unique element in the post-World War II story was represented by the huge Japanese involvement. It is appropriate that there are two contributions to this volume on Japanese companies in America, those by Jean-François Hennart, Thomas Roehl and Ming Zeng and by Ken'ichi Yasumuro (Chapters 11 and 12). Just as Americans were unfamiliar with the Japanese, the Japanese had much to learn about the United States.

As regards FDI in the United States by different nationalities, it is worth considering in the context of globalization how the experiences of firms of the various nationalities, with distinctive historical traditions, were transformed in the process of having FDI in America (and operating in this environment). Did these investments aid in creating more convergence in corporate behaviour on a global scale, changing the business conditions within the home countries as well as in the United States? It would seem so.

Industries

FDI in the United States has been across industries, but stands out more in certain sectors than in others. Because the American economy is so big, many figures fail to capture the significance of foreign business; thus, in 1997, US affiliates of foreign companies accounted for only about 6 per cent of US private-industry gross product and less than 4 per cent of civilian employment (*Economic Report of the President* 2000: 208, 348). These proportions are, to be sure, greater than in times past – some might marvel at them – but these aggregates are hardly dramatic. Nevertheless, foreign enterprise has been of major consequence, if we look at international trade and particularly when we view *specific* sectors within the economy. In 1997 US affiliates of foreign companies accounted for roughly 20 per cent of American exports and 30 per cent of American imports (ibid.: 208).

Table 2.2 provides a comparative overview for 1999 and 1950 of FDI in the United States by industries. Regrettably, the 1999 and 1950 data are not fully symmetrical. For 1950 there is no detailed break-down within the

Table 2.2 Foreign direct investment in the US (in US$ billions) by industry, 1999, 1950

	Amount (in billions (thousand millions) of US dollars)	
Sector	*1999*	*1950*
Manfacturing	391 (of which 103 was in chemicals and allied products)	1.138 (no break-down available)
Services	404 (of which 109 was in wholesale trade, 112 in banking and finance, 102 in insurance)	1.065 (only includes 'finance and insurance'; wholesale trade and other services were included with other industries)
Other industries	192 (of which 56 was in petroleum)	1.189 (of which .405 was in petroleum)
Total	987	3.391[a]

Sources: 1999: *Survey of Current Business* (2000b: 68); 1950: US Department of Commerce (1962: 36).

Note
a Column does not total because of rounding.

manufacturing sector; 'services' excludes wholesale and retail trades and banking (it is confined to finance and insurance); 'other industries' covers everything (except depository institutions) not included under the rubrics 'manufacturing' and 'finance and insurance.' The figures suggest that in 1950 33.6 per cent of inward FDI was in manufacturing.

The 1999 data are more complete (*Survey of Current Business* 2000b: 68). They indicate that 39.6 per cent of the inward FDI was in the manufacturing sector. In 1999, more than one-fourth of the stakes in manufacturing were in chemicals and allied products, with the composition by nationality in chemicals and allied products as follows: the British ($22 billion), Germans ($20 billion), Dutch ($16 billion), Swiss ($16 billion), and French ($12 billion). The level of FDI in 'the service sector' exceeded that in manufacturing (holding definitions constant, this would have been true in 1950 as well, since the service sector in 1950 was more narrowly defined). In 1999 about 80 per cent of the FDI in the service sector was concentrated in wholesale trade, banking and finance, and insurance. Oil industry direct investments were a larger share of total inward FDI in 1950 than in 1999; this is worth noting, but in my view has no profound significance (it is perhaps indicative that the oil industry was one of the earliest truly international ones); what it does demonstrate is that in the post-World War II years, inward FDI in general has risen faster than that of foreign oil enterprises in the United States (these figures should not, however, distract us from the fact that the US oil industry continues to be thoroughly internationalized and major investments from abroad have been made in this sector throughout the postwar years).

Indeed, once again, this overview for 1999 tells us little about the vast internationalization of the US economy. Yet, foreign business has been fundamental in the metamorphosis of the US economy in the last three decades, and this is not only true in the chemical and pharmaceutical industries, but in many other key sectors where foreign MNEs have come to rank among the leading players. Although this is particularly dramatic in chemicals and pharmaceuticals, foreign companies have also been highly significant in automobiles, rubber tyres, electronics and, of course, the oil industry. They have been important in transforming US steel production. Foreign companies have been involved, in addition, in a major manner in 'services', from advertising to movies, from banking to insurance.

At the start of the twenty-first century, the US economy was very different from what it had been in 1945. Marina v.N. Whitman has described the 'transformation of the large American corporation from the secure, paternalistic, and globally-dominant organization of the 1950s and 1960s to the lean, mean, and nimble global competitor of the 1990s' (Whitman 1999: 1). Competition from foreign MNEs within the United States in many different industries has jarred US corporate complacency. The introduction by foreign companies with their FDI of new products and processes – of new technologies – helped usher in the 'new economy.' By

1980, of all corporations (domestic and foreign), foreign ones took out 41 per cent of US patents; a decade later that percentage had climbed to about 50 per cent. By 1997, however, as Americans regained competitive vitality and as the number of new patents reached new peaks, the patenting by foreign corporations constituted a slightly lower share, or roughly 46 per cent of the total (*Statistical Abstract of the US 1999*: Table 893). These numbers are impressive.

New products and processes, along with new patents, spurred change in the US economy.[11] The Japanese role was critical: whether it involved the ingenious consumer electronics of Sony, or the attention to quality in the product and novelty in production processes by Honda, Toyota, and Nissan, the impacts were striking (Kenney and Florida 1993). It seems hard to remember that at the start of the 1990s, Americans were worried that the Japanese would come to dominate the semi-conductor industry (Tyson and Yoffie 1993). When deregulation came about, major advances in telecommunications were introduced by the Canadian Nortel and the German Siemens. Wilfried Feldenkirchen's Chapter 5 in this book shows the formidable role of Siemens, not only in telecommunications, but in a collection of innovative goods. The 'new economy' of information technology and of the Internet was far from a purely domestic creation. It was stimulated by numerous ideas from abroad.

'Big changes' in US industry have occurred in biotechnology. Here, too, foreign companies have intermingled with domestic enterprises. Key European pharmaceutical firms collaborated with new start-up companies in the United States, while at the same time they developed their own research agenda. In 1990, the Swiss Hoffmann-La Roche acquired a 60 per cent interest in Genentech, 'the most successful of the biotech start-ups' (Galambos and Sturchio 1998: 263, 265). The dynamics of the involvements by foreign companies, the mergers and acquisitions, in the pharmaceutical, particularly the biotechnology industry, were complex, but the bottom line was a throughly internationalized industry, and this very internationalization added immeasurably to the technological drive within this sector.

In the oil industry, Shell Oil has been important in the United States from the second decade of the twentieth century; in the postwar period it was joined by British Petroleum (which had nothing aside from a New York office before World War II). These two companies are among the leaders in the US domestic oil industry (Shell has over the years also been significant in the American chemical industry). This book has chapters on both oil MNEs (Chapter 10 on Shell by Tyler Priest and Chapter 9 on BP by James Bamberg). Like the principal US-headquartered oil companies, Shell and BP in America were part of global businesses. Because Shell and BP were 'foreign', they encountered certain obstacles in the United States that domestic companies did not, but in the post-World War II period these were few and far between. Both Priest and Bamberg do show how difficult it was for the foreign parents 'to control' their huge American affiliates.

The spread of foreign companies into a wide range of services has reflected a general shift of the US economy from 'blue collar' to 'white collar'. The term 'services' is broad. Foreign direct investors have long taken part in providing a wide range of services, from those in distribution to those in insurance (for the general importance of MNEs in services, see Jones 1996). However, in 1945–50, there was no provision of power and light and telecommunication services by foreign companies in the United States; now foreign MNEs have established a new and growing presence. Technological innovation has made these services no longer a 'natural monopoly.' Deregulation opened the way for the acceleration of entries by foreign companies.

So, too, foreign banks play a totally different role within the US economy at the start of the twenty-first century from their role in the immediate postwar years. In banking and financial services, foreign companies have participated in and contributed to a vast transformation in America. To a large extent, in 1945–50 banking was a locally based activity in the United States. Today, banks can *operate* nationally. The wall between commercial and investment banking has crumbled. An array of new products are now offered by banks (for the vast change see Calomiris 2000). The line between various types of financial services has been redrawn. The announcement in July 2000 that UBS (a large Swiss bank) was buying America's fourth largest brokerage house, PayneWebber (for $10.8 billion) reflects the altered circumstances (Associated Press, 13 July 2000). Adrian Tschoegl's Chapter 8 is on foreign banks in the United States, recounting their experiences.

In many sectors, foreign companies have assumed a new place within the US domestic economy that is basic rather than on the fringe. In this context, it is important to consider the management of the foreign enterprises. It is not sufficient to study research and development or new technology or patents, as an abstraction, nor is it enough to document large take-overs. All of these occurrences are embodied in companies managed over distance. Innovative competitive foreign companies shattered American smugness. They have taken over American companies to transform them and also to learn from them. By the end of the 1990s, as indicated earlier, there no longer seemed to be a 'threat' from abroad. In countless cases, American companies restructured and met the challenge posed by the foreign MNEs. In new industries, new domestic companies emerged. Foreign companies helped create in America markets that were 'contestable.'

As foreign companies provided competition, they wrestled with how much of 'foreign' managerial styles could be superimposed on American start-ups and acquisitions. American corporate managers of affiliates of foreign firms frequently failed 'to follow directions,' formulating their own agenda. Foreign companies experimented with degrees of managerial control – always within constraints. The process involved ebbs and flows. Managing a business in the United States was not simple for domestic managers, nor for foreign ones.

In sum, foreign businesses have penetrated into many basic US industries and services. They introduced innovations and they also obtained knowledge from their US experiences. Whitman writes of the domestic economy that:

> The creation of conglomerates through mergers and acquisitions in the 1970s, corporate restructurings in the 1980s and 1990s, and foreign acquisitions of US companies since the mid-1980s have all intensified a shift of ownership and decision-making power from local communities to headquarters elsewhere, often in another state or country.
>
> (Whitman 1999: 110)

Yet, at the same time, one is struck by the number of new local start-up firms in new industries that continue to proliferate at the start of the twenty-first century. How quickly will they lose their 'local' roots? One is also struck by the absence of uniformity in foreign corporate penetration over time. In some industries, there has been a reduction in the importance of foreign companies, while in others the impact is just beginning; and, in still others, the impact is on-going and seems bound to accelerate. Always the consequences tend to be ones of shaking up complacency – and prompting change (perhaps not at once, but surely in the long-run) in numerous sectors.

As foreign businesses have internationalized America's domestic economy, discussions arose on 'Who is US?' (Reich 1990; Tyson 1991; Dunning 1998). Commentators note the blurring of the domestic and the foreign; the questions raised are appropriate in *certain* respects, but I would agree with those who argue that there persisted important distinctions to be made in analyzing foreign companies in the United States and those that are domestically headquartered. Perhaps even more crucial, however, is the point that 'foreign' companies are not alike. Not only are there differences by nationality, but major differences by industry, and differences that can be ascribed to the particular company and its management. The distinction between American and 'foreign' is only one of many.

Regions

As pointed out, the United States is a vast country; throughout the years from 1945 to the present, most of the inward FDI was designed to reach national markets. There was, however, considerable variation in where US headquarters and US plants owned by foreign multinationals were located. In the post-World War II years foreign investors to some extent mirrored trends in regional locations that were domestic in nature and to some degree they led rather than followed the trends. It is important that as foreign companies expanded in the United States, if they took over existing companies (as was frequently the case) a foreign enterprise might have a number of different US headquarters, related to separate product lines, supervising 'establishments' across the country and in some instances abroad; these US headquarters would then become subordinate to the foreign company's headquarters abroad.

Regional considerations for foreign companies in the United States related to history, nationality, and industry. Since many foreign firms in the United States were multi-plant and multi-functional enterprises, they were often 'located' in many states. Yet, it is possible to discern patterns and identify noteworthy regional differences, which I will attempt to do here. (As in the rest of this contribution, where there are no notes, this is based on Wilkins forthcoming and Wilkins in process.)

By 1945, every state in the United States, without exception, had attracted some FDI, but the main concentration had been in New York, New Jersey, Pennsylvania, and New England (principally, Massachusetts and Rhode Island). Illinois had for many years drawn in FDI, although to a lesser extent than these other states; much of this FDI had been in the Chicago area. The heavily industrialized Michigan and Ohio regions had little appeal for FDI, since historically there had been little FDI in the automobile or automotive parts industries; the one foreign tyre maker in the United States in 1945 (Dunlop) had its plant in Buffalo, New York; the important Swedish-owned bearings manufacturer, SKF, was in Pennsylvania.

Across the United States in 1945 there were long-standing investors on the West Coast, typically firms that had multi-unit operations in the United States. HongKong & Shanghai Bank, for example, had been in California since the 1870s; it also had a New York agency. Canadian banks were on the West Coast, and in New York. Shell Union Oil had operations across the United States: it had been in California since 1912. In 1945, because of the war, as noted, the pre-war Japanese banks and trading companies were absent; their West Coast presence would be revived in the 1950s.

As for the American South, foreign-owned textile firms had begun to migrate there (along with the domestic industry) in the 1920s and 1930s. Thus, in 1945 the Scottish thread producer J & P Coats had important manufacturing in Georgia. In 1945 there were other miscellaneous sizeable FDIs in the American South, from a huge British-owned cotton plantation in Mississippi (acquired before World War I) to the significant British American Tobacco Company's investment in Brown & Williamson (made in the 1920s), which had its principal plant and headquarters in

Louisville, Kentucky. Foreign firms that were national in their operations, such as Shell, had different kinds of involvements throughout the American South.

In 1976, in the US Department of Commerce's major study of FDI in the United States, the Conference Board in New York, on behalf of the Commerce Department, systematically identified the sites of foreign-owned plants in the United States (US Department of Commerce 1976, Vol. 3: A-120–280). The Conference Board found that some of the largest foreign-owned companies in the United States had as many as 40 or 50 plants within the nation, but that most foreign-owned firms active in manufacturing in the United States operated from a single production facility and that many of the latter were small firms by US standards, with their plants near their industrial customers or near raw material resources. The Conference Board identified 2,053 plants, located in every state within the country (ibid.: A-121).

The five states that in 1976 had the largest number of foreign-owned manufacturing plants were very predictable: New York led with the most plants (222, of which 41 were classified as in electrical machinery, 31 in chemicals and pharmaceuticals, 29 in non-electrical machinery, and 21 in fabricated metals). New Jersey ranked in second place (178, of which 59 were in chemicals and pharmaceuticals and 24 in fabricated metals). In third, fourth, and fifth places were Pennsylvania (125 plants, of which 28 were in fabricated metals and 21 were in non-electrical machinery); California (103 plants, of which 24 were in fabricated metals and 20 chemicals and pharmaceuticals); and Illinois (92 plants, of which 18 were in fabricated metals and 15 in food and kindred products). Notice that no southern state was in the top five, although North Carolina came very close, with 90 plants.

The Conference Board study provided the names of the companies with maps pinpointing the locations of the particular plants. In New York State, there was a cluster of plants around the New York Metropolitan area, but a sizeable number were up-state, near Buffalo, Niagara Falls, and Syracuse; Ogdensburg had 6 Canadian-owned plants, while Plattsburg had 12 Canadian-owned factories. New Jersey had foreign-owned facilities throughout the state with a heavy concentration in the areas just across the Hudson River, easily accessible to New York City. In Pennsylvania plants dotted the state. In California a notable collection of factories were in the vicinity of San Francisco and of Los Angeles. Sony had two plants in San Diego, making televisions, record changers, and colour TV tubes and employing 778, a harbinger of the 'new age'. As for Illinois, while many plants were in the Greater Chicago area, others were elsewhere in the state.

In the 1970s and continuing in the 1980s and 1990s, there was a 'southern shift' in the United States (Sale 1975, Wright 2000). The term 'rust belt' was used in the 1970s and 1980s to refer to the old industrial areas in the North and Mid-West. The new automobile industry investments from the 1980s onward were mainly in the 'South' or alternatively in rural areas in the Mid-West, not in the traditional industrial areas. Southern states drew in many new foreign investments. In 1969–70, Burroughs Wellcome moved from a location in New York on the Hudson River to the North Carolina 'Triangle'. Subsequently, Glaxo started up there. South Carolina was able to attract Michelin and a host of important foreign companies. Daimler would go to Alabama, and then national (with its 1998 acquisition of Chrysler). In addition, California and Oregon pulled in 'new economy' businesses. NAFTA encouraged facilities that could be linked in with North American operations. Clusters of companies became more frequent, with Japanese automobile companies, for example, attracting their suppliers. Foreign multinationals became associated with the transformation of regions, the building up of the 'New South' and the 'High-Tech' West Coast. To some extent they were following trends; in other ways, they took leadership and encouraged the on-going developments.

A 1999 study on regional *employment* patterns of 10,952 foreign-owned US manufacturing establishments found that in 1992 the top five 'economic areas' for foreign-owned establishments reflected the historical pattern and the consequences of foreign acquisitions. The 'areas' were (1) 'New York–Northern New Jersey–Long Island, NY–NJ–CT–PA–MA–VT', (2) 'Chicago–Gary–Kenosha, IL–IN–WI', (3) Los Angeles–Riverside–Orange County, CA–AZ', (4) 'San Francisco–Oakland–San Jose, CA' and (5) 'Philadelphia–Wilmington–Atlantic City, PA–NJ–DE–MD'. This was in keeping with US-owned establishments. The study also reported, once again based on employment, that 'foreign-owned manufacturing establishments are relatively more concentrated than US-owned manufacturing establishments ... particularly in the Southeast' – in Nashville (Tenn.), Greenville–Spartanburg–Anderson (SC), and Charlotte–Gastonia–Rock Hill and Raleigh–Durham–Chapel Hill (NC). It noted differences by nationality: Japanese-owned greenfield (new start-up) plants tended to be concentrated on the West Coast and along a corridor extending from Indiana to northern Georgia. German-owned greenfield factories gravitated to areas where there were other German-owned establishments, both older plants and those recently acquired. New British plants tended to be more widely dispersed, while new German and French factories were apt to be in the East, including Southeast locations (*Survey of Current Business* 1999a: 8–11). Nationality did seem to matter in foreign companies' location decisions related to manufacturing.

I have not seen any systematic studies on the impact of NAFTA on the regional configurations of foreign-owned plants and other facilities in the United States. It is clear that before NAFTA, American and subsequently foreign companies had taken advantage of the Mexican border industrialization programme (inaugurated in 1965) to link their US and Mexican facilities. Both American and foreign-owned firms have increased their

Mexican investments subsequent to NAFTA. There are interpretations that plants that would otherwise have been built by foreign companies in the United States are being sited in Mexico instead (the Volkswagen plant, for example). Exactly how important NAFTA has been, and will be, to regional plant choices is yet to be determined. There exist substantial data on individual companies' decisions to coordinate plants outside the United States with vertically integrated establishments (either for finishing or for sales) within the United States. Thus far, however, most foreign MNEs that wish to reach the US market and are making new investments to do so are investing in the United States rather than in Mexico (or Canada). In the late 1990s, however, Canada and Mexico together accounted for about one-third of America's total trade (*Economic Report of the President* 2000: 209) and foreign MNEs were very much participants in that activity.[12]

Foreign business in the United States did not invest only in manufacturing. As noted, foreign MNEs went into a large assortment of 'service' activities. The regional patterns of such foreign companies varied by the type of service. The movie business was, of course, in California, so that was where the foreign companies made their investments. Banking in the United States had in the past been confined to individual states; the entry of foreign banks assisted in eroding the 'local' character of American banking. For a time, foreign banks could operate across state lines, and American banks could not. I do not think foreign insurance companies (1945–2000) had much impact on the geographical distribution of economic activity in the United States; many foreign insurance companies in the United States (like their US counterparts) had long provided national coverage, and did business in many individual states. Lilian Nachum has concluded that it was a combination of location advantages and agglomeration economies that affected the choices made by foreign MNEs in financial and professional services in the United States in the 1990s (Nachum 2000: 380). What is clear is that while every section of the country attracted foreign-owned businesses, the distribution of the operations of foreign affiliates throughout the nation remained uneven, although there is evidence both in manufacturing and in financial and professional services that foreign firms tended to be more clustered, more concentrated in particular areas, than their domestic competitors.

Performance

Throughout the postwar period, as the presence and operations of foreign MNEs have on a net basis steadily expanded within the United States, these enterprises have found doing business in the American market to be 'difficult'. While some companies have had remarkable successes in market penetration and have obtained excellent profits, a substantial number have met with frustrations and some have exited. This has been true of both greenfield entries and of mergers and acquisitions. Several chapters in this book discuss the problems that foreign companies have had in the American market. John Dunning found in his 1960 survey (see Chapter 3) that the average profits of UK affiliates in the United States were substantially below the average profits of US domestic companies. Other authors have noted how poor the returns were to Japanese companies in the United States (despite remarkable success in market penetration). During the 1990s, studies looked at what appeared to be, in general, very low rates of return to foreign direct investors, in absolute terms and relative to US businesses in the same industries.[13] There have been attempts to ask why this has been the case (for example, Grubert, Goodspeed and Swenson 1993; *Survey of Current Business* 2000a). A recent article found, for example, that during the years 1988–97 the return on assets (ROA) on all foreign-owned non-financial companies was consistently below that of US-owned non-financial companies. The study divided the data by industry and reported that the average ROA of foreign-owned non-financial companies was below that of US-owned companies in 22 of 30 non-financial industries (*Survey of Current Business* 2000a).

Tax authorities have wondered whether such low returns were 'real', or were contrived to evade taxes and caused by conscious over-borders transfer pricing (intra-company price manipulations). Other investigators shared the view that the returns were not real, but examined transfer price explanations that had nothing to do with tax considerations (that related, for instance, to Japanese companies' avoiding dumping accusations or foreign companies' preferring not to gamble on exchange rate fluctuations in their profit remittances). A different set of explanations emphasized the newness of many foreign companies, which meant high start-up costs. Along the same line, some scholars speculated that because the US market was unfamiliar to the many new foreign investors, the returns were bound to be lower. Still others insisted that many foreign investors had purchased US assets at unrealistically high prices (particularly at the end of the 1980s) and that had been responsible for the poor returns (this explanation was revived at the end of the 1990s). There has been some evidence of an 'age effect', that is, that foreign companies that have been in the United States for a longer time 'learn', and experience contributes to better performance (on the age effect, see *Survey of Current Business* 2000a: 55). On the other hand, others have shown that companies long in the United States have gone through new generations of products and management and their 'experience' can become outmoded over the passage of time. A different set of hypotheses on low returns has evaluated the topic from the vantage point of 'markets for corporate control'. American companies have been under intense pressure to bring up earnings ratios; foreign companies that are part of a larger MNE may be, the argument went, immune from these pressures and able to sustain low returns for a longer period; at this stage, the arguments branch: (1) the foreign company is not particularly eager to enlarge profits, having other strategic goals, or (2) the foreign company is ready to accept years of low profits or losses so as to achieve in the long-run market penetration and later obtain far higher returns. Geoffrey Jones explained the unsatisfactory performance of British multinational banks in the US market to failures in strategy (bad judgements in their acquisitions), absence of a real advantage in the United States 'beyond the ability to finance acquisitions', along with problems of managements inadequate to cope with the unfamiliar, competitive, and 'complex' US market conditions (Jones 1993: 367, 370). In his recent study of Unilever in the United States, Jones found that parent company managers were often unable to rectify continuing low profits, which persisted for years.

I know of no careful studies on whether the demonstrated poor performance was systematically related to the mode of entry: greenfield or take-over. In both circumstances, perhaps for different reasons, foreign MNEs encountered difficulties in doing business in America. Indeed, there seems to have been a wide variety of reasons for the often observed financial weaknesses of foreign affiliates in the United States (and the above paragraphs omit several explanations).[14] It is very clear, however, that the low returns were not exclusively or even mainly caused by tax evasion, as some experts on taxation initially believed. Often, in fact, the low returns (or losses) were very real, and some foreign companies found survival impossible. There have been a number of exits over the entire post-World War II period. Occasionally, the losses in the United States were so severe as to imperil the parent (some of the troubles in the Japanese economy in the 1990s have been blamed on the poor performance of the Japanese firms' affiliates in the United States) (Wilkins in process). When there were take-overs, if the foreign company was unable to add some kind of competence, profits were frequently below expectations. Foreign companies that came to the United States *to learn* from the enterprises that they bought had to have a core basis to digest the acquisition; if not, failures often followed. Yet, even when the foreign company had core competence in an industry, conducting business in America often proved not as easy as expected. Case studies of foreign direct investors in the United States are strewn with stories of the problems facing foreign MNEs in the United States and the absence of 'appropriate' profits. Frequently, the parent company did not know how to raise the returns (cost reductions often sacrificed efficiency, etc.). Yet, often foreign direct investors in the United States persisted, poor performance notwithstanding, since they saw the importance of 'being in America' no matter what. Some changed managements regularly, seeking to cope with unsatisfactory US results. New foreign companies entered, undeterred by the problems faced by their predecessors; the US market was too promising to forego. There was an element of prestige associated with being in America.

Public policies

There has never been a US 'public policy' toward foreign MNEs, but rather there have been different policies, most of which have altered over time (some in fundamentals, others in detail or implementation). There have been Federal, and also state and local government policies. Even though the US constitution leaves to the Federal government matters affecting foreign policy, many state and local policies (particularly in relation to land laws, taxation, banking, and business incentives) have affected foreign MNEs in the United States. Some policies have targeted foreign investors; others that are general have had a differential effect on FDI (sometimes the distinction is not clear).

When World War II ended, the key public policies within the United States that affected foreign MNEs in this country were the following.

1 Those that related to the war: 1940–1 foreign funds control; a loan that had FDI as collateral (the 1941 Reconstruction Finance Corporation loan to the United Kingdom); and the activities of the Office of the Alien Property Custodian. These matters needed to be unscrambled and were very specific to foreign companies in the United States. Some involved prolonged diplomacy and negotiations. Not until the 1960s were most resolved.
2 A set of anti-trust cases that had been inaugurated as part of the late New Deal attack on big business (and that had, in the main, been suspended during the war years): anti-trust cases were in the immediate postwar years revived and new ones initiated. This wave of anti-trust enforcement that affected both American companies and foreign ones continued on into the 1950s, with profound impact on the activities of foreign MNEs in the United States (Wilkins 1974, forthcoming, in process). Anti-trust law covered both US and foreign companies, but had, I would argue, a markedly differential effect on foreign enterprises that had their experiences in 'negotiated' environments. Indeed, US anti-trust policies set the stage for a highly competitive American economy of later years. In the late 1940s and 1950s, it became clear to European companies (and any American ones who had not already understood this) that cross-border division-of-market agreements were unacceptable in the United States.
3 A long-standing body of legislation related to foreign-owned corporations' ownership of American land, shipping, broadcasting, air transport, and eligibility for mineral land leasing; these laws remained on the books. Their enforcement would surface periodically to influence foreign business in the United States. American banking laws were not especially friendly to foreign direct investors.
4 In addition, and important, with the advent of the Cold War, laws and regulations associated with national defense that affected foreign companies would be clarified, new ones passed, and regulations increased.

Such matters aside, in the immediate postwar years, through the 1950s, the United States was interested in encouraging American business abroad (outward FDI) and would pay far less attention to formulating and implementing public policies toward inward FDI. The general thrust of America's postwar philosophical stance was toward worldwide recovery and global liberalization – in short, dismantling the autarchic policies around the world that had in the interwar and war years interfered with the free flow of trade and investment. The assumption was that democracy and economic liberalization went in tandem. Abroad, capital controls impeded foreign MNEs' expansion over borders (and home priorities took front stage).

In the early 1960s, when the US Department of Commerce reported on foreign business investments in the United States, it commented on the absence of 'a sustained increase in the rate of flow of foreign industrial capital to the United States', while indicating that the Commerce Department as well as various States were 'developing programs to bring opportunities here to the attention of foreign industrialists . . .' (US Department of Commerce 1962: 4).

In 1976, by which time 'the rate of flow' of foreign business to America had greatly accelerated, the US Department of Commerce undertook a major nine-volume study of FDI in the United States. Volumes 6 through 9 furnished information on existing US public policies and captured what were then seen as fundamentals. Volume 6 was on taxation: it quoted Robert V. Roosa, former Under Secretary for Monetary Affairs and at that time a partner in Brown Brothers, Harriman, as concluding that 'in our view, the present [withholding] tax [on income on foreign investments in the United States] discourages foreign investments at a time when it [inward foreign investment] should be encouraged' (US Department of Commerce 1976: VI, J-39). The volume examined US tax policies and their impacts on 'possible' US public policy aims, i.e. 'attracting foreign investment to the United States' (which the Treasury Department and many others wanted to do), differentially deterring certain foreign investments, obtaining information on FDI, securing reduction of taxes on American business abroad (reciprocity goals), and achieving traditional tax policy objectives of neutrality, equity, revenue, and 'administrability'. The volume also reviewed the existing tax treaties and their policy implications. Volume 7 offered a lengthy discussion of Federal and state laws affecting inward FDI, covering general investments, defence, transportation (shipping, aviation, railroads), communications, energy resources, power, banking, and insurance. Volume 8, which dealt with foreign investment in land, had a section on land law, while Volume 9 had a contribution on policies, laws, and regulations of other industrialized nations concerning inward FDI (for comparative purposes); interestingly, there was no exploration of industrial nations' policies toward *outward* FDI that might aid or impede FDI in the United States, nor was there attention to the general removal of foreign capital controls that was and would continue to open the way for new FDI in the United States. We know from case studies that American law protecting minority shareholders and fears of minority shareholder suits impacted foreign managers' ability to maintain control; this matter was not typically discussed in the general literature.

However, numerous books and articles (for example, Marans, Williams and Griffin (eds) 1980) regularly summarized the rules, regulations, and limits on FDI in particular US industries (banking, aviation, communications, shipping). These were historical barriers (see Wilkins 1989, Wilkins forthcoming). In banking, a major change occurred with the International Banking Act of 1978, designed for the first time to develop a comprehensive scheme of Federal regulation of the activities of foreign banks (Marans, Williams and Griffin (eds) 1980: 333). In the other areas, much of the older legislation was retained, but often not enforced (as in the case of the numerous state alien land laws). In the late 1970s and early 1980s, the application of anti-trust law to foreign companies in the United States remained important. Congress with the Hart-Scott-Rodino Act (passed in 1976) required that after September 1978, participants in large mergers had to notify the Federal Trade Commission and the Antitrust Division of the Justice Department and then wait a designated period to see whether the anti-trust regulators decided to challenge the planned transaction (ibid.: 168–9). This law applied to domestic as well as foreign take-overs and left available the path of negotiations and revised merger proposals, so they would become acceptable. As foreign business in the United States grew, strictly foreign mergers (that is a merger between two MNEs headquartered abroad) would have spill-over effects within the United States, and the merging parties routinely provided the FTC or Justice Department notification.

On the whole, however, within the United States in the 1960s, 1970s, and 1980s, the general policy had become one of 'Invest in the United States'. The Commerce Department encouraged FDI. States tried to lure investment, offering incentives. Thus, while many of the older restrictions still applied, and some new ones were added, they did little to impede the rising FDI. In the 1960s, the Federal government had wanted FDI in the United States for balance of payments reasons. State and local governments desired such investments to encourage employment. Increasingly in the 1970s, state and local governments sent missions abroad to bring in new FDI. By the 1980s and particularly in the 1990s, state and local incentives (involving site development, infrastructure, worker training, and the like) reached formidable proportions. In 1993, to woo Daimler and its Mercedes plant to Tuscaloosa, Alabama, and an investment of $300 million, incentives came to $250 million (an estimated $167,000 per employee), while in 1994 to get a BMW plant in Spartenburg and an investment of $450 million, South Carolina offered incentives of $130 million (which would come to an estimated $108,000 per employee) (*World Investment Report* 1995: 296–7).

At the same time, as the state and local governments were seeking to pull in new investments, mounting FDI would prompt episodes of alarm, resulting in the passage of important legislation. The Exon-Florio Amendment (to the Defense Production Act), enacted as a part of the Omnibus Trade and Competitive Act of 1988, gave the President of the United States certain powers to block mergers or acquisitions of US companies by foreign interests, when such actions were held to be a threat to national security. Under this amendment, the Committee on Foreign Investment in the United States (CFIUS) could undertake investigations of such mergers or acquisitions and recommend to the President that he forbid (or undo) the transaction. The CFIUS had been established in 1975 to monitor the increasing incoming FDI; the Exon-Florio amendment seemed to give this inter-agency committee 'clout'. When the Exon-Florio authority lapsed in the fall of 1990, it was re-instituted (and made a permanent part of US law) in August 1991 and that year new regulations were promulgated. The 1992 Byrd amendment to the National Defense Authorization Act *required* an investigation of a foreign investment where the acquirer was controlled by or acted on behalf of a foreign government and the acquisition could affect the national security of the United States; the Bingham Amendment forbade foreign government-owned companies from purchasing US defence contractors engaged in contracts requiring access to certain classified information. Under all these new procedures, only one investment has been blocked. In 1993 President George Bush required a Chinese government-owned firm to divest its holdings in a Seattle-based aircraft parts manufacturer (Graham and Krugman 1995: 126–34; Sidak 1997: 110; US Department of Treasury undated 1999–2000?; Kaye Scholer 2000). Throughout US public policy deliberations, frequent concerns had arisen about foreign *government* involvement in commercial (as well as national security-related) activities in America and whether that implied sovereign immunity and sovereign 'power'. The worry was that a foreign government-owned company acted – by definition – in an undesirable manner, by involving non-commercial considerations in its investment strategies (for the anxieties of the 1970s, for example, see Lamont 1979).

Perhaps the biggest US public policy change in the 1980s and 1990s came with the general trend toward deregulation within the United States (and deregulation and privatization around the world). It was away from regulation in the United States. New US policies meant foreign banks were able to enter with fewer restrictions. Altered public policies and the Telecommunications Act of 1996 opened the way for added FDI (although some of the older impediments lingered on) (Sidak 1997). Anti-trust applications to foreign joint-ventures with American companies and foreign mergers and acquisitions, which over the years had gone through 'ups and downs', became in the mid-1990s highly permissive. However, as the twentieth century ended and the new millennium began, after a flood of foreign inward mergers and acquisitions, there appeared to be once more a revival of a more active anti-trust stance, with applications to both domestic and international mergers alike. Anti-trust was never dormant, yet its time on a 'back-burner' opened the way for unprecedented foreign take-overs of American companies.

Accordingly, while, in general, America has been open to inward FDI in all except a very few specific sectors, and while there was in the 1970s, 1980s, and 1990s much interest by states and localities in attracting new investments with the goal of providing employment, there continued to be threats of new restrictions. Early in July 2000 Senator Ernest 'Fritz' Hollings (Democrat from South Carolina) introduced legislation to take away from the Federal Communications Commission (FCC) the ability to approve a Deutsche Telekom acquisition of a major US telecommunications company; the Senator argued that no company more than 25 per cent-controlled by a foreign *government* should be able to own a controlling interest in a company in broadcasting (a vital sector). When Senator Hollings' legislation was introduced, there had been no take-over offer, only a *rumor* that Deutsche Telekom was interested in the large company, Sprint; not long afterwards (on 23 July 2000), Deutsche Telekom announced it would buy VoiceStream, a 1-year-old wireless phone company (for $50.7 billion). The FCC Chairman (William Kennard) pledged he would give the proposal 'close scrutiny'. Alarm over foreign government-owned companies once more resurfaced, even in the age when privatization was moving forward (albeit not fast enough for some American critics) (*Miami Herald* 4, 24, 25 July 2000; Sidak 1997 for the history of the FCC authority). Senator Hollings insisted 'we didn't deregulate the telecommunications market to put it under German government control' (*Wall Street Journal*, 5 Oct. 2000).[15]

To what extent were foreign investors able to influence Federal, state, and local government policies; or were these investors passive accepters of exogenous governmental mandates? The answers vary considerably – by foreign investor and foreign investment, by policies, and by period. Clearly, foreign investors bargained with state and local governments for concessions and better incentive structures. They have monitored US, state, and local policies. Their attorneys or accountants alerted them when adverse tax policies were pending. When mergers occurred and the FTC and the Justice Department reviewed them, the companies had a say in their own defence, albeit many seemed so set in their merger plans that they were willing to accept divestments that might imperil the value of the merger. On employment conflicts and equal opportunity disputes, foreign firms sometimes turned for help in Washington. Some foreign affiliates have joined in associations to meet certain goals. Periodically, Americans have become upset over foreign companies' participating in national politics and suggested legislation to restrict such involvement. Currently, the formal limits on political action by foreign affiliates are almost identical to those facing US-owned corporations: lobbyists have to register; political action committee (PAC) donations are limited, and so forth. On the other hand, when foreign-owned businesses do make contact with US Senators or Representatives, or regulators, or ask for help, frequently suspicions arise, apparently more than would be the case when the overall legitimacy of corporate political action is also under fire (Getz 1998: 245–9). As a consequence, there is the Organization for International Investment (OFII), a Washington-based trade association that represents US affiliates of companies based abroad. It is 'dedicated to ensuring that US subsidiaries receive nondiscriminatory treatment under US Federal and state law' (Organization for International Investment 1998). To generalize, clearly, the economic impacts of the inward FDI have been far greater than any political consequences, although an indirect political outcome might be that the now formidable presence of foreign MNEs has served to encourage American policy to remain open. Large foreign companies have recognized a need to have a Washington office, a Washington representative (usually a law firm), and/or a Washington trade association, for information purposes and to ward off legislation and public sentiments potentially harmful to their interests. What emerges in several chapters in this book is that the advice of American lawyers, interpreting American law for the foreign MNE, has had substantial effect on the management of foreign-owned affiliates and has created an interesting principal-agent problem, with the American management arguing that American law and conditions are so special that only the 'agent' (Americans) can understand, while the 'principal' (the foreign parent) is less informed and less secure in its judgements.

Conclusions

Americans in 1945 had just emerged from a long war. By every criterion, the United States had the strongest economy in the world. The nation was ready to take leadership in dealing with the immediate priorities of global recovery and reconstruction. The pervasive belief in the United States was that economic growth abroad was good for the US economy. American companies made direct investments in foreign lands, contributing to the well-being of many countries.

Behind the scenes there was inward FDI in the United States, remnants from before the war and soon new entries, but from 1945 to roughly 1970, it was outward US direct investments that captured major attention in the United States and in the rest of the world (Wilkins 1974). This changed dramatically in the concluding three decades of the twentieth century, as FDI in the United States mounted rapidly and as the US domestic economy became thoroughly internationalized. It changed at the time when outward US direct investments continued to exceed inward ones. In the 1970s and 1980s Americans were anxious about their nation's competitive position and the entry of foreign MNEs seemed symbolic of the uncertainties. The British remained in first place among the inward investors throughout 1945–2000. During the 1970s and particularly the 1980s, the rise of Japanese investments in new processes and products was, however, spectacular. With the American economy in the doldrums in the 1970s and part of the 1980s, there was talk of Japan as 'Number One'.

Foreign companies increasingly became multi-product, multi-plant operations in the United States, so that there were not merely new entries but growth, additions through acquisitions, and also restructuring and some exits (often partial, sometimes full). Control from abroad was centralized and decentralized, with ebbs and flows. Alliances and contractual relationships, involving varying degrees of equity (or no equity at all) were part and parcel of the complex overall net expansion. Foreign companies experimented with Americans and expatriate (imported foreigners) managers as managers and granted differing degrees of autonomy to their US affiliates. Management was difficult, owing to the scale and scope of the inward FDI, but the patterns mirrored the more general historical experiences of MNEs where adjustments in managerial structures were always essential in the face of the dynamics of change (a point made on the expansion of US MNEs in Wilkins 1974: 419–22).

The internationalization of the US economy created new competition within the United States (as well as abroad), it brought new challenges, and after a time of 'shock', in the late 1980s and 1990s many American companies responded. They accepted the consequences of corporate restructuring. The country remained open to foreign trade and investment (new restrictions on trade were ad hoc; aside from new monitoring and reporting requirements there were no substantial extra US impediments to inward FDI); the country endorsed the North American Free Trade Area; it joined the World Trade Organization.

In the 1990s with the US economy performing well, concerns that inward FDI might have a damaging effect dissipated. In the background (and sometimes in the foreground), however, some Americans worried over 'globalization'. Inward FDI is closely associated with the globalization trends. As the United States entered the twenty-first century, it was a major recipient of new inward FDI (principally in the form of mergers and acquisitions). Foreign MNEs contributed to the nation's unprecedented prosperity.

Notes

1 I want to express my appreciation for the suggestions from so many of the chapter writers in this volume, especially Geoffrey Jones, Lina Gálvez-Muñoz, Jean-François Hennart, and John Dunning. In addition, my thanks go to Marina v.N. Whitman, Tetsuo Abo, and Al Chandler for their valuable insights.

2 Terra Networks was 70 per cent owned by Telefónica (*Economist* 20 May 2000). On Telefónica's international business, see Toral 1999: 169–200. The predecessor of Telefónica was founded in the 1920s as a subsidiary of International Telephone and Telegraph Corporation; it was nationalized in 1944.

3 In 1987, the French Thomson had purchased the consumer electronics business of General Electric, including the GE and RCA brand names. Thomson made TVs in the United States. In 1998, however, Thomson shut its large RCA plant in Bloomington, Indiana, and moved its basic TV output from there to Ciudad Juarez, Mexico. It appears to have continued to make picture tubes in the United States, and it sold the TVs in the United States (Wilkins in process). Bayer had done business under the Bayer name in the United States before World War I (Wilkins 1989); after that war, the rights to the Bayer name in the United States had passed to Sterling Products; in 1988 another American company, Eastman Kodak, acquired the US rights to the name Bayer; in 1994 a British MNE SmithKline Beecham obtained the US rights, which it in turn sold that same year, 1994, to the German Bayer (Wilkins 2000, forthcoming, and in process). Thus, from the end of World War I to 1994, a consumer of Bayer Aspirins in the United States was *not* buying a product of German Bayer, the name notwithstanding.

4 Terra Network would not be the first foreign investor in a US Internet access company, nor the first to envisage the potential of the Spanish language market in the United States. In 1997, the Mexican investor, Carlos Slim (the entrepreneur involved in the newly privatized Mexican telephone company, Telmex) had purchased Prodigy, one of the pioneer US Internet service providers and at this point an ailing firm; Slim sought to develop Prodigy's Spanish language capabilities. Slim also acquired in 2000, for $800 million, CompUSA, an important but financially troubled retailer of computers (*Financial Times* 2000b). The $800 million price tag made this a relatively 'small' acquisition in the start of the twenty-first century milieu.

5 Note, however, that in 1998 and 1999, *measured by market value*, FDI in the US did exceed US FDI abroad; in 1998 and 1999, measured by historical cost and by current cost, US FDI abroad was larger than FDI in the US (*Survey of Current Business* 1999b: 48, 50, 2000b: 57). My generalizations are based on historical cost measures, although prior to 1998 the generalizations would have held for all three measures.

6 Foreign portfolio investment was also always a two-way street: this was *not* a distinctive feature of FDI, as was once believed (Wilkins 1999b).

7 Texasgulf was a diversified mineral (and chemical) products company, which at the time of the CDC acquisition earned two-thirds of its income from Canadian sources. The US alarm was over the role of the Canadian *government* in this transaction.

8 Even earlier, there had been an attempt to stop the immigration of Japanese to the agricultural lands of the Pacific Coast through a 'gentlemen's agreement' that President Theodore Roosevelt had in 1907 negotiated with the Japanese government (Freidel 1960: 47).

9 In 2000 in the United States there was much concern over the treatment of Japanese-Americans during World War II and their internment – and many apologies.

10 The 1920 Mineral Lands Leasing Act had a reciprocity provision: no foreign company could lease American public oil lands if the nation from which the company came did not grant similar privileges to American investors. The Lands Leasing Act was an impediment to Royal Dutch Shell's American plans in the 1920s (Wilkins forthcoming).

11 Patents are one but not the sole index of technological vibrancy. Certain activities involved patents; others did not. Many economists argue that it is technological change that spurs economic growth and development.

12 When the French Thomson acquired the consumer electronics business of RCA (in 1987), the latter already had a large plant in Ciudad Juarez (Mexico),

established in 1968. Thomson-RCA greatly expanded its Mexican facility in the 1990s (Cowie 1999: 116, 124, 142, 151). The market for the output was in the United States. The Japanese-owned Toshiba factory in Ciudad Juarez began production in 1987, long before NAFTA. In 2000 this Toshiba factory had one customer: the Toshiba operation in Tennessee.

13 Over the years, rate of return calculations have been given, or can be made, based on data in the *Survey of Current Business* (*Survey of Current Business* 1950–2000). Using these data, Robert Lipsey showed that a dramatic decline in income as a percentage of the beginning-of-the-year inward FDI position occurred between 1985 and 1991 (Lipsey 1993: 142). For the 1990s studies, some scholars had access to aggregate tax data. Daniel Nolle, an economist at The Office of the Comptroller of the Currency, found in 1995 that over the prior 10 years, foreign banks had, as a group, consistently produced lower returns on assets than their US counterparts (reported in *Financial Times* 1995).

14 One explanation offered (and not mentioned in my text) related to the drop in the value of the dollar in the late 1980s: Japanese firms (which showed particularly low returns and even negative ones) were heavy importers into the United States; they had to price the imports on their US books at an inflated value that, in turn, reduced their US profits. Another explanation identified 'herd' instincts: many of the late 1980s moves by foreign MNCs into the United States seemed not well designed and more part of a 'fashionable trend', with the returns low because of bad planning at the start. As the 1998–2000 mergers and acquisitions multiplied, more explanations revolved on the inability of foreign MNEs to manage effectively the big businesses that they acquired and the seemingly 'preposterous' prices.

15 Senator Hollings' proposed legislation has not passed (and at the time of writing seems unlikely to pass). As of 1 December 2000, the merger of Voice-Stream and Deutsche Telekom remained 'subject to US regulatory approvals and clearances by the Federal Communications Commission, the multi-agency Committee on Foreign Investment in the United States, approval by Voice-Stream shareholders, and customary closing conditions'. The quotation is from a VoiceStream Press Release, 6 Sept. 2000; I have checked that nothing changed between 6 Sept. and 1 Dec. 2000.

References

Associated Press (13 July 2000) 'UBS Buying PaineWebber'.

Brayer, H.O. (1949) 'The influence of British capital on the western range cattle industry', *Journal of Economic History* Suppl. 9: 85–98.

Calomiris, C.W. (2000) *US Bank Deregulation in Historical Perspective*, Cambridge: Cambridge University Press.

Carreras, A. and Tafunell, X. (1997) 'Spain: Big manufacturing firms between state and market, 1917–1990', in A.D. Chandler, Jr., F. Amatori and T. Hikino (eds) *Big Business and the Wealth of Nations*, Cambridge: Cambridge University Press.

Clements, R.V. (1953) 'British-controlled enterprise in the west between 1870 and 1900 and some agrarian reactions', *Agricultural History* 27: 132–42.

Cowie, J. (1999) *Capital Moves: RCA's Seventy-Year Quest for Cheap Labor*, Ithaca: Cornell University Press.

Crowe, K.C. (1978) *America for Sale*, Garden City, NY: Doubleday.

Dunning, J.H. (1960–1) Unpublished notes on the history of British companies in the United States, Dunning's files, University of Reading, Reading, England.

—— (1998) 'Does ownership really matter in a globalizing economy?', in D. Woodward and D. Nigh (eds) *Foreign Ownership and the Consequences of Direct Investment in the United States: Beyond Us and Them*, Westport, Conn: Quorum: 27–42.

Economic Report of the President (2000) Transmitted to Congress February.

Economist (20 May 2000) Story on Terra Networks.

Faith, N. (1971) *The Infiltrators: The European Business Invasion of America*, London: Hamish Hamilton.

Financial Times (1995) 'The end of an awful story . . . the $3.56 bn sale of NatWest Bancorp', 20 Dec.

—— (2000a) New stories on Vivendi, 16, 17, 20, 21, 22 June.

—— (2000b) 'A Mexican with the Midas touch', 10 July.

—— (2000c) 'Lycos investors back merger with Terra', 28 Oct.

Frantz, D. and Collins, C. (1989) *Selling Out: How We are Letting Japan Buy Our Land, Our Industries, Our Financial Institutions, and Our Future*, Chicago: Contemporary Books.

Freidel, F. (1960) *America in the Twentieth Century*, New York: Alfred A. Knopf.

Galambos, L. and Sturchio, J.L. (1998) 'Pharmaceutical firms and the transition to biotechnology: A study in strategic innovation', *Business History Review* 72, Summer: 250–78.

Getz, K.A. (1998) 'Politically active foreign-owned firms in the United States: Elephants or chickens?' in D. Woodward and D. Nigh (eds) *Foreign Ownership and the Consequences of Direct Investment in the United States: Beyond Us and Them*, Westport, Conn: Quorum: 231–53.

Glickman, N.J. and Woodward, D.P. (1989) *The New Competitors*, New York: Basic Books.

Graham, E.M. (1998) 'A retrospect on FDIUS', in D. Woodward and D. Nigh (eds) *Foreign Ownership and the Consequences of Direct Investment in the United States: Beyond Us and Them*, Westport, Conn: Quorum: 43–8.

Graham, E.M. and Krugman, P.R. (1989) *Foreign Direct Investment in the United States*, Washington, DC: Institute for International Economics.

—— (1991) *Foreign Direct Investment in the United States*, 2nd edn, Washington, DC: Institute for International Economics.

—— (1995) *Foreign Direct Investment in the United States*, 3rd edn, Washington, DC: Institute for International Economics.

Group of Thirty (1999) *The Evolving Corporation: Global Imperatives and National Responses*, Washington, DC: Group of Thirty.

Grubert, H., Goodspeed, T. and Swenson, D. (1993) 'Explaining the low taxable income of foreign-controlled companies in the United States', in A. Giovannini, G. Hubbard, and J. Slemrod (eds) *Studies in International Taxation*, Chicago: University of Chicago Press: 237–75.

Jackson, W.T. (1968) *The Enterprising Scot: Investors in the American West After 1873*, Edinburgh: Edinburgh University Press.

Jones, G. (1993) *British Multinational Banking 1830–1990*, Oxford: Clarendon Press.

—— (1996) *The Evolution of International Business*, London: Routledge.

Kaye Scholar (2000) Kaye Scholar, Fierman, Hays and Handler LLP, 'Memo on the Exon Florio Process', Jan.

Kenney, M. and Florida, R. (1993) *Beyond Mass Production: The Japanese System and Its Transfer to the United States*, New York: Oxford University Press.

Kerr, W.G. (1976) *Scottish Capital on the American Credit Frontier*, Austin, TX: Texas State Historical Association.

Lamont, D.F. (1979) *Foreign State Enterprises: A Threat to American Business*, New York: Basic Books.

Lipsey, R. (1993) 'Foreign direct investment in the United States: Changes over three decades', in K. Froot (ed.) *Foreign Direct Investment*, Chicago: University of Chicago Press: 113–70, and discussion: 170–2.

McGovney, D.O. (1947) 'The anti-Japanese land laws of California and ten other states', *California Law Review* 35: 7–60.

Marans, J.E., Williams, P.C. and Griffin, J.P. (eds) (1980) *Foreign Investment in the United States 1980*, Washington, DC: District of Columbia Bar.

Miami Herald (4 July 2000) Associated Press Story, 'Lawmakers react to Sprint rumor'.

—— (24, 25 July 2000) Stories on Deutsche Telekom and VoiceStream.

Moser, J.E. (1999) *Twisting the Lion's Tail: American Anglophobia between the World Wars*, New York: New York University Press.

Nachum, L. (2000) 'Economic geography and the location of TNCS: Financial and professional service FDI to the US', *Journal of International Business Studies* 31, 3: 367–85.

Organization for International Investment (1998) *Investing in American Jobs*, Washington, D.C.: Organization for International Investment.

Reich, R. (1990) 'Who is Us?', *Harvard Business Review* 68/Jan.–Feb.: 53–64.

Sale, K. (1975) *Power Shift: The Rise of the Southern Rim and Its Challenge to the Eastern Establishment*, New York: Random House.

Sidak, J.G. (1997) *Foreign Investment in American Telecommunications*, Chicago: University of Chicago Press.

Spence, C.C. (1958) *British Investments and the American Mining Frontier*, Ithaca: Cornell University Press.

Statistical Abstract of the US (1999).

Survey of Current Business (1950–2000), various issues.

—— (1999a) 'Regional patterns in the location of foreign-owned US manufacturing establishments', May: 8–25.

—— (1999b) 'Direct investment position for 1998', July: 48–59.

—— (2000a) 'An examination of the low rates of return of foreign-owned US companies', Mar.: 55–73.

—— (2000b) 'Direct investment position for 1999', July: 57–68.

Telefónica (2000) Data on Terra Network's plans to take-over Lycos, CNET News.com, 16 May; Reuters 16 May; *Miami Herald* 17 May.

Toral, P. (1999) 'The direct investments in Latin America and the Caribbean in the 1990s of multinational enterprises headquartered in Spain', MA thesis, Florida International University (a revised version will be published by Ashgate, under the title *The Reconquest of the New World*, probably in 2001).

Tolchin, M. and Tolchin, S. (1988) *Buying into America: How Foreign Money is Changing the Face of Our Nation*, New York: Times Books.

Tyson, L.D'A. (1991) 'They are not Us: Why American ownership still matters', *American Prospect* Winter: 37–49.

Tyson, L.D'A. and Yoffie, D.B. (1993) 'Semiconductors', in D.B. Yoffie (ed.) *Beyond Free Trade: Firms, Governments, and Global Competition*, Boston: Harvard Business School Press: 29–78.

Ulan, M. (ed.) (1991) 'Foreign investment in the United States', *The Annals* 516: July.

US Congress (1982) House of Representatives, *Federal Response to OPEC Country Investments in the United States (Part 2 – Investment in Sensitive Sectors of the US Economy: Kuwait Petroleum Corp. Takeover of Santa Fe International Corporation,* Hearings before a Subcommittee of the Committee on Government Operations, 97th Cong., 1st sess.

US Department of Commerce (1937) Bureau of Foreign and Domestic Commerce, *Foreign Investments in the United States.*

—— (1962) Office of Business Economics, *Foreign Business Investments in the United States.*

—— (1976) *Foreign Direct Investment in the United States,* 9 volumes.

US Department of Treasury (undated, 1999–2000?) Office of the Assistant Secretary of International Affairs, Office of International Investment, 'Exon Florio Provisions', www.treas.gov/oii.

VoiceStream (6 Sept. 2000) Press release.

Wall Street Journal (5 Oct. 2000) Story on 'VoiceStream deal'.

Whitman, M.v.N. (1999) *New World, New Rules: The Changing Role of the American Corporation,* Boston: Harvard Business School Press.

Wilkins, M. (1970) *The Emergence of Multinational Enterprise: American Business Abroad from the Colonial Period to 1914,* Cambridge, Mass: Harvard University Press.

—— (1974) *The Maturing of Multinational Enterprise: American Business Abroad from 1914 to 1970,* Cambridge, Mass: Harvard University Press.

—— (1989) *The History of Foreign Investment in the United States to 1914,* Cambridge, Mass: Harvard University Press.

—— (1990) 'Japanese multinationals in the United States: Continuity and change, 1879–1990', *Business History Review* 64, Winter: 585–629.

—— (1993) 'The history of French multinationals in the United States', *Entreprises et Histoire* 3, May: 14–29.

—— (1999a) 'Swiss investments in the United States, 1914–1945', in S. Guex (ed.) *La Suisse et les Grandes Puissances 1914–1945/Switzerland and the Great Powers 1914–1945,* Geneva: Droz: 91–139.

—— (1999b) 'Two literatures, two story-lines: Is a general paradigm of foreign portfolio and foreign direct investment feasible?', *Transnational Corporations* 8, April: 53–116.

—— (2000) 'German chemical firms in the United States from the late 19th century to post-World War II', in J. Lesch (ed.) *The German Chemical Industry in the Twentieth Century,* Dordrecht, Netherlands: Kluwer: 285–321.

—— (forthcoming) 'The history of foreign investment in the United States, 1914–1945', book length manuscript.

—— (in process) 'The history of foreign investment in the United States after 1945', book length manuscript.

—— (ed.) (1977) *Foreign Investment in the United States,* New York: Arno Press.

Woodward, D. and Nigh, D. (eds) (1998) *Foreign Ownership and the Consequences of Direct Investment in the United States: Beyond Us and Them,* Westport, Conn: Quorum.

World Development Report (1999–2000).

World Investment Report (1995).

Wright, G. (2000) 'Old South, New South, Sunbelt South', presentation at Business History Conference, 10 March.

3 Revisiting UK FDI in US manufacturing and extractive industries in 1960

John H. Dunning

Introduction

This chapter will be mainly concerned with the scope, pattern and consequences of British participation in US manufacturing and extractive industries in 1960. It is based on data obtained by the author from UK parent companies and/or their US affiliates in the early 1960s. Information concerning the US investments of all British companies known to have a substantial interest in these fields was sought, and in all but seven cases – only two of which we believed to be significant omissions – it was readily granted. As our original list of firms was checked for coverage with official sources both in the UK and in the United States, the data compiled and presented here are believed to give a reasonably comprehensive picture of the role of UK enterprises in these particular sectors of the US economy. Moreover, since the investment by UK firms in the manufacturing and extractive sectors, taken together with that of British insurance companies, was thought to comprise between 85 per cent and 90 per cent of the total UK direct capital stake in the US in 1960, the overall picture can be calculated quite easily. The balance of the British stake in that year was made up of (a) land related investments – the more important of which can be traced without much difficulty – and (b) various sales and marketing outlets, which, though numerous, involved comparatively little capital.

Before revisiting the data earlier obtained, it may be helpful to trace briefly the chief features of the development of British direct investment in the US up to World War II.

An historical excursion

In the first stages of American colonization, viz. the seventeenth and eighteenth centuries, virtually all the capital for settler investment (required for the transport of colonists, their early subsistence and defence) was supplied from the United Kingdom. By means of immigrant capital, speculative investment, long-term loans and trade credit, financed both by private enterprise and the English government itself, the foundations of modern

America were laid and its development assured. More particularly, the establishment and growth of the colonial iron, tobacco, shipbuilding and naval stores trades – four of the basic colonial industries – relied almost entirely directly or indirectly on British capital. By the time of the Revolution, the colonies had accumulated debts to England estimated at $40 million.[1]

Yet perhaps the first half of the nineteenth century is best remembered as the period in which the most pronounced impact of British finance on American economic growth was made. By 1828 one-quarter of the US national debt was held in England; eight years later the majority of the cotton estates were mortgaged to London merchants. Initially most of the British capital was invested in state and corporation stocks and bonds; later, with the opportunities widening, it helped finance the development of America's transportation network. While there was comparatively little direct investment by British firms in US industry at this time, indirectly by their purchase of state bonds, not only was such capital often subsequently channelled into such ventures, but domestic savings were released for more speculative endeavours.

Between the end of the Civil War and 1914 a much more diversified structure of British capital exports to the US evolved. Again, portfolio rather than direct capital was the main form of finance and, again, railways were the main source of attraction. But as important as the railways themselves were the avenues for further investment that they opened up. For example, British capital made a noteworthy contribution to the great westward movement of people and economic activity in the middle and latter part of the nineteenth century. In the trans-Mississippi west it is estimated that 1,500 British companies were set up between 1865 and 1900. These were also the years of the vast speculative investments by British companies in cattle raising, mining, land and breweries – projects long since forgotten but exerting a vital influence on US economic development at the time.

More significant, however, for our present interests, it was during this period that the first British companies began to establish branch plants and subsidiaries in US industry. Among these were the embryonic ventures of some of the giant investors of 1960, e.g. Courtaulds, Lever, Coats, English Sewing Cotton and Shell, and a host of British insurance companies. The path for the British investor was by no means smooth; there were severe losses as well as profits. Nevertheless, by 1914, the stock of UK investment had reached an all-time peak of £755 million ($3,650 million at the then rate of exchange) out of a total foreign investment in the US approaching $7,000 million. The share of the British stake represented by corporate investment is not known, but there is no doubt that its volume was considerably greater than the corresponding investment by US companies in Britain at the time. In particular, UK affiliates were already making a significant contribution to the development of some of America's newer industries, e.g. rayon and petroleum.

During World War I and the years immediately after, Britain liquidated about 70 per cent of its dollar investments and, although later these were partially rebuilt, the value of Britain's portfolio holdings never reached its pre-war level. Direct investments, however, continued to gain in importance, and by 1937 accounted for $833 million of a total UK investment stake of £2,743 million. At the beginning of World War II it was estimated that there were over 600 branch enterprises or associated companies of British firms operating in the United States.

Only one large direct investment was compulsorily sold between 1939 and 1945, viz. that of Courtauld's 91 per cent interest in American Viscose, then the largest man-made fibre concern in the world, for the sum of £54 million, a fraction of its true market value. Other direct investments and some securities were pledged as security for a loan to Britain of $425 million by the Reconstruction and Finance Corporation. A further $700 million of securities were sold by the UK government who had the power to acquire holdings as and when needed.

According to a US Congressional report, Britain had $2,000 million invested in the United States in mid-1947. Of this figure, direct investments accounted for about $1,000 million. By 1950, this latter figure had risen to $1,168 million and by 1960 had more than doubled to $2,248 million. Further details are set out in Table 3.1, which *inter alia* reveals the important role played by UK investors in the finance and (particularly) insurance sectors. Table 3.1 also gives details of the relative importance of the UK as a foreign direct investor in the US.

The 1960 (Southampton) survey

In the second half of 1960 (prior to the completion of the first major survey by the US Department of Commerce on Foreign Direct Investment in the US), the present author initiated (at the University of Southampton) a comprehensive survey of all UK firms known to have direct investments in US manufacturing and extractive industries. At the time, drawing upon a variety of US and UK sources, we put the number of such firms at between 100 and 110, and the number of their affiliates in the US at between 150 and 200. Of the UK firms approached, 80 agreed to participate in our survey. Of these 74 were interviewed, some in the UK, some in the US, and some in both countries. Each completed a questionnaire about their US operations, and the questionnaires and interviews provided the data for our analysis.

Some of the results of this survey were subsequently published but, in the light of advances in knowledge about the determinants of foreign direct investment (FDI), and the strategy of multinational enterprises over the past 40 years, we thought it interesting to revisit some of our original data, and re-examine some of our earlier findings.[2]

In Table 3.2 we give some details about the extent, significance, age

Table 3.1 Value of foreign direct investment in the US by area and industry, 1950, 1955 and 1960 (US$ millions)

Areas and industries	*1950*	*1955*	*1960*
All areas, total	**3,391**	**5,076**	**6,910**
Petroleum	405	853	1,238
Manufacturing	1,138	1,759	2,611
Finance and insurance	1,065	1,499	1,810
Other	784	965	1,251
Canada	**1,029**	**1,542**	**1,934**
Petroleum	56	196	203
Manufacturing	468	711	932
Finance and insurance	153	179	246
Other	352	456	553
Europe, total	**2,228**	**3,369**	**4,707**
Petroleum	349	657	1,028
Manufacturing	669	1,040	1,611
Finance and insurance	870	1,272	1,504
Other	340	400	564
United Kingdom	**1,168**	**1,749**	**2,248**
Petroleum	95	204	339
Manufacturing	337	510	722
Finance and insurance	554	836	953
Other	182	199	234
Other Europe, total	**1,059**	**1,620**	**2,459**
Petroleum	254	453	689
Manufacturing	332	530	889
Finance and insurance	316	436	551
Other	158	201	330
Other areas, total	**134**	**165**	**269**
Petroleum	–	–	7
Manufacturing	1	8	68
Finance and insurance	42	48	60
Other	92	109	134

Source: US Department of Commerce (1961).

Note
Individual statistics may not add to totals because of rounding.

and ownership pattern of UK FDI in the US. Items 1–4 give our estimates of the total UK capital stake, and items 5–12 are based on data from the Southampton survey. The data set out in Table 3.2 are largely self-explanatory. We would, however, highlight the following points.

1 The UK FDI stake in US manufacturing and extractive industry in 1960 was highly concentrated. Six firms (Unilever, Shell Transport and Trading, British American Tobacco, Bowater, Coats and Clark

Table 3.2 Some features of British foreign direct investment in US manufacturing and extractive sectors *c.* 1960

1		Number of UK firms with US affiliates	100–110
2	a	Value of stock of UK direct investment (net assets)[a]	*c.* $1,250 million
	b	% of all UK direct investment in US	55.6
	c	% of all foreign direct investment in manufacturing and extractive sectors	24.5
3	a	Numbers employed in UK-owned subsidiaries	90–100,000
	b	% of US labour force	0.6
4	a	Value of sales of UK-owned subsidiaries	$4 billion
	b	% of all US sales	1.1
5	a	Average profitability[b] of UK-owned affiliates (1958–60)	5.8
	b	Average profitability[b] of all US firms	9.3
6		% of 2a accounted for	
		largest 6 firms	>65
		largest 12 firms	>80
7		Percentage of wholly owned subsidiaries	66.7
		majority-owned joint ventures	27.4
		minority-owned joint ventures	5.9
8		Percentage of UK subsidiaries originating by way of	
		greenfield ventures	62.2
		purchase or part purchase of US company	37.8
9		Number of US States in which UK subsidiaries were represented	34
10		About one quarter of US subsidiaries began operations in US before World War I; and a third were set up or aquired by UK firms between 1945 and 1960.	
11		While in most cases production costs per capita were higher in the US subsidiaries than in their parent companies, labour productivity in the former was higher than, or about the same as, the latter in four cases out of five	
12		The average percentage of the total of UK subsidiaries exported was under 10% in 1960. The import propensities of such subsidiaries were also very low, except in the case of some raw materials (e.g. cotton, yarn, etc.)	

Source: Southampton survey.

Notes
Items 1–4 US Department of Commerce (1961); items 5–12 for 74 firms participating in Southampton survey.
a Book value.
b Net profit (after tax) as % of net assets (capital employed).

and Borax (Holdings)) accounted for two-thirds of the total UK-owned capital stock, and the largest twelve firms for over four-fifths (item 6).

2 About three-quarters of the US affiliates of UK firms were first set up after 1918, and a third between 1945 and 1960 (item 10).

3 Just over three-fifths (62.2 per cent) of US affiliates originated as greenfield ventures; the balance took the form of a purchase or part purchase of an existing US company (item 8).

4 Two-thirds of US affiliates were branch plants of, or wholly-owned by, their parent companies. Some 27.4 per cent were majority-owned ventures, and 5.9 per cent minority-owned ventures (item 7).

5 In 1960, the total FDI stake by (all) UK firms in the US was only 0.5 per cent of the US gross national product. Latest figures released by UNCTAD in October 2000 (UNCTAD 2000) show the corresponding percentage was 5.2 per cent in 1998. In the manufacturing and extractive sectors, employment in UK-owned affiliates accounted for 0.6 per cent of the total labour force in the US in 1960.

6 The US affiliates of UK firms were represented in 34 states in 1960. However, about two-fifths of all affiliates were sited along the Eastern seaboard, while textile firms tended to cluster in Rhode Island and Georgia, mining firms in the mid-West, machine tool firms in New Jersey, metal using firms in the mid-West, pharmaceuticals and toiletry firms in New York and New Jersey, and tobacco and tobacco product firms in Virginia (item 9).

In Table 3.3 we list the 25 leading UK direct investments, classified by the name of US affiliate, product lines and the date of setting up a greenfield venture or acquisition of (or merger with) a US firm.[3] The towering importance of such firms as Shell Oil Company, Lever Bros., Bowater, Brown and Williamson, US Borax and Chemical Corporation and Coats and Clark is clearly seen from this table.

Motives for UK FDI in US

The contemporary literature on the determinants of foreign-owned production suggests that there are four main motives for such multinational enterprise (MNE) activity. Two of these are *supply* oriented, viz. to source inputs for value added activity, and to gain access to created assets (especially technology, managerial capabilities and markets); one is *demand* oriented, viz. to better serve existing, or penetrate new, markets; and the fourth is *efficiency* oriented, viz. to better organize the geographical spread of the activities of the investing firm, so as to benefit from the cross-border economies of scale, scope and integration.

Until the 1980s, most attention of international business (IB) scholars was directed to examining the role of FDI in *exploiting* the home-based competitive advantages of the investing firms, and in efficiently combining these advantages with those of foreign located assets and capabilities. It has only been in the last two decades or so, with the emergence of the knowledge-based economy, that the focus has shifted to viewing FDI as a modality of *protecting* or *augmenting* their existing stock of tangible and intangible assets, and particularly their intellectual capital.

Examining the motives for their *initial* entry into the US identified by our respondent firms, and classifying these by broad industrial groups, Table 3.4 shows that the great majority (82.4 per cent) were of an asset exploiting, market seeking variety; although three of the largest British investors were also drawn to the US by the presence of critical natural

Table 3.3 Some leading UK foreign direct investments in US manufacturing industries, 1960

Name of US subsidiary	*Date est. in US*	*Products*	*UK-owned net assets US$m.*	*Employment*
Arkwright/Interlaken Inc.[b]	1883	Book and tracing cloths	4.8	300
American Thread Company	1898	Textile products	38.7	4,940
Arnold Hoffman & Co.[a]	1950	Chemical products	9.7	2,816
Baker Perkins Inc.	1920	Food and chemical products	*c.* 5.0	1,100
Beecham Products Inc.[a]	1954	Toiletries	*c.* 3.5	225
Bowater of North America Ltd[c]	1954	Paper and pulp products	*c.* 75.0	2,385
Bradford Dyeing Association[a]	1911	Textile piece goods	4.2	855
Brown & Williamson Inc.[a]	1927	Tobacco products	205.0	6,607
Burroughs Welcome & Co. (USA) Inc.	1908	Pharmaceutical products	11.3	1,000
Capitol Records Inc.[a]	1955	Gramophone records	13.2	1,750
Coats and Clark Inc.	1870	Sewing thread	56.5	5,568
Crosse & Blackwell Co. Inc.[a]	1927	Processed food products	*c.* 3.0	450
Courtaulds Inc.	1951[d]	Man-made fibres	35.0	800
Distillers Co. Ltd. (Delaware)	1930s	Gin and vodka products	10.0	300
Dunlop Tyre and Rubber Corp.	1923	Rubber products	24.2	2,550
Fibre Industries Inc.	not known	Man-made fibres	15.0	400
Foote Bros Gear & Machine Corp.[a]	pre-1900	Machine tools	4.6	1,235
Hope Windows[a]	1926	Metal windows	5.2	500
Keasbey & Mattison[a]	1934	Building products	25.0	1,800
Lever Bros.[b]	pre-1900	Detergents, edible fats	80.0[f]	10,100
Morganite	1910	Carbon brushes and metal based accessories	40.0	2,800
R.F. French Inc.[a]	1926	Spices, pet foods etc.	25.0	1,300
Shell Oil Company, New York[b]	pre-1900	Petroleum and chemical products	410.0[e]	35,600
Tetley Tea Co. Inc.	1913	Tea products	3.8	1,000
Yardley of London Inc.	1928	Toilet preparations	7.7	350

Source: Southampton survey.

Notes
a Entry into US via M&A.
b Entry both by M&A. and greenfield venture.
c Incorporated in Canada. The Canadian company is responsible for all US operations.
d Though an earlier venture was disposed of in WWII.
e UK share of FDI stake by Royal Dutch Shell, in US.
f Assumed 50% of FDI stake in Lever Bros. was UK owned. Includes investment in Thomas Lipton.

Table 3.4 Motivations for UK direct investment in US manufacturing and resource-based sectors, 1960

	Number	*UK-owned net assets 1960*	*%*	*Employment 1960*	*%*
1 Natural resource seeking [minerals, petroleum, etc.]	6	84.7	6.9	3,238	3.7
2 Natural resource/market seeking [petroleum/ chemicals, wood pulp/paper, tobacco/tobacco products]	3	690.5	56.5	44,592	50.4
3 Market seeking (a) *Processing* [Food, drink and tobacco, chemicals, pharmaceuticals and toiletries, textiles and clothing, rubber products, paper, building materials]	34	340.9	27.9	31,445	35.5
(b) *Fabricating* [Machinery, metal goods, industrial instruments, auto parts]	27	92.0	7.5	7,488	8.5
4 Strategic asset seeking [Industrial instruments, machine tools]	4	15.0	1.2	1,695	1.9
5 Efficiency seeking		None		None	
Totals	74	1,223.1	100.0	88,454	100.0

Source: Southampton survey (1960).

resources.[4] Reviewing the answers to our questionnaires 40 years on we could only identify four cases where the respondents cited asset augmentation as a specific reason for entering the US; however, as we shall see later in this chapter, at the time, a good proportion of UK firms perceived that, as a direct result of their presence in the US, they had benefited from a feedback of technological and marketing know-how and managerial competence.

Again, in marked contrast to recent FDI by UK firms in the US (mainly in the form of mergers and acquisitions (M&As)) we were unable to identify any cases of an initial entry into the US being part of a global strategy of the investing firms, or as a means of promoting a more efficient division of labour of value added activities between the UK and the US plants. Almost without exception, in 1960, UK corporate interests in the US were considered largely independent of those elsewhere in the world. *Inter alia* this is shown by the very small amount of trade between the UK affiliates and their parent companies, apart from the import of some specialized raw materials, component parts and semi-finished or finished goods, particularly in the case of more recently established affiliates.[5]

Table 3.5 Stated reasons for investing in US at time of entry (no. of times reasons mentioned)

	Types of investment[a]					
	1	*2*	*3*	*4*	*5*	*Total*
1 To gain access to natural resources	5	2	2	–	–	9
2 To gain access to US technology and other created assets	–	–	–	–	5	5
3 To overcome tariff barriers and/or transatlantic transport costs	1	–	19	14	2	36
4 To gain (better) access to US markets	–	3	7	9	3	22
5 To lower costs of production compared to UK plants	–	1	12	5	1	19
6 To take advantage of (perceived) economic growth in US	1	3	25	19	2	50
7 To counteract and/or preempt more of competitors	–	1	9	4	–	14
8 Break up (voluntary or otherwise) of Anglo-US licensing *et al.* agreements	–	1	3	6	1	11
9 To be 'on the spot' to take advantage of different requirements of US consumers, and/or provide speedier delivery and offer better after sales service.	–	–	9	8	2	19
No. of firms responding	5	3	33	25	5	71

Source: Southampton survey (1960).

Notes

a Key to headings 1–5, see Table 3.3.

Table 3.5 gives more details of the specific reasons for investing in the US identified by 71 respondents. Here it can be seen that 'defensive', 'aggressive' and US specific market seeking opportunities were the most mentioned reasons, although in the case of process-related FDI, the perception that production costs in the US would be lower than in the UK appeared to be quite an important consideration. Strategic related motives, as, for example, originally identified by Ray Vernon (1966) and Frederick Knickerbocker (1973), were mentioned by fourteen firms including those in the oligopolistic sectors, e.g. petroleum, metal windows (here two of the three UK firms demonstrated a 'follow my leader' strategy), man-made fibres and rubber tyres. Eleven firms indicated that the break-up of Anglo-US licensing and other technical agreements directly led to their US investments, while only fourteen of the 185 reasons identified by the 71 firms could be construed as being of a natural resource seeking or asset augmenting kind.

FDI in the US and the theory of MNE activity

For the most part, UK participation in US industry in the late 1950s was designed to earn profits for the parent company by protecting existing and/or penetrating new markets. In the great majority of greenfield ventures, prior to the FDI being made, the investing company was exporting to the US. In doing so, it demonstrated it possessed certain sustainable competitive (or ownership (O) specific) advantages over indigenous US firms. Sometimes – as in the case of most consumer goods firms – these advantages related to the nature of the products being supplied; sometimes, as in the case of most producer goods, to unique or superior processing and fabricating technologies. Whenever and wherever it was in the interests of companies to add value to (i.e. exploit) such intangible assets in the US rather than in the UK (or another location), *and* also to internalize the transatlantic markets for them, then FDI became the preferred modality of transfer.

The exploitation, by UK investors, of home-based O advantages, first by exports and then by FDI, is entirely consistent with Vernon's product cycle theory, although because of the relatively higher wage costs in the US than in the UK, there needed to be other reasons (e.g. tariffs and transport costs, higher US productivity, easier access to local supplies and/or markets, better infrastructure) to induce a westward (in contrast to an eastward) transatlantic investment flow.[6] Certainly, however, the asset-based O advantages cited by UK firms in our sample were consistent with those later identified by the resource-based theory of the firm (Wernerfelt 1984; Barney 1991). For example in 1960, UK FDI in the US was strongly concentrated in sectors in which the UK, relative to the US, had a revealed technological advantage (RTA) in the following decade (Cantwell and Hodson 1991).[7] There is also some suggestion that these were also the sectors in which the UK had a revealed comparative advantage (RCA) in exports (Dunning 1978). In relatively few cases, however, would it appear to be the case that UK firms entered the US market to gain the advantages of transatlantic product or process integration.

While our research revealed little evidence that the companies investing in the US considered alternative locations, some parallel work we undertook in the early 1960s on UK FDI in Canada did suggest that several UK investors preferred to service the US market from a Canadian location. Mainly this seemed to be because they perceived Canada to be culturally more similar to the UK and that (real) labour costs were lower there.

However, within the US, and in congruence with modern location theory (e.g. Wallace 2000) there was some suggestion that UK firms preferred to agglomerate in particular states or districts within states. Thus textile firms were drawn to Rhode Island and Georgia, pharmaceutical firms to the New York, New Jersey area, metal-using firms to the industrial conurbations of the East Coast and mid-West, and firms seeking to

Table 3.6 Some determinants of UK direct investment in US manufacturing and extractive industries, 1960

(1) OWNERSHIP (O)-SPECIFIC ADVANTAGES (OF THE UK PARENT FIRM)	(a) Manufacturing techniques and marketing experience of US parent companies, e.g. in drink products, edible fats, building products.
(i) Property right and/or intangible asset advantage (Oa)	(b) Access to UK product and production technology; and innovatory capacity, e.g. in processing sectors, e.g. chemicals, food, drink and tobacco, textiles. (c) Access to UK managerial philosophy, attitudes and techniques; and 'bank' of human learning, expertise and experience, e.g. in petroleum refining. (d) Privileged possession of patents, trademarks and/or brand names, e.g. consumer goods such as processed foods, toiletries.
(ii) Advantages of common governance, learning experiences, and organisational competence (Ot)	(a) Those that branch plants of established enterprises enjoy were *de novo* firms, e.g. those associated with size, economies of scope, spreading of overhead costs and product diversification of parent companies; those which allow affiliates access to resources and experience of parent companies at marginal cost; and synergistic economies (not only in production, but in R&D, purchasing, marketing, financial arrangements. These were of only limited importance in case of UK firms investing in the US.
(2) LOCATION (L) SPECIFIC ADVANTAGES OF US RELATIVE TO OTHER LOCATIONS, FOR VALUE ADDED ACTIVITIES OF UK DIRECT INVESTMENTS	(a) Tariff and non-tariff barriers. Important for most consumer goods. (b) Exchange controls. (Not important) (c) Limitations on dividend, remission and capital repatriation. (Not important) (d)*Transatlantic transport and communication costs (e.g. in tobacco products, gramophone records). (e) Domestic market size and growth potential. (f) Presence of related firms, including other foreign affiliates (e.g. in metal windows sector).
(3) INTERNALIZATION (I) INCENTIVE ADVANTAGES (OF THE INVESTING FIRMS OR POTENTIAL INVESTORS)	(a) Avoidance of search and negotiating applicable particularly in case of smaller UK investors. (b) To avoid costs or moral hazard, information asymmetries and adverse selection; and to protect reputation of internalizing firm.

(c) Buyer uncertainty (in US), about nature and value of inputs (e.g. technology) being sold, e.g. in respect of metal-based products.
(d) Lack of suitable licences in US, e.g. in textiles and some foodstuffs.
(e) Need of seller to protect quality of intermediate or final products; especially important in case of some consumer goods.
(f) Company policy to own foreign affiliates wherever possible, e.g. as evident in case of textile, drink and tobacco firms.
(g) To control supplies and conditions of sale of inputs (including technology), e.g. petroleum and pulp paper products.
(h) To control market outlets (including those which might be used by competitors) e.g. in petroleum products.

---

augment their technological and managerial capabilities to the knowledge intensive states of California, New Jersey and Massachusetts. In addition, outside the resource-based sectors, three out of every five US affiliates were concentrated within a 60-mile radius of a major East or West Coast port.

Our survey did not specifically address the question as to why UK firms wished to own value added facilities in the US rather than to engage in licensing agreements with US firms, but based upon the rationale for internalization identified in the literature it is not difficult to rationalize why, in fact, UK firms chose the former route for exploiting and organizing their core competences.[8] Some of these reasons, together with the O and L advantages which helped facilitate UK FDI in the US in the mid-1950s and before, are set out in Table 3.6.

Managerial procedures and control patterns

Before considering the performance of UK firms in the US in the second half of the 1950s, let us briefly analyse our respondents' replies to two questions. The first of these is 'To what extent are managerially related questions, procedures, and functions in US plants "strongly", "partially" or "negligibly" based on their UK equivalents?' The second is 'Are major decisions on these procedures and functions – in so far as they relate to the operations of the US affiliates – only taken after receiving approval from the UK parent company, or are they taken by the management of the affiliate independently of the parent company?'

Table 3.7 sets out the answers to these questions. While, in the case of overall management philosophy and strategy, capital expenditure and

Table 3.7 Managerial procedures and control patterns with respect to UK affiliates in US manufacturing and resource based sectors, 1960

	Procedures in US plants (a) strongly, (b) partially or (c) negligibly based on UK techniques (% of total)			*Major decisions in US taken (a) only after approval from UK, (b) independently (% of total)*	
	(a)	*(b)*	*(c)*	*(a)*	*(b)*
1 Overall managerial philosophy and strategy	42.3	36.5	21.1	74.5	25.5
2 Capital expenditure	42.0	30.0	28.0	69.8	30.2
3 Product innovation and development	26.0	28.0	46.0	43.3	56.7
4 Production planning and budgetary control	15.4	30.8	56.0	15.1	84.9
5 Plant supervision and manufacturing methods	18.4	26.5	55.1	13.5	86.5
6 Wages policy and labour relationships	6.3	10.4	81.2	10.7	89.3
7 Distribution and marketing practices	6.4	21.3	72.3	19.2	80.7

Source: Southampton survey (1960). Based on replies of 70 firms.

product innovation, the procedures in the US plant are, for the most part, 'strongly' or 'partially' based on UK practice, for the other four functions identified, and particularly in respect of labour related policies and marketing procedures, such practices are clearly modified and adapted to the particular needs of the US economy. Moreover, the great majority of respondents claimed that the US-based line managers had full authority to take decisions on these matters independently of their opposite numbers in the UK.[9] However, decisions relating to the overall management strategy and capital expenditure of the US affiliates was strongly centred in the UK; although, somewhat surprisingly, (in the case of less than one-half of the respondent firms) the major decisions on product innovation and development in the affiliate were taken without reference to the parent company. As might be expected, there was some suggestion that the older and larger affiliates were more autonomous in their decision-taking relative to their younger and smaller counterparts; while decision-taking in 100 per cent owned affiliates tended to be more centralized than in joint ventures. At the same time, the fact that there was little product, process or marketing integration between the UK parent and its US affiliates, suggests that the latter, in 1960, had considerably more freedom in their managerial decision-taking than, for example, do UK affiliates of Japanese and US firms now producing in an integrated European market.

More generally, most respondents felt there were relatively few substantial differences between the managerial and control procedures adopted by US firms and their UK counterparts which could not be explained by size, experience and industry specific factors. Perhaps the most common perceived difference was the tendency for US firms to adopt more explicit or detailed control procedures and make more use of committees and task forces. At the same time, the style of management in the US was thought to be less formal and paternal than that in the UK.

Some results of UK direct investment in the US

Earlier in this chapter we indicated that the great majority of the firms participating in our survey perceived that the results of their US investments had come up to their expectations. Those who were not satisfied – all but one of which had been set up between 1948 and 1959 – identified four main reasons:

- i competition in the US was greater than they had anticipated;
- ii the start up costs of producing in the US were higher than they had thought;
- iii the market for their products had not expanded as had been hoped;
- iv in the case of some takeovers, the costs of adjustment and upgrading the acquired plant had been miscalculated.

At the same time, data on the profitability of some 54 respondent firms, over the 5 year period 1955–60, show that their performance was well below that of indigenous firms in all sectors.[10] Some details are set out in Table 3.8. The below average performance of the UK-owned affiliates

Table 3.8 Comparative rates and return[a] in US manufacturing industry, 1955–60

	Net profits US	
	UK affiliates	*US firms*
Chemicals and allied trades	6.4	15.0
Food and kindred products	8.2	10.5
Iron and steel products Non-ferrous metals	9.0	10.3
Textiles and clothing	5.0	6.5
Pulp and paper	7.9	10.6
Other manufacturing	5.2	n.a.
All manufacturing	7.3	11.7

Sources: UK firms – Southampton survey
US firms – First National City Bank of New York.

Note
a Rate of return defined as net profits (before tax) as a % of net assets (= total assets less current liabilities).

were in complete contrast to the higher than average performance of US-owned affiliates in the UK at the time (Dunning 1998). How is this to be explained? *Prima facie,* it seems to be in conflict with the proposition that FDI is undertaken by firms with superior competitive or ownership (O) specific advantages relative to those of the indigenous firms in the countries in which they operate (Hymer 1960).

In an earlier contribution (Dunning 1970), we examined four possible reasons for the variation in the profitability of UK affiliates. These were the size structure of the investment of the two groups of firms, differences in their age profile, the form or origin of the investment, and the financial and managerial relationships between the affiliates and their UK associates. In summarizing our conclusions on the first three factors we found that

a relative to their indigenous counterparts, larger UK affiliates did less well than smaller UK affiliates; yet, at the same time proportionately fewer larger affiliates experienced losses in the 1955–60 period than did smaller affiliates;
b there was no clear relationship between profitability and age of investment, except that those affiliates set up or acquired in the later part of the postwar period did less well than those set up or acquired before 1939;
c there were no significant differences in the performance of acquired firms as against greenfield ventures; nor between that of 100 per cent owned UK affiliates and Anglo/US joint ventures.

As to the fourth possible reason, we sought to test the following proposition. If the poor performance of UK-owned affiliates in the US was a reflection of the inferior quality or lack of dynamism of UK management, then one might expect those affiliates which were (a) strongly controlled by their parent companies in decision taking, and (b) which adopted their managerial practices and control procedures, would record lower profitability rates than those which were independent of UK governance, and whose philosophies and strategies were largely US influenced.

Our findings were as follows.

1 UK-owned affiliates with a UK chief executive in charge recorded considerably higher profits/net assets ratios than those with a US chief executive.
2 In general, UK affiliates which followed the managerial procedures of their parent companies earned a higher rate of return than those which did not. As Table 3.9 shows, the average of the seven sets of profitability ratios identified for firms which were markedly influenced by UK procedures worked out at 8.8 per cent, for those partially influenced at 6.3 per cent, and for those negligibly influenced at 7.1 per cent.

Table 3.9 Profit/capital ratios of UK affiliates in US manufacturing and extractive industries by control/influence exerted by parent companies

	Procedures in US plants (a) strongly, (b) partially or (c) negligibly based on UK techniques (% of total)			*Major decisions in US taken (a) only after approval from UK, (b) independently (% of total)*	
	(a)	*(b)*	*(c)*	*(a)*	*(b)*
1 Overall managerial philosophy and strategy	8.6	5.7	7.0	7.2	7.6
2 Capital expenditure	7.0	7.2	7.3	7.0	8.4
3 Product innovation and development	8.1	5.3	7.1	8.1	6.7
4 Production planning and budgetary control	7.8	6.3	7.1	7.8	7.1
5 Plant supervision and manufacturing methods	7.1	11.1	7.6	10.2	6.7
6 Wages policy and labour relationships	11.6	4.0	7.2	13.9	5.7
7 Distribution and marketing practices	11.2	4.9	7.0	11.4	5.7

Source: Southampton survey. Based on replies of 65 firms.

Similarly, in five out of the seven functional areas, affiliates which have to refer back to their parent companies before major decisions are taken are seen to have earned a higher rate of return on their capital than their autonomous counterparts; and even in respect of overall management policy, the difference in the performance of the two groups of firms was only marginal.

On the basis of these data then, there is only limited support for the proposition that the inappropriateness of UK managerial practices or inefficiency of control procedures was a significant factor in explaining the below average profitability of UK-owned affiliates in the US during the later 1950s. This does not mean that there may not have been other areas of managerial inefficiency; for example to do with the timing, form, location and choice of investment, weaknesses in transatlantic communication flows and organizational patterns, and the failure of UK firms to gauge properly the supply constraints and competitive challenges of the US market; only that the philosophy, policies and practices of UK management at that time were not greatly out of line with those of their US counterparts.

Why then did so many UK firms in 1960 appear to be satisfied with their US direct investments? For in the second half of the 1950s, the rate

Table 3.10 Knowledge feedback from US to UK as a result of UK FDI in the US

(1) Innovatory activities

- 45% of UK-affiliates did some R&D in US in 1960: and 89% of those with US-owned assets of $5 million or more.
- Only a handful of firms did any fundamental research in US.

(2) Knowledge feedback

- 70% of UK firms explicitly identified some feedback of technical, organizational, managerial, and marketing expertise.
- From their presence in US, 21% of foreign investors regarded this as important or very important; 39% of those which had assets of $5 million or more.

of return on domestic (UK) investments was, on average, considerably higher than that in the US. The answer, we believe, lies in other benefits which the UK firms perceived they derived from a presence in the US. Here we see (*ex post*) some of the earliest examples of asset augmenting FDI, even though, at the time of their entry into the US, most investing firms had other objectives in mind.

Re-examining the data from our 1960 survey, Table 3.10 shows that 45 per cent of the 74 respondent firms did some research and development in the US, and no less than 89 per cent of those with assets over $5 million. Admittedly the great majority of the innovatory activity of UK affiliates took the form of product adaptation, process development and machinery design. Only a handful of companies, notably Coats and Clark, Royal Dutch Shell, British American Tobacco, Dunlop, Lever Bros. and Burroughs Welcome, said they undertook any fundamental research in the US, and only two located their central R&D facilities in that country. For the most part, in 1960, the knowledge-related liaisons between the UK subsidiaries and their parent companies was considerably less than that reported by US firms with subsidiaries in the UK (Dunning 1998).

However, at the same time, and this is the point we wish to emphasize, no less than 70 per cent of British firms explicitly identified some technical feedback which they attributed to their presence in the US. Some 21 per cent of all firms regarded this as important or very important; these included 39 per cent of those companies with US assets of $5 million or above. While some of these benefits were a direct result of the R&D undertaken by UK affiliates in the US, even more important were the perceived knowledge enhancing gains resulting from tapping into the technological, managerial and organizational capabilities of US industry. Such a 'window' into American innovatory capacity and innovatory systems, product and process technology and machinery design, as well as the more general cross-fertilization of ideas and managerial methods, appeared to be especially important in the case of high technology UK firms, and particularly those in the pharmaceutical, electrical equipment and industrial instruments sectors.

We conclude then. Although the main motive for West-bound transatlantic FDI up until the 1960s was to exploit the *existing* competitive advantages of the investing firms, there was, nevertheless, a fair amount of innovatory activity undertaken by UK affiliates in the US; and a growing recognition of the value of direct access to the scientific and technological competencies of that country. While at the time no attempt was made to quantify these benefits, a study undertaken by the Department of Applied Economics in the 1960s calculated that UK firms investing abroad (mainly in Europe and the US) gained a return equivalent to 1.2 per cent of their net assets, and 11.5 per cent of their after-tax profits, as a direct result of the feedback of new knowledge of one kind or another (Reddaway, Potter and Taylor 1968).

Conclusions

The level and pattern of the FDI stake by UK companies in the US in 1960 strongly reflected the relative competitive (or O specific) advantages of UK and US firms; and the comparative advantages of the resources and capabilities of the US relative to that of the UK.

Second, the fact that the export/FDI ratio of UK firms investing in the US was so much higher than in the case of US firms investing in the UK in 1960 (Dunning 1993) reflected the relative locational (L) advantages of the two countries, and, in particular due to lower labour costs and the shortage of dollars, the greater the attraction of the UK as a location for most US-owned value added activities. Nevertheless, as a powerhouse for technological, managerial and other innovations the US was becoming increasingly attractive to asset seeking FDI from the UK and other parts of Europe.

Third, while there was some licensing activity between UK and US firms, the majority of UK economic involvement in the US was via FDI. The particular reasons why UK firms preferred to internalize their intermediate product transatlantic markets have been set out in Table 3.6. Of these 3a, b, e, f and g of Table 3.6 were the most frequently identified by firms.

The main motive for most FDI in the US was to exploit the US market more effectively than by other means. The extent to which managerial related practices and control procedures were UK or US-based varied according to function, although the overall philosophy and strategy of the UK affiliates strangely reflected that of their parent companies.

The main benefits of UK participation in US industry were the profits earned, plus an insight into US technology and other resources and capabilities. We found no compelling evidence that the relatively poor profit performance of UK affiliates could be put at the door of UK management practices and control procedures.

Notes

1 Although the actual amount granted by the British Parliament to those who had suffered losses in the Revolution was only $15 million.
2 For example, in Dunning (1961, 1970).
3 Though in twenty-eight (i.e. 35 per cent) of all instances this affiliate operated two or more production outlets.
4 We have always classified Brown and Williamson (which is owned by BAT) as a market seeking/natural resource FDI. However, the first manufacturing investment of BAT in the US took the form of the purchase of two US tobacco processing companies: T.C. Williams and David Dunlop, both of which were located at Petersburg in Virginia. Because of an earlier agreement with Imperial Tobacco Co. in 1902, these US-based companies could only supply non-UK export markets (Cox 2000).
5 Of sixty firms providing us with such data 56 per cent of US affiliates did not export from the US at all, and another 25 per cent exported 10 per cent or less of their gross output. Some 57 per cent of affiliates stated they imported nothing from the UK, and another 23 per cent less than 10 per cent of their outside purchases.
6 The Southampton survey suggested that the labour productivity of US plants was that in one-half of cases US productivity was higher and in a quarter of the cases about the same as in the UK; at the same time in three out of five cases, the unit production costs in the US were estimated to be 5 per cent or more higher than in the UK.
7 No data on RTA are available before 1969. Between that date and 1977, over four-fifths of the UK direct investment stake in the US was in sectors in which RTA_{UK}/RTA_{US} was greater than 1. The RTA of a particular sector is defined as a share of world-wide patents registered in the US, in that sector by a particular country, divided by its share in world wide patents.
8 As recently reviewed in Dunning (2000).
9 In about one quarter of cases these were opinions expressed by representatives of the UK parent concern; and the balance were those expressed by representatives of the US affiliates visited.
10 Excluding those in the hard minerals sectors.

References

Barney, J. (1991) 'Firm resources and sustainable competitive advantage', *Journal of Management* 17: 99–120.

Cantwell, J.A. and Hodson, C. (1991) 'Global R&D and UK competitiveness', in M.C. Casson (ed.) *Global Research Strategy and International Competitiveness,* Oxford: Basil Blackwell: 113–82.

Cox, H. (2000) *The Global Cigarette,* Oxford: Oxford University Press.

Dunning, J.H. (1961) 'British investment in US industry', *Moorgate and Wall Street,* Autumn: 3–23.

—— (1970) *Studies in International Investment,* London: George Allen and Unwin.

—— (1978) *Ownership and country specific characteristics of Britain's international competitive position.* University of Reading Discussion Papers in International Investment and Business Studies, No. 40, January.

—— (1993) *The Globalization of Business,* London and New York: Routledge.

—— (1998) *American Investment in British Manufacturing Industry* (revised and updated edition), London and New York: Routledge.

—— (2000) 'The eclectic paradigm as an envelope for economic and business theories of MNE activity', *International Business Review* 9: 163–90.

Hymer, S. (1960) *The International Operations of National Firms. A Study of Direct Investment*, PhD thesis, MIT (published by MIT Press in 1976).

Knickerbocker, F.T. (1973) *Oligopolistic Reaction and the Multinational Enterprise*, Cambridge, Mass: Harvard University Press.

Reddaway, W.B., Patten, C. and Taylor, S. (1968) *The Effects of UK Direct Investment Overseas*, Cambridge: Cambridge University Press.

UN (2000) World Investment Report: *Cross Border Mergers and Acquisition*, Geneva and New York: UN.

Department of Commerce (1961) 'Foreign Business Investments in the United States', *American Economic Report*, December: 6–8.

Vernon, R. (1966) 'International investment and international trade in the product cycle', *Quarterly Journal of Economics* 80: 190–207.

Wallace, L. (2000) 'Foreign direct investment in the US', in J.H. Dunning (ed.) *Regions, Globalization and the Knowledge Based Economy*, Oxford: Oxford University Press.

Wernerfelt, B. (1984) 'A resource based theory of the firm', *Strategic Management Journal* 5: 171–80.

4 Canadian companies in the United States

A survey and a case study[1]

Graham D. Taylor

Overview

Few countries are more closely integrated economically than the United States and Canada. Historically, in terms of trade, each has evolved as the other's largest partner since the early twentieth century, despite the presence of protective tariff structures on both sides of the border that began to be attenuated shortly before World War II. The negotiation of the Canada-US Free Trade Agreement (FTA) and North American Free Trade Agreement (NAFTA) in the early 1990s accelerated this process, even in the context of a dramatic growth of global trade for both countries. In 1999, 85 per cent of Canada's exports went to the United States and 76 per cent of its imports came from that source. Similarly, Canada was the largest single-country source of imports (20 per cent) and market for exports (22 per cent) in 1999, larger than all of the western European countries.

No less important as an integrating force has been the growth of cross-border direct investment between the US and Canada. In 1999 capital investment in both directions came to $275 million (Cdn), equal to the dollar value of imports and exports, supplemented by other forms of investment that totalled over $640 million (Cdn). In the case of Canada, the US share represented 72 per cent of total foreign direct investment, overwhelmingly the largest source, and somewhat larger (by 5 per cent) than its share in 1990, before FTA and NAFTA. Canadian direct investment in the US was 9 per cent of the total; this reflected a decline from 1992 when it was the third largest single country source of direct investment, but it remained a major player on the American scene, led only by the United Kingdom, Japan, Germany and The Netherlands (*Survey of Current Business* March 2000; Zeile 2000).

The role of US direct investment in shaping the Canadian economy has long been recognized, particularly in the period between the late 1960s and mid-1980s when US firms were reckoned to control almost half the manufacturing assets and close to 60 per cent of the mining, oil and gas industries in Canada, and the degree of foreign ownership became a salient political issue in Ottawa, leading to the imposition of measures to review and restrict foreign direct investment and an ambitious (and short-lived) 'national energy programme'. By the end of the 1980s the political appeal of these issues had receded, although the presence of foreign (and especially US)-owned companies did not diminish. In 1999, of the top twenty 'private companies' (i.e. companies not listed on Canadian exchanges) in the rankings by the *Toronto Globe & Mail*'s 'Report on Business', eleven were foreign-owned, nine by US firms – most notably in the auto industry where the 'Big Three' continued to earn revenues that exceeded even the largest Canadian financial and non-financial institutions (Taylor and Baskerville 1994: 450–9; 'Report on Business' 2000).

The Canadian preoccupation with the presence of foreign multinationals obscured, until fairly recently, recognition of the development of Canadian multinationals, and particularly the movement of Canadian direct investment to the United States. James Darroch has provided a perspective on the strategies of Canadian banks entering the US market. Canadian banks not only rebuffed foreign entries successfully up through the 1980s, but through mergers and the establishment of national branch systems in the early twentieth century developed the capabilities to move aggressively into foreign markets in the 1960s. By 1989 between 20 and 40 per cent of the assets of Canada's five largest banks (Royal Bank of Canada, Bank of Montreal, Bank of Nova Scotia, Canadian Imperial Bank of Commerce and Toronto-Dominion Bank) were held outside the country, with the largest proportion in the United States. Particular features of Canadian banks – the image of 'soundness' based on generations of stable growth, their ability to provide a wide range of financial services, due to deregulation in Canadian banking in advance of the US – proved to be critical advantages in this era (Darroch 1992: 153–72). According to its Annual Report, in 1999, 36 per cent of the total earnings of the Bank of Montreal were held in the United States. The comparative figures for the others of the 'Big Five' (except Toronto Dominion Bank) were: Bank of Nova Scotia (18.8 per cent); Canadian Imperial Bank of Commerce (25 per cent); and Royal Bank of Canada (11.8 per cent).

International expansion has by no means been restricted to the Canadian financial sector, and the United States has been a major recipient of Canadian direct investment. Although, as noted below, Canada's proportion of foreign direct investment measured in terms of assets has declined in the past two decades (reflecting the entry of companies from Europe, East Asia and elsewhere since the 1970s), Table 4.1 indicates that Canadian affiliates in the United States have grown steadily in that period in terms of sales and investment in research and development.

Table 4.2 provides a view of the level of US investment by Canada's ten leading non-financial institutions in 1999, in terms of both assets and revenue generation. While the proportion of US assets varies considerably among them, all (except Bell Canada Enterprises) have US holdings as

Table 4.1 Canadian share of foreign affiliate activities in the US, 1980–97 (%)

	1980	*1990*	*1997*
Assets	16.4	14.6	8.7
Sales	8.6	10.7	11.6
Employment	14.3	14.6	11.7
R&D	6.9	7.3	8.6

Sources: Rao, Legault and Ashfaq 1994: 96–9; Bezirganian 1993: 89–113; Zeile 2000: 21–54.

Table 4.2 US assets/revenues as a percentage of total for the 10 leading Canadian non-financial corporations, 1999 (all figures in $ million (Cdn))

Company	*US assets*	*As % of total*	*US revenues*	*As % of total*
Power Corp.	20,979	37	5,091	35
BCE[a]	72	>1	8,110	30
Seagram	15,093	58	5,917	48
Nortel	n/a	n/a	12,758	57
Canadian Pacific	3,723	18	3,879	34
Canadian National	3,043	17	1,020	16
Bombardier	281	15	5,497	48
Thomson[a]	10,588	85	5,178	82
Alcan	2,008	20	3,229	41
Brascan[a]	4,161	13	1,347	19

Sources: *Report on Business* 2000; Annual Reports of companies.

Note
a Marks 1998 Reports; all others are 1999 Reports.

large as or considerably greater than those of the five leading Canadian banks. Revenues from US operations (which include both cross-border sales and those of American affiliates) are significant for all of the companies. While BCE (parent company of Bell Canada) seems a small player in the US, its former manufacturing wing, Nortel (Northern Telecom) is a global company with over 24,000 employees in 100 locations in the United States; Nortel's expansion is discussed in more detail below.

In at least two cases (Seagram and Thomson Corporation), the US investment substantially exceeded the asset value of company holdings in Canada or indeed in any other country. Seagram, which began as a distributor of alcoholic beverages, acquired a substantial position in DuPont and Conoco when the second generation of the founding family, the Bronfmans, decided to diversify into petrochemicals in the 1980s. Subsequently, the dominant family figure, Edgar Bronfman, took a liking to the entertainment business and in 1995 the petrochemical investment was discarded so that Seagram could invest in Universal Studios, supplementing a 15 per cent share in the US media giant, Time-Warner. In June 2000

Seagram merged with the French media/communications firms Vivendi and Canal Plus. The Thomson Corporation, also essentially a family-dominated operation, began in the radio and newspaper field in the 1930s, building up a large media empire in Britain and Canada. When the founding father, Roy Thomson, died in 1976, his son, Ken Thomson, expanded substantially into the US newspaper market, while also acquiring control of Canadian retail firms, including the Hudson's Bay Company. Beginning in 1999, however, Thomson decided on another shift into Internet communications and has been selling off its 128 newspapers in the US, valued at over $4 billion (Cdn).

In terms of profitability, Canadian affiliates in the United States have done well. In 1997, the net return on investment for Canadian firms was comparable to that of British and German investors, and better than Japanese ventures. A study conducted in the early 1990s concluded that Canadian companies had performed better in terms of productivity than the American affiliates of other foreign countries in 1980 and 1990, and that the profitability of Canadian firms with direct investment abroad (including the US) was significantly better than that of companies primarily serving the domestic Canadian market in this period. Strong Canadian performance vis-à-vis other countries' affiliates was particularly notable in the manufacturing and financial services areas, which accounted for 33 per cent and 29 per cent respectively of all Canadian direct investment in the United States at the end of the 1990s (Zeile 2000: 48–9; Rao, Legault and Ashfaq 1994: 96–100).

Canadian foreign direct investment is not a recent phenomenon. According to Jorge Niosi, Canadian direct capital exports exceeded those of Japan, Germany and Italy in the 1930s and (not surprisingly) Canada emerged from World War II as the third largest country in foreign direct investment, behind the US and Britain. Even in the mid-1970s, Canada remained a major player in this field despite the recovery of Japan and Western European countries (Niosi 1985: 44–5). As Table 4.3 indicates, the United States has been the major recipient of Canadian direct investment, although it is interesting to note that in the past decade there has

Table 4.3 Canadian FDI in the US as a percentage of total Canadian FDI ($ million (Cdn))

Year	*FDI in the US*	*% of total FDI*
1929	259	61
1950	814	78
1960	1,716	61
1970	3,518	54
1980	17,849	63
1990	60,049	61
1999	134,287	72

Sources: Statistics Canada 1997: 38; Statistics Canada 2000: 34.

been a reversal of what had been a fairly stable rate of US investment in the previous 30 years. The dramatic increase in the magnitude of Canadian direct investment in the US in the period since 1970 is also worth noting: even taking into account inflation rates and the shift in exchange rates, particularly in the 1970s, the rate of increase is impressive. Even though Canada's position as a direct investor in the US declined from 13 per cent to 9 per cent between 1981 and 1999, the volume of Canadian investment increased almost six times over in these two decades.

The earliest Canadian multinationals emerged at the turn of the twentieth century in the field of electric utility development; building on expertise acquired in the construction of hydro-electric power sites in Canada, promoters provided capital and technical support to communities seeking to develop their own electrical systems. For the most part these ventures focused on Latin American countries. The largest of these was Brazilian Traction Light & Power which began establishing electric tramways and lighting systems for São Paulo and Rio de Janeiro in the early 1900s, becoming one of the largest companies in the country within the next two decades. After Brazil nationalized electric power in the 1950s, the Canadian company was transformed into Brascan, a diversified holding company which currently owns Noranda, one of Canada's largest mining operations. Similar electric power ventures flourished in Mexico, Cuba and other Latin American countries between 1900 and the 1940s. The 'utility multinationals', however, made no effort to enter the United States, although in its later manifestation Brascan acquired paper and lumber mills and oil and gas properties in the United States (MacDowall 1988; Armstrong and Nelles 1988).

Similarly, the large mining companies of Canada, when they ventured abroad (for the most part not until after World War II), went into Latin America, Africa and East Asia rather than into the United States. This pattern shifted after the mid-1970s when some of the mining firms began to develop more integrated operations. Alcan Aluminium, which began as a subsidiary of the US firm, Alcoa, a relationship that was officially terminated in the 1950s, expanded aluminium fabricating capacity in the US in order to meet competition (from its former parent firm, among others) a decade later. The largest expansion came in 1985 when Alcan acquired the aluminium capacity of Atlantic Richfield Company. Noranda, founded in 1922 as a copper and gold mining enterprise in Quebec, also moved into the US in the 1960s for much the same reason, to compete downstream in the aluminium fabricating field; it set up a major reduction plant in Missouri in 1971, augmented by mills acquired from Revere Copper & Brass in Alabama in 1985, and a large fabricating plant in Tennessee in 1998. In that same year Noranda and Falconbridge, another large Canadian mining operation, partnered with Du Pont in the US in a joint venture to resell the sulphuric acid output of all three companies (Niosi 1985: 110–18).

The Alcan example reflects another interesting feature of Canadian multinational expansion in recent decades: the maturing of companies which began as affiliates of foreign investors and subsequently evolved into strong international competitors. Perhaps the most dramatic demonstration of this evolution is the recent history of Nortel Networks, formerly Northern Electric, the manufacturing arm of Bell Canada, both of which were tied to the US telecommunications giants, American Telephone & Telegraph and Western Electric, through much of their early development from the late nineteenth century through the 1950s. During this period Northern Electric depended largely on Western for new technology and restricted its operations to serving the needs of Bell in the Canadian market. After US regulatory authorities eliminated the right of Western Electric to maintain exclusive patent agreements in 1956, Bell Canada bought Western's share in Northern Electric and began developing that company's in-house technological capabilities, focusing in particular on the area of digital technology in the 1970s. Rechristened Northern Telecom, the company became an aggressive international competitor in telecommunications systems by the 1980s, outbidding more established firms such as Ericsson and ITT in Saudi Arabia and East Asia. In the United States, Northern Telecom moved quickly into the local service telephone market after the breakup of AT & T in 1984, providing the regional Bell operating companies with digital systems; by the end of the decade it held a 40 per cent share of the US market in central office switching systems and its international sales (primarily in the US) accounted for more than two-thirds of its total revenues (Taylor 1994: 133–40; Amesse, Segian-Dulude and Stanley 1994: 421–3).

Up to the 1970s, Canadian direct investment in the United States was incremental and reflected moves by a wide variety of firms in the manufacturing and service as well as financial sectors; after that point we begin to see industry-wide strategic trends, particularly in the financial and resource extraction (mining and petroleum) areas. A study of the distribution of Canadian direct investment in the early 1930s provides an interesting snapshot of the range of operations as well as identifying some longer-term players in the US market. The study indicated 110 companies with affiliates in the US: twenty-two were in the financial sector, including five banks. The largest was the Canadian Bank of Commerce (the future CIBC) with two American West Coast branches. Other Canadian players came from a variety of backgrounds. The two major Canadian railroads (Canadian National (CN) and Canadian Pacific) owned spur or feeder lines into the US, mostly along the borders in New England and the Middle West. It is interesting to note that in 1911 Charles Hays, general manager of the Grand Trunk Railway (a predecessor of Canadian National) contemplated a gigantic integration of rail lines across Canada and the American Middle West – a vision that finally came to pass with the merger of CN and the Illinois Central Railroad in 1998. An attempt to extend this US foray further through a merger with Burlington, Northern and Santa Fe Railroad has been (temporarily perhaps) stymied by US regulatory authorities. Similarly, Canada's major steel manufacturers, Stelco and Algoma, owned US coal and ore mines integrated with their manufacturing operations.

More interesting are companies that set up operations specifically to function in the American market. The largest of these are still active there, albeit with varying fortunes. The Moore Corporation, manufacturer of business forms and packing boxes, may be one of the most long-lived Canadian firms in the US. In 1884, Samuel Moore, a printer in Toronto, established a factory to produce sales books in Niagara Falls, New York. In 1899 Moore acquired Kidder Press in New York City, predecessor to its business equipment division, and 10 years later a large box company, F.N. Burt, in Buffalo. Moore operates at the end of the twentieth century as a multinational with $2.7 billion in sales (Marshall, Southard and Taylor 1936: 175–97).

Another early entrant was the farm implement manufacturer, Massey-Harris of Ontario, which acquired several US firms in 1911–17 and set up a full American subsidiary in 1929 with $12 million in assets. The company went on to flourish in the middle of the century as a major multinational, Massey-Ferguson; it continues to operate, albeit in much diminished form, as Varity Inc. On a much smaller scale, a Canadian biscuit-maker, George Weston, made a somewhat ill-advised foray into the US in the late 1920s, selling its assets (two plants in New Jersey and Massachusetts) to its US affiliate in 1933. At the end of the twentieth century Weston is the largest food distributor in Canada, with significant international linkages. Finally, the early 1930s marks the point at which the Canadian distillers – particularly Hiram Walker and Seagram – moved directly into the US as the repeal of Prohibition eliminated the lucrative cross-border bootlegging business.

There is, then, a rich and diverse history of Canadian companies in the United States, but there is a relatively small literature on the subject. As noted earlier, Canadian historians have devoted a fair amount of attention to the 'utility multinationals' in the exotic climes of Latin America, but the more mundane American market has no chroniclers. E.P. Neufeld gave some attention to the expansion of Massey-Harris into the US in the early twentieth century, but the focus of his work was on the Anglo-Canadian merger, Massey-Ferguson. The Seagram story has been largely traced through the vicissitudes of the Bronfman family with relatively little attention paid to the management of the company. On the other side of the border, Mira Wilkins has provided valuable information on the operations of Canadian firms in the US, particularly in the finance sector, up to 1914. However the history of Canadian direct investment in the United States, particularly with regard to the internal organization and management of these firms in the twentieth century remains largely uncharted territory (Neufeld 1969; Marrus 1991; Wilkins 1989: 453–89).

The following section provides a detailed study of an Ontario-based company in New York State during the first 12 years of its operations. The company, Fisher Gauge Ltd, is admittedly not one of the major players on the North American scene; but it does occupy a significant niche market in the tool-and-die industry and has developed markets in North America, Europe and Japan. It is worth noting that while the continental activities of companies like Seagram commanded headlines, there has also been a steady flow of smaller firms operating across the border. The figures provided in the 1932 study of Canadian direct investment in the US indicate that the average capital investment per company was less than $800,000. A study of Canadian multinationals in the early 1990s indicated that more than one-third of the affiliates of Canadian firms operating in the US had assets of less than $1 million, and half were capitalized at less than $5 million (Marshall, Southard and Taylor 1936: 176; Chow 1994: 42–7). Fisher Gauge is not a 'small company' in this context and it has a history of operations in the US that goes back for more than 40 years.

One other feature of Fisher Gauge may also contribute to its 'typicality': it is a family firm, with ownership closely held and family members sprinkled across the management. As noted above, these are characteristics that can be found in even the largest Canadian multinational (and other) enterprises: the Bronfmans, Thomsons, Irvings, McCains, Westons and others continue to play a major role in the affairs of their companies.

Case study: Fisher-Gauge in New York, 1964–76

Fisher Gauge Ltd is a Canadian tool-and-die company specializing in two areas: the Fisher Cast Division manufactures zinc die castings which are used for a variety of purposes, from precision components for machine gears to cables for ski boot fasteners – a Fisher-Gauge casting, for example, is embedded in every Gillette safety razor. The Fisher Tech Division builds semi-automatic and automatic machines for producing cable system terminators and other equipment for small component assembly production. In 1999 it had sales exceeding $100 million (Cdn), of which more than 80 per cent were outside Canada, in North America, Europe and Japan. The company has over 700 employees, more than half in three plants in Peterborough, Ontario, and two affiliates: the first, in Watertown, New York, has been in operation since 1964. The second, in Welshpool in the United Kingdom, was opened in 1994.

Fisher Gauge is very much an entrepreneurial and proprietary firm. It was established in 1942 by William F. Fisher, literally in the basement of his family's home in Peterborough. Incorporated in 1952, Fisher Gauge remains a family enterprise and the founder continued to play a major role in its operations through his retirement in 1997. In certain respects, the company can be seen as an offshoot of the American-owned firm, Canadian General Electric (CGE), which came to Peterborough in 1890, lured by its hydroelectric potential and exemptions from municipal taxation. Peterborough was a centre for a variety of manufacturing enterprises – also US-owned – from the early twentieth century through the 1990s, including the American Cereal Company (later Quaker Oats), Westclox, Vermont Marble and Outboard Marine Co.; but CGE was the principal industry and employer in the community (Jones and Dyer 1987: 40–2).

Bill Fisher's father, Fred Fisher, emigrated with his family from Birmingham, England after World War I to work in the CGE plant as a toolmaker. Bill, his eldest son, apprenticed at CGE in the 1930s, as did his brothers, Chester and Frank. A talented artisan, Bill contracted with CGE to make insulating posts for military aircraft radio in his spare time. After working for a year for Ottawa Car and Aircraft, he returned to Peterborough in 1942 and set up his own business in his family's home. His first contract was with Massey-Harris, to design gauges for De Havilland Mosquito bomber aircraft – which led to the christening of the company as 'Fisher Gauge'. But the most important contract for the nascent firm came in 1945, again with CGE, to design and build a machine that could provide precision castings for metal discs for meters used to measure electric power use. This became the standard equipment used for production of watt meters for households throughout North America. By this time his younger brother, Frank, had left CGE to join the company. Through the 1950s, Frank assumed responsibility for managing shop operations, leaving Bill to do his preferred technical design work. Another brother, Chester, came to Fisher Gauge in 1955 after working for 16 years with CGE, particularly in its nuclear reactor programme. When Frank died suddenly in 1959, Chester effectively became the chief operating manager of the company. Throughout this period as well, Fisher Gauge benefited from a stream of employees who had been trained at CGE (*Fisher Findings*; Willcox interview, May 30 2000; Belsey interview).

Meanwhile, the company was looking for a more secure base as the design of machine tools had a relatively limited market. Fisher-Gauge sold its watt-meter machine to Ferranti-Packard in Canada and 12 machines to Westinghouse in the US, marking a first entry into that market. At the same time Bill Fisher, as a designer of the Edison mould, toyed with the idea of entering the consumer market with an egg-beater, but decided to stick with the more predictable producer-goods field.

In 1950, CGE contracted with Fisher to produce casting machines that could produce small precision gears. Based on this success, Fisher Gauge began producing casting machines for other manufacturers, but soon determined that their clients were less interested in the machines than in the gears themselves. By 1959, the Fisher brothers decided to move into the direct production of die castings in addition to building the equipment. This represented a major move that transformed Fisher Gauge into a major production facility, and also laid the groundwork for the decision to establish a plant in the United States.

In 1957, the company celebrated the fact that it had at that point sold $1 million of products since its inception in 1942. By 1965, Fisher Gauge was reporting sales of $1 million per year. Although the major value-added elements of its sales comprised the gauging and casting machines, the die castings themselves provided a volume of sales unprecedented in the company's history. Initially, die castings were targeted at Canadian buyers, but by the early 1960s the US had emerged as the major market for a wide variety of castings, many of them quite small, for use in telephone equipment, clocks, computers, automobiles and motorcycles and other industrial products. One area that used zinc die castings in great quantity was the toy industry, and through the 1960s and 1970s this was one of the largest markets for Fisher Gauge in the US, making, among other things, the small playing pieces used in the game of 'Monopoly'. Many US die casting producers tended to concentrate near major customers in the iron and steel industry and to focus on larger castings. Fisher Gauge chose to emphasize smaller 'miniature' castings which had lower transport costs, and in the 1950s–60s most of their US clients congregated in the New York City and western New England areas (Belsey interview).

Although US import duties posed a barrier, this was offset to some extent by a favourable exchange rate for the Canadian exporters. Nevertheless, by the early 1960s the Fisher brothers were considering the possibility of establishing a plant in the US, to bypass both duties and 'red tape', and also to provide a site for maintenance service of the casting machines they were exporting there. The precipitating factor, however, was not the result of any American measures but rather a sales tax levied by Ottawa in 1963 on production machinery used by Fisher Gauge in its casting business; this effectively increased costs by 11 per cent and left the company vulnerable to US competitors in that market.

Once they began looking seriously at locating a plant across the border, other advantages also emerged. Federal (US) income taxes were not only lower than Canadian, but included an investment allowance that allowed for deduction of up to $25,000 annually for new equipment. New York State (the most likely site for a new factory) had a 'flexible' business tax that could be reduced if profits fell. In addition, both the Federal and state governments were prepared to assist in the financing of new business start-ups and had commercial officers actively seeking Canadian firms to relocate across the border. Through the US Small Business Administration, Fisher Gauge was able to arrange financing at an interest rate of 1.5 per cent below the rates charged it in Canada.

One other factor involved location. The Fishers looked at three well-established industrial centres in upstate New York: Buffalo, which had a number of Canadian as well as US electrochemical and electrical utility forms; Rochester, best known as the home of Eastman Kodak Co.; and Syracuse, which had a range of industries including jet engines and chemicals, and was a financial and market centre for the north-central region of the state. Curiously, the Fishers opted for Watertown, a smaller city north of Syracuse which had relatively little industry and was regarded as a depressed area. In an interview in 1965, Bill Fisher indicated several considerations, most notably its convenience to the Canadian border and Peterborough, only three hours' drive away. In addition Watertown may have been attractive as a 'depressed area' because of the possibility of special support, including financial assistance from New York State for the construction of the plant through the Job Development Authority ('Canadian Businessmen Tell Why They Established a Branch Plant in New York State,' *Business in New York State*, November 1965, CWFP, Box 15).

Although these may have been compelling reasons at the time, in retrospect the choice of Watertown had some longer-term problems. Watertown is in a fairly remote location, with no direct access to an international airport, and it proved hard to recruit the best qualified workers since educated young people preferred to move to larger urban centres; this placed limits on the capacity of Fisher-Gauge to transfer more sophisticated technical operations to Watertown. Although initially Bill Fisher suggested he might move some machine-tool production to Watertown, the American plant remained largely tied to die castings, focusing on smaller, less intricate products in its early years (Belsey interview).

Fisher Gage Inc. was established on 18 August 1964 with a capitalization of 10,000 shares at $10.00 (US), all held by Fisher Gauge in Canada. Initially the company set up operations in an unused airplane hangar at the Watertown airport which the city had converted into a quondam industrial park. Fisher-Gauge sent Earl Belsey, who was foreman of the die casting operation in Peterborough, to manage the new plant. Over the ensuing 4 years, production rose from 1 million die castings to 60 million castings by 1969. By this time, the plant was using eight casting machines with more than fifty employees (*Fisher Findings*).

The system of communication and coordination between the two organizations could be characterized as essentially *ad hoc*. Belsey went to Peterborough once a month to report on production issues. Bill Fisher, who had little interest in routine management issues, rarely went to Watertown. Chester Fisher, as General Manager of Fisher Gauge, was more directly involved. In 1968 the scale of operations justified expansion into a larger factory. Chester Fisher played a major role in this development, acquiring 60 acres of land outside the city and setting up an affiliated company, Fisher Gage Realty, which held the lease on the new Fisher-Gage plant. Chester Fisher preferred this location to a site near other (older) industries in downtown Watertown, and appears to have conceived of developing the land as an industrial park, although ultimately all the land except that occupied by the Fisher-Gage works was sold back to the Watertown public development corporation ('Notes on Meeting with Representatives of Jefferson County Industries re Fisher Gage Industrial Park,' Aug. 24, 1970, CWFP, Box 24; Belsey interview).

There were some occasions of friction in these early years, reflecting inconsistencies in management coordination. Following a visit to Watertown in 1967, Chester Fisher noted that the two plants 'must not attempt to compete with one another' for US business by engaging in 're-quoting' each other's rates. In 1969 Earl Belsey reported that 'Watertown feels that they are Peterborough's largest customer, but we are not getting the consideration a large customer deserves', being charged 'exorbitant' replacement valuations and charges for items that Watertown regarded as defective but Peterborough believed to have been mishandled. These were minor irritants; after the first year of operations, and a short downturn in 1967, the Watertown plant under Belsey's direction steadily expanded sales and produced net (after tax) profits that rivalled Peterborough. (C.W. Fisher, Review with Earl [Belsey], [handwritten notes – no date, *c.* 1967]; K.S. Stewart 'Watertown Relations,' March 24, 1969 [Stewart was supervisor of production controls at the Peterborough plant], CWFP, Box 16).

At this point, however, more sweeping changes were in the works for the entire Fisher-Gauge organization. The company had expanded dramatically in the late 1960s, almost tripling its overall asset value, posting sales that exceeded $2 million annually by 1969–70, diversifying into new product lines with the move into die casting, as well as establishing a US factory. Expansion in turn created a challenge for the organizational capacity of the enterprise. It is fair to say that Fisher Gauge was a company built on 'shop floor management'. All of the Fisher brothers and many of the other senior managers in the late 1960s had begun as apprentices, working their way up in tool-and-die production with relatively little experience outside the company or the industry. Bill Fisher himself, as noted earlier, had entrepreneurial instincts but was principally interested in design issues and resolving technical puzzles. There were others in the firm with good managerial qualities, such as Earl Belsey (who helped direct the Peterborough operations through difficult times in the mid-1970s after returning from Watertown), but had no formal training in finance or organization. Chester Fisher was certainly the most capable person in terms of understanding management needs, particularly in labour relations, and he had experience working with a much larger organization, Canadian General Electric, before coming to Fisher Gauge. But Chester was also aware of his own limitations and believed that a more systematic approach to management was required to enable the firm to cope with its larger, more complex operations.

In 1969, Chester persuaded his brother to bring in Price Waterhouse to review the organization of Fisher Gauge. Price Waterhouse recommended recruiting a professionally trained manager to lead the reorganization effort. Fortuitously, the management company itself recommended a person that Chester Fisher already knew: Tod Willcox, trained in engineering at the University of Saskatchewan, had worked with Chester in the jet-engine division of CGE in the 1950s. Willcox then worked at the CGE plant in Scarborough, outside Toronto, in its nuclear power division; in 1970 the Scarborough plant closed down after CGE lost a large Ontario Hydro contract and Willcox was available. He was brought in as General Manager while Chester 'stepped aside' as Executive Vice President (Willcox interview, June 5, 2000).

Under Willcox a number of changes were brought to Fisher Gauge in 1970–1. New supervisory levels were set up to relieve senior managers from dealing with routine shop floor problems, and an executive operations committee established to develop longer-term plans. A document system, based on the CGE model, was introduced. The emergence of two distinctive product lines was recognized through the establishment of divisions. The marketing and sales operations were reorganized, as described below. In terms of production, Willcox began pushing the company to move toward larger die castings with greater added value, particularly for the auto industry in Ontario. He advocated broadening the company's international sales efforts, an idea that appealed to Bill Fisher who became an assiduous participant in international trade fairs in Europe and Japan, making contacts that would significantly extend Fisher Gauge's markets and led eventually to the establishment of the factory in Wales in the 1990s. (Willcox interviews, June 5 and June 13, 2000; 'Fisher Gauge Main Problem Areas' [no date, *c.* 1970]; 'Fisher Gauge Limited, Long Range Facilities Planning Project' January 1971, CWFP, Box 16).

These changes inevitably had a substantial impact on the Watertown operation. Willcox believed that the Watertown plant was no better organized than the home company, that communications between Peterborough and Watertown were inadequate and that the New York plant needed people with better technical capabilities on the spot to ensure continuous quality production. He began travelling to Watertown weekly, often taking specialists from Peterborough to facilitate changes. As in the case of Peterborough, new layers of supervision were set up to oversee tools and equipment, casting operations, engineering and quality controls. The Watertown factory was to be integrated with Peterborough in terms of the document system. Inventories were reduced and there were some staff reductions to 'place the business on a sound footing'.

Willcox also took steps to streamline sales operations. In place of direct sales from Peterborough and Watertown (with a small sales force), he set up a system of regional contracts with manufacturers' representatives across North America, paid on commission. Sales guides were to be developed by staff at Peterborough and all orders coordinated through the central offices of the two divisions, under the management of Eric Graham (for machine tools) and Fred Jay (for die castings). This eliminated potential inter-plant competition and allowed for a huge expansion of sales capacity over the next two decades (Willcox interview, June 13, 2000; T. Willcox to E. Belsey, F. Jay, E. Graham and G. Reader 'Interim

Working Arrangements between Watertown and Peterborough' April 13, 1970; Fisher Gage Organization May 15, 1970; Willcox to Belsey, 'Adjustments Planned for Watertown Operation' May 21, 1970, CWFP, Box 16). It is fair to say that the measures introduced were intended both to reduce the autonomy of Watertown and to promote a greater integration of sales and production, reversing what appears to have been the trend in the first 5 years.

Hard on the heels of this reorganization, a new challenge arose that would enhance this process of integration and demonstrate the value of the US investment. In August 1971 the US government, faced with chronic and growing balance of payments problems, simultaneously moved to devalue the US dollar through suspension of gold payments while imposing surcharges on imports of a range of items, and also providing an investment tax credit for American manufacturers to further protect them from foreign competition. These 'Nixon Shocks' were intended primarily to counter perceived threats from Japanese (and Western European) competition, but the impact was felt strongly by Canadian exporters and, in contrast to the practice of the preceding decade, no 'special treatment' was accorded them.

All of these measures affected Fisher Gauge as the 10 per cent surcharges included die castings and machine tools (except in the auto and military-related industries, neither of which were significant markets for Fisher-Gauge products at that time). The tax credit would benefit US competitors and devaluation pushed the Canadian dollar toward (and above) parity with the American, where it hovered up to 1976. More than 40 per cent of the die casting output from Peterborough went to the US market. Although the machine tool side was less dependent on exports, the casting machines were tied in with the US market. In a memo to Fisher Gauge employees, Chester Fisher warned:

> Our company faces what is undoubtedly the most serious crisis in its history. It is a confrontation with high costs, general business slowdown, changing currency values and economic sanctions. All these factors are marshalled against us and are the more severe because we are so highly involved in exports.
>
> (C.W. Fisher, Memo to Fisher Gauge Employees Aug. 30, 1971, CWFP, Box 7)

The 1971 crisis was not entirely unprecedented or unexpected. In 1969, Chester Fisher had arranged for the transfer of production of timers for cooking stoves and ranges to Watertown in anticipation of a 'substantially higher and prohibitive import duty' by US Customs. He recognized that production of timers is 'difficult from both the standpoint of production and quality as well as customer relations and will undoubtedly try the Watertown capability'. Apparently the transition was successful, as by 1974 Fisher

Gage in Watertown had sales of about $300,000 in this area (representing slightly less than 10 per cent of total sales) and it represented a step toward more complex production operations (K. Stewart to C.W. Fisher Mar. 14, 1969; C.W. Fisher to E. Belsey April 17, 1969, CWFP, Box 16).

In 1971, the shifting of appropriate work to Watertown became the centrepiece of the company's strategy. All casting jobs which could achieve savings of 15 per cent through transfer to Watertown were moved. Three new casting machines scheduled for Peterborough operations were detailed off to New York along with ten specialized employees, and efforts were undertaken to procure more zinc dies from US sources. On a more ambitious scale, Willcox contemplated reorganizing the Watertown operation so that it could become a 'subcontractor on [US] defence contracts', and more lyrically, Watertown was envisaged to 'eventually serve as the casting manufacturing plant for North and possibly South America' (with Peterborough to be 'the base from which to spawn overseas operations'). However, there was no attempt to move the machine tool side of the company to Watertown; instead the emphasis in marketing would be placed on Fisher Gauge quality and focus on exports to new regions (T. Willcox, 'Business Strategy for Fisher Gauge' Aug. 23, 1971, CWFP, Box 7).

The more ambitious schemes floated for Watertown in August 1971 did not come to pass, although some other ideas about international expansion did emerge over the next two decades. On the other hand, the transfer of the larger portion of die cast work to Watertown was a successful move in the short term. Sales by Fisher-Gage Inc. of New York jumped from $1.1 million (Cdn) in 1970 to $1.8 million in 1972 and over $2 million the following year, while sales from Peterborough fell by almost $1 million (Cdn) in 1971, returning to slightly above 1970 levels the next year. While US-based production helped the shareholders (i.e. the Fisher family) circumvent the impact on profits in Peterborough, there was another element that helped the parent company. In 1970, a new item, 'Intercompany Overhead' was introduced in the Fisher-Gage accounts, apparently part of Willcox's measures to integrate cross-border operations. In 1971 this item was quadrupled and 'overhead' (part of which reflected increased costs tied to the transfer of equipment to Watertown) helped cushion what would otherwise have been a significant loss for Fisher-Gauge (Fisher Gauge Annual Reports 1971–3).

Watertown never did become the centrepiece for hemispheric expansion of Fisher Gauge. During the mid-1970s the continuing recession in the US damaged its markets, and the plant had to retrench, laying off more than half its employees. The Canadian plant also experienced tough times, but by 1976 its sales were picking up, assisted in part by the decline of the Canadian dollar, and a major expansion was underway in Peterborough. By the end of the decade Willcox's strategy of expanding the diecasting business into more lucrative, value-added lines was taking shape for Peterborough: in 1978 almost one-quarter of Fisher Gauge's sales were going to the automotive and defence industries. By contrast, Watertown's output was primarily in the established fields of electrical components and small parts for domestic appliances: Watertown had no defence contracts and less than 4 per cent of its sales went to the auto industry (Jim Taylor [business analyst] to T. Willcox, 'Historical Financial Information: Fisher Gage Incorporated, Watertown' June 12, 1979, FR, Box 13). While on the Canadian side of the border two new factories were built in the 1980s, the New York plant remained essentially as it had been in the 1970s, growing with the business but sidelined from both the mainstream of the US market and the new directions of the parent firm. In 1973, Watertown accounted for 35 per cent of the asset value of the entire Fisher Gauge operation; by 1991, it represented 24 per cent (Fisher Gauge Ltd. Consolidated 1991 Financial Statement, FR, Box 15).

It is interesting to note that although Fisher Gauge is a relatively small, proprietary firm, the history of its relationship with the Watertown company is similar in many aspects to the experience of much larger enterprises operating across borders. While trade barriers were not a direct factor in the Fishers' decision to enter the US, the experience in 1971–2 demonstrated the utility of that decision; indeed, Fisher Gauge was in an advantageous position in that it had already made its initial investment prior to the emergence of the barrier. In more recent years this particular rationale has less resonance and it is not clear that Watertown has the degree of saliency to Fisher Gauge's future that it did in the early 1970s.

The Watertown operation was so small in its early years that there was little impetus towards a more autonomous status, as has been the case with affiliates in larger organizations; but there were certainly tendencies toward rivalry between the Peterborough and Watertown plants which might have developed further in the absence of the centralization that occurred in the firm in 1970–1. Despite occasional gestures thereafter, it would appear that the parent firm retained control over the more high-value operations, with the expanding Peterborough plants absorbing much of the new business in larger more complex castings and entirely controlling the equipment production (Fisher Tech) side of the operation. To the extent that when research and development takes place in Fisher Gauge, it takes place in Peterborough.

Tod Willcox's speculations about the future of Watertown in Fisher Gauge's strategy are interesting as a kind of embryonic version of a regional mandate form of organization with Watertown as the major 'hemispheric' player. Although Fisher Gauge moved in the 1980s into a more globally defined sales approach, production has not followed this path. To some extent, this may reflect the particular circumstances of the post-1976 period, when a low-value Canadian dollar encouraged a focus on exports rather than cross-border production growth. But this situation also reflects the essentially marginal position of Watertown in the US market, particularly as the industries which form Fisher Gauge's clientele migrated to the American South and West. In this context the convenience of proximity to Peterborough was less compelling. Curiously, the Welshpool operation is also in a fairly marginal location in relationship to the principal European markets for Fisher Gauge. If the company had evolved a genuinely global production strategy neither of these branch operations would have been likely to emerge where they did. But businesses are shaped by their history and sometimes investments that made sense at the time persist long past the point where their 'strategic' purpose is self-evident.

Final comments

The experience of Fisher Gauge was not atypical for Canadian companies venturing into the United States up to the mid-1970s, and in many respects for many small to medium-scale companies operating across the border through the present. There were few formal barriers to movement and the traditional influences on direct investment – tariff levels and exchange rates – at best explain only part of the story. Although the trend in cross-border tariff rates was downward on a more or less steady rate from the 1930s following two Reciprocity treaties, duties on particular items could influence specific investment decisions; in the 1960s–70s exchange rate differentials diminished to the point where the Canadian dollar was above parity. In the more recent period, declining tariffs culminating with the Free Trade Agreements and a lower Canadian dollar provided disincentives for Canadian direct investment, but, as has been noted earlier, the volume of investment grew steadily throughout these decades. A variety of factors affected company relocations: transportation costs (particularly sensitive to shifting markets), comparative labour costs, access to government programmes set up for 'American' companies, and other considerations, including the personal idiosyncrasies of proprietors, all played a part.

Canadian companies not infrequently benefited from the boosterism of local chambers of commerce and municipal authorities in the US, as was the case for Fisher Gauge, and encountered a business environment that was less restrictive and conservative than their home base. For English-Canadian firms relocation posed few cultural challenges, and by the 1980s managers of firms on both sides of the border could draw increasingly on shared or comparable educational experiences and common approaches to business issues. French Canadian companies faced more significant barriers of language but, again, by the 1980s there was a much greater degree of cultural integration of the Francophone business community into North American business practices than had been the case prior to Quebec's 'quiet revolution' of the 1960s. A notable example is Bombardier, which began as a quintessential French Canadian proprietary enterprise, selling snowmobiles to rural *Quebecois* in the 1940s. A generation later the company diversified into a range of transport fields, including construction of subway cars (for New York City among other clients worldwide) and aircraft, and bought Lear Jet of Kansas City in the 1990s, among its other international acquisitions.

Although Canadian direct investment in the United States has grown steadily since World War II, the case can be made that a 'sea change' of sorts took place some time between the mid-1970s and the 1980s, stimulating the kind of strategically far-ranging and tactically aggressive incursions of companies such as Bombardier and Nortel. Before that point, Canadian companies tended to move cautiously into the larger and more volatile US environment; even firms that became quite large in terms of their American operations, such as the Moore Corporation, Massey-Harris, or New Brunswick's Irving Oil, grew incrementally and usually built slowly from a regional cross-border base such as New York State or New England. There were, to be sure, exceptions, particularly in the distilling industry where both Hiram Walker and Seagram moved aggressively into US production when Prohibition was repealed in the 1930s. But for many firms an attitude of constraint could provide an effective barrier to expansion in the absence of physical or cultural barriers. The history of Fisher Gauge in Watertown provides an example of this constraint at work.

This change may reflect a number of elements: the 'maturing' of formerly foreign-owned companies; the experience of Canadian companies in other offshore settings, providing greater confidence in dealing with the US business environment; and the emergence of a generation of managers trained in the United States or in US-influenced institutions, perhaps reflecting in a broader sense the development of a 'North American' set of business practices and attitudes. On this subject, however, as on the whole area of the Canadian direct investment in the United States, much more work remains to be done.

Note

1 I would like to acknowledge the work of Bill Brydon and Jo-Ellen Brydon, who set up the Fisher Gauge Archive over the past several years and provided assistance in accessing the company records and oral history materials. Thanks also to Earl Belsey and Tod Willcox for their participation in interviews, and also to Douglas Fisher, chief executive of Fisher Gauge, for his support for the development of the archive and for the research on this paper.

References

Primary sources

Fisher Gauge Archives, Peterborough, Ontario.

Chester W. Fisher Papers (CWFP).

Fisher Findings, June 1994.

Fisher Gauge Annual Reports.

Fisher Gauge Financial Records (FR).

Interviews
Earl Belsey, July 17, 2000.
Tod Willcox, May 30, 2000; June 5, 2000; June 13, 2000.

Statistics Canada (1997) *Canada's International Investment Position 1926–1996*, Ottawa: Statistics Canada.

Statistics Canada (2000) *Canada's International Investment Position 1999*, Ottawa: Statistics Canada.

'Report on Business' (2000), *Toronto Globe & Mail*, July.

Secondary sources

Amesse, F., Segian-Dulude, L. and Stanley, G. (1994) 'Northern Telecom: A case study in the management of technology', in S. Globerman (ed.) *Canadian-Based Multinationals*, Calgary: University of Calgary Press.

Armstrong, C. and Nelles, H.V. (1988) *Southern Exposure: Canadian Promoters in Latin America and the Caribbean, 1896–1930*, Toronto: University of Toronto Press.

Bezirganian, S. (1993) 'US affiliates of foreign companies: Operations in 1991', in *Survey of Current Business*, May: 89–112.

Chow, F. (1994) 'Recent trends in Canadian direct investment abroad: The rise of Canadian multinationals', in S. Globerman (ed.) *Canadian-Based Multinationals*, Calgary: University of Calgary Press.

Darroch, J. (1992) 'Global competitiveness and public policy: The case of Canadian multinational banks', in G. Marchildon and D. MacDowall (eds) *Canadian Multinationals and International Finance*, London: Frank Cass.

Jones, E. and Dyer, B. (1987) *Peterborough: The Electric City*, Burlington: Windsor Publications.

MacDowall, D. (1988) *The Light: Brazilian Traction, Light & Power Company, 1899–1945*, Toronto: University of Toronto Press.

Marrus, M. (1991) *Mr. Sam: The Life and Times of Samuel Bronfman*, Toronto: McClelland & Stewart.

Marshall, H., Southard, F. and Taylor, K.W. (1936) *Canadian-American Industry: A Study in International Investment*, New York: Carnegie Foundation.

Neufeld, E.P. (1969) *A Global Corporation: A History of the International Development of Massey-Ferguson*, Toronto: McClelland & Stewart.

Niosi, J. (1985) *Canadian Multinationals*, trans. R. Chodos, Kitchener: Garamond Press.

Rao, S., Legault, M. and Ashfaq, A. (1994) 'Canadian-based multinationals: An analysis of activities and performance', in S. Globerman (ed.) *Canadian-Based Multinationals*, Calgary: University of Calgary Press.

Taylor, G. and Baskerville, P. (1994) *A Concise History of Business in Canada*, Toronto: Oxford University Press.

Taylor, G. (1994) 'Negotiating technology transfers within multinational enterprises: Perspectives from Canadian history', *Business History* 36: 133–40.

Wilkins, M. (1989) *History of Foreign Investment in the United States to 1914*, Cambridge: Harvard University Press.

Zeile, W. (2000) 'Foreign direct investment in the United States: Preliminary results from the 1997 Benchmark Survey', in *Survey of Current Business*, July: 21–54.

5 Siemens in the US

Wilfried Feldenkirchen

Although Siemens began doing business in the US in the nineteenth century, it scarcely maintained a presence in the market after failing in its efforts to open and operate a factory in Chicago in the 1890s. Up until the 1950s, the company largely limited its US activities to representative tasks and to the exchange of patents and know-how with American partners. The one exception was the field of medical engineering, which remained the company's most important source of sales in the US until the 1970s. During the past two decades, Siemens has systematically penetrated the American market with the help of acquisitions of numerous US companies. Today all of Siemens core segments operate in the US – which is the company's largest foreign market – and generate a volume of sales equal to that in Germany.

The beginnings of Siemens' business in the US

In over 150 years of its existence, Siemens has been active and successful in both domestic and foreign markets. Ever since the founding of the Siemens & Halske Telegraph Construction Company (S&H), international commitment has been a key element of company policy. Formed in 1847, Siemens began systematic efforts in the mid-nineteenth century to move into foreign markets in a way few other German companies had ever done. Its foreign activities were in part dictated by economic necessity (Feldenkirchen 1994), but they also reflected the political convictions of Werner von Siemens and his brothers Wilhelm and Carl, who were also partners in the business.

In the period before 1880, Siemens' activities in America were limited to patent applications and licensing agreements drawn up by the London branch (Feldenkirchen 1995: 876–900). Apart from an order for railroad telegraphs that Siemens & Halske supplied to Philadelphia in 1854 (Matschoss 1916: 108), and assorted minor orders, no substantial business transactions were conducted in the US. Although the American market offered opportunities for foreign companies, the import of foreign products was hampered by high protective tariffs as well as by patent laws which

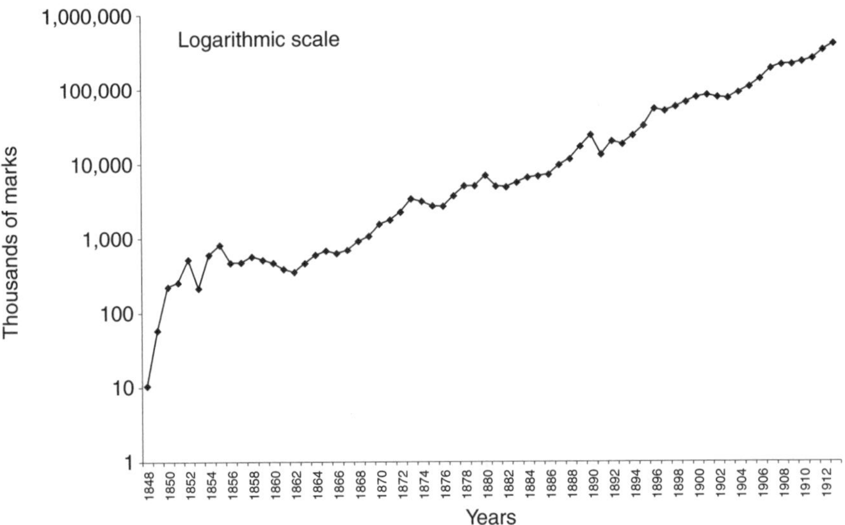

Figure 5.1 Sales of Siemens 1848–1913.

Source: Siemens Archives.

prohibited the import of apparatus and machines that were already patented in the US (von Weiher 1990: 143). In order to set up its own manufacturing facilities in the US, Siemens & Halske would also have been obliged to raise capital, a step which the family-owned enterprise was initially unable and unwilling to take (Feldenkirchen 1993: 156 f.). In addition, lengthy conflicts over competences between the London company of Siemens Brothers and the Berlin headquarters on how to handle overseas business prevented an early commitment in the US. However, an important business contact with Thomas Edison did take place in the 1880s. Siemens & Halske licensed the carbon filament lamp Edison had invented in 1880. A personal friendship between Edison and Werner von Siemens developed from this business tie. Edison stayed a number of days at Werner von Siemens' home in Berlin-Charlottenburg during his visit to Germany in 1889.

When the Siemens & Halske Electric Co. of America was finally formed in Chicago in 1892, the moment for successfully penetrating the American market had already passed; American competition was strong and Siemens & Halske had lost its technical lead. Siemens & Halske Electric Co., which was to manufacture electric machines and equipment, railway motors and dynamos and market them in the US and Canada, had to contend from the outset with financial difficulties that necessitated two capital increases within as many years. At the same time, the company was reluctant to invest additional capital in what was considered, even at the time of its launching, a highly controversial and risky venture far from

Berlin. Conflicting ideas on how to conduct business – flexible American management methods often met with resistance from an unwieldy administration in Berlin – and the sheer distance alone made communication difficult. Personal differences between O.W. Meysenburg, the American president of the company, and its technical manager Dr. Alfred Berliner also inhibited smooth business operations. When a fire completely destroyed the Chicago factory in August 1894, the heavy financial blow ended all dreams of accessing the American market. The company was finally wound up in 1904, after generating millions in losses up to 1898.

In 1908, Siemens' virtually non-existent activities in the US were revived and an information office was opened in New York under the direction of Dr. Karl Georg Frank. The company's activities focused on acquiring and passing on information. Large-scale sales operations were not envisaged, nor was the New York office equipped to handle them.

Activities in the US between the wars

As a consequence of World War I, Siemens lost its extensive patent rights in the US. In addition, research deficiencies in some areas of electrical engineering, as well as outdated organizational procedures, had caused Siemens and the whole of the German electrical industry to fall behind its major, chiefly American, competitors, who had been able to develop unhindered. The awareness of a technological gap led to a flurry of fact-finding visits by German industrialists and engineers to the US in the early 1920s. Carl Köttgen, Chairman of the Managing Board of Siemens-Schuckertwerke (SSW), visited numerous American companies to study their factory organization and examine ways of applying it at SSW (Köttgen 1926: 599–605, 1924a: 238–9, 1924b: 4–6, 1925).[1] Some of Köttgen's rationalization measures resulted from these visits. Apart from Köttgen, Hermann Reyss was another SSW director who endeavoured to renew old contacts in the US. During a visit in 1922, Reyss revived the contacts with Westinghouse which had existed before the war. This subsequently led to an agreement on the regular exchange of patents and technical assistance in 1924.[2] The initial agreement ran for 10 years and was renewed in 1934.[3]

The first major pooling of information arising out of this agreement concerned the Benson boiler, named after the former holder of the patent. After Siemens had acquired the patents from Benson in England in 1923, Hans Gleichmann succeeded in constructing a superpressure steam generator for Siemens-Schuckertwerke's cable plant in 1927, largely on the basis of experience acquired by Westinghouse.

Despite the technological lag of German companies, large American electrical engineering companies were in principle interested in cooperative arrangements of this kind. German companies could contribute important know-how, at least in some fields. At the same time, these companies, although major competitors in the world market, did not pose a competitive threat in the American market, which was by far the most important arena for US companies. The agreement with Westinghouse thus defined separate spheres of interest: Siemens was not to operate in Westinghouse's areas of activity in the US and Canada, while Westinghouse refrained from doing business in Europe. This provision effectively prevented Siemens from undertaking any major business activities in the US. In fact, SSW abandoned plans for a cooperative agreement with General Electric in 1927 in order not to jeopardize its Westinghouse alliance.

More large-scale negotiations on the division of overseas business and spheres of influence were held in 1931. The talks, in which the world's leading competitors in the energy sector took part, resulted in the International Notification and Compensation Agreements (INACA) between AEG, SSW, BBC, the British companies Metropolitan Vickers, General Electric, English Electric and Thomson-Houston, as well as Westinghouse and General Electric in the US.

Despite repeated attempts, Siemens also failed to gain access to the US market between the wars. Although a liaison office was maintained in New York (Feldenkirchen 1999: 199 f., 592 f.) until 1941 and personal contacts took place with high-ranking representatives of the American electrical industry, the existing agreements with Western Electric, Autelco, Westinghouse and other companies not only failed to yield any export business, but even restricted it severely.

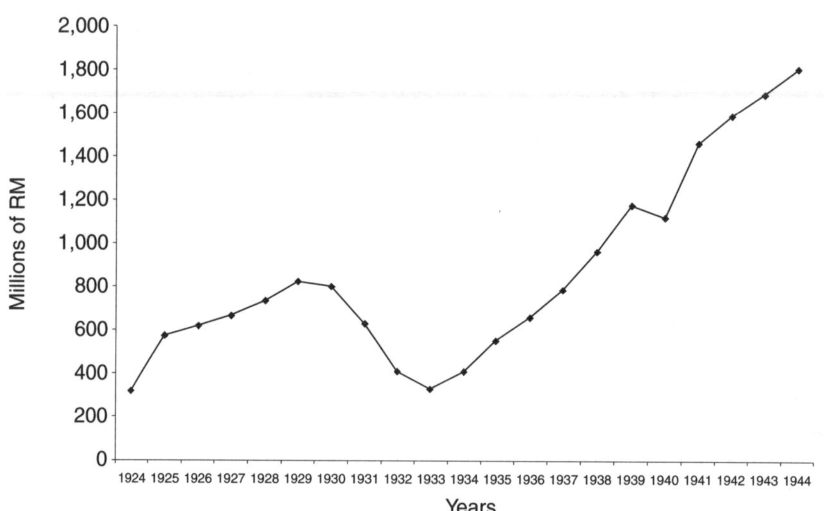

Figure 5.2 Sales of Siemens 1924–44.

Source: Siemens Archives.

Siemens in the US after World War II

By the end of the 1940s, Siemens representatives had made various trips to the US to explore sales opportunities and had decided that the American electrical goods market was an extremely attractive arena for Siemens (Tacke 1977: 205–12). Nevertheless, the absence of distribution channels, divergent industrial standards, differences in technical infrastructures, the lack of financial resources, and different business and marketing methods weighed the scales against a major commitment to the US. All the same, reciprocal visits were made to laboratories and technical colloquia were held with American companies following the currency reform. These events attracted numerous Siemens engineers, physicists and legal experts to the US.

These fact-finding visits and the resumption of contacts with US companies quickly spurred SSW to seek reactivation of the License and Technical Assistance Agreement with Westinghouse, which was signed in 1924, extended in 1934, and finally interrupted by the war. Initiated in 1953, the negotiations came to fruition in 1954 with an agreement between SSW and Westinghouse on the free exchange of patents and know-how (License and Technical Assistance Agreement).[4] A decisive role in the rapidly concluded negotiations may have been played by earlier contacts and by the special political situation created by the Cold War. The agreement prohibited the companies to launch products in each other's domestic markets. In addition to working with Westinghouse, Siemens concluded patent licence agreements with ITT, Western Electric and RCA in the telecommunications and power-engineering equipment sectors, as well as in the fields of transistors, diodes, television and radio. Finally, the License and Technical Assistance Agreement of 1954, which had been extended by 10 years in 1966, was terminated by mutual consent in 1970. The exchange of patent licences was not immediately affected by the termination of the cooperation, and both sides extended the licence rights until 1972. The relationship with Westinghouse had already become somewhat relaxed in the 1960s. But the main reason for terminating the agreement was that the cooperation between Siemens and AEG within the framework of the Kraftwerk Union AG (KWU) and Transformatoren Union AG (TU) could have led to an exchange of know-how between Westinghouse and General Electric, which had a 12 per cent stake in AEG.[5] This was prohibited by Germany's anti-trust legislation. In addition, the agreements with Westinghouse were so worded that the domestic markets of each company enjoyed special protection, a situation which could have been challenged under the new anti-trust regulations.[6]

Founding the regional company

After the war, Siemens first focused on re-establishing its traditional markets base in Europe and South America. During that period, the company confined its activities in the US to representative functions, apart from license and technical assistance agreements. In the 1950s, Siemens New York functioned as an 'embassy' or 'base' and did no more than advise headquarters about business opportunities. It did not perform the functions of a distribution company, such as warehousing, service, billing and bookkeeping. This arrangement lasted until a Siemens Regional Company was formed in 1960. Up to that date, Siemens had merely operated a 'speciality business' in the US, whose sales did not even reach DM 30 million by fiscal 1960. Chiefly as a result of stepped-up operations in the US by Wernerwerk für Messtechnik and Siemens-Reiniger-Werke (SRW), the activities of Siemens New York thereafter increasingly assumed the character of a normal business with such necessary facilities and services as warehouse, maintenance, spare parts and an office organization.[7] SRW's activities were a key factor in the company's development into a true subsidiary as it penetrated the US market with its range of speciality products. The passive components and measuring equipment business also showed strong growth.

In 1963, the medical business was detached from the Regional Company and incorporated as Siemens Medical Systems at a new location in New Jersey. Seven years later, it was again consolidated in organizational terms with the other sales units in Siemens Corporation.

Developments during the 1970s

Despite the oil and currency crises, the 1970s were clearly a decade of increasing world trade for Siemens. In fiscal 1974–75, half the company's

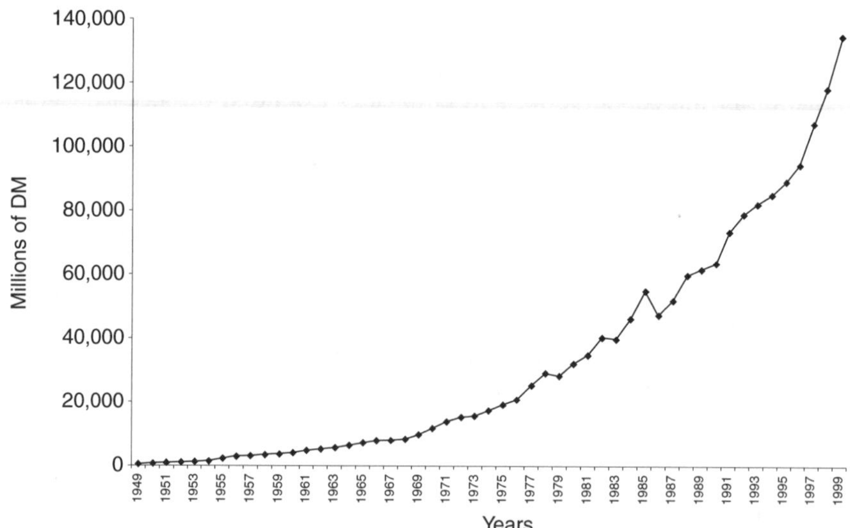

Figure 5.3 Sales of Siemens 1949–99.

Source: Siemens Archives.

sales were recorded abroad for the first time. Over a half of this international business was accounted for by Western Europe, whereas the other two large markets of the triad, namely America and Asia, shared equal proportions of 15 per cent but were significantly under-represented in comparison with the company's European business. Africa, Australia and Eastern Europe accounted for about the same lesser shares in the Siemens world business of around 5 per cent (Feldenkirchen 2000: 334).

Siemens' US business doubled in the 1960s, yet this success was not attributable to a fundamental change in business policy towards the American market. Only in the early 1970s, when Bernhard Plettner was CEO, was the US included seriously in the company's general sales and investment policy and seen as a strategically important sales market. This change of direction was prompted by the realization that, as Paul Dax, head of Corporate Sales, put it: 'There is no way of bypassing' the US. 'Our . . . activities in the United States will be . . . a new touchstone of our capacity to perform and adapt.'[8]

In the early 1970s, almost a third of the world's electrical market was accounted for by the US. In 1971 the American electrical market attained a value of DM 175 billion, compared with DM 44 billion for the Federal Republic of Germany. The US electrical market was thus four times as large as that of the Federal Republic and about half as big again as the entire EEC market.[9] US electrical imports were almost exactly DM 10 billion in 1971, i.e. almost a quarter of the electrical market of the Federal Republic. Measured by Siemens sales in fiscal 1971–2 of DM 200 million, the company's market share in the US was 0.1 per cent and its share of electrical imports some 1.4 per cent. These figures alone show that Siemens ran a pure speciality business in the US which was made up almost exclusively of imports.

This situation was described at a meeting of the Central Committee in summer 1973 as extremely unsatisfactory, especially as sales of German products to the US were seen as being greatly jeopardized in many sectors due to the falling value of the dollar. In future, therefore, the business was to focus on local manufacture of equipment or the procurement of products from the dollar zone.[10] The unanimous opinion of the Central Committee was that Siemens would have to penetrate the US market more strongly and also gain a production foothold there, in addition to purely marketing interests; the following reasons supported this view.

1 The most important of these was the drop in the value of the dollar, which had made exports to the North American market from Germany considerably more expensive. Many foreign companies who merely had marketing operations in the US were now faced with a stark choice: either to pull out of the US – the world's largest single market – altogether or to gain a stronger foothold there. The answer

for Siemens was unequivocal: 'We must emancipate ourselves as quickly and extensively as possible from exclusive deliveries from the DM zone by setting up manufacturing facilities in the US.'[11]

2 Costs were rising more quickly in Germany than in the US.
3 The danger of restrictive import barriers set up by the US.
4 The need for closer links to the technological advances made in the US, especially in those fields in which American technology was the worldwide standard, such as the electronics sector.
5 The recognition that in the long run Siemens could operate a broad-based business in many sectors only if it could demonstrate its resolve to establish itself firmly on the American market.
6 The pressure from the market for shorter delivery times and technical adaptation to the special requirements of local customers.

It was clear that in order to be involved more strongly in the US electrical market, the company had to increase its commitment on the manufacturing front. Because Siemens lacked both the financial and personnel resources to take this path alone in view of the dimensions of the American market, it was obliged to set up joint ventures with suitable US partners. A good starting point was created by numerous agreements on licensing and the exchange of technical assistance. In the early 1970s, Siemens was linked to over 200 US companies in this way; among the most important were ITT, Western Electric, IBM, RCA, Texas Instruments, Motorola, GTE, Westinghouse and Allis-Chalmers. With a few exceptions, the cooperation between Allis-Chalmers and Siemens extended across the entire range of electrical technology. In the early 1970s, Siemens concluded a licensing agreement with the Allis-Chalmers Corporation in Milwaukee in the sector of power engineering. This was followed in 1978 by the joint founding of a company known as Siemens-Allis Incorporated in Milwaukee/US in which Siemens initially had a 20 per cent share. This was increased by another 30 per cent in January 1979.[12]

Good prospects were also seen for Kraftwerk Union AG, which was already able to achieve success on the US market in the mid-1970s and had acquired orders for large turbo-generators worth over a billion DM in cooperation with Allis-Chalmers Power Systems Incorporated.[13] At a meeting of the Supervisory Board held at the end of 1975 it was noted

> that the US power supply industry has a keen interest in a third manufacturer in addition to General Electric and Westinghouse and that the technology offered by KWU has met with a good response there, so that it is by no means illusory to aim for a US market share in the order of 15–20 per cent. We believe that the opportunity which exists as a result of these successful sales in the United States should not be allowed to slip out of our hands.[14]

However, medical engineering continued to occupy a special position in the company's US commitment. It remained the best-selling sector until the expansion of the company's activities in the 1970s. Here too, partners were sought, particularly for large installations such as X-ray equipment and computer tomographs. But the company's own manufacturing capacity was also extended by setting up an X-ray plant in Cheshire (Connecticut), in addition to Siemens Medical Laboratories Inc. in Walnut Creek, which manufactured electron accelerators for medical applications.

Although the US business was certainly successful in some sectors, it was not without its problems. Among these were cultural differences: the distinct American and German mentalities, difficulties in mutual understanding, language barriers, diverging technical standards and different requirements of the users. In other words 'where business matters were mixed strongly with sociological questions involving interpersonal relationships' – to quote from a meeting of the Managing Board held in summer 1976 – business activities were rendered more difficult at times.[15] The speaker continued:

> Let us not forget that the United States has already been the world's foremost economic power for several decades, will certainly continue to occupy that position in the future and is at the forefront of many technological fields. This has led to Americans developing a justified and surely understandable feeling of their own high competence in both technical and organizational matters which makes them disinclined to listen to outside advice. Because our German technical departments and employees share much the same attitude, meetings with Americans often lead to a collision of two worlds. Both of them consequently respond with a psychological defense reaction mixed with a claim to leadership, known today by the term 'not invented here ("n.i.h.")' which should under no circumstances be restricted to technical matters.... It seems to me that we can acquire a solid footing in the US only if the German Groups develop a deeper understanding of the peculiarities of the American market and the methods and mentalities prevailing there. This is certainly no easy task, and in approaching it they must in no way give up their identity as members of the parent company.[16]

Developments in the 1980s

The long-term strategic considerations applied in the early 1980s responded to an increasingly global business climate in which the company could no longer limit its activities to the European market if it was to attain or maintain a leading position. The US, which made up 30 per cent of the world electrical market in the early 1980s, was extremely attractive above all from the standpoint of regional strategy.

The largest homogeneous electrical market in the world – with a common language, uniform standards of electrical technology and largely uniform consumer habits – it was extraordinarily dynamic and innovative in a number of specific electronic markets, such as telecommunications and data technology. Other contributory factors were the country's relatively high political and economic stability as well as the extensive accessibility to foreign trade, investments and capital which it offered.

Since 1980, the US has been among the most flourishing export markets for Siemens. Whereas Siemens US still accounted for only 10 per cent of the company's total export business in 1980, this had already risen to 20 per cent in 1988 and grew further in the ensuing period. A status report on Siemens AG from 1982 showed that the company employed 13,600 people in the US and recorded sales there of some DM 2.6 billion.[17] The Siemens group in the United States, with sales and service branches in all major US cities, comprised thirteen majority holdings and five minority holdings with a total of 32 factories and development laboratories. By that time, the US business had reached a size which made it increasingly difficult to manage from as far away as Munich or Erlangen, the company's German headquarters. Problems in transatlantic communication and the different working habits of Germans and Americans in the operative business called for a fundamental reorganization geared toward stronger local links and decentralization. Bernhard Plettner, the Chairman of the Supervisory Board at that time, was a particular advocate of this move: in a memorandum from the year 1982, he wrote:

> If we examine our own export business to find out why we are successful in many places and less so or not at all at others, then it soon becomes apparent that we do well in Europe wherever we succeed in recruiting strong local management and in adapting plants, workshops and assembly departments to local requirements.... The United States of America shows us an extreme case of a situation already familiar to us from the industrial nations of Europe. We can set up a trade agency; but if we wish to manufacture there, we can only do so with American managers and American management methods and by excluding the German proprietor entirely from the day-to-day running of the business.... In other words, a certain distance must be maintained at organizational level, and this can only be done by having an American holding with a president at its head whom we dare not overrule; a president who ensures that the Executive Vice Presidents of the Group are solely responsible to him for the conduct of business and who gives them the backing they need to protect themselves from any meddling from Munich and Erlangen.[18]

A few years later, these considerations would also be reflected in the new company structure of 1989 which strengthened the autonomy of the local companies. At that time Siemens was represented in about 130 countries – some of them with national management – but the central decisions were nevertheless always taken in Germany. The organization of the large foreign companies was now upgraded and their autonomy was increased by having them report directly to the Managing Board (Feldenkirchen 2000: 335).

The increasing acquisition of various companies after the 1980s under the motto 'all business is local' made a significant contribution to the company's growth in the US. In the sector of communications technology, Siemens founded the Rolm Company in Norwalk (Connecticut) in 1989 together with IBM for marketing private communication installations manufactured by Rolm Systems in Santa Clara (California). It has since become a part of Siemens Business Communication Systems Inc. In 1988, the BiiN joint venture was set up in Hillsboro together with the Intel Corporation for manufacturing systems for networked computer applications. The same year, Allied-Signal Inc. acquired the Bendix Electronics Group, thus giving Siemens a presence in the automotive technology sector too.

Siemens-Allis Inc. contributed a third to Siemens US sales and had to compete against cheap imports on the stagnating market for conventional power engineering as a result of the strong dollar. The company was extensively restructured in 1985 and its automation technology activities were extended to become the focus of its product range. After the acquisition of its remaining shares, the company became a wholly-owned Siemens subsidiary and trades under the name of Siemens Energy & Automation Inc.

In the sector of medical engineering, the US share of the world market accounted for more than 40 per cent in the early 1980s.[19] New orders received by Siemens in the US comprised 27 per cent in fiscal 1981–2 and thus pushed domestic business to second place for the first time. Siemens acquired the nuclear diagnostics division of Searle in 1980 and merged it with a new company known as Siemens Gammasonics Inc. (Since 1982, the medical engineering business has been run as a subsidiary of Siemens Capital Corp. via Siemens Medical Systems Inc.) The reorganization resulted in the development, production and sales of medical engineering equipment in the US now being concentrated at Siemens Medical Systems Inc.

Developments from the 1990s to the present

The regional structure began to move in the early 1990s. The European business declined slightly during the previous years and then recovered again in 1993–4, but had dropped in terms of market share, whereas the other regions were able to show a significant increase. The international business was now distributed uniformly over the world's three largest economic regions known as the triad of North America, Western and Central

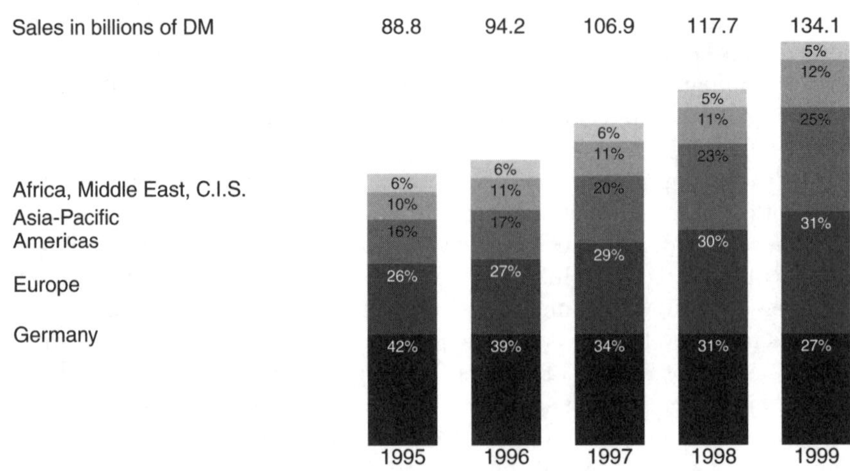

Figure 5.4 Sales of Siemens in Europe, the Americas and Asia-Pacific, 1995–9.

Source: Siemens Archives.

Europe, and the Far East. Particularly high growth rates were recorded in Eastern Europe and South-East Asia, where the volume increased more than threefold in 4 years (Feldenkirchen 2000: 335).

As markets increasingly opened up and competition became tougher in the age of globalization, the German electrical industry was faced with a major challenge in the 1990s, namely 'to quickly build up a strong position in its west European home market and at the same time to create a solid presence in North America', in the words of then CEO Karlheinz Kaske 1990.[20]

> However, we cannot attain the volumes needed in our core sectors – the critical mass – in Europe alone. We need the North American market as our second mainstay. We must expand our market position strongly in our core sectors in North America during the coming decade and must aim to double our sales share in this region to 20 per cent by the year 2000.[21]

As a vision of the future, it was quite realistic for Kaske that the company would 'conduct parts of its business from the US, from our European neighbours or possibly also from the Far East in the year 2000 . . .'.[22]

However, the US business was not expanded merely to secure an additional market for the company. Siemens also had to be present in this market because of the pioneering role it still played in many essential technologies. Another reason for the company's commitment to the US was to strengthen its position as a global supplier in all parts of the world and to secure it over the long term.

After the company had succeeded in the early 1990s in giving its American business a secure footing with sales of more than DM 6.5 billion and around 31,000 employees (1990 status), it aimed for further high growth in this market.[23] Siemens enhanced its international competitiveness by means of various forms of strategic alliances with other companies and continued its policy of acquisitions and mergers which contributed significantly to its growth in the US.[24] Thus the merger of Siemens Communication Systems Inc. with Stromberg-Carlson in 1990 resulted in eight large operative companies with several subsidiaries which employed 29,000 people. Other foundations included Siemens Transportation Systems Inc. (1990) in the sector of transportation technology, Siemens Industrial Automation Inc. (1991) in the automation engineering sector and Siemens Power Corporation in the power plant sector as a result of the merging of four US companies (1992).

The company's market presence in the US has expanded strongly up to the present, with annual growth exceeding 12 per cent in the past decade. The share of Siemens US in the export business, which was already 20 per cent in 1988, grew by a total of over 40 per cent between 1992 and 1996. The better overall result recorded in fiscal 1995–6, despite continuing earnings problems in data systems, was due to the buoyant economy and the important contribution made by Osram Sylvania Inc.; this company was formed in 1993 after the acquisition of the Sylvania lamp business from the GTE Corporation. Early in 1999 Siemens AG established Unisphere Solutions, Inc., a Siemens company, to target leadership in converged voice/data and Internet networking solutions. Unisphere Solutions is a wholly-owned subsidiary of Siemens and belongs to the Information and Communication Networks (IC Networks) Group. In addition, Siemens acquired Argon Networks, Inc., and Castle Networks, Inc., which together with several units of Siemens Information and Communication Networks, Inc., US, forms the basis of the new company. By creating Unisphere Solutions and acquiring specialized start-up companies, Siemens has strengthened its position in the market for converged network technology.

Today, the US represents the world's largest and technologically most important market for Siemens and is of particular strategic importance within the scope of globalization. Siemens US recorded sales of DM 26.4 billion in fiscal 1998–9 – some 20 per cent of the company's global sales. Thus the business volume transacted in the US is making up an ever larger share of the company's overall sales. In fiscal 1999–2000 sales in the US were for the first time ever higher than in Germany. Siemens expect sales to increase faster than average in the years ahead.

The holding company of Siemens Corporation, with headquarters in New York City, has a decentralized structure and comprises more than 100 operational companies and holdings in the sectors of power, industry, information and communications, medicine, transportation, light as well

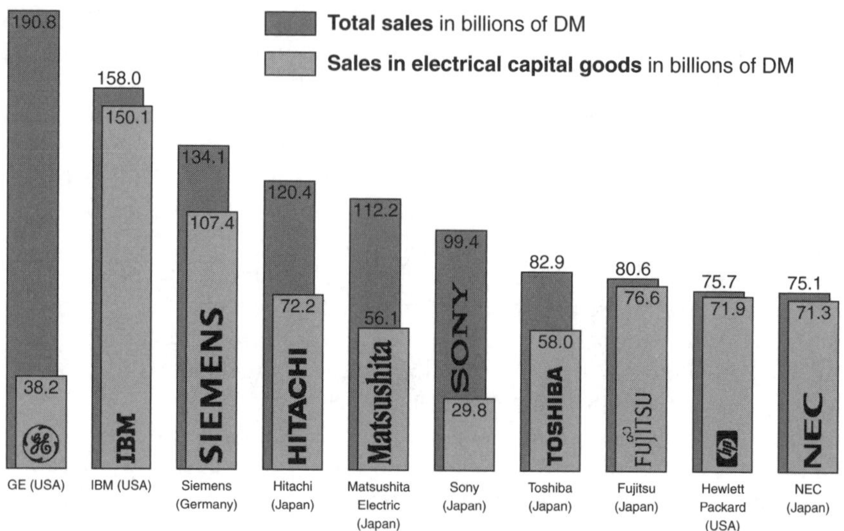

Figure 5.5 The top ten companies in world electrical engineering and electronics in 1999.

Source: Siemens Archives.

as research and development and financial services.[25] Among its companies with the highest sales shares are Siemens Westinghouse Power Corp., Osram Sylvania, Siemens Medical Systems Inc., Siemens Energy & Automation Inc., Siemens Information & Communication Networks Inc. and Siemens Building Technologies Inc. Together, they make up approximately 80 per cent of the total sales of Siemens Corporation.

Siemens has more than 100 manufacturing facilities as well as some 525 sales and service offices in the United States of America. It has a presence in 27 US States, with a regional focus in Florida, Georgia and California. Of the company's more than 64,000 employees (30.9.1999) in the US, some 5,000 work outside the country. The company, which is preparing for its planned listing on the New York Stock Exchange in the year 2001, is among the largest foreign multinational employers in the United States.

Siemens is planning a radical reorganization in the US during 2001 in advance of a major push into the market. The company will reinforce cooperation between its 30 US operating businesses with joint ventures and a common holding company to take on the administration. In the US, Siemens will concentrate on organic growth, centralizing back office procedures such as controlling, human resources and accounting. It will also extract synergies from creating four customer clusters in the fields of healthcare, airports, e-commerce fulfilment and logistics, and high-technology campuses and business centres. The new shares will be used only to fund small, targeted acquisitions.

Conclusion

In spite of trying to start an American business as early as the 1890s, Siemens has been a relative late-comer in becoming a significant market player in healthcare, energy and power, information and communications, lighting and precision materials, and industry and automation. Due to the historical reasons outlined above, efforts were only intensified since the 1970s when Siemens began acquiring American companies in various fields. In trying to conquer the most important market in electricals and electronics Siemens heavily relied on external growth while staying away from setting up greenfield plants. Major acquisitions and internal growth have helped to turn the US into Siemens' most important single market and to make the company one of America's biggest foreign multinationals.

Notes

1 In 1903, 'Elektrizitäts-Aktiengesellschaft vorm. Schuckert & Co.' merged with the power engineering interests of Siemens & Halske. Siemens thus consolidated its position in the sector of power engineering, especially vis-à-vis its greatest competitor, AEG. Siemens-Schuckertwerke, a stock corporation since 1927, became a wholly-owned subsidiary of Siemens & Halske in 1939.

2 SAA 4 / Lf 656; SAA 54 / Lb 2; SAA 21 / Li 95; SAA 11 / Lf 367, 11 / Lf 384 and 11 / Lf 179, Köttgen papers: correspondence on the Westinghouse agreement (1923–7); NA RG 26017-242-3-1 (National Archives, Washington).

3 SAA 6957: Agreement between Westinghouse and SSW on the delimitation of the business sectors of November 10, 1934; SAA 21 / Lg 645; SAA 54 / Lb 2.

4 SAA 7489, Vol. 14: Main Westinghouse agreement of 1954 with changes 1964; cf. also SAA 7394; SAA 7449. The planned contractual partners were Westinghouse Electric Corporation and Westinghouse Electric International Company on the one side and S&H, SSW, Siemens-Reiniger-Werke AG (SRW) and Vacuumschmelze AG (VAC) on the other. The set of contracts dealt with exclusive and non-exclusive licences for patents and technical assistance in the work sectors of S&H, SSW, SRW and VAC.

5 Kraftwerk Union AG and Transformatoren Union AG were set up in 1969 jointly by Siemens and AEG in order to strengthen their competitiveness. KWU built both conventional thermal as well as nuclear power plants in addition to manufacturing turbines and generators. TU supplied the corresponding transformers.

6 The relationships between Siemens and Westinghouse were revived in 1998 when Siemens took over the fossil-fuelled power plant business from Westinghouse when it acquired Westinghouse Power Generation.

7 Siemens-Reiniger-Werke AG was set up in 1932. In the 1930s, it was the world's largest company specializing in electromedical products.

8 Talk given by Paul Dax on May 27, 1974 on investments in the US, quoted from Gerd Tacke (Tacke 1977: 212). The most important of these was the founding of Siemens-Allis in 1978, a joint venture with Allis-Chalmers in the sector of power engineering. As early as 1970 Allis-Chalmers had concluded a licensing agreement with Siemens in order to use Siemens know-how to extend the range of its electrical engineering products.

9 Cf. Interim Report on the US concept to the Central Committee on 23.7.1973, p. 2. (Siemens Archives).

10 Cf. ibid. p. 16.
11 Cf. ibid. p. 4.
12 Cf. talk given by Bernhard Plettner at the meeting of the Supervisory Board of Siemens AG in Nuremberg on July 5, 1976, p. 5; Documents for the meeting of the Supervisory Board in Zurich held on July 7, 1977, Annex 1, p. 5; Dr. Plettner's report on the state of the company in July 1979, pp. 11 f. (Siemens Archives).
13 DM 1.2 billion, cf. Bernhard Plettner at the meeting of the Supervisory Board on 11.11.1975, Annex 1, p. 9 and talk by Dr. Plettner at the meeting of the Supervisory Board of Siemens AG in Munich on November 8, 1974, p. 9. (Siemens Archives).
14 Cf. Bernhard Plettner at the meeting of the Supervisory Board on 11.11.1975, Annex 1, pp. 9 f. (Siemens Archives).
15 Cf. Annex 1 to the meeting of the Managing Board on 29.6.1976, p. 29. (Siemens Archives).
16 Cf. ibid., pp. 26 f. (Siemens Archives).
17 Cf. report by H.-G. Neglein on the state of the company in June 1982, p. 13. (Siemens Archives).
18 Cf. Bernhard Plettner: Comments on 'Manufacturing facilities abroad' of March 2, 1982, pp. 2 f. (Siemens Archives).
19 Cf. Meeting of the Managing Board in Erlangen, June 21, 1983, Annex 1, p. 1. (Siemens Archives).
20 Cf. K. Kaske: Parliamentarians' discussion in Bonn, 14.2.1990: Responses by the German electrical and electronics industry to the challenges of the nineties, p. 3. Cf. also Hermann Franz: Neustrukturierung der Weltelektroindustrie – Notwendigkeit von Allianzen und Kooperationen, meeting of the Supervisory Board July 5, 1990, p. 5. (Siemens Archives).
21 Cf. K. Kaske: Siemens in the nineties. Siemens-Tagung 1990, p. 20 f. (SAA 64/Lm 210).
22 Cf. ibid. p. 20.
23 Cf. ibid. pp. 6 f.
24 In view of the unsatisfactory business performance of Siemens-Allis Inc. as a result of stagnating markets and cheap imports, the company was comprehensively reorganized in 1985; automation technology was extended to become the focus of its product range; after the acquisition of the remaining shares, the company became a wholly-owned Siemens subsidiary and traded under the name of Siemens Energy & Automation Inc. The following additional companies were founded or acquired: BiiN, Hillsboro, as a joint venture with Intel Corp., Santa Clara (computer systems for networked applications, 1988); Bendix Electronics Group from Allied-Signal Inc., now known as Siemens-Bendix-Automotive Electronics (automotive technology, 1988); merger of Siemens Communication Systems Inc., Boca Raton, with Stromberg-Carlson, Lake Mary (1990); Siemens Transportation Systems Inc. (transportation technology, 1990); Siemens Industrial Automation Inc., Atlanta, by adding automation technology and the stored-program control business previously operated by Texas Instruments Inc., Dallas (1991).
25 The Siemens business in the US comprises the following operative companies: Siemens Automotive Corporation, Siemens Building Technologies, Siemens Business Services, Siemens Corporation, Siemens Corporate Research, Siemens ElectroCom, Siemens Energy & Automation, Siemens Financial Services, Siemens Hearing Instruments, Siemens Information and Communication Networks, Siemens Information and Communication Mobile, Siemens Medical Systems, Siemens Power Corporation, Siemens Power Transmission & Distribution, Siemens Procurement & Logistics Services, Siemens Real Estate, Siemens

Shared Services, Siemens Solar Industries, Siemens Transportation Systems, Siemens Westinghouse Power Corporation, ADB (airfield technology), Infineon Technologies Corporation (semiconductors), Opuswave Networks, Osram Sylvania (lighting), Unisphere Solutions (highly-integrated communications solutions) and White Oak Semiconductor.

References

Feldenkirchen, W. (1993) 'Unternehmensgeschichte und Unternehmenskultur am Beispiel Siemens', *Archiv und Wirtschaft* 26: 153–62.

—— (1994) *Werner von Siemens. Inventor and International Entrepreneur,* Columbus: Ohio State University Press.

—— (1995) 'Die Anfänge des Siemensgeschäfts in Amerika', *Wirtschaft – Gesellschaft – Unternehmen,* Festschrift for Hans Pohl on his 60th birthday, Wilfried Feldenkirchen (ed.), Frauke Schönert-Röhlk, Günther Schulz, 2 vols. (Vierteljahrschrift für Sozial- und Wirtschaftsgeschichte, Beiheft 120 a/b), Stuttgart.

—— (1999) *Siemens 1918–1945,* Columbus: Ohio State University Press.

—— (2000) *Siemens – From Workshop to Global Player,* Munich: Piper.

Köttgen, C. (1924a) 'Produktionsmethoden Fords', *Organisation* 26, 13/14: 238–9.

—— (1924b) 'Facharbeiter und Fordsche Fabrikationsmethoden', *Siemens-Mitteilungen* 59: 4–6.

—— (1925) *Amerika und Gemeinschaftsarbeit,* Talk held at the Cologne Industry Conference on 18 June 1925 (manuscript in the Siemens Archives: SAA VVA Köttgen).

—— (1926) 'Das wirtschaftliche Amerika', *Jahrbücher für Nationalökonomie und Statistik,* No. 124, 3rd series, 69: 599–605.

Matschoss, C. (1916) *Werner Siemens. Ein kurzgefasstes Lebensbild nebst einer Auswahl seiner Briefe,* Berlin: Julius Springer.

Tacke, G. (1977) *Ein Beitrag zur Geschichte der Siemens AG,* unpublished printed manuscript in the Siemens Archives.

von Weiher, S. (1990) *Die englischen Siemens-Werke und das Siemens-Überseegeschäft in der zweiten Hälfte des 19. Jahrhunderts,* Schriften zur Wirtschafts- und Sozialgeschichte, 38, Wolfram Fischer (ed.), Berlin: Duncker & Humblot.

6 French direct investment in car and truck manufacturing in the US

A story of failure and success[1]

Ludovic Cailluet

Introduction

As world leaders of the sector in the 1890s, French automobile companies have been active direct investors in America since the very beginning of the twentieth century. Renault set up sales, repair and spare parts depots in New York and on the West Coast in 1906. Michelin operated a tyre factory in New Jersey in 1907, rapidly turning into an early and serious competitor to the domestic tyre industry (Wilkins 1993: 18). During the interwar period the prosperity of French manufacturers in the US declined due to the changing nature of the demand (Fridenson 1986). Post-1945, conflicting images of early successes were darkened by later failures. In the long run, automobile manufacturers have not been successful in their multiple attempts to turn export successes into durable distribution and manufacturing operations. Renault's American ventures in the late 1950s and the 1980s exemplify these downturns. The story, however, is not limited to the nationalized company. Peugeot, Simca and Citroën, though on a lower scale, have also been successful in importing cars into the US. The combined market share for all French automobile manufacturers nevertheless remained rather marginal.

The story for commercial vehicles is different. The commercial arm of the Renault Group – Renault Véhicules Industriels (Renault VI) – has been a success, manufacturing and selling in the US since 1977 through its alliance with Mack Trucks Inc.[2]

The story started in 1977 with a mere commercial alliance, to end with a 100 per cent ownership of Mack Trucks by Renault VI since the early 1990s. The Renault VI–Mack Trucks alliance provides an excellent case study of multinational co-operative strategies. Looking at the relationship, one can observe various steps in the building of an international strategic alliance (Dussauge and Garette 1995). Considering the previous failures of French motor industrialists, especially within the Renault Group, it is interesting to look at an experience of successful North American investment within the same corporation. If organizations are capable of memory, they should be able to learn from and capitalize on past experiences of failures and successes (Koenig 1994). However, this might not be the case inside diversified corporations between different activity-based divisions. As a result, some basic questions to be reviewed by French industrialists when considering an American venture still remain at the beginning of the twenty-first century (Franck 1997).

Jones (1996) has given an excellent overview of the enormous literature produced about multinational enterprises (MNEs) and foreign direct investment (FDI) in recent decades. Furthermore, foreign investments by European multinationals in historical perspective have been thoroughly researched (Wilkins 1989; Chandler 1997) for earlier periods. Unsurprisingly, due to difficulties in accessing sources, works dealing with more contemporary issues are rarer. Wilkins' contribution to the present volume (Chapter 2) is a welcome exception.

Nevertheless, the business history literature rarely looks at effects of FDI on the strategic practices and the corporate culture of firms. Among the available business histories of European and French multinationals (Beltran, Daviet and Ruffat 1995), very few focus on the managerial impact of FDI (Gleize 1993). Finally, despite a respectable number of publications about the global motor industry (Fridenson 1999; Loubet 1998, 1999, 2000), there are very few academic work available on truck manufacturing (Banville 2000; Glimstedt 2000).

The motor vehicle industry is often considered as a whole, although truck manufacturing is indeed a very different activity from automobile manufacturing. The truck sector is poorly known and researched, except for the trade press (*Fleet Equipment, Fleet Owner, Modern Materials Handling, Traffic Management*) and for books focusing mainly on the product itself (Chanuc 1993). Truck plants have served as research field for social historians (Terrail and Tripier 1986), and statistical surveys are easy to access (Steck 1990) especially through professional associations (CCFA 1999). Looking at more contemporary and strategy oriented works, Laure (1988) and Grevet (1996) have published a general perspective on the concentration movement of the 1950–70s, and Banville and Chanaron have looked at supplier–manufacturer relationships (1995). Durand (1995) has studied the international joint ventures of Berliet. However, the literature is poor and may even be misleading. As an illustration, in a chapter describing the supposed 'failure to grow outside Europe' of Renault, the author dedicated only five lines to explaining that the acquisition of Mack had made Renault the second biggest world producer of utility vehicles. This chapter aims to fill some of these gaps by means of empirical research.

The French automotive industry in the US

After World War II, the French automotive industry took some steps to export cars to obtain a share of the promising North American market.

The European automobile industry at the time was obviously handicapped by market and customer base differences. Despite these factors, British (Jaguar, MG, Triumph) and German (Volkswagen) manufacturers had some successes in the US from the late 1940s onwards. These examples pushed French companies to bet on the US market for cars, especially in the so-called 'economy' segment. The government and the national planning agency encouraged such initiatives in order to get much needed US dollars to improve the trade balance. Renault's first attempt in 1948 was in association with John Green, a Californian businessman. From 1948 to 1952, the latter sold annually on behalf of the French company between 860 to 1500 Renault '4 CVs'.[3]

This trial was a failure for two reasons. Green was primarily a salesman who was not able to set up any after-sales and maintenance organization (Loubet 2000: 126). Besides, parts prices were terribly high and their availability extremely irregular.[4] Replacement tyres for the '4 CV' and later the 'Dauphine' had dimensions that were not manufactured in the US. They had to be imported from France and cost the client up to 60 per cent more than the Chevrolet equivalent (Loubet 1998). In 1952, Green almost faced bankruptcy. More than 700 unsold cars lay abandoned by dealers in lots all over the US.

Renault had to repaint the cars and try to sell them in Canada and elsewhere with huge losses. The CEO of Renault, Pierre Lefaucheux, decided then to stop the American disaster and to withdraw. He was at this point subject to political pressure to keep a foot in the US. In fact, the government considered the presence of French cars 'in the streets of New York' necessary prestige. Renault as a state-owned company and national economic icon resumed exports to the US, the Ministry of Finance providing an 18 per cent subsidy on the cost of each car (Loubet 2000). After a few years of artificial exports boosted by economic policies, French manufacturers turned back to their domestic markets for almost a decade.

In 1957, a new move by economic planners changed motor industrialists' strategy once more. The French government needed foreign currency to pay for the colonial war in Algeria. As a consequence, the Ministry of Finance was eager to have industrialists sell abroad at all costs. Paul Ramadier imagined a fiscal incentive mechanism to force domestic manufacturers to go international (Loubet 1999: 293).[5] From 1957 to 1960, exports by French car manufacturers rose from 24 to 43 per cent of their total output. Renault and Simca sold many cars thanks to low-cost products and a good initial image. In addition, sales in Europe were in decline due to the Suez Canal crisis of 1956 and thus Renault decided to redirect European exports to the US.

The result was outstanding with 117,000 Renault cars sold in 1959 in the US, 25 per cent of the company's output for the year! The key success factor in the US market was mainly the price of the cars sold, with an average difference of $600 to $700 compared to American equivalent segment products. In 1959, for the first (and last) time, Renault Inc. sold more cars in the US than Volkswagen of America. To enlarge its offer, the company even accepted to sell its competitors' products. Peugeot '403' type cars were sold through Renault's American dealership.

Despite these successes in volume, however, the financial performance was very bad. The American operations were constantly generating losses during the 1950s. Marketing and inventory costs inflated considerably and added to the heavy spending already implied by logistics.[6] Meanwhile, Renault Inc. was accused by federal authorities of anti-competitive practices.[7] Last but not least, the product appeared to be inappropriate to the driving practices and conditions of North America. In 1960, after four years of trials, Renault Inc.'s 'Estafette' commercial van failed to pass Federal road tests. The van was banned from motorways for its inability to maintain a minimum speed on full load (Loubet 1998).

Renault's failure proved very quickly to be complete. The diagnosis was clear. The product, despite an enthusiastic welcome by the market due to its uniqueness, was not sufficiently adapted to the American market. The heating system was, for example, the same for Californian and Canadian cars (Loubet 1998: 220). Moreover, to satisfy volume targets, the local subsidiary had built up a weak network of dealers too rapidly. Renault Inc., in fear of missing sales, had signed dealership agreements with car sellers unable to service and maintain a foreign car with uncommon features. In contrast, Volkswagen of America gradually organized its own network, certifying dealers only when their ability for after-sales performance was proved.

The lesson was a severe one for Renault. The impact on the firm's image remained disastrous for years, reinforced by press campaigns organized by major American competitors. From 1959 to 1962, Renault's exports to the US were reduced by two-thirds. In 1961, the inventory was equivalent to 8 months of sales; the consequences at home were high with 3,000 redundancies in French plants and resulting riots. The network remained but with marginal sales of 10,000 cars a year on average until the 1970s.

Most attempts failed in the long run due to quality problems and difficulties in adapting products to local needs. The Renault cars of the 1970s were almost unsaleable in the US markets. Moreover, success in such a large country was very much linked to the quality of the commercial network. It was mainly Renault Inc.'s inability to develop a proper national network of dealers, ready to service the cars and supply exchange parts that led to most failures. Potential buyers were rapidly disappointed and the French manufacturers' reputation was tarnished for a long time. In that respect, the poor management of the AMC/Renault joint venture in the 1980s represents a second case study.

Renault and AMC: dreams and reality

Renault has had relations with the American Motors Company (AMC) since the early 1960s when Pierre Dreyfus, CEO of Renault, tried to convince AMC to back the French company's commercial efforts. In 1978, severely damaged by the competition from Japanese economy cars, AMC was in very poor shape except for its Jeep division (Loubet 1998). The company looked for an alliance with a manufacturer with a product range including cars with lower gasoline consumption. AMC negotiated with many possible partners including Peugeot. Renault remained the last option, and was very keen to renew its American presence. It bought a 22.5 per cent stake in the capital of AMC at a cost of $350 million. This strategic move was motivated by the oil crisis and its supposed consequences on the habits of American drivers. Peugeot had started to sell more of its diesel engine cars ('504' and '604' models) thanks to the rising cost of gasoline in the US; this was felt to be a lasting phenomenon. It was nevertheless to be a very short success; sales plummeted to 6,500 cars in 1988 and Peugeot withdrew definitively from the US market in 1990 (Loubet 1997: 319).

Renault bet on the commercial network of AMC supplying the company with supposedly suitable models. Renault 'Alliance' and 'Encore' derived from European designs (R9 and R11) and received good reviews in 1982–3; the sales were impressive with 200,000 cars in 1984. From then onwards, however, the story repeated itself. The offer to the market was limited to two models when the competition was supplying dealers and clients with a complete range of cars for all segments. More crucially, Renault failed to adapt its offer properly. Cars were fitted with European engines less powerful than the American equivalents and handicapped by the anti-pollution equipment (lower emission engine) added to the original block. The air conditioning units, popular in the US but very rare in Europe, decreased engine performance. On top of that, the exchange rate of the dollar proved to be very problematic in the mid-1980s for goods partly imported from France.

Ultimately, Renault under-evaluated the manufacturing costs of parts and engines at AMC and later neglected monitoring manufacturing quality in its American plants. Ultimately, the company did not properly support its distribution network, and the consequences were disastrous in terms of image and warranty costs. On the financial side, AMC's situation rapidly proved disastrous, with losses of $180 million in 1980. The economic crisis of the period added to the inadequacy of the AMC product range reinforced the bad results. In 1981 Renault was practically forced to take over 46.4 per cent of AMC's shares to save its subsidiary from bankruptcy. The cost was very high – $200 million – but the reward was complete control of the board of AMC.[8] In 1986, AMC started to be profitable again with good results on 'Medallion' and 'Premier' models. However, liabilities remained very high, and the Renault group decided to benefit from the reversal of fortune. The new group CEO, Raymond Levy, was not convinced by the American strategy that he had inherited. He sold AMC to Chrysler whose objective was to obtain the Jeep division; the Renault/AMC product range was quickly abandoned. Chrysler eventually ended all collaboration with the French group, paying a financial penalty of $211 million in 1992. In 1987, Renault brought its 8-year career as an American car manufacturer to a halt.

In automobiles, the outcome was very bad for French companies in the US. They had repeated some of their errors of the 1950s in underestimating the importance of having an appropriate range of vehicles to offer to the dealers. In their attempts to build a proper commercial network, French automobile manufacturers ignored important differences with their usual domestic practices. American car dealerships were seldom brand exclusive, neither were they affiliates or employees of the car manufacturers as in Europe. Their allegiance had to be won, and control on the quality delivered by the distribution network was very difficult to obtain for a non-established foreign brand. Finally, the AMC venture confirmed the problems of currency exchange risks in international operations, particularly in times of inflation.

Renault VI and Mack Trucks, anatomy of an alliance: 1977–90s

Since the late 1980s, Mack Trucks Inc. has thus remained the only automotive manufacturing industry asset owned by a French investor in the US. This story has been a surprisingly durable one with a collaboration that has lasted almost a quarter of a century. To explain this durability, one needs to go back to the origins of the agreement between Renault and Mack.

Renault, a state-controlled automobile manufacturer until 1996, has never really been a specialist of commercial vehicles. However, for political reasons and since the 1950s, Renault had led the concentration of the commercial vehicle sector in France. Through its Saviem subsidiary, the group took over most independent truck manufacturers during the 1960s. The last remaining independent company, Automobiles Berliet, closed the list in 1975. From that last merger was born the new commercial vehicles division of the Renault Group, known as Renault Véhicules Industriels or Renault VI.

The operation was sensitive in terms of corporate culture. Long-time fierce competitors, Saviem and Berliet were very different companies with few evident synergies. Since World War I, Berliet had developed a strong brand of quality heavy trucks and buses with a high level of industrial integration ('Detroit in Lyon'). In the mid-1970s, Berliet was a major player in Africa and, since the early 1950s, the company has had many experiences of FDI, mainly in developing and socialist countries. On the other hand, Saviem had developed a strong commercial network in France and Europe but was lacking a coherent line of products, particularly in the upper end of the market: heavy trucks. It mainly specialized in assembly, purchasing major components from third-party suppliers. What were the apparent motivations of Renault VI in its alliance with Mack?

The newly created Renault VI was suffering from a very diverse set of facilities inherited from past mergers and acquisitions of Saviem and the very specific and regional nature of Berliet's integrated plants (Durand 1995). The strategic intent of Renault VI was to expand into foreign markets to become a significant challenger to world-leader Daimler-Benz. A strong incentive to such a strategy was to absorb over-capacity output in France where it was difficult to consider brutal restructuring of facilities.

In that respect and because development costs rose in the 1970s, Saviem had started to build various alliances with MAN, Volvo and others. They developed through the so-called 'club of four' a common cabin for mid-sized cab-over-engine trucks (COE).[9] The second stage of the strategy was to grow in terms of industrial presence and to lower production costs. Saviem had strong positions in France and Africa but was threatened by Daimler-Benz in all its markets. In the mid-1970s, Saviem had problems of scope and size compared to its German rival, and in an open European market there was no way to secure a French monopoly.

As a consequence, Renault's experts started to consider the idea of a reinforcement. The project of an alliance with a foreign manufacturer of heavy trucks was born at Saviem (Renault) and preceded the 1976 merger with Berliet. The architect of the merger and head of Saviem from 1968, François Zannotti, was a man with a vision for the French commercial vehicle industry. He regarded Mack as one of the many acquisitions to be made to develop the firm into a global player, a company that could compare with Daimler-Benz. In fact several options were considered. Renault negotiators held discussions with Iveco, Scania, Mack and White.[10] The latter was taken over by Volvo, and Mack was finally chosen.

The North American market was preferred because of its size and prestige which could not be ignored. Moreover, the mid-range trucks produced in America were usually powered by gasoline (as opposed to diesel fuel) and performed only moderately well. Volvo had also started to distribute a 'class 6' truck in the US very similar to Renault VI products, proving that there was a market for such a product in North America. There was also a fiscal incentive, as 'incomplete trucks' (without body fitted) were only taxed at 3 per cent when imported into the US from Europe.

Renault VI was also influenced by a popular management motto of the time: the experience curve theory. In-house experts calculated that only the cumulative experience curve of Renault VI and Mack would be competitive with Daimler's in the long term. Moreover, according to a Boston Consulting Group report, the American market was considered a very promising one within a 15-year perspective. Renault VI's choice of

Mack was motivated by its commercial network and good image in the American market. Mack was also the only American truck company to manufacture its own engines; an alliance with the 'Bulldog' would thus mean possible joint development of components and engines.

Aside from Signal's[11] own motivation to focus on other activities, Mack's motivation was to help its network of dealers to expand their market base with a broader offer including an already developed class 6–7 product. Contrary to the European situation, the truck dealerships were independent companies; as a consequence truck manufacturers were in a weaker position with regard to distribution. Lastly, except for International Harvester, American truck manufacturers were not experts in diesel truck engines, and in the aftermath of the oil crisis the market was ready for a switch from gasoline to diesel.[12]

The idea of Zannotti, then CEO of Renault VI, was to use Mack to expand sales of its mid-range class 6 and 7 trucks in the US and other markets.[13] Renault VI would use its European marketing network to sell Mack trucks and thus enlarge its product offer in the upper end and specialized segments (fire department engines, oil industry, etc.). Moreover, it was hoped that further co-operation would enable the use of Mack engines on heavy duty Renault VI trucks. Eventually, the 'Midliner' truck would give a much needed workload to the Renault VI Bainville plant in Normandy.

'Built like a Mack truck'

Mack Trucks was created in 1900 in New York. The company erected a truck manufacturing plant in Allentown, PA, in 1905, and gained a reputation for reliability during World War I. In the 1950–60s Mack developed its expertise in direct injection diesel and turbo-charged engines (e.g. Thermodyne, Maxidyne). The brand rapidly became an icon of popular American culture with sayings such as 'built like a Mack Truck'.

In 1967, Mack was controlled by Signal. Until 1975 at least the truck manufacturer was a 'cash cow' for Signal, contributing between 30 and 75 per cent of the group benefits. There was no significant capital investment during the period and the profitability declined steadily from 9.2 to 4.1 per cent.[14] In 1976, Signal was determined to sell at least part of the company and wanted the news to be spread. Lazard's Félix Rohatyn was the man who forwarded that information to Renault.

Mack was then a relatively 'small' vehicle manufacturer compared to Ford or General Motors Corp. (GMC). However, the Pennsylvanian company was known on the commercial vehicle market for higher end quality products. In 1977, Mack accounted for 17.8 per cent of the class 8 trucks sold, close behind International Harvester (21.8 per cent), but leading Ford and GMC (13.8 and 12.2 per cent). The 'bulldog truck' was a favourite with construction companies, fire departments and municipal services on the East Coast of the US. During the mid-1970s, Mack was the first American exporter of diesel trucks. Contrary to its domestic competitors, its operations were highly integrated with four plants in the US and a CKD operation in Canada. The company's strength was also in its international and domestic commercial presence.[15]

Evolving co-operation

Renault first took a 10 per cent interest in Mack Trucks Inc. to secure a commercial and development agreement.[16] Mack was originally to import Renault VI products in the US. That modest start was motivated by the firm belief that Mack and its clients were not ready to accept any foreign – not to mention European – interference in the firm's management. The French were warned by their advisors and the owner of Mack, respectively Lazard and Signal, that the integration would be a long process. Interestingly enough, Mack management was hardly involved in the negotiation.[17]

Mostly due to the sequels of its own organizational problems, Renault VI did not really take any major interest in the management or performance of Mack. Except for their representation on the board of the company (including Elios Pascual from 1983 onwards), Renault directors were not members of any Mack internal sub-committee.[18] In 1983, adding $118 million to its initial investment, Renault became a 44 per cent shareholder (Fixari 1993). This move was partly motivated by the withdrawal of Signal, Mack's major shareholder and partly by fears that another European producer might take over the company, as Volvo Trucks of Sweden had done in 1981 with White Motor Corporation.[19]

In 1990, Renault would use its right to purchase the remainder of the Signal shares in Mack, and the company was transformed into a private company, a 100 per cent subsidiary of Renault VI. It was at the time perceived as a bitter bargain for Mack employees as the very popular company share saving plans meant that many American employees had invested in the company. Their first perception of the French ownership was to have been given an unfair price for their Mack shares at $6.25 (almost half of their value in the 1980s).

Common project and cross-cultural challenges

During the first years of the Renault major shareholding, John (Jack) B. Curcio, who was Mack president since 1980, conducted a turnaround had been policy including plant closings, layoffs, upgrading of engine and transmission plant, and construction of an $80 million, high technology, non-unionized plant in South Carolina.

From the mid-1980s onwards, the two companies accelerated joint development of components and engines in order to fill obvious commercial/product gaps in each other's product range. They then discussed the possible design of a common product, the 'Baby 8' or CS400, for 1987. The truck was a European design adapted to the American market and standards (i.e. lower emission engine). This was to be a major marketing error according to one of the managers of the project. There was no local market for such a product either in Europe or in the US. Other common development products of the 1980s included E6 and E9 heavy duty engines for European buses and various military applications.[20]

Co-operation at that stage was not easy for various reasons. Mack engineers and their Renault counterparts were not enthusiastic at the development of common products and faced strong professional and cultural differences. Reports on visits by French managers or engineers were full of negative comparisons with French plants, repeatedly mentioning the poor organization of Mack shops and methods:

> The industrial performance of Mack looks poor: large inventory, low personnel productivity, product diversity, demerits ... the union agreements 'one man per machine' involves workers reading books seated nearby their machines.[21]

However, the comments were not all bad and Renault engineers or managers sometimes reported that they ought to look closer at some of the best practices of Mack. That was the case, for example, in 1984 with Mack's materials resource planning (MRP) system. It was suggested that Renault did rapidly transfer, taking into account social and national differences, whatever could be quickly transferred in terms of planning and procurement systems 'in the same way the company has done in Japan recently'.[22]

Despite the existence of joint committees from the early 1980s, it was difficult to find French individuals willing to be expatriated in the US and even more difficult to find Pennsylvanian engineers or managers willing to spend some time in France.[23] The language and the cultural differences represented a real challenge. As an illustration, French engineers commonly used the word 'demands' in their memos – a false cognate meaning 'wishes' in French, whose sense is milder and which came across as very brutal to their American colleagues.

Americans were also surprised by the habit of their French colleagues to raise their voice to make their point. Mack employees were also having problems finding their way through the Renault VI plethoric organization and their multiple counterparts. Product development systems were also very different in terms of methodology and philosophy, opposing a schematic pragmatic and action-focused American side to a more perfectionist French engineering spirit. These cultural differences were partly overcome by a small flow of staff exchange, but not before the early 1990s.

The evolution of the French presence in the US

The first French team to be set up at Allentown so-called world headquarters was comprised of less than five technicians and marketing people. In the late 1970s they were acting as a liaison team for the US distribution of the 'Midliner' truck built by Renault in France. They were people with previous experience of expatriation. Some were US educated, had previously worked with the American automotive branch of Renault or had worked in other foreign countries for the French company. Their status was not extremely well established, as witnessed by their basement office location. Even their American secretary was considered an outsider, since a New Yorker was not always looked at with sympathy by her Mack colleagues in Pennsylvania.

During the 1980s, participation in various joint committees was a good opportunity for cross-cultural experiences. However, few people at Mack were used to foreign contacts, just as, despite a wider foreign exposure, few people at Renault VI were able to work in English.

The restructuring of Mack and the complete take-over of 1990

In 1986, Mack had a net loss of $30.5 million. Renault meantime had problems of its own with a capital restructuring to avoid bankruptcy. It was not until 1989–90 that Renault started to show major losses reaching $185 million in 1989 and $285 million in 1990 (Le Boucher 1990).

Mack was suffering from major problems of productivity, underinvestment, work relations management and control. There was almost no automation process in its old Allentown plant and parts were moved with forklifts. The labour costs were very high compared to other regions of the US due to the strong positions of UAW. Renault was familiar with the management of a highly unionized workforce, but the American environment was very different and the UAW difficult to compare with the Communist-inspired Confédération générale du travail (CGT). In the 1980s, the union question at Mack had became almost an obsession for management. Mack's Chairman and CEO Jack Curcio led a bitter fight against the UAW. The union made Mack a special target of national interest in its attempt to avoid de-unionization in the truck industry. Curcio was defeated in his attempt to establish a non-union low labour cost plant in Winnsboro, South Carolina in the late 1980s (McGough 1989). In that period Mack Truck headquarters became a fortress with a seemingly paranoid anti-union atmosphere. Moreover, the problems at Winnsboro delayed the launch of a much needed new product line; this threatened the survival of the company as a whole. As a consequence and at the initiative of Renault, Curcio had to relinquish the title of CEO to Ralph Reins, a former executive of the automotive industry (Rockwell, ITT). In

February 1990, the *Wall Street Journal* described Mack Trucks as 'one of the best examples in American heavy industry of how to take a bad situation and make it worse'.

That was the first interference of Renault in the management of its American subsidiary. Reins, with an industry reputation of 'turnaround artist', brought in a new breed of managers commonly called 'Detroit people' by Mack employees. He repeatedly affirmed that Renault did not appoint him to liquidate Mack but to 'cut out the crap and fixing [sic] the root cause of problems'. Quality became a major issue, with authority given to the director of corporate quality to halt production to meet quality standards and thus lower warranty costs and demerits (Bearth 1990). Profitability and cost cutting were put forward along with a will to make peace with the UAW. Recognizing the 'victory' of the union in the Winnsboro conflict, Reins hired William Craig, former vice-president of human resources at Volkswagen of America. Many more executives at Mack were fired in order to change the way the company was managed. However, according to several managers, Mack Trucks was not a company big enough to fulfil Reins' corporate and financial ambitions. Elios Pascual replaced him in 1990. He was the first French CEO to manage the company, which since then has continuously been led by top managers transferred from Renault.

Business culture, management and knowledge transfer

Pascual had extensive experience in engineering, design and supply chain management. According to witnesses of the time he adapted his management style to become a quasi-American boss involved not only in figures but also with morale. He had to break away from the illusions of the old Mack culture and to build on the turnaround move of Reins' team in the 'Detroit style'.

Except for senior VP finance and treasurer Guy Claveau, Pascual did not bring in any other French executives. Rather, he hired new American managers from other regions in order to fight the supposedly paralysing Pennsylvania Dutch mentality. This was a big cultural move, as Mack traditionally recruited local people even at management level.

Pascual also took a new perspective regarding negotiation with unions. It did not imply softer policies, however, as job cutting on a large scale resulted in a 30 per cent reduction of the workforce in the early 1990s. Productivity was to be the new credo with specialists temporarily imported from France to train plant workers and foremen. This was to be the third sub-culture introduced at Mack (see Table 6.1).

The corporate culture transformation at Mack took place in multiple stages and should not be attributed to one executive hero. Jack Curcio did bring about some change in the 1980s. He insisted on the international development of the company, and its Winnsboro project of new plant

Table 6.1 Three subcultures and the turnaround of Mack in the 1990s

Mack	*Detroit*	*Renault*
Product oriented	Market oriented	Process oriented
Hard working	Profitability	TQM/JIT/Procurement
Pennsylvanian	Work relations	Ergonomics + Team work
Conservative	Cost reduction	International
Brand/corporate culture	Foundation of quality	Pride
Arrogance		

included some modern just-in-time (JIT) and inventory methods. Under his reign the company also introduced a (modest) supplier certification programme.[24]

Renault VI used its own experience of restructuring process during the European crisis of the mid-1980s to reorganize Mack processes. Job description analysis was imported for the first time to Mack by Renault automotive experts. This was a turnaround in factories where union agreements had ruled the organization of work for decades. Ergonomics specialists showed union leaders and workers the benefits of proper distribution of work in the shop. They introduced mechanization and renewed the flows of component in the old plants to introduce JIT-like systems.

The knowledge of Japanese manufacturing methods acquired in the 1980s by Renault motorcar division, the parent company of Renault VI, was crucial to the success at Mack in terms of knowledge creation. Simultaneous engineering, supply chain management and statistical process control were gradually introduced and came as a cultural shock in a very conservative firm. Total quality management through teamwork was, for example, a complete innovation for Mack workers, whose working relations were organized by a detailed and relatively antiquated 1972 UAW agreement. Renault VI not only used neo-Fordist models, but also such very classical Taylorian tools as time and motion studies. Suppliers were reduced from 2,000 to 1,200 and inventory cut by 35 per cent in 18 months (Farhi 1992). Quality auditing as well as the use of a demerits index was made systematic.

The productivity of Mack plants in 1990 was half that of comparable Renault VI European plants. Through reorganization of shop plans, productivity at Winnsboro improved dramatically in 1990–92. It took 124 hours to assemble a truck in 1990 at Winnsboro as against 76 hours in 1992 (Farhi 1992: 59).

Quality training programmes available at Renault were not considered usable by American personnel as such and needed adaptation. They were not only translated but adapted in a more ‘hands on’ and practical way. The quality movement was not a complete French import, however: Mack engineers did set up their own programme. They borrowed from Renault VI but also from other leading automotive companies, trying to benchmark programmes. They even used systems developed in a nearby Pennsylvanian financial services company.

It is worth noticing that Pascual later insisted that the new methods imported in the early 1990s were accepted because the crisis was so deep that Mack people felt it was their last chance; nor was it presented as a 'lesson from France', as there were very few French people in Mack plants.

Integration and global organization at work

It was only in the late 1990s that Renault VI decided to place French managers at key positions at Mack, as the subsidiary had eventually became an essential element of Renault's global commercial vehicle strategy. Purchasing 100 per cent of the shares and making Mack Trucks a private company, Renault VI took a new path. Efforts are now being made to integrate the two organizations with cross-functional project management.

In 1999, Mack ranked third (13.1 per cent) in the class 8 market with eight consecutive years of progression in the US. The company yielded 42.6 per cent of Renault VI group turnover and contributed $204 million to the operating profits of Renault VI in 1999, up from $105 million in 1998. It has became a strong asset of the Renault VI group and was central in the decision of Volvo to merge its truck activities with Renault.

Since the late 1990s, Mack has been integrated in the so-called Renault VI-Mack Group. Under French top management, Mack is changing to incorporate Renault VI's methods. Some central functions such as internal auditing are held by French managers trained in the Renault organization. Moreover, intercultural awareness was included in the training of Mack employees at the end of the 1990s and is felt to be a major asset in improving the integration of Renault VI and Mack into a single company. It came along with a growing flow of expatriate French and American managers. Contrary to the 1990s, the unification tools at the turn of the twenty-first century are in the area of corporate reporting and management systems such as ERPs and of product development systems such as computer-aided design (CAD). As in other large companies, the globalization of markets has been translated into a more integrated organization. It took Renault a very long time to gain complete control of its American subsidiary and to benefit from synergies at the origin of the first agreement of 1977. Almost a quarter of a century passed before the French investors were able to send in managers and assume the top management of an American company. Despite a very cyclical market, Mack proves to be an important part of the Renault VI Group today on a par with its French owner in terms of market position. Cultural problems are still present and efforts are being made to improve cultural awareness on both sides. However, the nationality of the ownership does not matter much to American managers, and workers are relatively fatalistic so far as Mack continues to thrive.

Mack illustrates the complexity of organizational learning and management method transfer. Total quality programmes, production process improvement and customer relationship management have not been implemented by the will of a single top manager; nor have they been imported using standard foreign models. Rather, important steps were taken at a time of crisis when change was accepted as a measure of salvation with no alternative available.

Conclusions

Internationalization is considered as a risky option by business strategy scholars. Renault and other French manufacturers have faced very tough challenges through their attempts to gain access to the North American market for motor vehicles since the 1940s. What have they lacked to succeed? The answers should be segmented in terms of time period. In the ventures of the 1940–60s the problems were of strategic and marketing nature.

In defining strategy there was a double and somewhat contradictory motivation in the period: generate quick revenues in dollars and at the same time establish long-term positions. The French government was eager to bring in foreign currency, and used its power to influence manufacturers. Corporations were urged to sell abroad and to sell a lot and fast through fiscal incentives. The state represented at that point a negative influence integrating foreign policy factors, such as prestige in the strategy of the companies, while artificially assuring financial performance via public subsidy of exports. On the other hand, in times when Renault badly needed funds to recapitalize its US assets in the 1980s, the state provided necessary support.

On the marketing side, the French motor vehicle manufacturers were experienced exporters – but in markets where there were no adaptation efforts to be made. At home, they had lost any need for real marketing efforts and were used to a rationed environment where buyers were queuing to buy whatever car was available. Confronted with a demanding and mature market like the American one, French managers looked rather naïve. They had enormous problems in building a proper commercial network, and lacked the right product range and the experience of the American market and business environment, unlike Volkswagen of America.

The other foreign direct investment of the Renault Group in the US, i.e. commercial vehicles, has been very different indeed and reflects another mode of entry and strategic choice. Most international business textbooks tell us that in order to conquer foreign markets, most companies first seek out alliances with local partners. That was the attitude of Renault VI when the company started to look at the North American market. The Renault VI/Mack alliance and later integration has in fact been a success story of its own in terms of durability. It seems evident that in some sectors, like the motor vehicle industry, there are compulsory entry modes. Renault VI was successful in buying a market share and a brand, and in then proceeding progressively to integrate its American operations.

Interestingly enough, there did not seem to have been many contacts or much transfer of knowledge between the various divisions of the Renault group during that period, nor any attempt to set up an international division in charge of providing central support to divisions dealing with America. It raises the question of the much-praised synergies and knowledge transfer capabilities in diversified groups.

Notes

1 The author would like to acknowledge the support of GDO, the research group at Toulouse University Graduate School of Management (ESUG-IAE) and to express his gratitude to the individuals who helped in the research and/or accepted to be interviewed during the research in Allentown, Macungie, Lyon and Paris. Renault VI archives held at Fondation de l'Automobile Marius Berliet in Lyon are quoted as 'Berliet/RVI Archives'.

2 The research has been conducted through the corporate archives of Renault VI, partly held by the Fondation de l'Automobile Marius Berliet in Lyon, France, and using the documentation of the Mack Museum at Allentown, PA. It has been completed by several interviews with employees and former employees of Renault, Renault VI and Mack Trucks in Paris and Allentown, PA.

3 The 4 CV was a rear-engined small family car.

4 The French consul in Detroit wrote personally to the CEO of Renault to get a replacement carburettor for his own 4 CV!

5 Paul Ramadier (1888–1961), a Socialist politician, was Prime Minister many times in the 1940s and 1950s and Minister of Finance in 1957–8. As such he 'invented' a car tax.

6 Renault bought twelve former liberty-ships and created a dedicated transportation company to handle the transatlantic flow of its cars from Le Havre to New York.

7 US customs accused Renault Inc. of dumping due to state subsidies. At the same time the State Department contested attempts by the French company to impose exclusivity contracts on dealerships (Loubet 1998: 213).

8 Renault avoided a complete majority shareholding of AMC to retain its character as an American company in order to be able to compete in military procurement contracts.

9 Cab-over-engine trucks (COE) are rarer than trucks with the engine fitted in front of the driver, which are therefore known as 'conventional' in North America.

10 'Etude sur les hypothèses d'association avec Mack et Scania', P. Carfantan, Direction planification et produit Renault VI-SEE, 29 avril 1977. RVI/Berliet Archives.

11 Signal was a diversified group of companies operating several activities in engineering and mechanical products.

12 See Duncan T. (1978), 'Rolling into the fleets' *Fleet Owner*, December: 67–71.

13 The 'Midliner' was manufactured by Renault VI at Blainville with engines produced at Vénissieux or Limoges. There were two models: class 6 (MS200, 170 HP) and lower end of class 7 (MS300, 210 HP) fitted with supercharged engines. They were equipped with US compulsory components (battery, lamps, filters, tanks, etc.). The cabin was decorated with Mack signs.

14 Dossier M. Grob, Bureau de Centralisation des Plans, Mack 1968–81. Berliet/RVI Archives.
15 'Le plan véhicules industriels', 25 mai 1977. RVI/Berliet Archives.
16 C25 'Contrats RVI-Mack 1984'; 'Negotiation and agreements 1977–83'. Berliet/RVI Archives.
17 Report by V. Grob on a meeting between Renault and Signal at Lazard NY, June 1, 1977. RVI/Berliet Archives.
18 Appropriation review, corporate management, conflicts, foreign payments review, contributions, management operating council, corporate information steering, product, strategic planning, production rate, product regulation compliance, target plan committee(s).
19 'Mack, Organisation des accords 1979–83'. Berliet/RVI Archives.
20 'Minutes of the sixteenth Mack/RVI cooperation meeting', June 18, 1987. Berliet/RVI Archives.
21 Visite chez Mack 3–4 décembre 1981. Berliet/RVI Archives.
22 'Etude 10–14 septembre 1984' (report by French experts on Mack's planning and procurement system). Berliet/RVI Archives.
23 'Minutes of the Fourth Mack/RVI cooperation meeting', March 28, 1984. Berliet/RVI Archives.
24 Schauer D. (1988) 'Manufacturers Quality Programs ... Hype or Substance?' Fleet Equipment, December: 22–26.

References

Banville, E. De (2000) 'Le poids-lourd oublié du monde automobile?', *La Lettre du Gerpisa* 141: 7–8.

Banville, E. De and Chanaron, J.J. (1995) *Poids lourols et partenariat*, Grenoble: IREPD.

Bearth, D.P. (1990) 'Mack revamps, Renault offers aid', *Transport Topics*, 29 January.

Beltran, A., Daviet, J.-P. and Ruffat, M. (1995) *L'histoire d'entreprise en France essai bibliographique*, Paris.

Chandler, A.D. Jr., Amatori, F. and Hikino, T. (eds) (1997) *Big Business and The Wealth of Nations*, Cambridge, Mass: Cambridge University Press.

Chandler, A.D. Jr. (1990) *Scale and Scope: The Dynamics of Industrial Capitalism*, Cambridge, Mass: Cambridge University Press.

Chanuc, L. (1993) *Camions: chroniques d'un siècle*, Boulogne-Billancourt: Éditions MDM.

CCFA (1999) 'Comité des constructeurs français d'automobiles', *Analyse & Faits. Le Marché Mondial.*

Durand, C. and Gillain, C. (1985) *Le processus de prise de décision dans les entreprises Industrielles: Branche Construction Lécanique*, monographie Renault Véhicules Industriels, unpublished report.

Durand, J.D. (1995) 'Paul Berliet, un industriel lyonnais en Chine', *Cahiers d'Histoire*, juillet–décembre: 431–44.

Dussauge, P. and Garette, B. (1995) *Les stratégies d'alliance*, Paris: Editions d'organisation.

Farhi, S. (1992) 'Mack mis au régime RVI', *L'Usine Nouvelle*, 2359, 9 avril.

Fixari, D. (1993) *Historique du financement de Renault*, Armines, unpublished document.

Franck, G. (1997) *A la conquète du marché américain*, Paris: Odile Jacob.

Fridenson, P. (1986) 'The growth of multinational activities in the French motor industry, 1890–1979', in P. Hertner and G. Jones (eds) *Multinationals: Theory and History*, Aldershot: Gower.

Fridenson, P. (ed.) (1999) 'Bibliographie sur l'automobile', *Actes du Gerpisa* supplément, 28.

Gleize, G. (1993) 'La gestion des cadres expatriés: le cas de la Régie Renault (1958–1993)', *Entreprises et Histoire*, 3, mai: 30–46.

Glimstedt, E. (2000) 'Creative cross-fertilization and uneven Americanization of Swedish industry: Sources of innovation in post-war motor vehicles and electrical manufacturing', in J. Zeitlin and G. Herrigel (eds) *Americanization and its Limits*, Oxford: Oxford University Press: 180–208.

Grevet, J.-F. (1996) *Berliet, Renault et les autres ... Pour une histoire de l'industrie française du poids-lourd des origines à 1974*, Université Charles de Gaulle, Lille III, DEA d'Histoire.

Jones, G. (1996) *The Evolution of International Business*, London: Routledge.

Koenig, G. (1994) 'L'apprentissage organisationel: repérage des lieux', *Revue Française de Gestion*, janvier–février: 76–91.

Laure, V. (1988) 'Concentration, accords commerciaux et centralisation financière dans l'industrie du poids lourd en France (1950–1978)', *Actes du GERPISA* 3 octobre: 69–80.

Le Boucher, E. (1989) 'Mauvaise conjoncture et "mauvaise gestion": Lourdes pertes pour les camions américains Mack (Renault)', *Le Monde*, 16 November.

—— (1990) 'Déjà propriétaire de 45% des actions Renault veut prendre le contrôle total des camions américains Mack', *Le Monde*, 9 July.

Loubet, J.L. (1998) *Renault, cent ans d'histoire*, Paris: ETAI.

—— (1999), *Citroën, Peugeot, Renault et les autres. Histoire de stratégies d'entreprise*, Paris: ETAI.

—— (2000) *Renault, histoire d'une entreprise*, Paris: ETAI.

McGough, R. (1989) 'Union bites bulldog', *Financial World*, 14 November: 28–30.

Schauer, D. (1988) 'Manufacturers' quality programs ... hype or substance?', *Fleet Equipment*, December: 22–6.

Steck, B. (1990) 'Les véhicules utilitaires dans le monde', *L'Information Géographique*, mars–avril: 66–7.

Terrail, J.P. and Tripier, M. (1986) 'Destins ouvriers, cultures d'entreprise, pratiques syndicales, rapport de recherche ATP vie sociale dans l'entreprise', II, *L'acier et les Camions*.

Wilkins, M. (1989) *The History of Foreign Investment in the United States to 1914*, Cambridge, Mass: Oxford University Press.

—— (1993) 'French multinationals in the United States: An historical perspective', *Entreprises et Histoire*, 3: 14–29.

7 Managing US subsidiaries from non-traditional foreign direct investors

Spanish stainless steel companies

Juan José Durán and Fernando Úbeda

Introduction

This chapter analyses the strategies followed by two Spanish multinational steel firms operating in the United States. These companies are Acerinox and Tubacex, which are respectively the fifth world producer of stainless steel and the second world producer of non-welded stainless-steel tubing. The experience of these firms is interesting because Spain has not been a large investor in the US. During the period 1993–2000 the proportion of Spanish foreign direct investment (FDI) in the US was only about 4 per cent of the total.[1] However, out of a sample of 174 Spanish multinationals, 25 per cent had at least one subsidiary in the US (Durán and Úbeda 2001).

The low proportion of Spanish FDI in the US can in part be explained by the fact that Spain was a latecomer as a developed economy, and this in turn was reflected in its pattern of multinational investment. Spain closely followed the so-called Investment Development Path suggested by Dunning (Dunning 1988, 1993, 1997; Narula 1996; Dunning and Narula 1996). Until the 1960s the Spanish economy had very little inward or outward FDI, but during that decade as the economy was opened up, so Spain attracted considerable inward FDI. Following rapid economic development, by the second half of the 1970s, direct investment abroad by Spain began to achieve substantial levels (Durán and Sánchez 1981), continuing through the expansion of the 1980s and accelerating after joining the European Economic Community in 1986. Until the mid-1990s Spain was a net receiver of FDI, but during the second half of that decade Spanish outward FDI rose rapidly (Durán and Úbeda 1998, 2000; Úbeda 1999).

During the fast expansion of outward FDI in the late 1990s it was Latin America rather than the US which attracted most Spanish outward FDI beyond the European Union. This was due to major shifts in the locational advantages of Latin America for foreign investors, as technological process eroded the position of public services such as telecommunications as natural monopolies, while deregulation and privatization opened new opportunities for foreign firms. Spanish companies had become quite competitive in these sectors in the 1980s, boosted by major investments in

Spain in infrastructure, both economic and social (health, education etc.), by reorganization (gains in scale and efficiency), and by the greater attention paid to research and development. Because of linguistic and cultural factors, Spanish firms often chose to invest in Latin America first before growing elsewhere (Durán 1999). However, Spanish companies also undertook significant multinational investment, especially in qualitative terms, in Organization for Economic Cooperation and Development (OECD) countries and in less developed countries (LDCs). Although the main Spanish multinational enterprises (MNEs) are in the service sectors (telecommunications, electricity, gas, water, banking and finance, hotels, construction), there are several cases in manufacturing, including automotive, textiles, machinery, electronics and steel.

The two Spanish multinational stainless-steel firms operating in the US examined in this chapter serviced a market niche. An examination of their strategies, mode of entry and management provides important insights into the technological cycle in the steel industries, as well as permitting a study of investments in the US by a non-traditional investor.

International stainless steel production

The steel sector has a mature, highly codified and standardized technology. It is a capital intensive sector that can be classified as non-differentiated Smithian (Ozawa 1996). It is closely correlated with economic activity and is a very important sector for development. Internationally, steel production has gradually moved towards the less developed countries (see Table 7.1). Competitive pressure in the developed world

Table 7.1 Changing structure of global steel production (%)

	1960	*1970*	*1980*	*1990*	*1995*	*1998*
Developed countries	*91.96*	*89.40*	*81.20*	*47.85*	*45.69*	*45.05*
Western Europe	45.22	38.59	35.04	20.93	20.36	20.39
US	37.36	28.51	22	12.64	12.68	12.60
Japan	9.38	22.30	24.16	14.28	12.65	12.06
South Korea	n.a.	0.11	1.86	3.96	4.89	5.16
Taiwan	0.05	0.07	0.92	1.97	1.54	2.18
Russia	n.a.	n.a.	n.a.	3.9	6.9	5.48
Ukraine	n.a.	n.a.	n.a.	4.5	3.0	3.03
China	n.a.	n.a.	n.a.	11.2	12.7	14.74
Brazil	0.95	1.29	3.32	1.39	3.34	3.33
India	1.36	1.50	2.06	2.61	2.92	3.08
Others	n.a.	n.a.	n.a.	22.59	19.11	17.94
World production in tons[a]		595	716	648	752	775.3

Source: D'Costa (1999) and IISI (2000).

Note

a Million metric tonnes finished steel products.

n.a. not available.

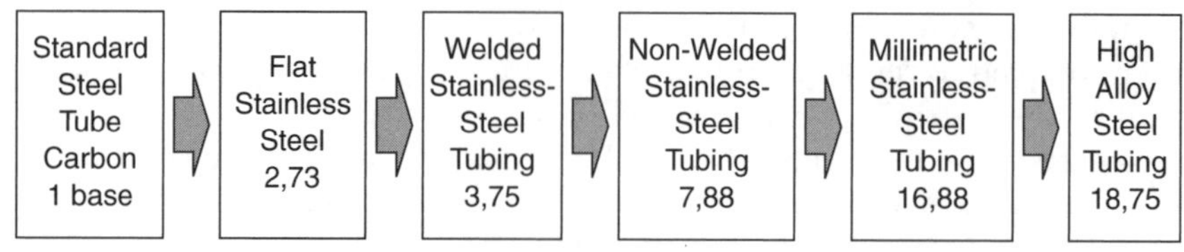

Figure 7.1 The specialization path in the steel sector. Price-per-kg comparison for standard products.

Source: Personal interview with Tubacex.

can be seen as a determinant factor for diversification toward stainless steel. This segment is technologically more intensive and value added, with a highly concentrated demand in the more advanced countries. Thus, not only have the traditional steel firms incorporated stainless steel in the portfolio of products, but also new specialized firms have been established.

In Figure 7.1 we show the specialization path in the steel sector from the point of view of steel tubing. The price of a very specialized product such as non-welded stainless-steel tubing is almost eight times higher than that of standard steel tubes. The higher price restricts demand to the developed countries. To be able to compete in terms of cost in a given market segment, the company must be large enough to supply the world market.

The higher level of technological specialization has intensified the concentration of both the demand and the supply for stainless-steel products; indeed, it may be seen that while the production of carbon steels is shifting to recently industrialized countries, the production of stainless steel is rising in the developed countries (see Figure 7.2).

Mergers and acquisitions have changed the scale of European companies engaged in the flat-products stainless-steel segment. According to the 1999 figure and the forecast for 2000–4 (see Table 7.2), the leader in Europe is KTS, with 2.2 million metric tonnes a year, this company having arisen from the merger between the German company KTN and the Italian company Acciai Speciali Terni (AST). Second place is held by Avesta-Polarit, formed through the merger of the Swedish (Avesta), British (Sheffield) and Finnish (Outokumpu) companies. The French company Ugine, a subsidiary of the French steel company Usinor, specializing in stainless steel, is the third most important producer. Coming in at fourth place, with over a million tons a year, is Acerinox. After completing its investment in its North American subsidiary NAS, Acerinox will reach a figure of 1.8 million tonnes a year. Completing the list of European producer is ALZ, a subsidiary of Arbed (a Luxembourg steel company).[2]

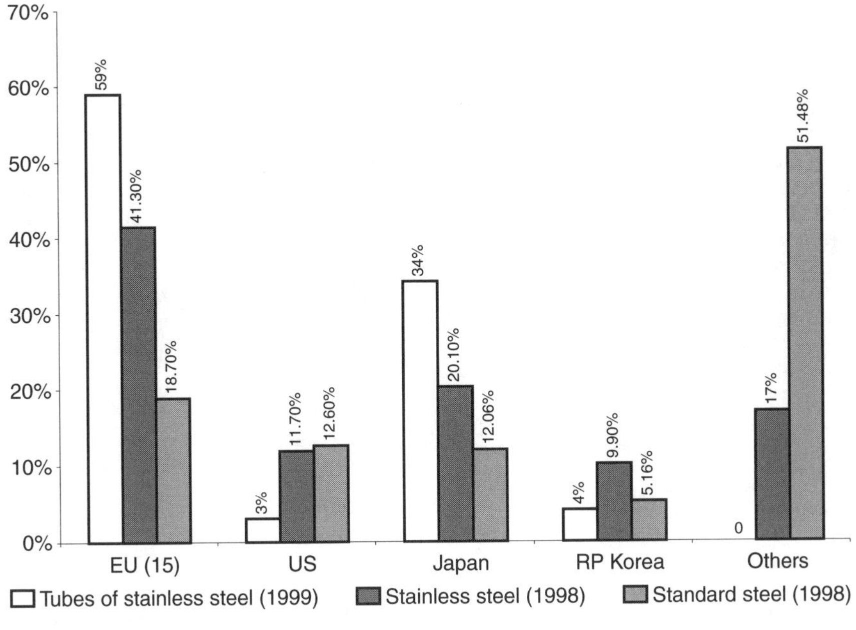

Standard steel: 775.3 million metric tonnes.
Stainless steel world production: 17.18 million metric tonnes.
Stainless steel tubes world production: 180,000 metric tonnes.

Figure 7.2 The worldwide geographical distribution of stainless-steel production and stainless-steel tubing production, 1998.

Source: Personal interviews with Acerinox and Tubacex.

For the producing companies, stainless steel is just one more product in their range, and so their production facilities are not designed for optimizing costs in stainless-steel production. In most cases, they have improvised structures under the wing of their main production system, i.e. these companies are not highly specialized in the production of stainless steel. This reinforces the competitive advantage of Acerinox, based on its integrated production system.[3] By way of example, we could mention that the Acerinox plant in Algeciras (south Spain) employs a staff of 1,600, plus a further 2,000 engaged in administrative and marketing work, while Avesta-Sheffield, with an output of 200,000 tonnes more a year, has some 7,000 employees.

The Japanese companies Nisshin Steel, Kawasaki and Nippon Stainless, the Korean company Posco and the Taiwan company Yieh United are the most direct competitors for the European companies in third markets, but not in their markets of origin.[4] There are two main markets needing to buy in stainless steel: the US, which is currently the main market and is a net importer of stainless steel, even though it has its own producers (J&L, Allegheny and AK Steel), and Southeast Asia, with China being particularly

Table 7.2 The main European stainless-steel producers in 1999 and forecasts for 2000–4 (tons)

	Production			*Forecast*		
Company	*1999*	*2000*	*2001*	*2002*	*2003*	*2004*
KTS Group	**2,220**	**2,350**	**2,450**	**2,900**	**3,150**	**3,300**
KTN, Germany	1,200	1,200	1,200	1,200	1,200	1,200
AST, Italy	800	800	900	1,300	1,400	1,500
SKS, China	220	350	350	400	550	600
Avesta-Polarit	**1,799**	**1,849**	**1,849**	**1,969**	**2,129**	**2,249**
Outokumpu, Finland	600	650	650	770	930	1,050
Avesta, Sweden	747	747	747	747	747	747
Sheffield, UK	452	452	452	452	452	452
Usinor Group	**1,763**	**2,225**	**2,225**	**2,275**	**2,425**	**2,475**
Ugine, France	1,050	1,200	1,200	1,200	1,200	1,200
Fafer, Belgium[a]	123	305	305	305	305	305
Acesita, Brazil	220	350	350	400	550	600
J&L, US	200	200	200	200	200	200
Thainox, Thailand	170	170	170	170	170	170
Acerinox	**966**	**1,000**	**1,120**	**1,560**	**1,800**	**1,800**
Spain	966	1,000	1,000	1,000	1,000	1,000
NAS, US			120	560	800	800
ALZ, Luxembourg	**577**	**600**	**600**	**720**	**850**	**1,000**

Source: Heinz H. Parisier & Co. (2000).

Note

a Capacity includes also other alloy steels.

prominent. Producers such as the French company Ugine, the Korean company Posco and the Japanese company Nisshin Steel have set up there.[5]

The non-welded stainless-steel tube products segment has also undergone a process of mergers and acquisitions, particularly among European companies: Sandvick, the current world leader, acquired the British company Sterling; Tubacex, the second-ranking world producer, acquired the Austrian company SBER in 1999; and the third-ranking company is DMV, which arose from the merger involving three companies (the Italian company Dalmine, the German company Manesmann and the French company Vallourec). There are only two Japanese companies left alongside these, Sumitomo and Sanyo (see Figure 7.3).

Of the companies cited, only the Spanish company Tubacex, the Swedish company Sandvick and the Japanese company Sumitomo have integrated production of non-welded stainless-steel tubing. The advantages of this production process lie partly in the way it gives greater control over the production process, thus ensuring that the steel has the

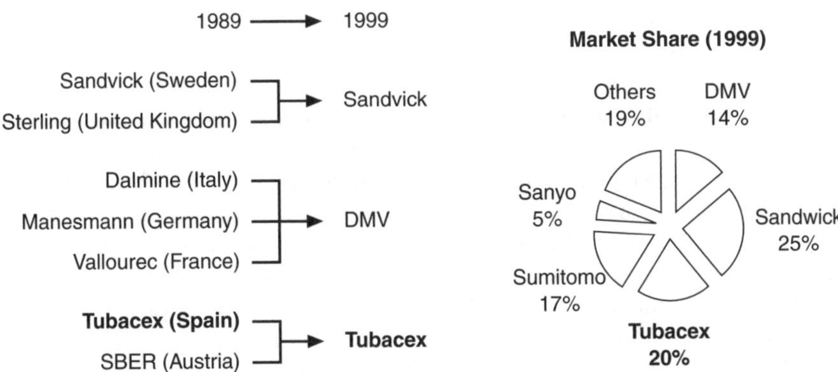

Figure 7.3 The process of concentration in the European non-welded stainless-steel tubing segment.

Source: Personal interview with Tubacex.

quality required for tube production, and partly in bringing savings of around 10 per cent in respect of the competition. The production process in itself is a strong barrier to entry, on account of the investment involved and the 2 years it takes to set up a new plant up and get it running.

Acerinox and Tubacex: the past

From the developmental point of view (Nelson and Winter 1982), the qualities that make a company different are the result of a unique knowledge-accumulation process (Cantwell 1989). The past history of companies is relevant in explaining why they decide to invest in the US, how they move in, and how relations with the subsidiary are arranged.

In 1969 the Spanish government called an international tender for setting up a plant to make stainless steel in Algeciras (in Campo de Gibraltar in the south of Spain), this being the origin of Acerinox.[6] The award went to a consortium that brought together a large Spanish bank (Banesto) as the financial partner (two-thirds of the capital), a Japanese stainless steel company (Nisshin Steel) as the technology partner transferring the very latest technology, and a Japanese trading company (Trader Nissho Iwai), which contributed with experience in exporting output that exceeded the requirements of the home market.[7] The two Japanese companies accounted for a third of the capital of Acerinox. At present nearly 60 per cent of the capital is quoted on the Stock Exchange, and the main shareholders are the banking group BBVA (14 per cent) and Nisshin Steel (12 per cent).

The company's competitive advantage came from the integrated-production design, through which the three essential processes in making stainless steel were brought together in a single region with a sea port: steel-making, hot rolling and cold rolling.[8] This brings considerable savings in transport, logistics and coordination, with greater control over the entire production process and thus better quality in the end product, while it also facilitates the learning process. At present, Acerinox is the stainless steel company with the best productivity rates in the world, and the world's largest factory for flat stainless-steel products. The company has developed along incremental lines, introducing the most advanced technology in mini-steelworks. During the first stage the cold-rolling system – the last process in the production cycle – was installed, thus making it possible to use semi-finished products and to produce short runs of high added-value stainless steels. During the second stage, which was the most important in investment terms, hot-rolling was added, and then in the third stage a continuous electric furnace was brought in for converting raw materials (mainly iron and nickel) and scrap into stainless steel for subsequent treatment (see Figure 7.4).[9] Moving from each of these stages on to the next entails a sharp rise in dead time, and so exporting to international markets was essential.

The initial management team at Acerinox was made up of graduates who had recently entered the employment market, so these managers were given intensive training in Japan. This created strong company loyalty. Furthermore, a variable-remuneration system was established in the 1970s, a system that was very unusual in Spain at the time: 30–40 per cent of the remuneration paid depends on the volume of output and on

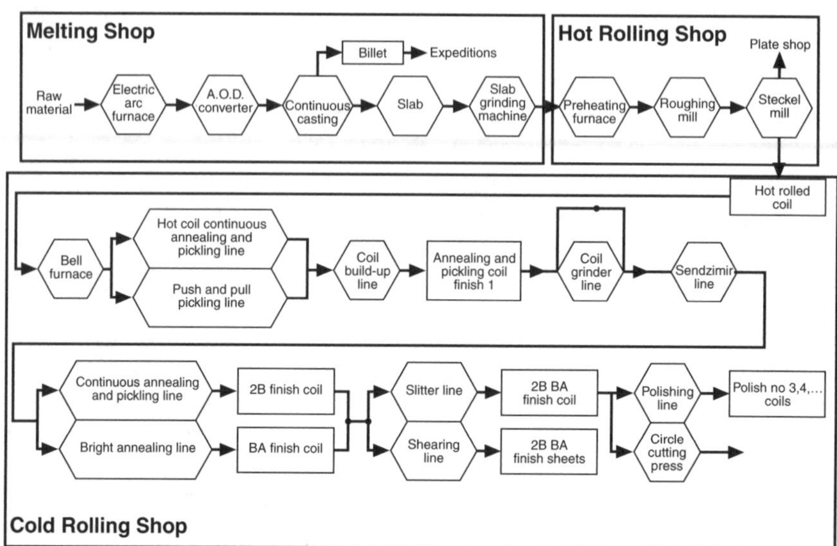

Figure 7.4 The production process at Acerinox.

Source: Personal interview with Acerinox.

the quality achieved, and over the period 1990–7, the correlation coefficient for manufactured volume against staff costs per employee was 95 per cent, showing clearly how this remuneration system affords flexibility to the company, while at the same time providing an incentive mechanism.[10]

Although the path of Tubacex differs from that of Acerinox, its competitive advantage is also based on specializing its productive capacity in a single product: stainless-steel non-welded tubing. The Group was founded in 1963 with an extrusion plant in Llodio (in the province of Alava, in the north of Spain), a plant that produced non-welded steel pipes up to 8 inches thick.[11] Its main customers were in the petrochemical, chemical and shipbuilding sectors, and they were engaged in economic expansion.

During the 1970s, the company developed on an essentially national scale, thanks to the good performance of home demand despite the recession of 1973. It was during this decade that the company embarked on internationalization, and thus achieved production levels that were high enough to invest in an electric furnace and to set up an integrated production system. Moreover, a strategy of diversification was pursued, since the surplus steel produced by the furnace and not used for making tubing was rolled and marketed externally.

The competitiveness of Tubacex during the 1980s was based on two external variables: the exchange rate and tax incentives for exporting. When Spain joined the European Community, this situation could no longer be sustained. In this context, the rise of the peseta and the elimination of export incentives brought a 40 per cent reduction in exports to European Community countries. The company reacted by abandoning the less profitable products. Shrinking demand in 1992 resulted in losses of 8,900 million pesetas and technical bankruptcy.

This technical bankruptcy marked the starting point of far-reaching restructuring. The strategy pursued reduced the company's vulnerability to external factors, bringing it positive results in the lower part of the economic cycle. It was a two-pronged strategy for action: concentrating resources and capacities solely on activities that generated value, and seeking out markets. Success naturally depended on remedying the financial situation, and this was achieved thanks to an issue of convertible bonds, most of which were taken up. Now nearly all the company capital is quoted on the Stock Exchange, there being no significant reference finance partner. In the case of Tubacex, there is a clear divorce between ownership and control: it is a managerial company.

Reallocating resources and capacity to value-generating activities meant specializing the product range and downsizing. Steel production was abandoned, as was the production of all tubular products other than non-welded stainless-steel tubing, which meant closing down two production plants and cutting back the workforce by 30 per cent.[12]

As in the case of Acerinox, the competitive advantage of Tubacex lies in the integrated production system and in product specialization. The raw material is processed into billet form at the northern Spanish steelworks Aceria de Alava SA (Aceralava) using an electric furnace.[13] At the Llodio and Amurrio works (also in the north of Spain), the billets are used in the extrusion process, which produces non-welded stainless-steel tubing. Lastly, another group subsidiary in Aceniega (Tubos Taylor Accesorios) produces the stainless-steel curved products that are needed if the customer is to be offered an integral service. The extrusion press is the most valuable strategic asset, and it is here in fact that a bottleneck may form in the company's growth.

Gradualist internationalization at Acerinox and Tubacex

Acerinox has had an international outlook right from its inception, partly because of the nature of the two founding partners, and partly through the requirements of the project itself. In 1969, Spain's consumption of stainless steel amounted to 30,000 tn/year, and in 1974 Acerinox had an output capacity of 350,000 tn/year, which necessarily entailed exporting. During the first year of production, cold coils were exported to nine countries, a number that had grown to fourteen a year later, with the US amongst them. The percentage of the output devoted to exports reached a watershed value in 1988, when the volume of sales abroad exceeded sales to the home market. The development of Tubacex ran on similar lines: sales abroad amounted to 30 per cent of total sales in 1973, and the dynamism of the foreign markets enabled the company to embark on an expansion plan through which it doubled its productive capacity. By 1976, its export activity accounted for between 40 and 60 per cent of its output.

The high concentration of demand made it necessary to export almost simultaneously to the two main markets for any European company: the European Union (EU) and the US. The lesser degree of specialization of Acerinox enabled it to achieve greater diversification in its product range stemming from the demand from emerging markets – Latin American markets in the 1970s, and Southeast Asia, specifically China, over the following two decades. This high concentration and the industrial nature of the product reduces the need to generate knowledge of the context in the internationalization process, which explains why no gradualist internationalization can be observed from a geographical point of view.[14] (See Table 7.3 for geographical distribution of both companies' sales in 1999.)

The need to get closer to the customer, and thereby to provide a more personalized service better adapted to each customer's needs, entails setting up a network of marketing subsidiaries. During the 1980s, both companies set up such a network, with a strongly European character. The marketing strategies implemented by Acerinox and Tubacex were different: the

Table 7.3 The geographical distribution of Acerinox and Tubacex sales in 1999 (%)

Acerinox		*Tubacex*	
Spain	31	Spain	19
Abroad	69	Abroad	81
Europe	45	Europe	46
Americas	13	US-Canada	24
Asia	10	Far East	4
Other	1	Middle East	1
		Other	5
Sales (US$ millions)	1,045	Sales (US$ millions)	177

Source: Personal interviews with Acerinox and Tubacex.

former opted for vertical integration, selling directly to the end customer, while the latter used the wholesaler network. Thus the marketing subsidiaries, owing to their nature, differ both in function and dimension.

Acerinox has worked hard to adapt its products in such a way as to suit the needs of the customers through highly qualified after-sales services.[15] The work of the marketing subsidiaries in this strategy is crucial, and they are in many cases backed by service centres in which cutting, polishing and finishing operations are performed.[16] This network facilitates the logistics of the company, and enables future requirements of the customers to be spotted. The time path traced by the marketing subsidiaries is in line with the gradualist hypotheses with regard to psychological distance (Johanson and Wiedersheim-Paul 1975; Johanson and Vahlne 1977, 1990).

Acerinox's first subsidiary was located in France, which is very close in geographical, cultural and institutional terms. This was the first component in the European network that has been set up gradually from 1980. The second subsidiary was formed in Latin America in 1979, specifically in Chile, a country that is close from a cultural point of view, and which has an emerging economy. In 1982 a subsidiary was set up in the US, the second most important market for the company. The marketing network was finally rounded off with subsequent investments in Europe and in Southeast Asia. In this case, we can see a clearly gradualist trend in the forming of the network, naturally consistent with the characteristics of each of the markets concerned.

In the early 1990s, both companies had a strong international marketing base that was underpinned by the competitiveness of their products. Their growth was dependent on their production capacity, and the time had come to start out on the third phase of the internationalization process: locating production capacity abroad. From the gradualist perspective, this stage would bring the greatest complexity and would

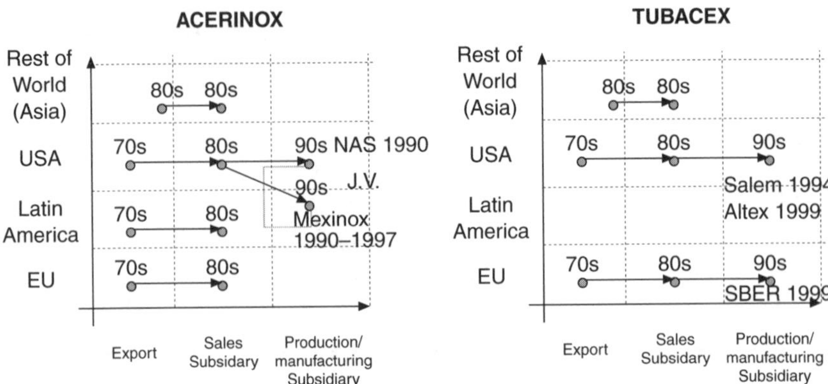

Figure 7.5 The development of internationalization over time at Acerinox and Tubacex.

Source: Personal interviews with Acerinox and Tubacex.

require great capacity for managing and coordinating activities on a multinational basis (see Figure 7.5).

The Tubacex marketing strategy, based on the use of specialized wholesalers, reduces the role of the subsidiaries to an essentially sales-related activity in which product differentiation is achieved through brand reputation. This way a lightweight commercial network can be maintained, since a marketing staff of one to three members is employed at each subsidiary. These circumstances explain why no clearly gradualist path can be seen in the formation of the Tubacex network, since it was dependent on the concentration of wholesalers. The Dutch subsidiary (Tubacex Europe BV) coordinates the subsidiaries located in France and Italy. The subsidiary in the US (Tubacex Inc.) handles 31 per cent of the consolidated sales of the group. These two networks are supplemented by a number of sales offices located in less developed countries (LDCs) that have some oil-related activities or that show a potential market (see Figure 7.5).

Entry in the US market: a real option with strategic value

In the United States there was an oligopolistic market controlled by private capital, and strong economic growth during the 1950s prompted an increase in local productive capacity and in steel imports. Since there was no real competition, companies had no incentive to invest in technological innovation, which meant that the new plants set up did not incorporate oxygen converters (BOF), opting rather for traditional technology in order to exploit their knowledge base.[17] It is paradoxical to note that the technology gap between the United States on the one hand and Europe and Japan on the other began to widen at a time of strong growth.

The oil crisis of 1973 and the recession which followed it showed up the weaknesses of the steel industry in the United States. Companies there not only had to face up to the problem of productive overcapacity, but they also had to make up for having lagged behind in technology, with greatly fallen costs and losses.[18] This situation was aggravated by structural problems, such as the strong geographical concentration in the north and east of the US and excessively high wage levels.[19] The consequences became evident straightway: overcapacity, increasing debt ratios, company closures and investments in technological adaptation.[20] The result of the restructuring process was unbalanced supply. It was decided to reduce the production of intermediate products of lesser added value, these being imported from Brazil, while steels of higher added value were imported from Japan and Europe on account of the technology gap.

The search for niche markets based on technological superiority is the main reason for direct investment in the US for the two companies studied here. For Tubacex and Acerinox, producing in the US means that they can provide better service, since they can substantially cut delivery times, eliminate the costs of maintaining a store, overcome the trade barriers and win the badge 'made in USA'.[21] It also put the companies in a position to meet latent demand in Latin America.

The steel industry in the US has an oligopolistic structure, with supply concentrated in three US companies (J&L, currently controlled by the French company Ugine, Allegheny, and Armco, which was acquired by its competitor AK Steel in 1999). These companies have often proved their ability to prompt a protective reaction from the institutions (higher tariffs, quotas, environmental barriers).[22] In addition, it must be remembered that the US has a stainless-steel deficit, receiving supplies from Europe and Japan.

The objective of Acerinox was to replicate the Spanish production system (Algeciras) in the US and thus be able, at the first stage, to supply its stainless-steel import quota while avoiding the entry barriers. However, the American situation in terms of production and institutions entailed high risks on the institutional front, since a reaction from the oligopoly and environmental legislation could prevent the full development of the project, which, as we mentioned, involves three successive stages: cold rolling, hot rolling and steel making. In view of this situation, Acerinox designed an interesting country-risk cover strategy, which we will set out to analyse by examining the implicit real options.

The cold-rolling plant enabled products of high added value to be obtained, and also entailed two real options: vertical integration (call option), or abandoning the project (put option), bearing in mind that the cold-rolling plant is the stage requiring the least investment effect, thus reducing start-up costs.

A Joint Venture is an agreement which not only reduces the volume of resources committed, but also provides two real options (Kogut 1991;

Kogut and Kulatilaka 1994). Any of the partners can either (a) expand its participation to the point of achieving majority or outright control, i.e. executing the call option, or (b) abandon the project by selling the participation to the local partner, i.e. executing the put option. These decisions depend on the confluence of four different factors: relations between the partners, internal uncertainty, external uncertainty, and the value of the Joint Venture for the partners concerned.

In this context, Acerinox set up a cold-rolling plant in 1990 in Carrollton, Kentucky.[23] For this purpose, a 50 per cent Joint Venture was arranged with a local producer, Armco, called North American Stainless (NAS). This way of entry is justified by the need to have a local partner to lessen the risk of a strategic reaction by local producers, and it also makes it easier to become familiar with the context. Armco is more than just a hedge against country risk: it also reduces asset commitments and facilitates the execution of the call or put options that were part and parcel of the investment decision.

In view of the strategic importance of the North American market for Acerinox, the company completed its entry strategy by acquiring a sale option and a purchasing option in Mexico, i.e. it created an alternative Joint Venture called Mexinox in 1990. The trade negotiations between Mexico and the US lasted from 1986 to 1990, and the free trade agreement negotiations from 1990 to 1994 (CEPAL 2000). In this way, and once Mexico joined NAFTA, this country offered an appropriate institutional environment for arranging supplies to the US market.[24] In addition, the geographical proximity and the Mexican advantage in terms of the cost of the production factors must be borne in mind. Thus, together with Krupp Thyseen Niroska (KTN), Acerinox tendered for and won the award for the privatization of the Mexican company Nafinsa, which possessed a cold-rolling plant. The share capital of Mexinox was split into equal parts between the two foreign companies (Acerinox and KTN) and the Nafinsa executives, who still handled the management, which initially posed an internal-uncertainty problem.

This simultaneous investment in two cold-rolling plants by Joint Venture can be seen as the acquisition of two real options for developing an integrated system in one of the two countries. This strategy gives us four possible scenarios: maintaining both Joint Ventures if the uncertainty endures; taking up the purchase option in one location, which would imply executing the sale option in the other; or abandoning NAFTA by executing both sale options. Trends in internal and external risks, relations with the partners and the strategic value of the subsidiary would determine the life of the two subsidiaries (see Table 7.4).

In the case of Mexico, one of the terms of the privatization arrangements involved taking in the former managers as local partners, who would retain management of the company. This was a problem for knowledge transfer, particularly since relations with that partner were clouded

Table 7.4 Four possible scenarios of the country-risk hedge strategy designed for Acerinox

	Risk (internal/external)	*Relation with partner*	*Strategic value of subsidiary*
Maintain both joint ventures	USA: high external risk MEX: high internal risk	USA: equilibrium in bargaining power MEX: equilibrium in bargaining power	USA: high MEX: high
Call USA and put MEX	USA: low external risk MEX: not relevant	USA: Acerinox has a high bargaining power MEX: Not relevant	USA: high MEX: low
Put USA and call MEX	USA: high external risk or institutional intervention MEX: low internal risk	USA: Acerinox has a low bargaining power MEX: Acerinox has a high bargaining power	USA: low MEX: high
Put USA and put MEX	USA: high external risk or institutional intervention MEX: high internal risk	USA: Acerinox has a low bargaining power MEX: Acerinox has a low bargaining power	USA: low MEX: low

by the lack of transparency and the detection of certain irregularities. After long negotiations between the parties, requiring the intervention of the Paris Clearing Chamber, KTN acquired the stake held by the local partners in 1997 and a large part of the share capital of Acerinox (23 per cent), thus becoming the majority partner. Acerinox now has 10 per cent of the share capital, which gives it the right to remain on the Board of Directors and underpins its position as a supplier of black coil.

Though also not without their tensions, relations between Armco and Acerinox are regarded as very good. However, Acerinox executed its call option in 1994, acquiring the 45 per cent of the company capital that was held by the local partner for 73 million dollars.[25] NAS was deemed to be an American company, which reduced the external uncertainty. The reason for Armco's departure was its financial weakness: it could not face up to the high investments required for the second phase of the project, according to a personal interview in Acerinox.

By the end of 1998, the hot-rolling capacity of NAS stood at 800,000 tn/year, which accounts for 30 to 40 per cent of the group's production capacity. The third phase of the project, the building of the steelworks, is now being implemented, and this will make Acerinox the third-ranking European producer of stainless steel. The decision to establish the system in the US had a direct impact on the strategic value of Mexinox, which declined, and this, along with the management difficulties referred to above, makes the abandoning of Mexico in 1997 understandable.[26]

In 1994, Tubacex acquired Salem Tube Inc. in Greensville, Pennsylvania, a company that has a plant engaged in the production of non-welded stainless-steel tubes and nickel para-alloys that was on the verge of bankruptcy.[27] The institutional context that Tubacex was facing was different from the context confronting Acerinox, since there were no local producers, and thus the institutional risk was absent; in addition, relations with the local authorities are excellent (as they are also in the case of Acerinox). The acquisition of a plant also made sense from a technical point of view, since it takes 2 years to start up an integrated system for producing non-welded stainless steel.

A year after its acquisition, the subsidiary was posting profits. After restoring its financial position, a plan was launched to expand the installed capacity by means of a Pilger type cold-rolling system for tubing. Automation and optimization procedures were also introduced in the production processes and have improved the subsidiary's productivity. In 1997, sales by the North American subsidiary accounted for 31.7 per cent of Group sales, and a 103 per cent increase in sales in the US market had been achieved in just 2 years. In 1999 the company continued its international expansion by acquiring two companies, with different objectives: an Austrian company (Shoeller Bleckman Edelstahlrohr (SBER)) and the assets for tube manufacturing of the American company Altech, which were used to form Altx Inc.

The objectives pursued with these latest acquisitions were different. The Austrian company SBER has 150 years' experience behind it in the cold and hot manufacture of stainless-steel tubing, and a solid presence in Central and Eastern Europe, complementing the Tubacex sales network. SBER has a market share of 6 per cent and a brand of great international prestige. It also has a technology that complements Tubacex's, since it specializes in small-sized high-alloy tubing of high added value. The purchase of SBER was prompted in the first place by the acquisition of two strategic assets: the technology for products of higher added value, and the brand image. In this context, the transfer of knowledge could work both ways.

Altech is one of the two plants in the US for making hot-extruded stainless-steel tubing, and it has also bought capacity for cold drawing and rolling. The implicit logic of this acquisition is similar to that of Salem: the acquisition of market share in the US, low-cost assets, and the badge 'made in USA' (see Figure 7.6).[28]

The two FDIs arranged by Tubacex in the US improve the company's efficiency since through them the steel surplus produced in Spain (Acer-

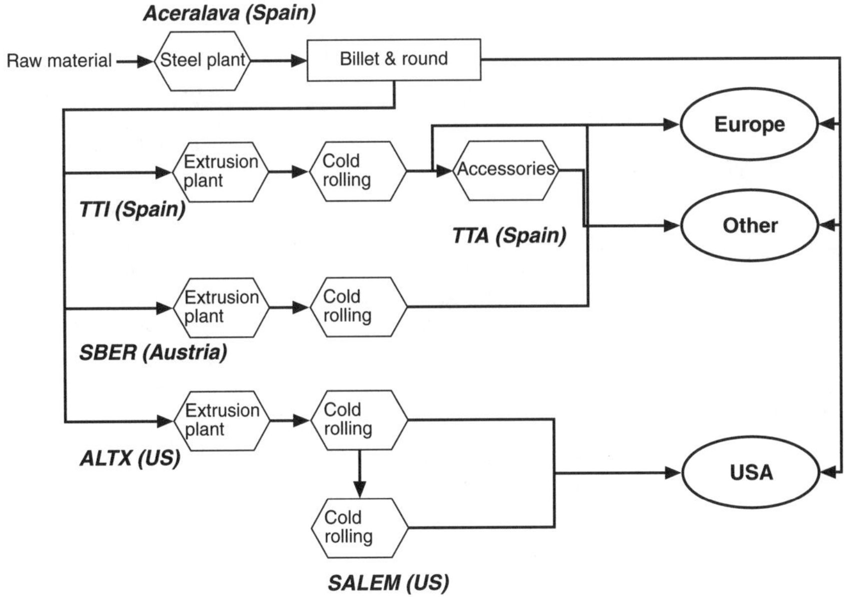

Figure 7.6 The international production process of Tubacex.

Source: Personal interview with Tubacex.

alava) can be turned to good account, reducing the effect of nickel price fluctuations on the company's profitability.[29] Moreover, the product range has been extended through the acquisition of SBER, with higher specialization within the range, while a multi-brand strategy has also been adopted.

Management of the US subsidiaries

Multinational subsidiaries can be classed in terms of the relative importance of the location and in terms of the resources allocated to, and the abilities of each subsidiary: black hole, contributor, implementer and strategic leader (Barlett and Goshal 1989). In Figure 7.7 we show the main differences between these types of subsidiary. Both Acerinox and Tubacex have made major investments in the US and have arranged a considerable allocation of organizational capabilities and resources (technological, financial etc.) for their respective production subsidiaries. Along with the sector forecasts and interviews, the performance of the US subsidiary indicates that NAS, Salem and Altx are all strategic leaders for both multinationals.[30]

Both companies have achieved good results through investing in the

		Black hole	***Strategic leader***
	High	• Minimal capabilities in a strong market. Is not an acceptable strategic option.	• Legitimate partner with headquarters in developing and implementing broad strategic thrusts.
Strategic importance of local environment		***Implementer***	***Contributor***
	Low	• Have just enough competence to maintain their local operations in a nonstrategic market. The majority of national units play this role. • Not contribute much to the strategic knowledge of the firm. • They maintain the commercial viability of the company. • Generate resources.	• Subsidiary with high competence and capabilities, these are captured and applied in the rest of worldwide operations.
		Low	*High*
		Level of local resources and capabilities	

Figure 7.7 Generic roles of multinational subsidiaries.

Source: Adapted for Bartlett and Ghoshal (1989).

US, and this is reflected in the profits turned in by their subsidiaries and in the improvements in their consolidated indicators. In addition to being profitable, the North American subsidiaries of both companies enjoy good labour relations and are appreciated in their locations – by the local institutions and the local society as well.

The primary reason cited by both companies for entering the US market was the large market size, since they had confidence in the competitiveness of their product and in their superior technology (see Figure 7.8). The question was how to enter the market. Both companies followed a different path. However, both companies perceived that, once located in the US, the country provides more opportunities than threats for their subsidiaries.

Acerinox shows an ethnocentrist approach (Perlmutter 1969), since it follows a home-country oriented management style, indicated by the use of an expatriate from the home country rather than a local person to manage the subsidiary. On the other hand, Tubacex follows a more polycentric or host-country approach. Both companies reported that their managers have sufficient autonomy from the subsidiaries, although both firms exchange extensive personal visits between parent and subsidiaries. Both of them, but especially Acerinox, also bring executives and all the technical people to Spain to learn about production and management. All

	ACERINOX	TUBACEX	
EUROPE		PRODUCTION CAPACITY AND INTANGIBLE ASSET SEEKING *(Acquisition)*	→ EFFICIENCY GAINS
US	MARKET SEEKING *(Greenfield)*	MARKET SEEKING ASSET SEEKING (Physical capital) *(Acquisition)*	
FUTURE			
China Mercosur	MARKET SEEKING *(Joint venture)*	MARKET SEEKING *(Joint venture)*	

Figure 7.8 Internationalization of production of Acerinox and Tubacex by region.

Source: Personal interviews with Acerinox and Tubacex.

this reflects the dependence on technology of US operations. The technology transfer between parent and subsidiary is, in both cases, production-based, although in the case of Acerinox it is also management-based.

In this, the high social content of these policies can be seen, reinforced by the activity pursued by the expatriates now occupying the senior management posts. Although the socialization systems facilitate communication between the subsidiary and the parent company, knowledge transfer is still essentially asymmetric. While the subsidiary has considerable autonomy in the marketing sphere, strategic decisions are the sole province of the parent company. This situation is understandable, since the subsidiary is still engaged in an initial learning process and the degree of autonomy is necessarily lower than it would be in the case of a full 'strategic leader'. The subsidiary strategic-leader is in training.

The NAS will have a plant that is more productive than the Algeciras plant, since it features latest-generation technology and the accumulated experience of the firm. According to the parent company, only 650 employees are required for the same output capacity that now requires 1,600 in Algeciras.[31] In view of the importance of the US market and the potential of Latin America, the Company's socialization process and transfer of resources and capabilities make it likely that the subsidiary will very soon be taking an active part in strategic decision-making and in the generation of organizational and technological knowledge.[32]

Executive trips and exchanges are less frequent in Tubacex than in Acerinox, and there are fewer expatriates. This points to a lower commitment to socialization, which results in the use of coordination and control systems based essentially on formal tools, particularly management by objectives. Hence the degree of autonomy of the Tubacex subsidiaries is greater, which is consistent with statements made by the multinational's executives in Spain.

The distribution channel of Acerinox in Europe is shared almost equally between wholesalers and its own commercial networks. In the US Acerinox sells about 80 per cent of its products through wholesalers. Acerinox had tried to develop its own commercial network but it was not successful due to local wholesaler control of the market.

As explained above, Tubacex acquired existing companies in the US, which makes the corporate-culture or socialization transfer process more complex than in the case of Acerinox. Furthermore, there is the fact that Tubacex has little international experience. A corporate division was set up in 1999 with the main function of co-ordinating the international subsidiaries and proposing management measures to generate synergies, prominent amongst which are the development and consolidation of the idiosyncratic transactional advantages of making the company multinational.

The marketing system of Tubacex comprises four independent networks (Tubacex, Salem, Altx, SBER) each with its own brand – brands that are clearly differentiated in the North American market. The company plans to continue with a multi-brand strategy that is to be compatible with rationalizing the network in order to avoid duplications and increase the synergies generated.

The two main difficulties facing Tubacex in its US investment were the environmental legislation and the shortage of trained human resources. Entry into the North American market also required some adaptation work on the dimensions of the tubing to bring them into line with local legislation.

Conclusion

In this chapter we have analysed some of the mechanisms through which a mature technology is gradually transferred from the country of origin to recently industrialized countries. In an appropriate institutional environment, this can result in competitive companies that start out on an internationalizing path. These two circumstances – the sector having a mature technology and the country being recently industrialized – help us to see that Acerinox and Tubacex have similarities with multinationals belonging to the second wave of FDI from LDCs (Cantwell and Tolentino 1990; Dunning, Hoesel and Narula 1999), although they do have one distinguishing feature: their competitive advantage is based on a more specialized product.[33]

Acerinox represents the closing of the technology cycle for steel. Its competitive advantage lies in a technology that was initially developed in the US and then transferred to Japan (to the emerging economy that Japan was in the 1960s) through the use of licences. This technologically perfected knowledge was then transferred from Japan to Spain (emerging economies in the 1970s) by Acerinox's technology partner, the Japanese company Nisshin-Steel. The cycle was closed in the 1990s when Acerinox set up a production subsidiary in the US. One particular cycle of technology-knowledge management can be seen in this.

The strategies of product specialization and seeking out a market niche were the source of the competitive advantage of the companies studied here, corroborating the evidence of Hoffman (1988) on the typology of European companies investing in the US. Moreover, certain realities glimpsed in this exploratory study are encountered again: difficulties in obtaining skilled labour, good relations with the local authorities, and a high degree of autonomy in marketing-related decision-making. However, differentiating elements are also noticeable, possibly as a result of the business activity itself, such as the great uncertainty perceived, stemming from restrictive environmental legislation and from the power of the established oligopoly in the case of Acerinox.

From the standpoint of entry paths, the country-risk cover tool designed by Acerinox is noteworthy: it efficiently combines the real options that were implicit in the joint ventures set up as a way of entry. Tubacex was essentially seeking production capacity already installed in the US by acquiring companies facing financial difficulties. The need to control the technology-transfer process justifies the company's retaining 100 per cent of the share capital of all its subsidiaries.

The subsidiaries have received a great deal of knowledge-transfer, the expatriates having played a crucial role in this. The different approaches to international reality have had a bearing on the work done by those expatriates. Acerinox has a more ethnocentric attitude, and has thus made special efforts to transfer both technology and organizational culture (values and company decision-making systems), i.e. a control and co-ordination mechanism based on socialization is being designed. However Tubacex, had a more polycentric approach with the expatriates fundamentally having a more technological profile. In order to make the productive process profitable, great autonomy was given to the management of the subsidiary, using formal control mechanisms.

Both companies work with a demand that is clearly regional in structure. There are two markets in which they have a strong commercial presence, Europe and the United States, while in the Asian market their penetration is low, the closed market of Japan being prominent there, as is China, which currently shows strong growth potential. On this subject, Acerinox commented to the authors of this article that they are considering entering China in alliance with Nisshin Steel.

In this context, both Acerinox and Tubacex look set to create an international production network with productive activity in all three of the regions mentioned. To this end, the US is a location of high strategic value for the companies, both of which have gone to great lengths to provide their subsidiaries with resources and capabilities. These subsidiaries can be regarded as *strategic leaders* for the network.

Notes

1 The data have been calculated by the authors based upon data from the Spanish Secretary of Commerce.
2 Arbed has taken a major stake in Aceralia, the Spanish steel company that arose from the restructuring in the 1980s and 1990s.
3 The Finnish company Outokumpu has an integrated production system.
4 There is a unwritten pact among stainless-steel producers based in exporting countries not to interfere in each other's home markets.
5 AK Steel acquired the fourth producer, Armco, in 1999.
6 In the late 1960s, having a stainless-steel plant was a strategic objective for the Spanish government, since it would lead to an improvement in the balance of payments by reducing imports, boosting exports, and creating jobs in an area with little in the way of industrial development.

Locating the company away from Spain's traditional metal-industry region was peculiar. The need for a port as competitive as the port of Algeciras, the last European port for America and Asia, the intention to set up an integrated project and thus one less dependent on the other producers, and political considerations regarding job creation in an area that had been left out in industrial terms were all decisive factors behind this choice of location.
7 In the 1970s, the most competitive steel industries were the Japanese ones.
8 Only one European company currently has an integrated stainless-steel plant: the Finnish company Outokumpu.
9 Acerinox's geographical location gives it cheap access to the world scrap market, but using scrap also enables the company to attenuate the cost impact of rising nickel prices. Seventy per cent of the raw material now used is scrap.
10 Bringing in variable remuneration met with strong opposition from the trade unions. Nevertheless, one year on, the workers declared themselves satisfied with the system. This system was truly innovative then.
11 The only Spanish companies that were producing non-welded hot-rolled pipes were the affiliate of the British firm Babcock & Wilcox and Tubos Forjados, these two companies merging in 1968 and thus forming the new company Tubos Reunidos.
12 An example of the drive to differentiate products by specializing in high value-added, knowledge-intensive products was the company's participation in a world project to develop bimetal tubing, designed to withstand high temperatures and the mix of highly corrosive substances that pipes are exposed to when drilling for oil and gas. The development of this piping brought it approved status among the main oil companies. In 1989 the Tubacex workforce numbered 1,463, while in 1998 the total was 822.
13 The price of nickel is a crucial factor in the costs of the end product, amounting to 70 per cent of the value of the billet, and between 30 and 35 per cent of the cost of the tube. Tubacex is not competitive in billet production since it is not produced by continuous casting: they have to use ingot moulds and then make the tubes. Despite this, surplus steel production is sold to the end market. The growth strategy pursued by Tubacex seeks in part to reduce billet surpluses by stepping up tube production.
14 The gradualist approach is based upon a dynamic relationship between the mode of entry, the localization factors and international experience. These relationships have been studied from four different approaches: the perspect-

ive of internalization (Buckley and Casson 1986; Rugman 1981; Casson 1986), the transaction cost (Magee 1977; Contractor 1984; Teece 1986; Hennart 1988; Anderson and Gatignon 1986), the named School of Uppsala based on market knowledge and international resources commitment (Johanson and Wiedersheim-Paul 1975; Johanson and Vahlen 1977, 1990) and finally the approach from the theory of organizational capabilities (Madhok 1997, 1998).

15 Each batch delivered to the customer has an identification number, and the company keeps a sample. The sample is then used to carry out tests and trials, obtaining results that are supplemented by the studies on the behaviour found in the steel throughout its life. This activity has enabled the company to keep track of the quality of the steels over their history and to ascertain customer requirements, all of which enables the products to be improved. In 1997, Acerinox had 18 industrial-property registrations for patents and trademarks. Personalized customer treatment and diversification in the product range has enabled the company to maintain an operating margin ranging from 35 to 45 per cent.

16 In the case of Acerinox, the marketing subsidiaries must keep their operating costs below 0.5 per cent of total sales. Those subsidiaries are also interconnected, in order to achieve integrated order management and thus to achieve delivery times of under 3 months.

17 These technologies have given rise to three main production systems: integrated (blast furnaces), minimills and high-quality alloys and special steels.

18 Productive capacity had risen by 30 per cent over the previous decade.

19 The steel industry had become concentrated in the north and east of the US to take advantage of economies of scale and skilled labour, i.e. the cluster-specific externalities. This meant that the west coast lacked installed capacity of its own, and could thus seek supplies from anywhere in the world owing to the sharp drop in sea-transport costs – one of the endemic causes of the trade deficit in steel in the North American economy (D'Costa 1999).

20 The first plant to use an oxygen converter was set up in the mid-1960s, 15 years after commercial use of that technology had arrived in Austria. The industry made major efforts to bring in the new technology, with average annual investments of 2000 million dollars between 1960 and 1965, steel produced by the use of BOF technology representing 50 per cent of national production (D'Costa 1999).

21 One example of the practices of the US authorities is the accusation of dumping levelled at Acerinox by the Special Steels Institute of North America (SSINA), a charge that was dismissed (Espina 1997).

22 In the Wilkins' Chapter 2, we can understand that although the institutions are interested in the entry of foreign direct investment, there is a sufficiently complex legal framework to give the foreign investor a strong sense of administrative risk.

23 A small city near the main centres that buy in steel, with a major river port. All this recalls the origin of the company in Algeciras (Spain) – and indeed the small size of the city meant, as had happened in Algeciras, that strong identification bonds formed between the city and the company, reaping the economies of scale associated with an industrial district (Espina 1997).

24 In this case, we have an example of how NAFTA affects the shaping of a new economic space for the foreign investor, as suggested by Wilkins. A similar strategy had been followed by another Spanish firm in the specialized steel products, Sidenor, which acquired 51 per cent of two Mexican companies (Atlax and Metamax). Through these two firms Sidenor will export to the US market.

25 The setting up of a network of six sales offices that were independent of the

Armco network, since control over distribution brings a major sales-margin transfer, led to confrontation between the partners in view of their clear divergence of interests (Espina 1997).

26 The sale of the company's participation in Mexinox led to an extraordinary profit of 10 million dollars, this sum being used on expanding the NAS facilities.

27 With the accumulated losses on the acquisition price, this company was acquired for 7.3 million dollars.

28 The aim with Altx is to achieve a 25 per cent market share in the US.

29 An investment of 1,400 million pesetas was made in the period 1999–2000 to bring in a round-finishing line in order to supply the hot-rolling plants of SBER and Altx.

30 Acerinox executives mentioned that they do not have any problem at all with Nisshin Steel exports to the US but they do not produce in this country.

31 NAS has a 40 per cent saving in the cost of electricity supplies compared to Algeciras.

32 It must be stressed that Acerinox is engaged in a continual-improvement process in search of solutions to make the production process less costly or more flexible. Modifications are made to the conventional equipment and, when they have proved themselves, they become new technical requirements for suppliers. This enables innovation to be arranged in conjunction with the equipment makers. The most prominent success was the joint patent with Chugairo (a capital-goods producer) for the second bright-annealing line.

33 Greater specialization in the products offered is perhaps something to be borne in mind when analysing the characteristics of a direct-investment issue involving countries engaged in the fourth stage of the IDP.

References

Athreye, S.S. (1994) 'The spread of technology and the level of development: A comparative study of steel mills using the electric arc furnace technology in India and Britain', unpublished PhD dissertation, Science Policy Research Unit, University of Sussex.

Anderson, E. and Gatignon, H. (1986) 'Modes of foreign entry: a transaction cost analysis and propositions', *Journal of International Business Studies* 17, autumn: 1–26.

Barlett, C.A. and Ghoshal, S. (1989) *Managing Across Borders: the Transnational Solution*, Boston: Harvard Press.

Buckley, P.J. and Casson, M.C. (1981) 'The optimal timing of a foreign direct investment', *Economic Journal* 91 March: 75–87.

Cantwell, J. (1989) *Technological innovation and multinational corporations*, Oxford: Basil Blackwell.

Cantwell, J. and Tolentino, P.E. (1990) *Technological accumulation and third world multinationals*, Discussion Papers in International Investment and Business Studies, University of Reading.

Casson, J. (1986) 'Contractual arrangements for technological transfer: new evidence from business history', *Business History* XXVIII: 5–35.

CEPAL (2000) *La Inversión Extranjera en América Latina y el Caribe*, Santiago de Chile: United Nations.

Contractor, F.J. (1984) 'Choosing between direct investment and licensing: theoretical considerations and empirical test', *Journal of International Business Studies* 15, winter: 167–88.

D'Costa, A. (1999) *The Global Restructuring of the Steel Industry*, London: Routledge.

Dunning, J.H. (1981) 'Explaining the international direct investment position of countries: Towards a dynamic or development approach', *Weltwirtschaftliches Archiv* 11, 1: 30–64.

—— (1986) 'The investment development cycle revisited', *Weltwirtschaftlicher Archiv* 122: 667–77.

—— (1988) 'The eclectic paradigm of international production: a restatement and some possible extensions', *Journal of International Business Studies* 19, spring: 1–32.

—— (1993) *Multinational Enterprises and the Global Economy*, London: Unwin Hyman.

—— (1997) *Alliance Capitalism and Global Business*, London and New York: Routledge.

Dunning, J.H. and Narula, R. (eds) (1996) *Foreign Direct Investment and Governments*, London: Routledge.

Dunning, J.H., Van Hoesel, R. and Narula, R. (1998) 'Third world multinationals revisited: new developments and theoretical implications', in J.H. Dunning *Globalisation, Trade and Foreign Direct Investment*, Oxford: Pergamon.

Durán, J.J. (1999) *Multinacionales Españolas en Iberoamérica, Valor Estratégico*, Madrid: Pirámide.

Durán, J.J. and Sánchez, P. (1981) *La Internacionalización de la Empresa Española: Inversiones Empresa Española en el Exterior*, Madrid: ICEX.

Durán, J.J. and Úbeda, F. (1998) 'The investment development path: A reassessment', paper presented in the 24th Annual Conference of European International Business Academy (EIBA), Jerusalem, 13–15 December.

—— (2000) *The direct investment path: a new empirical approach and some theoretical insights*, Working Paper, Centro Internacional Carlos V, Universidad Autónoma de Madrid.

—— (2001) *Estrategias de Multinacionalización de la Empresa Española*, unpublished manuscript, Centro Internacional Carlos V, Universidad Autónoma de Madrid.

Espina, A. (1997) 'Especialización y autofinanciación, palanca para la internacionalización: el caso Acerinox', in J.J. Durán (ed.) *Multinacionales Españolas II: Nuevas Experiencias de Internacionalización*, Madrid: Piramide.

Gatignon, H. and Anderson, E. (1988) 'The multinational corporation's degree of control over foreign subsidiaries: an empirical test of a transaction cost explanation', *Journal of Law, Economics and Organization* 4, 2: 305–36.

Heinz H. Parisier & Co. (2000) Alloy metals & steel productions, Weekly Service, no. 650.

Hennart, J.F. (1988) 'A transaction costs theory of equity joint-ventures', *Strategic Management Journal* 9: 361–74.

Hoesel, R. (1992) *Multinational enterprises from developing countries with investment in developed economies: some theoretical consideration*, Discussion Paper 1992/E/6, Center for International Management and Development – Antwerp CIMDA, University of Antwerp.

Hoffman, R.C. (1988) 'The general management of foreign subsidiaries in the USA: an exploratory study', *Management International Review* 28, 2: 41–55.

Hymer, S. (1960) *The International Operations of National Firms. A Study of Direct Investment*, PhD thesis, MIT (published later by MIT Press in 1976).

IISI (International Iron and Steel Institute) (2000) Published on the Internet: http://www.worldsteel.org

Johanson, J. and Mattson, L.G. (1988) 'Internationalization in industrial systems –

a network approach', in N. Hood and J.E. Vahlne (eds) *Strategies in Global Competition*, New York: Croom Helm.

Johanson, J. and Vahlne, J.E. (1977) 'The internationalisation process of the firm: A model of knowledge development and increasing foreign market commitments', *Journal of International Business Studies* 8, 1: 23–32.

Johanson, J. and Vahlne, J. (1990), 'The mechanism of internationalisation', *International Marketing Review*, 7, 4: 11–25.

Johanson, J. and Wiedersheim, P.F. (1975) 'The internationalisation of the firm. Four Swedish cases', *Journal of Management Studies* October: 305–22.

Jones, G. (1996) *The Evolution of International Business*, London and New York: Routledge.

Kogut, B. (1991) 'Joint venture and the option to expand and acquire', *Management Science* 37, 1: 19–33.

Kogut, B. and Kulatilaka, N. (1994) 'Operating flexibility, global manufacturing and the option value of multinational network', *Management Science* 40, 1: 123–39.

Lall, S. (1996) 'The investment development path: some conclusions', in J.H. Dunning and R. Narula (eds) *Foreign Direct Investment and Governments*, London and New York: Routledge.

Madhok, A. (1996) 'Know-how, experience and competition-related considerations in foreign market entry: an exploratory investigation', *International Business Review* 5: 339–66.

Madhok, A. (1987), 'Cost, value and foreign market entry mode: The transaction and the firm,' *Strategic Management Journal* 18, 1: 39–61.

Madhok, A. (1998) 'The nature of multinational firms boundaries: transaction costs, firms' capabilities and foreign market entry modes', *International Business Review* 7: 259–90.

Magee, S.P. (1977) 'Multinational corporations, the industry technology cycle and development', *Journal of World Trade Law* 11: 297–321.

Narula, R. (1996) *Multinational Investment and Economic Structure: Globalisation and Competitiveness*, London and New York: Routledge.

Nelson, R.R. and Winter, S.G. (1982) *An Evolutionary Theory of Economic Change*, Cambridge: Harvard University Press.

Ozawa, T. (1996) 'Japan: the macro-IDP, meso-IDPs and the technology and technological development path (TDP), in Dunning, J.H. and Rajneesh Narula, (eds) *Foreign Direct Investment and Governments*. London and New York: Routledge.

Perlmutter, H.V. (1969) 'The tortuous evolution of the multinational corporation', *Columbia Journal of World Business* January–February: 9–18.

Rugman, A.M. (1981) *Inside the Multinationals: The Economics of Internal Markets*, New York: Columbia University Press.

Teece, D.J. (1977), 'Technological transfer by multinational firms: The resource costs of transferring technological know-how', *Economic Journal* 87, 2: 242–61.

—— (1986) 'Transaction cost economics and the multinational enterprise', *Journal of Economic Behaviour and Organization* 7: 21–45.

Tolentino, P.E. (1987) *The global shift in international production: the growth of multinational entreprises from developing countries*, unpublished PhD dissertation, University of Reading.

Úbeda, F. (1999) *La senda de la inversión directa exterior: una nueva aproximación metodológica*, unpublished PhD Thesis. Universidad Autonoma de Madrid.

Williamson, O. (1975) *Market and hierarchies: analysis and antitrust implications: a study of the economics of internal organizations*, New York: Free Press.

8 Foreign banks in the United States since World War II

A useful fringe

Adrian E. Tschoegl[1]

Introduction

Foreign banks have had an organizational presence in the United States since the early 1800s. Until after World War II, the foreign banks' presence was generally limited. They engaged in trade finance, and in some cases ethnic banking. Their growth really dates from the mid-1960s to 1990. The growth in demand for their services was itself the consequence of the growth trade, the Eurodollar market, foreign exchange trading and non-financial foreign direct investment in the US.

First, the General Agreement on Trade and Tariffs (GATT) and its successor, the World Trade Organization (WTO), facilitated the rebound of trade from its collapse during the Great Depression. Since the end of World War II, world trade has grown more rapidly than world GNP, and this has generated an increase in the demand for trade financing and the execution of trade payments. Second, liberalization of capital flows and the growth of the Eurodollar market from the late 1950s on, led many foreign banks to want to have a presence in the US money markets, and therefore New York, and perhaps a dollar deposit base as well, to be able to fund their customers' demand for US dollar loans. Third, the breakdown of the Bretton Woods systems of fixed exchange rates led to the development of foreign exchange trading, with New York again appearing as a leading centre. Lastly, as companies in Europe and Japan recovered from World War II, they first rebuilt their domestic operations. By the mid-1960s (Europe) or mid-1970s (Japan), many of these companies were ready to establish operations in the US. As they did so, they wanted their bankers to accompany them.

As we shall see below, this period of rapid growth in the presence and role of foreign banks in the US is over. Although the share of foreign banks in US Commercial and Industrial (C&I) loans reached a peak of 35 per cent in 1995, we are now seeing a retreat.

In Chapter 2, Wilkins suggests five perspectives for examining FDI in the US, of which four are relevant to this study: the role of regulation, the regions affected, the nationality of the investors, and the performance of the investors. The second section describes the legal and regulatory background to the foreign banks' presence and some legislative milestones. The third section focuses on the agencies and branches of foreign banks, and deals with the geography of their presence. The fourth section focuses on the foreign banks' subsidiaries; this section deals more with the national origins of the foreign banks and the banks' performance. The last section is the conclusion.

Some legal and regulatory background

The legal form of the foreign banks' presence

To examine the impact of foreign banks in the US I will consider separately the activities of what I will call the integral forms and the equity forms of presence. Representative offices, agencies and branches of foreign banks are not separate legal persons but are, instead, an integral part of their parents. However, affiliates, consortia and subsidiaries are separate legal persons. Integral forms trade on the basis of their parents' capital; their commitments are automatically their parents' commitments. An integral form cannot go bankrupt unless the parent goes bankrupt; however, if the parent is bankrupt, so are its branches and agencies. An equity form trades on the basis of its own capital. As a separate legal person, an equity form can go bankrupt even when its parent remains solvent and may remain solvent even when the parent is bankrupt.

Under the Basle Agreement, prudential supervision of integral forms is primarily the responsibility of the regulatory authorities of the parent bank's home country. Supervision of the equity forms is primarily the responsibility of the regulatory authorities of the entity's country of incorporation, which is generally the host country. This division of duties follows logically from the legal status of the two sets of forms.

This legal distinction also parallels an operational distinction in terms of the activities the banks undertake and hence the markets that they serve. Heinkel and Levi (1992) establish an empirical link between the legal form of a foreign bank's presence in a country and the activities that it undertakes. Earlier, Cho *et al.* (1987) found that foreign banks' agencies and branches in the US engaged primarily in trade finance, corporate banking, foreign exchange dealing, and money market activities.

Grubel (1977) distinguished three markets for multinational banking: wholesale, corporate, and retail. Agencies and branches are an appropriate form for banks wishing to participate in wholesale capital markets, as they permit the parent bank to trade on its own capital rather than the smaller capital base of a subsidiary. The same considerations apply in the case of corporate lending; under most regulatory regimes, the capital base restricts the size of the loan a bank may make and hence agencies and branches may make larger loans than may a subsidiary. Typically, banks use subsidiaries for retail banking to disengage the operation from the parent and to bring it under local regulatory supervision which qualifies it for deposit insurance, should that be available.

Of course, frequently host country or home country laws and regulations constrain the foreign banks' choices (Tschoegl 1981; Engwall 1992). For instance, New York will not permit foreign banks from countries that do not permit New York banks to establish branches or subsidiaries there to establish a branch in New York. It does, however, permit banks from countries with such immigration barriers to open representative offices and agencies; this is one factor behind the establishment of agencies in New York.

Some legislative milestones

Congress intended the 1978 International Banking Act (IBA) to remove some regulatory loopholes that permitted foreign banks to operate in more than one state while US banks were restricted (with only a few grandfathered exceptions) to one state (Hultman 1987). Before the IBA of 1978, banks such as Barclays Bank and Bank of Tokyo had established subsidiaries in New York and California, something that was denied to US banks. Even after the passage of the law, foreign banks could still have a subsidiary in one state and a branch in another.

The Depository Institutions Deregulation and Monetary Control Act (DIDMCA) of 1980 included provisions granting foreign banks' branches and agencies direct access to Federal Reserve services and privileges, including the discount window. However, it also subjected all foreign banking institutions accepting deposits to Federal Reserve rules.

In 1989, it was discovered that Banca Nazionale del Lavoro's agency in Atlanta had made unauthorized loans to Iraq in an amount in excess of US$5 billion. In 1990, the Bank of Credit and Commerce International went bankrupt as a result of massive internal fraud that involved top management. These shocks led to Congressional demands for tighter scrutiny of foreign banks. In 1991, Congress passed the Foreign Bank Supervision Enforcement Act (FBSEA). Before FBSEA, state authorities could license foreign banks to operate branches and agencies within their states with only a courtesy notification to the Federal Reserve (the Fed). Now, the Fed must approve all entries. The Fed apparently approves applications from banks from Europe and Japan quickly, but delays interminably in the case of banks from Latin America, the transition economies, and anywhere else where the Fed believes that regulatory supervision may be inadequate.

FBSEA limits deposit insurance to US-chartered depository institutions. It also bars foreign branches from accepting deposits of less than US$100,000 from US residents and citizens, although deposits from foreigners may be of any size. Lastly, FBSEA requires foreign banks acquiring more than 5 per cent of a US bank to notify the Federal Reserve (the previous limit had been 10 per cent). If the foreign bank owns or controls at least 25 per cent of the US bank, the Federal Reserve Bank must also approve the foreign parent bank as a holding company.

The most recent development has been the Interstate Banking and Branching Efficiency Act (IBBEA) of 1994 (Hultman 1997). This act took effect in 1997 and authorized interstate branching by domestic banks and the US subsidiaries of foreign banks. Foreign banks may also operate branches in more than one state without establishing a subsidiary unless the Board of Governors requires the bank to establish a subsidiary to ensure that the bank adheres to US capital requirements.

Integral forms: representative offices, agencies, and branches

This section first discusses the foreign banks' lending activities and then their contribution to the development of the major financial centres in the US.

The foreign banks' lending

As one can see from Table 8.1, total assets at the agencies and branches of foreign banks have grown 35 times since 1973, and peaked in 1997. Business loans grew 18 times, and peaked in 1993. The *share* of foreign banks in total banking system assets and loans peaked around 1991–2. It is no coincidence that this peak coincides with that in the number of Japanese banks in New York (and the US).

From the mid-1980s on, Japanese banks, buoyed by the strength of the Japanese economy, the yen and the effect of the stock market bubble on their capital base, expanded their presence throughout the world. Before the early 1980s, the Japanese, constrained by the Ministry of Finance in terms of the number of offices they could establish, were under-represented in world financial centres, relative to what one might otherwise expect (Choi *et al.* 1986). By 1990, the restraints had been lifted and they were over-represented (Choi *et al.* 1996).

As Baer (1990) found, foreign penetration of US wholesale banking markets was strongly linked to the market capitalization of foreign banks. At the time, the market capitalization (as a percentage of assets) of Japanese banks was almost three times that of US banks, and at least 50 per cent higher than that of the major Swiss, German and British banks. Market capitalization correlated strongly with the growth in foreign bank activity as the banks sought to add assets, explicitly by making loans and implicitly by issuing stand-by-letters of credit. At the same time as Japanese banks capitalization increased due to the rise in land values and stock prices in Japan,[2] the market capitalization of US banks suffered from a series of

Table 8.1 The assets and loans of the agencies, branches and subsidiaries of foreign banks in the US, 1973–99

	Agencies & Branches				*Subsidiaries*			
	Total assets		*Total business loans*		*Total assets*		*Total business loans*	
Year	*(US$bn)*	*(%)*[a]	*(US$bn)*	*(%)*[a]	*(US$bn)*	*(%)*[a]	*(US$bn)*	*(%)*[a]
1973	25	3	10	6	5	1	2	1
1974	34	4	15	8	10	1	3	1
1975	38	4	16	8	12	1	3	2
1976	46	4	16	8	14	1	4	2
1977	59	5	18	8	16	1	4	2
1978	87	6	27	11	20	2	5	2
1979	114	8	38	13	33	2	9	3
1980	147	9	46	14	50	3	13	4
1981	172	9	53	14	76	4	20	5
1982	207	1	57	13	89	4	24	6
1983	228	1	56	12	98	4	27	6
1984	272	1	64	14	119	5	32	7
1985	312	11	73	15	126	5	34	7
1986	397	13	90	17	124	4	35	6
1987	461	15	109	19	128	4	38	7
1988	514	16	125	21	132	4	41	7
1989	580	16	138	22	152	4	44	7
1990	627	17	147	24	160	4	45	7
1991	700	18	165	28	157	4	41	7
1992	712	18	168	29	154	4	40	7
1993	695	17	158	27	159	4	37	7
1994	740	17	171	27	203	5	45	7
1995	761	17	197	28	222	5	52	7
1996	821	17	222	27	170	3	43	5
1997	925	17	232	26	201	4	50	6
1998	901	15	223	23	217	4	57	6
1999	904	14	205	19	325	5	74	7
Δ73–99	**879**	**3,510**	**195**	**1,850**	**320**	**6,300**	**72**	**3,500**

Source: Board of Governors of the US Federal Reserve.

Note
a Percentage of total for all banks in the US, domestic and foreign.

regional downturns and the failure of many less-developed countries (LDC) borrowers to repay loans on schedule.[3]

However, as Peek and Rosengren (1997) found for the 1988–95 period, the sharp decline in land and share prices in Japan between 1989 and 1992, together with an increased regulatory emphasis on capital adequacy, led Japanese banks to reduce their lending. To limit the effect on long-standing customers the banks concentrated the reduction on overseas customers. Japanese branches in the US showed a statistically significant decrease in both total loan growth and business loan growth relative to assets as their parent banks' risk-based capital ratios fell. However, the US subsidiaries of Japanese banks did not show a similar reduction in lending.

Similarly, Laderman (1999) found that since 1992, Japanese banks' California branches and agencies share of the total business loans made by banking institutions based in the state plunged. However, Japanese-owned US-chartered banks headquartered in California held their share of business loans fairly steady during the same period. The difference is that loans by agencies and branches reflect the capital of the parent, whereas those of subsidiaries reflect their own capital.

Shrieves and Dahl (2000) found that US lending by Japanese banks fell in the years after 1989 due to a variety of factors, including developments in foreign exchange rates and exports to the US, but most importantly due to complementarities between the banks' domestic and US lending. They suggest that the complementarities could also reflect a correlation between the domestic and US borrowing needs of Japanese firms, or the banks' reassessment of their customers' creditworthiness. Again, the Japanese banks' subsidiaries appeared to be unaffected by their parents' capital or domestic lending.

In a later analysis, Peek and Rosengren (2000) found that the pullback by the Japanese branches had at least a temporary effect on the overall availability of credit in the US. However, this is part of a larger story. In the late 1980s a property boom swept across a number of countries. Ball (1994) argues that technical change in key service industries led to an upsurge in demand for buildings from the mid-1970s onward. Also, deregulation increased credit availability. Monetary authorities, attempting to rein in the credit expansion, ended the boom. Deflation of real estate values hit banking systems in Australia, Canada, Denmark, Finland, Japan, Norway, Sweden, the UK and the US (Ball 1994; Bartholemew 1994). Japanese lending abroad, including in the US, is part of the story, but whether it was the keystone or not is an open question.

Before leaving the topic of lending by foreign banks it is worth noting that the activities of the US agencies, branches and subsidiaries of foreign banks understates the activities of foreign banks. As McCauley and Seth (1992) point out, in the second half of the 1980s, US reserve requirements interacted with money market interest rates to give foreign banks an incentive to book loans offshore. When the regulations changed, foreign banks transferred or rebooked some of their offshore business to branches and agencies located in the US (Terrell 1993).

For 1993, Terrell's data shows that French, German, Swiss and British banks had both more loans and deposits than the onshore figures would suggest. The French were small net borrowers rather than small net lenders. The Germans and Swiss remained small net placers of funds in US domestic markets. The British had double the loans and deposits than their onshore figures would indicate, and the British too were small net placers. The Canadian banks had substantially more loans than onshore figures would indicate; their ability to take deposits in Canada meant that they did not book deposits in the offshore centres. Lastly, the offshore figures indicated a small increase in Japanese lending from offshore offices, but a large increase in deposit taking.[4]

The development of US financial centres

There is a circular causation between the presence of the integral forms of foreign banks and the development of a financial centre. The foreign banks plant their representative offices, agencies and branches in certain cities because they are financial centres, and it is the foreign banks presence and their activities that make the centre. In terms of the number of foreign banks with a presence in the city in the form of a representative office, an agency or a branch, Table 8.2 suggests that the six most important cities are New York, Los Angeles (LA), Miami, Chicago, San Francisco (SF), and Houston. Interestingly, of the top centres in 1980, all but New York have only held their place, or have lost ground. In the last 20 years, the dramatic growth has been in the South, with the rise of Miami and the entrance of Houston and Dallas into the ranks (Tables 8.2 and 8.3).

New York

Already in 1912, New York was the premier US financial centre. In 1957, there were sixty-seven different foreign banks with a presence in the city, of which three were subsidiaries and the rest were representative offices and agencies (Tamagna 1959). Between 1959 and 1961, Chase Manhattan Bank and Citibank led the Association of New York Clearing House Banks to sponsor a bill permitting foreign banks to open branches in New York. Both Chase and Citibank were meeting resistance to their expansion in Japan and Latin America on the grounds that New York did not offer reciprocity (Pauly 1988). More recently, Rosen and Murray (1997) urge New York (the city and the state) to encourage the government of the United States to work to increase openness abroad to the establishment of foreign banks. This is part of their strategy for enhancing the importance of New York as a financial centre.

In Figure 8.1, I have graphed the number of foreign banks in New York from 1970 to the present. There is some double counting of branches and subsidiaries, but the overall shape appears representative of developments in the US in general. Almost all foreign banks have a presence in New York if they have a presence in the US.

The turndown in the number of foreign banks in New York is due to three factors. First, there has been a decline in the number of Japanese banks. Second, mergers among the world's largest banks are resulting in some consolidation of operations. Third, increased regulatory caution is slowing the inflow of newcomers.

Table 8.2 Distribution of foreign bank offices in the US, 2000

City	*Representatives*	*Agencies*	*Branches*	*Total*
New York (NY)	89	20	174	**283**
Los Angeles (CA)	17	26	26	**69**
Miami (FL)	14		35	**49**
Chicago (IL)	11		29	**40**
San Francisco (CA)	9	5	10	**24**
Houston (TX)	16	9		**25**
Atlanta (GA)	4	7		**11**
Seattle (WA)	4		4	**8**
Portland (OR)			4	**4**
Washington (DC)	8		2	**10**
Dallas (TX)	6	2		**8**
Coral Gables (FL)			2	**2**
Boston (MN)	3		1	**4**
Flushing (NY)	1		1	**2**
San Jose (CA)	1		1	**2**
Alhambra (CA)			1	**1**
Aventura (FL)			1	**1**
Greenwich (CT)			1	**1**
Monterey Park (CA)			1	**1**
Stamford (CT)			1	**1**
Menlo Park (CA)	1	1		**2**
Beverly Hills (CA)		1		**1**
Honolulu (HI)		1		**1**
Huntington Park (CA)		1		**1**
Minneapolis (MN)	3			**3**
Jacksonville (FL)	2			**2**
Pittsburgh (PA)	2			**2**
Staten Island (NY)	2			**2**
Baltimore (MD)	1			**1**
Boca Raton (FL)	1			**1**
Buffalo (NY)	1			**1**
Charlotte (VA)	1			**1**
Cincinnati (OH)	1			**1**
Cleveland (OH)	1			**1**
Denver (CO)	1			**1**
Florence (KT)	1			**1**
Jackson Heights (NY)	1			**1**
Jersey City (NJ)	1			**1**
Memphis (TN)	1			**1**
New Orleans (LA)	1			**1**
Palm Beach (FL)	1			**1**
Philadelphia (PA)	1			**1**
Richmond (VA)	1			**1**
Rye (NY)	1			**1**
Somerville (MA)	1			**1**
Southfield (IL)	1			**1**
St. Louis (MO)	1			**1**
Total	**212**	**73**	**294**	**579**

Source: Board of Governors of the Federal Reserve (Mar 2000).

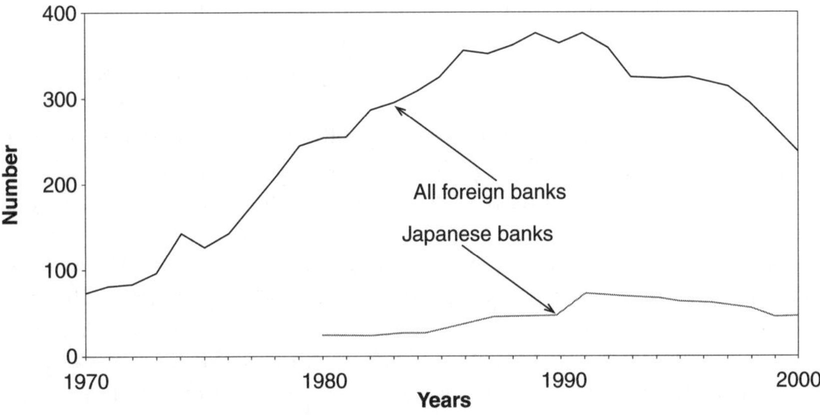

Figure 8.1 Number of foreign banks in New York, 1970–2000.

The second line on the graph is the number of Japanese banks in New York, net of double counting. The evident downturn is primarily a function of the decline in profitability in banking in Japan, which has caused several banks to cut back on unprofitable offices overseas. An increase in mergers, itself a consequence of the difficulties in the Japanese financial sector, is also a factor. Thus the merger of Bank of Tokyo and Mitsubishi Bank, both of which had New York branches, resulted in a reduction in the number of separate institutions by one.

Table 8.3 Changes in the distribution of foreign bank offices in the US, 1980–2000

	1980			*Mar 2000*			*Change (1980–2000)*	
State	*Agencies*	*Branches*	*Total*	*Agencies*	*Branches*	*Total*	*(No.)*	*(%)*
New York	59	74	133	20	175	195	61	47
California	79		79	34	39	73	−6	−8
Illinois		31	31		29	29	−2	−6
Florida	12		12		38	38	26	117
Georgia	9		9	7		7	−2	−22
Washington		8	8		4	4	−4	−50
Pennsylvania		5	5			0	−5	−100
Oregon		4	4		4	4	0	0
Massachusetts		4	4		1	1	−3	−75
Hawaii	2		2		1	1	−1	−50
Texas			0	11		11	11	
D. of Columbia			0		2	2	2	
Connecticut			0		2	2	2	
Total	161	126	287	72	295	367	80	28

Source: Board of Governors of the Federal Reserve.

Japan is not the only country to have seen mergers. Mergers and acquisitions (M&A) among large foreign banks appear to have increased in the 1990s. By my count, there was only one merger each in the 1950s and the 1960s that resulted in a consolidation in New York. In the 1970s there were six, in the 1980s five, and in the 1990s 31. Even allowing for the increase in the number of foreign banks in New York over the second half of the twentieth century, merger activity appears to have increased in the 1990s.

Lastly, while retreat from unprofitable operations and M&A have reduced the number of foreign banks in New York, the Federal Reserve has become more cautious in authorizing the entry of foreign banks. For instance, in 1992 the Fed blocked an application by the Banco Nacional de Mexico, the largest bank in Mexico, to open a branch in Florida, though state regulators had approved it the previous year.

Los Angeles and San Francisco

In 1910, San Francisco was the financial centre for the West Coast in that five foreign banks had a presence there, and none were in Los Angeles. The Canadian Bank of Commerce did operate in Seattle and Portland (Wilkins 1989) and other Canadian banks had short-lived offices elsewhere, but San Francisco was clearly the centre. In 1960, four of the five foreign banks in California at the turn of the century were still present and two others had joined them. By 1970, SF had 11 agencies of foreign banks and LA had three. By 1975, LA had pulled ahead with 23 agencies to SF's 20. Since then, LA has pulled even further ahead in terms of the number of foreign banks with a presence in the city, while SF has seen only slight growth.

Chicago

The first foreign bank in Chicago was a branch of the Bank of Montreal (BoM), established in 1861, closed thereafter before being re-opened in 1871 (James 1938). Other Canadian banks came and went but by 1914, Bank of Montreal was the largest bank in Illinois (Wilkins 1989). However, after a change in Illinois law in 1921, BoM was forced to restrict its activities and the branch lost its pre-eminent position. In 1952 BoM downgraded its branch to a representative office (Denison 1967). In the same year Dai-Ichi Kangyo (DKB) became the first foreign bank to enter after World War II when it established a representative office. In 1973, the Illinois legislature passed the Foreign Banking Office Act permitting foreign banks to open one branch per bank. The new law restricted the location of the foreign banks' branches to the area of the Loop (Chicago's town centre). The restrictions on foreign banks were consistent with Illinois' general banking laws, which restricted all banks to a single office (so-called 'unit banking'). Chicago's largest banks had backed the market-opening measure as they had found themselves restricted in their own international expansion when trying to enter countries, such as Japan, that required reciprocity. The large Chicago banks and the business community in general also favoured the development of Chicago as a financial centre for the middle of the country. The number of foreign banks apparently peaked at over 80 in the late 1980s, before dropping to the present 40.

Miami

Before 1972, foreign banks could own banks in Florida. Still, prior to 1972, only Canada's Royal Trust Company had acquired local subsidiaries (Wilkins 1979). In 1977, Florida passed the Firestone-Bloom bill, which authorized agencies of foreign banks starting in 1978. By 1979 there were 13 in the greater Miami area and by 1981 there were 21. By 1984 there were 48 but since then the number has stabilized. Grosfoguel (1995) argues that Miami emerged as a world city in the late 1970s as it became the core of the Caribbean system of cities on the basis, in part, of an infrastructure built to serve tourism. Óhuallacháin (1994) maintains that Miami now acts as node for flows of trade and investment between the United States, South America and Europe and as a centre for South America. In a process in which the banks played a pivotal role, Miami has emerged as a financial and business centre for Latin America.

Houston and Dallas

In 1985, the Texas legislature finally authorized foreign banks to operate as agencies. Prior to the passage of the Foreign Bank Agency Act (SB746), foreign banks could only operate via representative offices and Edge Act banks. The Act still limited the foreign banks to operating only within counties with a population of over 1.5 million. However, this limit included the two cities of greatest interest: Houston, with its Port of Houston – one of the busiest ports in the US – and Dallas-Fort Worth with its hub airport.

Atlanta

In 1972 Georgia authorized the entry of foreign banks in a bid to make Atlanta a financial centre. Originally there was some hope that Atlanta could provide a central base for foreign banks servicing foreign firms establishing manufacturing plants in the south. However, the rise of Miami and the Texas centres, and the increase in the number of cities with the presence of just a single foreign bank has probably come at some expense to Atlanta's role as a financial centre. The airports of Miami,

Dallas-Fort Worth, and Chicago equal Atlanta as hubs for access to the south.

We should not allow the focus on the quantity of lending by agencies and branches to overshadow completely the other contributions of these foreign banks' offices. For instance, foreign banks have been able to gather some correspondent banking business because smaller domestic banks consider them less of a threat in terms of stealing customers than large domestic banks (Goldberg 1992). On occasion this can extend to an invitation to participate in loans that are too large for the domestic bank to carry on its own. Probably the most important long-run role of the integral offices is their dispersal of specialized knowledge and expertise (including knowledge of their home countries). Face-to-face contact is important when banks produce specialized services for corporate customers. By locating in several cities throughout the US, the foreign banks reduced the cost of access to such services for smaller, local firms.

In the 1970s, the foreign banks in New York brought some expertise to the foreign exchange market, but by the 1980s, US banks dominated the rankings (Tschoegl 1999). Many of the Japanese banks that came to New York in the late 1980s and early 1990s came with the ostensible aim of learning to operate in the international foreign exchange, money, and debt markets. However, as Scher and Beechler (1993) point out, factors internal to the banks, especially personnel policies, worked to vitiate any learning.

Equity forms: consortia, affiliates and subsidiaries

Consortia, banks owned by several parent banks, have never played a large role in the presence of foreign banks in the US. This form was really a child of the late 1960s to the early 1980s, having peaked in popularity in the early 1970s.

The Federal Reserve data does not distinguish between affiliates and subsidiaries, as it takes a 25 per cent ownership stake as its dividing line for reporting purposes. There are many examples of foreign banks acquiring a minority position in a US bank. Usually these appear to be passive investments, the motive for which is idiosyncratic to the transaction. However, the most important equity presences of foreign banks, especially the ones we discuss below, are (almost) all subsidiaries.

The largest affiliates or subsidiaries

From Table 8.4 it is apparent that the five largest banks control 67 per cent of all the banking system assets accounted for by affiliates and subsidiaries of foreign banks. The next five account for 18 per cent of the assets. Thus the ten largest banks account for 86 per cent of all assets in affiliates and subsidiaries. The largest banks are almost all subsidiaries

Table 8.4 Concentration in the ownership of assets of foreign bank subsidiaries and affiliates, 1999

		Headquarters		*Parent Bank*		*Subsidiary assets*	
Rank	*US subsidiary*	*City*	*State*	*Name*	*World Rank*[a]	*(US$bn)*	*(% of Total)*
1	HSBC Bank USA	Buffalo	NY	HSBC	3	82.3	24
2	Bankers Trust	New York	NY	Deutsche Bank	18	46.3	14
3	LaSalle Bank	Chicago	IL	ABN AMRO	16	46.2	14
4	Union Bank of California	San Francisco	CA	Bank of Tokyo-Mitsubishi	4	33.1	10
5	Harris Trust	Chicago	IL	Bank of Montreal	63	20.5	6
	Top 5					*228.4*	*67*
6	AllFirst Bank	Baltimore	MD	Allied Irish	115	16.2	4
7	European American Bank	New York	NY	ABN AMRO	16	15.0	4
8	Michigan National	Farmington Hills	MI	National Australia Bank[b]	43	11.4	3
9	Bank of the West	San Francisco	CA	BNP Paribas	14	10.2	3
10	Sanwa Bank California	San Francisco	CA	Sanwa Bank	11	9.0	3
	Second 5					*61.8*	*18*
	Top 10					*290.2*	*86*
	Total					339.3	100

Sources: Board of Governors of the Federal Reserve (Mar 2000); *The Banker* June 2000.

Notes

a In terms of total assets in 1999.

b In November 2000 NAB announced that it was selling Michigan National to ABN AMRO.

whose growth came about by acquisition, typically with one major acquisition accounting for the bulk of the story.

Of these ten banks, three are in New York and California, and two are in Illinois. These three states are populous, wealthy and have diversified economic bases. They are also the homes to the United States' three largest cities, and the homes to the three most important financial centres.

The parent banks tend to be among the largest banks in the world; six are among the top 20, two among the next 80, and the smallest is still the 115th largest bank in the world. Most of the growth of these subsidiaries and affiliates is due to the acquisition, in the 1970s, or later, of one large domestic bank, supplemented by further acquisition. Although their growth is recent, three of the parents have been in the US since the nineteenth century, two entered during the first half of the twentieth century, and four entered since then.

Generally, the parent banks did not acquire their subsidiaries in order to achieve any learning. As Tschoegl (1987) argues, retail banking is an industry in which one should not expect foreign banks to possess any advantage vis-à-vis their local competitors. Instead, the foreign banks appear to have acquired their subsidiaries as part of a strategy of establishing a base in the US, to profit from the rehabilitation of their acquisitions. The one exception among the top ten subsidiaries is Deutsche Bank's acquisition of Bankers Trust. Deutsche Bank is attempting to build its international investment banking capability and the acquisition of Bankers Trust represented an attempt to acquire expertise. Bankers Trust is an interesting case: in the 1970s it had itself divested itself of its retail banking activities and had embarked on a reasonably successful attempt to transform itself into an investment bank.

A number of home countries are noteworthy for their absence. With the exception of Deutsche Bank, the major Swiss and German banks have eschewed forays into retail banking. All are universal banks and several had securities affiliates in New York. The banks feared that acquiring retail banks would push the Federal Reserve's tolerance to the limit, given the then separation between securities activities and commercial banking mandated of US banks by the Glass-Steagall Act. The British had a substantial presence but no longer do so. They withdrew after experiencing performance that ranged from mediocre at best to disastrous at worst (Jones 1993; Rodgers 1999).

The role and contribution of the foreign banks

A number of foreign banks established subsidiaries in the US to provide retail-banking services to emigrants from the bank's home country, or their descendants, and other co-ethnics. Examples include banks from Hong Kong, Greece, Israel, Japan, Korea, and the Philippines.

Some of these banks, such as the National Bank of Greece's Atlantic

Bank (which dates its origins back to the Bank of Athens Trust Company, established in 1926), or the Korean or Philippine banks (which arrived more recently), have not grown beyond their ethnic niches. At the other extreme, banks such as Bank of Tokyo-Mitsubishi and HSBC have retained their ethnic banking roots while growing well beyond them. In between are banks such as Sumitomo Bank of California. Like Bank of Tokyo, Sumitomo Bank re-entered California in 1953 to serve Japanese-Americans. At the time of the bank's sale to Zion Bancorp in 1998, 45 per cent of the depositors still were Japanese-Americans (Domis 1998). The contribution of the ethnic banks is clear: they provide immigrant communities with banking services that are more tailored to their needs than host country banks can or perhaps choose to provide. Customer service issues include matters of culture, language, and remittance facilities.

The foreign banks that have grown beyond their ethnic niche, or that have never attempted to serve an ethnic clientele, appear to behave just like domestic banks. The newspaper accounts of some of the more notable acquisitions, such as Bank of Tokyo's acquisition of Union Bank, are replete with quotes from Japanese executives assuring the public that nothing will change as a result of the change of ownership. All the evidence suggests that the foreign-owned subsidiaries are indistinguishable in their behaviour from the domestic banks. For instance, Aaker (1990) found that the Japanese banks in California chose not to export the Japanese service industry's culture and programmes. Instead, the Japanese firms tended to compete very much like American firms. The Japanese managers he interviewed doubted the feasibility and lacked the motivation to introduce 'the Japanese way' in the United States.

Unlike the case of the branches and agencies, it is clear from the data in Table 8.1 that, both in terms of assets and business loans, the subsidiaries of foreign banks did not exhibit growth and peaking. Assets have grown 63 times and business loans 35 times since 1973 and, in absolute terms, for both quantities 1999 represents the high. However, the shares of total assets or business loans appear to have reached a steady state in the early 1980s, at about 4 per cent and 6 per cent, respectively.

The largest foreign subsidiaries have grown by acquisition. This is part of a more general phenomenon. As Lichtenberg and Siegel (1987) argue, firms rearrange ownership of assets through the purchase and sale of operations. A firm lacking a comparative advantage with respect to a given operation will sell it to another firm. This process may lead both to internationalization by acquisition, and to exit by divestiture. As we have seen above, foreign banks have been on both sides of the process. They have bought operations, and some have subsequently sold them, having perhaps demonstrated to themselves that they did not have the comparative advantage they thought they did.

Numerous relatively recent studies have documented that foreign-owned banks are not as profitable as their domestic peers (e.g. Seth 1992 and Nolle 1995). Nolle also found that foreign-owned banks tended to be less cost-efficient than their domestic peers. DeYoung and Nolle (1996) pushed the issue further and found that the lack of profitability stemmed from the foreign banks' dependency on purchased funds. These findings are also consistent with earlier work (e.g. Hodgkins and Goldberg 1981 and Houpt 1983). Peek *et al.* (1999) find that the poor performance of foreign bank subsidiaries was not a result of the acquisition but that the banks' problems predated the acquisition. The foreign banks were generally simply unsuccessful at raising the acquired banks' performance levels to those of their domestic peers.

The first part of the story, that foreign banks tended to acquire poorly performing domestic banks, is clear. Such banks probably appeared cheap, as shareholders would have welcomed any offer in the absence of signs that existing management had credible plans to turn the banks around. The foreign acquirers, for their part, may have overestimated their own abilities and underestimated the scope of the problem. However, as Peek and his co-authors note, one must be careful about inferring too much from these studies of profitability. Reported profits are vulnerable to transfer pricing. DeYoung and Nolle (1996) found that foreign-owned banks tended to buy market share by offering good rates to high quality borrowers, and funded the loans through the use of bought funds. This ties in with Tschoegl's point (1988) that small adjustments to the interest rate paid on 'due to parent and affiliates' accounts could serve to transfer profits abroad.

One can find anecdotes of cases in which the acquired banks introduced innovations in retail or commercial banking products transferred from the parent after the acquisition. For example, Michigan National introduced a home mortgage product with numerous novel features after its acquisition by NAB (Serju 1997). Furthermore, Michigan National is attempting to build on this by acquiring HomeSide Inc., the Florida-based but nationwide producer and servicer of residential mortgages. However, we do not know if, one-time transfers aside, foreign-owned banks are any more (or less) innovative than domestically-owned ones. There has simply been no study that has attempted to define innovations in commercial banking and then determine whether there is a difference in the rate of innovation between the two types of banks.

Rosenzweig (1994), in one of the few extant studies of the problems confronting foreign firms seeking to operate in the US, identified two sets of problems at entry – the scale of the US market and its competitiveness – and three sets of problems post-entry, which he called the managerial, cultural and organizational. The scale of the US market is such that even the largest foreign banks have only a minor market share. Furthermore, to achieve scale, foreign banks often found themselves acquiring troubled banks that they they could not successfully rehabilitate (see below). With respect to competitiveness, we have already remarked that there was no reason to believe that the foreign banks could bring any special, durable advantage that would offset the liability of operating at a distance and in an unfamiliar environment. The post-entry managerial problem Rosenzweig identified was the difficulty in inducing high-calibre US managers to remain with or to join the subsidiaries. The cultural problem was related to this, and is the problem of managing the US managers' desire for independence. The US managers see their career development as involving a sequence of different firms, in part because of the low probability of achieving senior positions in the head offices of the foreign parent; they therefore desire autonomy in order to make their own mark, and in turn signal their abilities to their next employer. Giving the US managers too little autonomy led to a reduced ability to hire the best people; giving them too much could lead to disasters such as Midland Bank's massive losses on its acquisition of Crocker Bank (Jones 1993). The last problem Rosenzweig mentions, the organizational challenge of balancing integration and independence, is less of an issue in retail banking because it is, to a great degree, a multidomestic industry.

Perhaps the most important long-run impact the subsidiaries of foreign banks had on the US financial system was to force the pace of deregulation of interstate banking. As already mentioned, one problem was the loophole that the 1978 IBA closed. However, there was a more interesting problem. In those states that permitted foreign banks to acquire local banks, a foreign bank was frequently the only viable purchaser of local banks that were on the block. All US banks from other states were automatically barred from the sale. Frequently the largest local banks were not viable acquirers for anti-trust reasons. Small local banks might be unwilling or unable to take on the task, especially when the bank to be acquired was larger than they, and in difficulties. Hence, permitting a large, foreign bank to make the acquisition was often the only viable solution. The foreign bank would have the resources to rehabilitate the acquisition, and its entry would enhance competition rather than reduce it. However, the large, out-of-state US banks that were shut out of the bidding, objected. They argued that, because they were excluded from the bidding, the foreign bank was generally unopposed and that therefore shareholders of the acquired bank were not necessarily getting the best price. In time, this argument, together with a general trend towards deregulation, had its effect.

Conclusion

Although the total assets and business loans of foreign banks continue to grow, their shares of total domestic banking systems assets or business loans are off the peaks achieved in 1992. To understand this evolution it is necessary to examine separately the operations of the integral forms of foreign presence (representative offices, agencies and branches) and the equity forms (affiliates and subsidiaries).

The 1992 peak in the foreign banks' shares is due entirely to the activities of branches and agencies, and in particular to those of the Japanese banks. The bubble economy resulted in the Japanese banks having excess capital and hence lending capacity, which they deployed in the US. When the bubble burst, the Japanese banks cut back their lending, reducing credit availability in the US. However, the long-run contribution of the foreign banks is in the development of financial centres throughout the US, making specialized services more accessible to smaller firms. In this process, foreign banks have contributed to the development of the financial sector in the southern half of the US, especially Los Angeles, Texas and Miami.

As far as equity forms are concerned, nine parent banks and nine subsidiaries and one affiliate account for 86 per cent of all the assets in foreign banks' affiliates and subsidiaries. Although foreign banks have bought and sold subsidiaries and their positions in affiliates, the share of these banks in total domestic bank assets and business loans has been small and constant since the early 1980s. The foreign banks have contributed innovation and competition, especially in the market for control given the then rigidities in US law. Long-run, arguably the most important contribution of these banks has been to speed the deregulation of US banking, especially the dismantling of the barriers to interstate banking.

Notes

1 I would like to thank Lina Gálvez-Muñoz, Geoffrey Jones, Mira Wilkins, and the other participants at this conference for helpful comments on the previous draft. All errors and flaws remain my responsibility.

2 Japanese banks held large portfolios of stocks in companies or in their customers. Under the Basle rules, the Japanese banks could count 40 per cent of the unrealized capital gains on these shares as part of their capital base.

3 The US banks' LDC lending was particularly heavily weighted towards Latin America. The Japanese banks' LDC lending was particularly heavily weighted towards Asia. Latin America suffered a 'lost decade' from 1982 on. Asia saw the growth of the '4 tigers' until the Asian Crisis of 1997.

4 Loans to or deposits from non-banks at US banks' offices in the Bahamas and Cayman Islands were stable and very small throughout the 1983–92 period.

References

Aaker, D.A. (1990) 'How will the Japanese compete in retail services?', *California Management Review* 33, 1: 54–67.

Baer, H.L. (1990) 'Foreign competition in U.S. banking markets', *Fed. Res. Bank of Chicago Economic Perspectives* 14, 3: 22–9.

Ball, M. (1994) 'The 1980s property boom', *Environment and Planning A* 26: 671–95.

Bartholomew, P.F. (1994) 'Comparing depository institution difficulties in Canada, the United States, and the Nordic countries', *Journal of Housing Research* 5, 2: 303–9.

Cho, K.R., Krishnan, S. and Nigh, D. (1987) 'The state of foreign banking presence in the United States', *International Journal of Bank Marketing* 5, 59–75.

Choi, S.R., Park, D. and Tschoegl, A.E. (1996) 'Banks and the world's major banking centers, 1990', *Weltwirtschaftliches Archiv* 132: 774–93.

Choi, S.R., Tschoegl, A.E. and Yu, C.M. (1986) 'Banks and the world's major financial centers, 1970–1980', *Weltwirtschaftliches Archiv* 122: 48–64.

DeYoung, R. and Nolle, D.E. (1996) 'Foreign banks in the United States: Earning market share or buying it', *Journal of Money, Credit and Banking* 28: 622–36.

Denison, M. (1967) *Canada's First Bank: A History of the Bank of Montreal*, New York: Dodd, Mead.

Domis, O. (1998) 'Utah's Zions to buy Sumitomo of Calif. for 1.3 times book', *American Banker* March 27: 1.

Engwall, L. (1992) 'Barriers in international banking networks', in M. Forsgren and J. Johanson (eds) *Managing Networks in International Business*, Philadelphia: Gordon and Breach: 167–77.

Goldberg, L.G. (1992) 'The competitive impact of foreign commercial banks in the United States', in R.A. Gilbert (ed.) *The Changing Market in Financial Services*, New York: Kluwer Academic Press.

Grosfoguel, R. (1995) 'Global logics in the Caribbean city system: The case of Miami', in P.L. Knox and P.J. Taylor (eds) *World Cities in a World System*, Cambridge: Cambridge University Press.

Grubel, H. (1977) 'A theory of multinational banking', *Banca Nazionale del Lavoro Quarterly Review* 29: 349–63.

Heinkel, R.L. and Levi, M.D. (1992) 'The structure of international banking', *Journal of International Money and Finance* 16: 251–72.

Hodgkins, B.B. and Goldberg, E.S. (1981) 'Effects of foreign acquisitions on the balance sheet structure and earnings performance of US banks: Trends and effects', in R.F. Dame (ed.) *Foreign Acquisitions of US Banks*, Richmond, VA: US Comptroller of the Currency: 401–30.

Houpt, J.V. (1983) 'Foreign ownership of US banks: trends and effects', *Journal of Bank Research* 14: 144–56.

Hultman, C.W. (1987) 'The foreign banking presence: Some cost-benefit factors', *Banking Law Journal* 104, 4: 339–49.

—— (1997) 'Foreign banks and the U.S. Regulatory Environment', *Banking Law Journal* 114, 5: 452–63.

James, F.C. (1938) *The Growth of the Chicago Banks*, New York: Harper.

Jones, G. (1993) *British Multinational Banking, 1830–1990*, Oxford: Clarendon Press.

Laderman, E.S. (23 April 1999) 'The shrinking of Japanese branch business lending in California', *FRBSF Economic Letter* No. 99, 14.

Lichtenberg, F.R. and Siegel, D. (1987) 'Productivity and changes in ownership of manufacturing plants', *Brookings Papers on Economic Activity* 3: 643–73.

McCauley, R.N. and Seth, R. (1992) 'Foreign bank credit to US corporations: the implications of offshore loans', *Federal Reserve Bank of New York Quarterly Review* 17: 52–65.

Molyneux, P. and Seth, R. (1998) 'Foreign banks, profits and commercial credit extension in the United States', *Applied Financial Economics* 8: 533–9.

Nolle, D.E. (1995) 'Foreign bank operations in the United States: Cause for concern?', in H.P. Gray and S.C. Richard (eds) *International Finance in the New World Order*, London: Pergamon: 269–91.

Óhuallacháin, B. (1994) 'Foreign banking in the American urban system of financial organization', *Economic Geography* 70: 206–28.

Pauly, L.W. (1988) *Opening Financial Markets: Banking Politics on the Pacific Rim*, Ithaca: Cornell University Press.

Peek, J. and Rosengren, E.S. (1997) 'The international transmission of financial shocks: The case of Japan', *American Economic Review* 87, 4: 495–505.

—— (2000) 'Collateral damage: Effects of the Japanese bank crisis on real activity in the United States', *American Economic Review* 90, 1: 30–45.

Peek, J., Rosengren, E.S. and Kasirye, F. (1999) 'The poor performance of foreign bank subsidiaries: Were the problems acquired or created?' *Journal of Banking and Finance* 23: 579–604.

Rodgers, D. (1999) *The Big Four British Banks: Organization, Strategy and the Future*, London: St. Martin's Press.

Rosen, R.D. and Murray, R. (1997) 'Opening doors: Access to the global market for financial sectors', in M.E. Grahan and A. Vourvoulas-Bush (eds) *The City and the World: New York's Global Future*, New York: Council on Foreign Relations.

Rosenzweig, P.M. (1994) 'The new "American challenge": Foreign multinationals in the United States', *California Management Review* 36, 3: 107–23.

Scher, M.J. and Beechler, S. (July 1993) 'The internationalization of Japanese financial institutions: What went wrong?', Columbia University, unpublished paper.

Serju, T. (1997) '"Tailored home loan" gives you flexibility', *Detroit News* May 20: C5.

Seth, R. (1992) 'Profitability of foreign banks in the United States', Federal Reserve Bank of New York Research Paper, No. 9225.

Shrieves, R.E. and Dahl, D. (2000) 'Determinants of international credit allocation: An analysis of US lending by Japanese banks, 1988 to 1994', *Pacific Basin Finance Journal* 8, 1: 25–52.

Tamagna, F.M. (1959) 'New York as an international money market', *Banca Nazionale del Lavoro Quarterly Review* 49: 201–34.

Terrell, H.S. (1993) 'US branches and agencies of foreign banks: A new look', *Federal Reserve Bulletin* 79: 913–25.

Tschoegl, A.E. (1981) *The Regulation of Foreign Banks: Policy Formation in Countries Outside the United States*, New York University Salomon Brothers Center for the Study of Financial Institutions, monograph 1981–2.

—— (1987) 'International retail banking as a strategy: An assessment', *Journal of International Business Studies* 19, 2: 67–88.

—— (1988) 'Foreign banks in Japan', Bank of Japan, Institute for Monetary and Economic Studies, *Monetary and Economic Studies* 6, 1: 93–118.

—— (1999) 'National and firm sources of international competitiveness: The case of the foreign exchange market', The Wharton School: unpublished paper.

Wilkins, M. (1979) *Foreign Enterprises in Florida: The Impact of Non-U.S. Direct Investment*, Miami: University Presses of Florida.

—— (1980) *New Foreign Enterprise in Florida*, Miami: Greater Miami Chamber of Commerce.

—— (1989) *The History of Foreign Investment in the United States to 1914*, Cambridge, Mass: Harvard University Press.

9 OLI and OIL

BP in the US in theory and practice, 1968–98

James Bamberg

How does OLI apply to OIL? That is the question that this chapter addresses in applying theories of transnational corporations to BP's experience as a major foreign direct investor in the US. The theoretical elements in the paper come from John Dunning's 'eclectic paradigm', which argues that the impetus for firms to engage in international operations comes from the OLI combination of ownership (O), locational (L), and internalization (I) advantages (Dunning 1977, 2000). Ownership and internalization advantages belong to firms, while locational advantages belong to countries. The ownership advantages of firms, commonly called competitive advantages, stem from their possession of distinctive skills and assets such as superior technology, powerful brands, privileged access to raw materials, or management skills. Internalization advantages are derived from using internal administrative processes to effect transactions within the firm – for example, transfers of intermediate products, or of know-how – more efficiently than can be achieved in imperfect external markets. Locational advantages arise from the comparative endowments of different countries, such as cheap labour, plentiful natural resources, or growing markets.

The empirical evidence is drawn from research into BP's archives and interviews with BP managers on BP's large-scale entry into the US in 1968–70, and its subsequent expansion and consolidation in the US up to 1998.

Background

By the time that BP made its entry into the US, the company was already long-established as a major international corporation. Formed in 1909 to develop the oil resources of Persia, BP quickly developed into an international oil major, one of the famous 'Seven Sisters' which came to dominate the international oil industry (Ferrier 1982; Bamberg 1994, 2000; Sampson 1975). BP's international operations were based on all three of the ownership, internalization and locational advantages in the eclectic paradigm. Oil-producing countries, prospective and actual, attracted BP because of their favourable geology and ample oil reserves (i.e. locational advantages) which BP could exploit because of its ownership advantages of capital, technology, managerial capabilities, oil exploration skills, and access to markets. Oil-consuming countries had the locational advantage of ready markets, to which BP could bring its ownership advantage of access to plentiful supplies of low-cost oil. Equally, if not even more striking, were the internalization advantages which BP and the other major international oil companies gained through horizontal and, above all, vertical integration. BP and the other oil majors developed the strategy of vertical integration almost to perfection. As a result the international flow of oil, from oil fields through refineries and on to the final consumer, was channelled through the internal circuits of the majors' vertically integrated systems. Internal transfers took the place of intermediate product markets almost completely (Penrose 1968).

By the late 1960s BP had developed a highly centralized and integrated system of international operations, but was not by any means a global company. BP was essentially a national company with international operations, retaining a strongly British national identity, with a managerial hierarchy in which virtually all the senior positions were filled by Britons (Bamberg 2000: 4, 16–17, 71–3, 326, 328). In its overseas operations it was to a large degree a company of two regions: the Middle East for upstream oil production, and Western Europe for downstream markets (Bamberg 2000: 226). It was, most importantly for this paper, the only one of the oil majors which had no substantial presence in the US, a country which possessed unrivalled locational attractions (Bamberg 2000: 224).

Locational attractions of the US

The US was both a major oil producing and consuming country. Until the mid-twentieth century its production exceeded its consumption, and the US was a substantial oil exporter. By the 1950s, however, the US had became a net oil importer (Odell 1983: 38, 75). In 1958 BP, seeking markets for its vast reserves of low-cost Middle East oil, formed an alliance with the Sinclair Oil Corporation, the seventh-largest US oil company, which possessed a large downstream network in the US, but was short of crude oil. The primary purpose of the alliance was for BP to supply Sinclair with Middle East crude oil for refining and marketing in the US. This purpose was, however, soon frustrated by the US's adoption of mandatory oil import quotas in 1959, which placed restrictions on oil imports (Bamberg 2000: 122).

The introduction of the import quotas protected the world's largest oil market from low-cost oil imports and helped to make it a highly profitable place to be in the oil business, especially in comparison with the unprotected oil markets of Western Europe where competition was exerting strong downward pressure on prices and profits (Odell 1983: 40; Jacoby

1974: 141–3; Tugendhat and Hamilton 1975: 158). The US's combination of size and profitability, coupled with political stability and a private enterprise culture, made it the most desirable country in the world for investment by the oil majors. No other country offered comparable locational attractions. BP's absence from this most desirable location placed it at a substantial competitive disadvantage in relation to the other oil majors (Bamberg 2000: 271).

BP's entry into the US, 1968–70: agreement with Sohio

Although the BP Sinclair alliance was frustrated in its aim of importing large quantities of Middle East oil to the US, it also provided for the two companies to set up a joint exploration company to explore for oil in the western hemisphere (Bamberg 2000: 122). One of the areas they explored was Alaska. Disappointed by lack of early success, Sinclair decided against participating in bidding for acreage at Prudhoe Bay on the Arctic North Slope of Alaska. BP therefore went ahead on its own, securing large acreage at Prudhoe Bay, where the largest oil field ever found in the US was discovered in 1968–9. BP's possession of more than half of the supergiant Prudhoe Bay oil field gave it a powerful ownership advantage in the US (Bamberg 2000: 188–95).

BP, however, recognized that it lacked other ownership advantages that would be needed to fulfil its strategy of setting up a vertically integrated oil operation in the US. First, BP lacked the financial capacity that would be needed to develop its Alaskan reserves, to construct transportation facilities and to establish refining and marketing operations. Second, BP lacked an established US managerial organization capable of undertaking a large-scale entry into the US market. Third, BP was conscious of the need to assuage American worries that a large share of US oil reserves was falling into the hands of a foreign company. For these reasons, BP decided that it should commercialize its Alaskan oil reserves through the vehicle of a US company which possessed the ownership advantages of knowledge of the US market, strong management capabilities, financial strength, and a widespread American shareholding which would give some protection against anti-foreign sentiment.

After discussions with several US oil companies, BP came to an agreement in 1969 with Standard Oil of Ohio (Sohio), whose ownership advantages were complementary to those of BP. Although Sohio was engaged in a range of diversified activities, its core business was as a regional refiner and marketer in the state of Ohio, where Sohio held the dominant share (about 30 per cent) of the gasoline market, the fourth largest gasoline market in the US. Sohio was renowned as an efficient marketer, its management was highly regarded, it had about 50,000 US shareholders, and it was financially strong. Its main weakness was that it lacked its own crude oil reserves. The basis of the agreement between the two companies was therefore to combine BP's ownership advantages in the upstream sector, in which it possessed large crude oil reserves and strong exploration and production skills, with Sohio's ownership advantages of downstream know-how, strong US management, financial strength, and widespread American shareholders.

The agreement between the two companies came into effect at the beginning of 1970, when BP's part of the Prudhoe Bay oil field plus some ex-Sinclair downstream assets that BP had acquired in 1968 were transferred to Sohio. In return, BP received an immediate equity stake of 25 per cent in Sohio on the basis that this would rise by stages to a maximum of 54 per cent as Sohio's crude production from Prudhoe Bay increased to 600,000 barrels per day (Bamberg 2000: 272–8). Significantly, BP Alaska Inc., a wholly-owned subsidiary of BP, would continue as the operator of the part of the Prudhoe Bay oil field that was transferred to Sohio. BP's know-how in the Alaskan upstream sector would not therefore be lost. In addition, BP would be entitled to nominate at least two members of Sohio's board of directors (BP archives 10394, agreement 7 Aug. 1969; 81276, agreement 1 Aug. 1969).

While the agreement between BP and Sohio brought together their complementary ownership advantages, the prospects of realizing internalization advantages were constrained by Sohio's determination to retain its managerial independence and by American legal constraints. One of the negotiators of the agreement between the two companies later recalled that 'one of the most fiercely discussed items between BP and Sohio at the time of the proposed merger was the concern of Sohio that BP would wish to "interfere" with the day-to-day management of Sohio' (BP archives 10513, Adam 18 Aug. 1975). Sohio insisted, according to another BP negotiator, on 'very clear understandings about independence of management', for which US law provided substantial props.

In the US the relationship between a company and a partly-owned subsidiary was a legal minefield (BP archives 10514, Koerner 30 Aug. 1977; 10515, Carter 8 Oct. 1980; BP legal file on Project Swan Lake, Sullivan and Cromwell 13 Nov. 1980, Stapleton 28 Oct. 1983, Walder 6 Feb. 1984). Substantial barriers to internalization arose from the rights of minority shareholders, and from anti-trust laws. With regard to shareholders, a large or majority shareholder was under an obligation not to exercise its power over its partly-owned subsidiary to its own advantage and to the disadvantage of the minority shareholders. A minority shareholder who considered that the majority shareholder had taken wrongful advantage of its position could bring a law suit against the majority shareholder and against the directors on the subsidiary's board who had participated in the wrongful action. Minority shareholders' suits were most likely to be brought on the grounds that the major shareholder and the partly-owned subsidiary had entered into a transaction that was not fair to the minority shareholders, or that the major shareholder had usurped a business opportunity from its partly-owned subsidiary. For a transaction between a company and a partly-owned subsidiary to be fair, it had to be on terms which were as favourable to the subsidiary as would have been the case if the subsidiary had been dealing at arm's length with a third party. So far as corporate opportunity was concerned, it was unlawful for the parent company to use information obtained from the partly-owned subsidiary to take up a business opportunity which properly belonged to the subsidiary.

The US anti-trust laws also had to be taken into account in parent-subsidiary relations. Under the Sherman Act any combination or conspiracy in restraint of trade was unlawful. By definition, a single entity could not conspire or combine to restrain trade with itself. However, US legal precedents were not clear on the extent to which a company and its partly-owned subsidiary constituted a single entity for anti-trust purposes. If they were considered to be separate actors, it would be unlawful for a company and a partly-owned subsidiary to reach agreement between themselves on, say, prices or the division of markets.

There were precautions that could be taken by the parent company to reduce its exposure to minority shareholders' and/or anti-trust actions. For example, as long as transactions between the parent and its partly-owned subsidiary were negotiated at arm's length, as between third parties in an external market, it was unlikely that they would be challenged as being unfair to a subsidiary's minority shareholders. Other precautions against legal problems could also be taken. For example, the risk of corporate opportunity law suits could be reduced if there was a demonstrable restraint on exposure of the subsidiary's business opportunities to personnel in the parent company's organization. Another precaution against usurpation of opportunities was to avoid any overlapping activities by, for example, confining the parent company's and the subsidiary's respective operations to mutually exclusive geographical areas. However, while that would remove the possibilities of the parent usurping the subsidiary's opportunities, the agreement not to compete might itself constitute a conspiracy in restraint of trade, causing anti-trust problems. There were, therefore, some contradictions in the legal situation. On the whole, however, it could be said that the legal system militated strongly against the realization of internalization advantages between a company and its partly-owned subsidiary. The more arm's length the relationship, the less was the likelihood of encountering legal problems.

Although these legal considerations were important, there was no requirement that they should be mentioned specifically in the agreement between BP and Sohio. Nevertheless the agreement stated unambiguously that:

> The Board of Directors of Sohio and the Sohio officers elected by it shall have complete independence to discharge their duties in the interest of all Sohio stockholders including without limitation the

> right to develop and implement operating programs and related budgets, the right to determine appropriate financing programs, the right to determine all organizational and personnel matters, including management assignments, compensation and employee benefit plans, and the right to develop and implement marketing programs.
>
> (BP archives 10394, agreement 7 Aug. 1969)

The inclusion of this wording was indicative of the importance that Sohio attached to retaining its managerial independence.

In addition to this declaration of Sohio's independence, the two companies reached an unwritten agreement that Sohio should be BP's 'chosen instrument' in the US. The basis of the chosen instrument policy was that BP and Sohio would not overlap in their activities. BP would channel all its main activities in the US through Sohio, while Sohio would keep out of international operations (Adam, R.W. 1986, interview, 12 Aug.). The activities of the BP Group inside and outside the US would therefore be conducted by separate managements, operating at arm's length in segregated geographical zones. BP's entry into the US via its agreement with Sohio was thus based on a combination of locational and ownership advantages, but with a virtual prohibition on the internal transfers and transactions that are the stuff of internalization theory.

BP as minority shareholder in Sohio, 1970–8

After the BP–Sohio agreement came into effect at the beginning of 1970 BP initially appointed two nominees to Sohio's board as non-executive directors, adding a third in 1972 (BP archives 18589, Information Department 23 Jan. 1970; 10385, BP New York telegram 28 Apr. 1972). Below board level there was extremely little contact between Sohio and BP managers, and BP adopted a 'hands-off' policy towards Sohio's operations (e.g. BP archives 10254, Robertson 10 Jul. 1973, Frampton 14 Dec. 1973). At times, BP managers felt frustrated at the virtual ban on sharing knowledge and expertise between the two companies (e.g. BP archives 10495, Cazalet 7 Aug. 1974); but although BP and Sohio were separately managed, the absence of internalization advantages did not seem to trouble BP.

There were several reasons for this. First, the US domestic oil industry, protected by import quotas, was not integrated into the international oil industry. BP was not, therefore, seeking to integrate Sohio's operations into BP's highly centralized and integrated international operations. Second, BP and Sohio shared a common strategic interest in bringing the Prudhoe Bay oil field into commercial production as soon as possible. One of the features of this project was that it was an extremely large project in relation to the size of the firm undertaking it. Sohio was fully stretched, at times overstretched, managerially and financially, by the project. With its resources fully committed, Sohio had very little scope to enter into other substantial projects. So although Sohio was managed separately from the rest of the BP Group, there was little prospect of its going its own separate way. Both BP and Sohio were effectively tied into the same strategic goal. Third, BP remained responsible, through BP Alaska, for operations at Prudhoe Bay. BP therefore retained managerial control of this crucial upstream area, in which BP possessed much more expertise than Sohio.

There were, to be sure, some moments when Sohio's ability to bring the Prudhoe Bay project to fruition seemed to be in doubt, primarily because environmental concerns caused steep escalation in the costs of constructing the trans-Alaska pipeline, which was to transport crude oil from the Arctic North Slope of Alaska to a warm water terminal 800 miles to the south in the Gulf of Alaska (Roscow 1977; BP archives 10394, Whitehouse 31 Aug. 1970; 10388, Spahr 24 Apr. 1975). But despite the severe financial and managerial strains, the development of Prudhoe Bay was successfully completed, and the oil field was brought into production in 1977 (Roscow 1977: 199–204). Under the terms of the BP–Sohio agreement, as production from Prudhoe Bay increased, so did BP's shareholding in Sohio, and in June 1978 BP became Sohio's majority shareholder (BP archives 10514, BP press release 23 Aug. 1978). The aims of the original agreement between the two companies had thus been achieved, and Sohio was consolidated into BP's annual accounts in the same way as other subsidiaries in which BP held a majority shareholding. Consolidation into the accounts was, however, a far cry from integration into the BP Group, from which Sohio continued to stand apart.

The 'Chinese wall'

Discussions on what form the BP–Sohio relationship should take after BP gained its majority shareholding had already taken place before the majority shareholding became a reality. One decision was that BP Alaska, the wholly-owned BP subsidiary that operated Sohio's part of the Prudhoe Bay field, would be merged into Sohio. This was implemented at the beginning of 1978, when BP Alaska's staff were transferred to Sohio (Standard Oil Company 1977; BP archives 10495, Adam 26 Sep. 1974). As a result, BP was no longer involved in operating Sohio's part of the Prudhoe Bay oil field.

In agreeing to the merger of BP Alaska into Sohio, BP was naturally concerned to ensure that Sohio's management was as strong as possible. BP therefore sought to implant senior BP managers in some key positions in Sohio, and to establish the principle that there should be staff secondments and exchanges between the two companies. Sohio's attitude towards staff exchanges was, however, for the most part negative. BP did succeed in placing one of its top exploration and production executives on Sohio's board as the director in charge of Sohio's upstream activities, though significantly the executive concerned was required to give up his employment with BP and to become an employee of Sohio. BP also secured the appointment of one of its senior executives as president of Sohio Petroleum Company, the successor organization to BP Alaska. But BP did not succeed in securing the appointment of another senior BP executive to take charge of Sohio's oil supply and transportation operations. Sohio's top management opposed the appointment, and indeed the general principle of management transfers between the two companies, arguing that the transfer of BP executives to Sohio would cause discontent, and be seen as an attempt by BP to use its position as majority shareholder to dictate to Sohio. The scope for internal transfers of human resources, and the accompanying transmission of expertise, between BP and Sohio was therefore far from fully realized (BP archives 10379, Adam 7 Oct. 1975; 10380, Adam 25 Mar. 1976, Manson 3 Jun. 1976, Sohio news service 11 Nov. 1976; 10382, Whitehouse 17 Aug. 1976, Manson 17 May 1977, Adam 19 Sep. and 29 Dec. 1977, Cazalet 18 Nov. 1977; 10513, Spahr 14 May 1976, Manson 19 May and 10 Jun. 1976; 10514, Adam 9 Jan. 1978; Bexon, R. 1986, interview, 8 Oct.).

Similar obstacles to realizing internalization advantages were encountered by BP when it sought to integrate BP's and Sohio's capital investment planning. In 1977, with BP's attainment of a majority shareholding in prospect, a series of meetings was held between senior planners from BP and Sohio. Their basic purpose was to correlate the planning cycles of the two companies so that Sohio's planning procedures would mesh with those of BP. Sohio's planners appeared happy with this idea, but before it was implemented a top-level Sohio executive asked for a legal opinion on the grounds that a diminution in the role of Sohio's management was implicit in the proposed planning procedures (BP archives 10379, Adam 7 Oct. 1975; 10380, Adam 25 Mar. 1976; 10514, King 16 Aug. 1977; BP CRO 5D 7194, Thomas 14 Jun. 1977, Nicholson 15 Mar. 10 Jun. and 29 Jul. 1977). The draft legal opinion suggested that the flow of information from Sohio to BP should be highly restricted in order to minimize exposure to the risk of legal action from minority shareholders, who might claim that BP had misused the shared information. It would be desirable, argued the legal opinion, for there to be a 'Chinese wall' preventing the dissemination of information about Sohio's plans within BP (BP archives 10514, Sheedy 12 Aug. 1977). Further legal advice taken by BP also emphasized the legal risks that were inherent in the relationship between BP and Sohio (BP archives 10514, Koerner 30 Aug. 1977, King 16 Sep. 1977, Adam 10 Nov. 1977 and 19 Jan. 1978).

In the light of this legal advice and the determination of Sohio's top management to preserve its managerial independence, an agreement on planning procedures was reached that fell well short of integration, and left BP with little access to information on investment projects that were proposed within Sohio. Specifically, Sohio was not required to produce the Developmental Plans that were required from other BP subsidiaries. Instead, Sohio produced its own Corporate Long Range Plans which were submitted to BP in October each year, before they were put before Sohio's board for formal approval. Sohio also produced an annual Capital Budget which was submitted to BP in December each year. The BP board did not have the right to approve or disapprove of Sohio's plans and budgets, but could authorize its nominees on Sohio's board to vote in favour of, or against them (BP archives 10514, Adam, 3 Aug. 19 Sep. 10 Nov. and 29 Dec. 1977; BP CRO 4K 3281 *passim*).

An important aspect of these arrangements was that Sohio's Capital Budgets did not necessarily include full technical or economic justifications for the capital projects included in the overall budget. Indeed, approval of the budget was not in itself an authorization to proceed with specific projects. Applications for such authorization were made separately, with full supporting detail, through submission of Authorization for Expenditure forms (AFEs) to Sohio's board. Although BP received Sohio's Capital Budgets in advance of their final approval by Sohio's board, BP did not have prior sight of AFEs before they were submitted to Sohio's board (BP archives 10515, unsigned 11 Jul. 1980; BP CRO 4K 3281, Walker n.d.). In practice, therefore, BP's planning and authorization procedures in relation to Sohio gave the parent company less opportunity to bring its expertise to bear on Sohio's investment decisions than was the case in BP's normal parent–subsidiary relationships. As a senior BP executive noted in 1980, 'the level of knowledge about the justification of Sohio's main projects is significantly lower than for comparable projects in other parts of the BP Group' (BP archives 10515, Gillam 17 Nov. 1980).

Internalization advantages depend not only on free internal transfers and sharing of personnel and information, but also on the existence of a culture of trust which reduces the friction and costs of internal transactions. In the case of BP and Sohio this was diminished as a result of a top-level management succession in Sohio at the beginning of 1978, which resulted in the appointment of a new chairman and chief executive officer of Sohio in whom BP lacked full confidence (BP archives 10379, Adam 7 Oct. 1975; 10380, Adam 25 Mar. 1976; 10406, Strathalmond 14 Sep. 1971; 27809, Belgrave 29 Apr. 1976). There were, therefore, strong barriers to internalization advantages between BP and Sohio as the time approached when BP would gain a majority shareholding in the American company.

BP as majority shareholder in Sohio, 1978–86

After the Prudhoe Bay oil field was brought into production in 1977 Sohio was transformed in a very short time from a regional refiner–marketer into one of the US's largest companies. By any measure the transformation was spectacular. In the space of just 5 years from 1976 (the last full year before Prudhoe Bay came on stream) Sohio's net income rose from $137 million to $1,947 million, its revenues from $3,174 million to $14,104 million, and its employees from 21,100 to 56,700 (Standard Oil Company 1985). In 1981 Sohio's estimated oil reserves in the US were higher than those of any other company, including even Exxon, and Sohio's crude oil production in the US was surpassed only by Exxon's (*Financial Times* 1983). In the same year, Sohio came sixth in the ranking of US industrial corporations by net income (*Fortune* 3 May 1982). Within the BP Group, Sohio was easily the most important subsidiary, accounting for 63 per cent of BP's estimated oil reserves, 58 per cent of the BP Group's consolidated net income, and 42 per cent of its capital employed (BP 1981).

The engine of growth behind this extraordinary rise was the giant Prudhoe Bay oil field, whose prolific production generated a torrent of cash. With crude oil prices at record levels (rising from $13 to $30–40 a barrel in 1979–80 when Iranian production was disrupted during the revolution that overthrew the Shah), Sohio enjoyed an unpredicted bonanza, but at the same time faced the extremely difficult strategic challenge of how to invest its suddenly inflated income to provide future growth in the years after the Prudhoe Bay oil field went into its inevitable decline.

Over the next few years it would become increasingly clear that Sohio lacked ownership advantages in this new situation. In what would prove to be a classic case of managerial limits to the growth of firms, the rapid expansion of Sohio's income outstripped the capacity of its managerial resources to create and sustain new growth opportunities. In the words of a report in *Business Week*:

> Trained to operate a company of decidedly shorter horizons, they [Sohio's management] have only general notions about what to do with their riches and have implemented no plans to maintain their magnitude. The company has ballooned in size so suddenly that it lacks the staff, expertise and investment vehicles to make decisive use of its money.
>
> (*Business Week* 25 Aug. 1980)

The much larger managerial resources of the BP Group might have helped to resolve this problem, but they were kept apart from Sohio by a continuing lack of integration, and even co-operation, between the two companies. The resultant failure to achieve internalization advantages for the BP Group as a whole was manifest in several episodes, and became an increasing cause for concern.

The lack of co-operation between Sohio and BP was well illustrated by the problems that were encountered with crude oil supplies in 1979–80. In that year, BP found itself short of crude oil owing to the disruption to supplies during the Iranian revolution and the takeover of BP's producing interests in Nigeria by the Nigerian government (BP 1979). Sohio, on the other hand, possessed a surplus of crude. BP therefore approached Sohio to see whether a purchase of crude oil from Sohio could be arranged. In making this approach, BP was not seeking specially favourable terms from its majority-owned US subsidiary. Sohio, however, raised various objections to the proposed transaction. For example, Sohio argued that there were political problems in selling crude oil to non-US customers; that there were legal issues involved, particularly concerning the reaction of Sohio's minority shareholders to an intra-Group crude oil transaction; that Sohio's own supply position was too uncertain for it to enter into a commitment to supply BP; and that Sohio should seek to dispose of its surplus crude, not by outright sale, but in return for future crude oil supplies or exploration interests. After 18 months and at least ten meetings with Sohio on the subject, BP had still failed to obtain any crude oil from Sohio by the end of 1980 (BP archives 12940 *passim*; 10515, Wright 10 Nov. 1980; BP 114235, Gillam 15 Dec. 1980). As one senior BP executive put it, 'it is easier dealing with Exxon' (BP archives 10515, Gillam 17 Nov. 1980).

Another problem in relations between BP and Sohio was the 'chosen instrument' policy under which Sohio was to be BP's sole vehicle for activities in the US. For the BP Group as a whole, the US continued to offer the unrivalled locational advantages of a large natural resource base and a large domestic market, coupled with political stability and a generally benign attitude towards private enterprise. These locational advantages made the US an area of central importance for the realization of some of the BP Group's strategic objectives. In instances where Sohio's plans did not meet Group objectives, BP increasingly sought to expand or to establish its own operations in the US.

Although BP's direct interests in the US were very small in comparison to Sohio's, there was nevertheless an emerging tendency for the BP Group's US operations to be run by two separate managements, one of BP, the other of Sohio. For example, in the upstream sector, BP, having been denied crude oil supplies by Sohio in 1979–80, felt that it needed its own direct participation in US production (BP CRO 1A 0222, unsigned 12 Jan. 1981, Bexon 18 Feb. 1981). Alaska was regarded as one of the most prospective areas for oil exploration in the non-communist world, offering a large unexplored acreage with the potential of major discoveries. Moreover, with long experience of Alaskan exploration, BP possessed a knowledge of the area that gave it a competitive advantage over other companies (BP archives 11876, Hulf 15 Oct. 1981; 92761, unsigned strategy review paper Nov. 1981). BP therefore expanded its exploration interests in Alaska, and also obtained a direct interest in Alaskan production after the Kuparuk field, in which BP held a stake of nearly 30 per cent, came into production in December 1981. BP thereby obtained direct access to Alaskan crude for the first time (Standard Oil Company 1981; BP 1981; BP CRO 1A 0222, Jones 3 Feb. 1981, Bexon 18 Feb. 1981, Butler 5 Jun. and 3 Jul. 1981; 7U 2223, Law department 15 Mar. 1984; BP archives 10294, Adam May 1982).

In the downstream sector, BP's direct US operations were expanded through the activities of a subsidiary, BP North America Trading, which planned to become, in the words of a draft US strategy review paper in 1981, 'a broad based marketer and transporter of petroleum products in competition with the independent sector' (BP CRO 8B 4374, US strategy review paper section 4 1981).

BP's non-oil businesses were also becoming increasingly interested in the US. For example, by November 1980 BP Coal was looking to take a direct stake in US coal production. In the words of a senior BP executive, BP Coal

> are unwilling to be locked out of the US market by a decision to designate Sohio the chosen vehicle for US coal investment. They feel the need to be established in the US, which is the most important coal country in the non-communist world, and with the greatest export potential, if they are to become a major international coal company and coal trader.
>
> (BP archives 90684, Ross 3 Nov. 1980)

Specifically, BP Coal sought to acquire a US coal company capable of producing up to 5 million tons of coal a year for export to Europe (BP CRO 8B 4374, US strategy review paper section 4 1981; BP archives 90684, Jump 12 Nov. 1980, Pennant Jones 1 Dec. 1980; 10242, Smith 24 Feb. 1981).

It was not BP Coal's intention to compete with Sohio, which was already engaged in the US coal industry, or to usurp Sohio's opportunities for expansion in coal. Competition and usurpation were unlikely to be significant in view of the fact that BP Coal's emphasis was on the export market, whereas Sohio was interested primarily in the US domestic market. BP Coal therefore set up a branch office in the US with a brief to identify, and open negotiations to acquire, a US coal company in BP's chosen location of Southern Appalachia. BP informed Sohio about BP Coal's plans, making it clear that BP Coal would not compete with Sohio, 'that there was ample scope for co-operation between us', and that any assets which BP Coal acquired that did not fit its plans would be offered to Sohio (BP archives 90684, Jump 12 Nov. 1980, Pennant Jones 1 Dec. 1980; 10242, Smith 21 Jan. and 24 Feb. ('ample scope') 1981).

Sohio, however, countered with the argument that if BP Coal made its planned acquisition in the US, this 'would make our companies competitors in coal trade', and claimed that Southern Appalachia was an area of primary interest in Sohio's long-range coal plans (BP 10242, Whitehouse 25 Feb. 1981). This was tantamount to saying that Sohio could virtually indefinitely reserve a functional and/or geographical area for itself merely by naming it as an area of interest in a long-range plan. According to BP's lawyers, BP Coal would not, in this situation, be usurping a business opportunity from Sohio if it made an acquisition in Southern Appalachia. For a usurpation to be proved it would have to be shown not merely that Sohio had expressed a general interest in a particular market or activity, but that it had a real and identified investment opportunity which was usurped by its majority shareholder (BP legal file on Project Swan Lake, Sullivan & Cromwell 13 Nov. 1980). As one senior BP executive summed it up:

> we have for some time maintained a 'hands off' policy to enable Sohio to develop their own plans ... However, we have made it clear to Sohio that we cannot wait for ever. In order to meet our world-wide coal objectives we need access to US reserves and we have been urging Sohio to consult with us to try and coordinate investments in the United States for the maximum benefit of both parties. Our lawyers have advised us (and Sohio have copies of this advice) that this is a perfectly proper course of action.
>
> (BP archives 10242, Manson 6 Mar. 1981)

Subsequently, in 1981 BP and Sohio agreed that BP Coal could continue to seek out an acquisition in the US provided it was careful not to prejudice Sohio's plans to purchase some coal assets from US Steel (BP archives 10242, Jump 15 Apr. 1981). In fact, as events turned out, BP Coal did not make an acquisition, but the episode had provided yet another illustration of the frictions and tension between BP and Sohio, and the absence of internalization advantages in their relationship.

The failure to share information and expertise between Sohio and BP was perhaps at its most striking in Sohio's diversification into minerals through the acquisition of Kennecott in 1981. At that time the minerals industry was a very popular target for oil companies seeking to diversify out of oil. For example, in 1979 Amoco acquired Cyprus Mines, in 1980 Tenneco acquired Houston Oil and Minerals, and in the same year BP acquired Selection Trust. This was followed by a flurry of takeover activity directed at US minerals companies in the first quarter of 1981, when Chevron made a bid for Amax, Seagrams bid for St Joe Minerals, and Sohio made an agreed bid for Kennecott, the largest US producer of copper (*Financial Times* 6, 16 Mar. 1981). Sohio's desire to diversify into minerals was not, therefore, controversial, and BP in general terms supported the idea (BP legal registry WH19/11, Webster 14 Nov. 1980).

However, the specific proposal for Sohio to acquire Kennecott came to BP almost completely out of the blue, providing virtually no opportunity for BP to contribute to the assessment and evaluation of the proposal despite the fact that it involved an enormous expenditure of $1,770 million by Sohio. Specifically, when BP's board of directors met on 12 March 1981 one of the directors, who was also one of BP's nominees on Sohio's board, made a brief presentation on Sohio's proposal to acquire Kennecott for $1,770 million, and explained that the boards of Sohio and Kennecott would be meeting later that same day to consider the matter. The only other person present at the BP board meeting who had any prior knowledge of the proposal was the CEO, who knew about it only in general terms, and presumed that the BP director with responsibility for minerals knew the details. It therefore came as a shock when BP's minerals director said that he knew nothing about the proposal. His immediate reaction was that the price was high, and he was concerned about the large capital expenditures that would be required to modernize Kennecott's run-down plant if the acquisition went ahead. Following hurried consultations after the BP board meeting, BP agreed to go along with the decision of Sohio's board. Later that day Sohio's board duly approved the acquisition, as did Kennecott's board, and that same evening they jointly announced that the acquisition was to go ahead (Manson, W.A.L. 1986, interview, 5 Aug.; Adam, R.W. 1986, interview, 12 Aug.; Belgrave, R. 1986, interview, 1 Oct.; Bexon, R. 1986, interview, 8 Oct.; Steel, D.E.C. 1986, interviews, 21 Oct. and 6 Nov.; Birks, J. 1986, interview, 4 Dec.; BP company secretary's office, BP board minutes 12 Mar. 1981; BP archives 90684, BP press release 13 Mar. 1981). Thus, in the course of one day, BP had acquiesced in a very large acquisition of which most of BP's directors, including the head of BP's own minerals business, had been in ignorance that same morning.

The manner in which the acquisition of Kennecott was rushed through, with a minimum of information and consultation, was the most extreme example of what could occur as a result of the restricted flow of information across the 'Chinese wall' between Sohio and BP. Had the assets which Sohio acquired from Kennecott turned out to be profitable, an attitude of 'all's well that ends well' might have prevailed. But Sohio's minerals operations consistently made heavy losses, justifying criticism of the manner in which the acquisition had been handled.

One of the drawbacks of Sohio's diversification into minerals was that Sohio lacked ownership advantages in the minerals industry, as indeed did other oil companies, including BP, which ventured into minerals. In Sohio's case, it also lacked ownership advantages in oil exploration, in which it invested its surplus cash extremely heavily. In its attempt to discover new sources of oil to replace the Prudhoe Bay oil field, Sohio spent huge sums on oil and gas exploration, which was the centrepiece of Sohio's investment strategy (Standard Oil Company 1979–85). The results were extremely disappointing. A survey that was completed in 1984 found that Sohio's exploration record was the poorest in the industry, with Sohio displaying the lowest ability to replace ongoing production among oil companies of similar size. Unlike BP, which had a long history of being a top-rank explorer, Sohio was a newcomer to exploration. Before 1978 it had virtually no exploration activities, and in its attempt to replace Prudhoe Bay it entered into a crash programme, involving a rapid expansion in its exploration staff, its acreage, its geological and geophysical data, and its exploratory drilling. The essential problem was that exploration capabilitites could not be built up overnight. In the words of the 1984 survey:

> A successful exploration effort is a function of many things; in addition to good luck and large capital, it requires a highly disciplined and well conducted organization of talented people and a portfolio of promising leases. The few companies with a sustained record of profitable exploration have been assembling people and acreage for a long time. It is questionable whether the gap between them and a newcomer can be closed in a few years.
>
> (BP CRO 7U 2217, unsigned survey n.d.)

Reorganization, takeover and integration of Sohio, 1986–7

The consequences of Sohio's lack of managerial resources, its low ownership advantages in oil exploration and minerals, and the absence of internalization advantages arising from its lack of integration into the BP Group, were becoming all too apparent by the mid-1980s. In 1985, against a background of falling oil prices and profits, Sohio announced very large write-downs in some of its investments, primarily in minerals, coal, and oil and gas exploration (Standard Oil Company 1985). In the light of these events, followed by a precipitate fall in the crude oil price to only $10 a barrel in the winter of 1985–6, BP decided to enforce top-level management changes at Sohio. Specifically, Sohio's top management was replaced in April 1986 by a small team of high-powered executives from BP, including Robert Horton and John Browne, both of whom would later become CEOs of BP, and Colin Webster, the president of BP North America (*Financial Times* 28 Feb. 1, 3 Mar. 1986). To take up their new roles, these three resigned from BP and became employees of Sohio.

Sohio's new top management moved quickly to dispose of assets and businesses in which Sohio did not possess competitive advantages, and to reduce Sohio's costs so that the company would be more robust in an environment of volatile oil prices. About half of Sohio's undeveloped exploration acreage was relinquished, and exploration and production was focused on areas with good prospects, and in which Sohio possessed competitive advantages – primarily northern Alaska, the Gulf of Mexico, and the Anadarko basin in Oklahoma. In minerals, the new strategy was to concentrate on the Bingham Canyon mine, one of the richest copper ore bodies in the world, while disposing of other copper-mining properties. In the coal business, nearly half of Sohio's coal reserves were relinquished in

1986. Through these and other disposals, the new management sought to strengthen Sohio's ownership advantages. Sohio continued, however, to be managed separately from the rest of the BP Group, whose ownership of a majority shareholding in Sohio did not enable it to realize internalization advantages for fear of legal action from minority shareholders (BP 1986).

The remedy for this situation was implemented in 1987, when BP acquired full control of Sohio by buying the 45 per cent minority shareholding. This decision stemmed from BP's conviction that it could achieve greater value for its shareholders if it merged all the BP Group's US operations, including those of Sohio, under one management and integrated them into BP's international operations. This was duly achieved by merging the previously separate US activities of Sohio and BP into one organization, BP America, which accounted for about half the BP Group's fixed assets. By giving the BP Group access to the full potential of the US, this enhanced BP's ability to reap locational advantages. At the same time, BP was able to reap cross-border internalization advantages from the integration of BP America with the rest of the BP Group outside the US. To give just some examples, emerging production technologies developed in Alaska to extend the life of the Prudhoe Bay oil field were transferred to other fields in the North Sea and elsewhere; Sohio's world-leading technology in acrylonitrile was integrated into the BP Group's international chemicals businesss; and there was a significant influx of American managers into BP's London head office (BP 1987; Packham, D. 2000, telephone interview, 10 Jul.).

At the same time, senior BP executives who were expatriated to work in the US picked up American ideas about management which they brought back to Britain when they were later repatriated. The most dramatic example was Robert Horton, who returned to London from the US prior to his appointment as BP's chairman and CEO in 1990. Influenced by contemporary trends in US management, and particularly by the example of Jack Welch at General Electric, Horton launched a high-profile reorganization of BP, replacing the traditional command-control British hierarchy by a delayered 'flat' structure based on shared vision and values, which emphasized the importance of teamwork and the sharing of knowledge and ideas (Horton 1989; Guyon 1999; BP archives 104136, Project 1990 information pack 19 Mar. 1990).

Globalization

Having cleared away barriers to internalization, such as those which characterized the pre-1987 relationship with Sohio, BP in the 1990s placed great emphasis on the benefits of mutual support, learning and sharing knowledge, transferring skills, mobilizing technology, and diffusing best practices across the whole BP Group (BP 1995–9). These internalization advantages were considered an essential element in the strategy of globalization that was taken to a new level by the merger of BP and Amoco in 1998. The aim of the merger, wrote BP's chairman, was to create 'a global corporation for a global economy' (BP 1998). In a statement that wrapped up the locational, ownership and internalization advantages that BP was seeking to achieve, BP's CEO added that

> We now have the strength to take substantial positions in the key resource developments and markets of the world [locational advantages] and also the ability to combine our skills and know-how [ownership advantages], learning from each other and applying best practice across the whole of our combined asset base [internalization advantages].
>
> (BP 1998)

Retrospect and conclusion

To conclude, the eclectic paradigm of OLI combinations is certainly helpful in explaining BP's experience in the US. Of particular value, is the ease with which the OLI combinations of the paradigm can be reconfigured to explain dynamic situations. In BP's case, its entry into the US through Sohio was based initially on a combination of ownership and locational advantages, but with high barriers to internalization arising from Sohio's determination to retain its managerial autonomy and the legal constraints on internalization between a company and a partly-owned subsidiary in the US.

During the first phase of the BP–Sohio relationship, Sohio's ownership advantages were substantial in helping to manage and finance BP's entry into the US, and the absence of internalization advantages was not a major handicap while BP and Sohio shared a common commitment to bringing the Prudhoe Bay oil field into commercial production. This phase lasted from 1970 until 1977–8, when Prudhoe Bay came onstream and BP achieved a majority shareholding in Sohio.

When it came to the second phase, Sohio lacked ownership advantages to invest the vast inflow of cash from Prudhoe Bay, primarily because it was short of managerial resources to cope with such a rapid expansion of the firm. The sharing of information and expertise with BP might have helped to alleviate Sohio's lack of management resources, but internalization barriers prevented transfers of people and know-how. Much of the cash generated by Prudhoe Bay was spent on poor investments which had to be written down when the oil price fell in the mid-1980s.

That inaugurated the third phase, which started in 1986 when BP sent a high-powered management team to replace Sohio's top management. The new team rapidly implemented a strategy of concentrating Sohio's activities on areas where it possessed competitive (ownership) advantages, while disposing of other assets and businesses. Formidable barriers to internalization advantages continued, however, to exist until BP acquired Sohio's minority shareholding in 1987. That opened the way for BP's and Sohio's separate activities in the US to be merged under one management and integrated with the worldwide BP Group, enabling internalization advantages finally to be realized.

By the 1990s the barriers to internalization that had characterized the pre-1987 relationship between BP and Sohio were a thing of the past. The importance of internalization advantages was a leitmotif of BP in the 1990s, and a vital element, along with locational and ownership advantages, in the strategy of globalization that BP pursued, most notably through its merger with Amoco in 1998.

References

Unpublished sources

BP archives, BP Archive, University of Warwick, Coventry, England.
BP CRO (Company Records Office), c/o DSI, Hemel Hempstead, England.
BP legal files, Britannic House, 1 Finsbury Circus, London, England.
BP company secretary files, Britannic House, 1 Finsbury Circus, London, England.

Published sources

Bamberg, J. (1994) *The History of The British Petroleum Company: Volume II, The Anglo-Iranian Years, 1928–1954*, Cambridge: Cambridge University Press.

—— (2000) *British Petroleum and Global Oil, 1950–1975: The Challenge of Nationalism*, Cambridge: Cambridge University Press.

BP (1979–98) *Annual reports.*

Dunning, J.H. (1977) 'Trade, location of economic activity and the multinational enterprise: a search for an eclectic approach', in B. Ohlin, P. Hesselborn and P. Wijkman (eds) *The International Allocation of Economic Activity*, London: Macmillan.

—— (2000) 'The eclectic paradigm as an envelope for economic and business theories of MNE activity', *International Business Review* 9: 163–90.

Ferrier, R.W. (1982) *The History of The British Petroleum Company: Volume I, The Developing Years, 1901–1932*, Cambridge: Cambridge University Press.

Financial Times (1983) *Oil and Gas International Yearbook.*

Guyon, J. (1999) 'When John Browne talks, big oil listens', *Fortune* 5 July.

Horton, R.B. (1989) 'At the edge of the nineties: future challenges to management', Distinguished alumni speech to triennial Sloan Fellows convocation at MIT, 12–14 October.

Jacoby, N.H. (1974) *Multinational Oil: A Study in Industrial Dynamics*, New York: Macmillan.

Odell, P.R. (1983) *Oil and World Power*, 7th edn, Harmondsworth: Penguin Books.

Penrose, E.T. (1968) *The Large International Firm in Developing Countries: The International Petroleum Industry*, London: George Allen and Unwin.

Roscow, J.P. (1977) *800 Miles to Valdez: The Building of the Alaska Pipeline*, Englewood Cliffs, NJ: Prentice-Hall.

Sampson, A. (1975) *The Seven Sisters: The Great Oil Companies and the World They Made*, New York: Viking Press.

Standard Oil Company (of Ohio) (1977–85) *Annual reports*.

Tugendhat, C. and Hamilton, A. (1975) *Oil, The Biggest Business*, revised edn, London: Eyre Methuen.

10 The 'Americanization' of Shell Oil[1]

Tyler Priest

Americans tend to think of the oil industry as essentially American. In 1859, the first commercial oil discovery was made at Titusville, Pennsylvania. By the end of the century, an ambitious entrepreneur from Cleveland, Ohio, John D. Rockefeller, had created not only the largest oil business in the world, but indeed the largest industrial enterprise in the world. For the next 50 years, the United States led the world in both oil production and oil consumption. Five of the seven largest oil firms in the world – the famous or infamous 'seven sisters' – were American. Even as numerous other countries vastly surpassed the United States in oil production after World War II and gradually wrested control of their oil sources from the major oil companies, the idea of the oil industry as organically American has remained a staple of the nation's cultural identity, even up to the present.

What Americans do not often realize is that foreign direct investment (FDI) contributed significantly to the development of the US petroleum industry. In 1950, as Mira Wilkins notes in Chapter 2 of this volume, FDI in this industry was $400 million, nearly 12 per cent of total 'inward' FDI. Nearly all of this $400 million was accounted for by the Shell Oil Company, whose majority owner was the British-Dutch oil giant, Royal Dutch/Shell. Formed by the famous 1907 merger between Royal Dutch Petroleum and the English Shell Transport & Trading Company to compete against Standard Oil in world markets, the Royal Dutch/Shell Group grew to become one of the largest and most internationally dispersed enterprises in the world. A key aspect of this growth was the emergence of the Group's US affiliate as a major oil company in its own right.

Throughout most of its history, Shell Oil enjoyed a considerable degree of autonomy from its majority shareholder. During the 1940s and 1950s, Shell Oil both expanded and consolidated the many parts of its business in the United States. In the process, it projected a new public image, downplaying its majority foreign ownership and declaring Shell to be an American company, with American directors, and guided by American decision-making. 'We pitched this strongly', said a Shell Oil corporate secretary from this period, 'and we believed it'. The average American also believed it. Even to this day, many Americans think that Shell companies around the world are subsidiaries of the Houston-headquartered Shell Oil.

This essay explores the theme of Shell's 'Americanization'. More than just a public relations ploy, Americanization refers to a real assertion of independence by the American company from the Group after World War II. Explaining why and how this came about requires attention to contexts at both the national and international levels. It forces us to think about the United States as a 'host country' for foreign investment, an understudied aspect of the history of multinational enterprise. It also gives a new twist to the concept of 'Americanization', which has been used almost exclusively by scholars to describe the uni-directional transfer of American products, media, and cultural practices to foreign countries (Gienow-Hecht 2000; Kipping and Bjarnar 1998). Although the sources for this study are grounded in the American side of the story, this essay attempts to look at the evolution of Shell Oil from the Group's perspective and in terms of the international structure of the Group.

As Bamberg points out in Chapter 9, the international oil industry expanded in the twentieth century through strategies of vertical integration across national borders, which gave the oil majors tremendous 'internalization' advantages, to use Dunning's eclectic paradigm, in moving oil cheaply and efficiently from oil fields through refineries to consumers (Dunning 2000). Royal Dutch/Shell (RD/S) certainly was no exception to this trend, but the extension of its operations across national boundaries was not seamless, and for decades there was actually very little integration between the Group's operations inside and outside the United States. RD/S's initial entry into the United States had more to do with the two other kinds of advantages indicated by Dunning's paradigm: locational and ownership advantages. The locational advantages of the United States lay in its large petroleum resources and consumer market. The ownership advantages RD/S could bring to exploit opportunities in the United States included, most importantly, advanced engineering and technical proficiency. Investment in the United States also had strategic importance: it allowed the Group to become more competitive globally with chief rival, Standard Oil.

Although US oil developments greatly influenced global pricing, most oil production in the United States was for regional markets or the national market. Political, legal, and cultural constraints, in addition to industry structure, dictated clear administrative and operational divisions between the Group's US affiliate and the rest of its far-flung global empire. In an imperfectly integrated world economy consisting of many distinct national economies, and with a prospering and protected US oil market, this division suited the Group's increasingly decentralized approach to international investment and management during the post-World War II period. If British Petroleum can be described as 'essentially a national company with international operations' (Bamberg, Chapter 9), then Royal Dutch/Shell was essentially an international organization with national operations. But as the locational advantages of oil in the United States began to decline relative to other producing countries by the 1970s, and as the world economy became more thoroughly integrated, the advantages of internalizing the Group's US assets and operations grew in importance to its global strategy. Although their oil interests in the United States were quite different, British Petroleum and Royal Dutch/Shell faced many of the same barriers to internalization, which they both successfully overcame in the 1980s and 1990s when domestic and international conditions in the oil industry changed dramatically.

Operating in Standard's backyard

Royal Dutch/Shell first entered the United States on the eve of World War I. With the intensifying price wars between Standard and the Group in the Far East and Europe, the United States became increasingly important to the Group's global strategy. 'When our business grew to such international dimensions', explained Royal Dutch's brilliant but autocratic chairman, Henri Deterding, 'we obviously had to dig ourselves in as traders on American soil; otherwise we would have lost our foothold everywhere else. Until we started trading in America, our American competitors controlled world prices – because ... they could always charge up their losses in underselling us in other countries against business at home where they had a monopoly' (Beaton 1957: 58). The US Supreme Court's 1911 decision to dissolve the Standard Oil trust into 33 separate companies stiffened Deterding's resolve to 'operate in Standard's backyard'. He regarded the case as a clever legal gimmick that did not prevent the companies from acting in concert.

In 1912, Shell established a small marketing company in the Pacific Northwest, stretched down the coast into exploration and production in California, where it made famous discoveries at Signal Hill and elsewhere, and then broadened the hunt for oil into Oklahoma. Shell's rapid expansion threatened Standard Oil and its offspring, who maligned Shell as a foreign exploiter. Burgeoning numbers of tank cars and service stations painted in Shell's emblematic yellow and red colors provoked William Randolph Hearst to dub Shell the 'yellow peril', presumably at the behest of Shell's rivals ('Oil – Shell's Game' 1952: 21).

Deterding came to realize that building a large and powerful Shell organization in the United States might require enlisting American capital to keep the American public favourably disposed to it (Beaton 1957: 229). The Union Oil Company of Delaware presented Shell with such an opportunity. This company, which owned 26 per cent of the Union Oil Company of California, had fallen on hard times and was ripe for takeover. A merger between Shell and Union in 1922 brought all companies under a holding company called the Shell Union Oil Corporation, with approximately 65 per cent of the stock held by the Group (through another subsidiary called the Shell Caribbean Petroleum Company) and the remaining 35 per cent held by groups of US investors. Shell's move to 'go public' almost backfired, however. A majority of Union California's stockholders formed a bloc dedicated to preventing Shell's interest in their company from growing. The campaign even recruited national politicians who, preying upon anti-British sentiment leftover from World War I, charged Shell with being a tool of the British government. Shell Union weathered this storm by disposing of its Union California stock, but keeping the minority shareholding interests. The company then gained new public acceptance by maintaining a clean reputation during the oil scandals of the mid-1920s (Beaton 1957: 206–34).

During the interwar period, Shell built and acquired new refineries and pipelines, established affiliated companies in research and chemicals, and expanded marketing into the East Coast. The Group's American operations, however, consisted of several operating companies governed by two separate organizations, one east and one west of the Rocky Mountains. The company retained duplicate sets of vice presidents and department heads in New York and San Francisco. Each organization had its own philosophy and approach. Few moved between the two. Some individuals from the West had moved East, but not vice versa. Friendly competition existed between the regions, and those on the Pacific Coast exuded an air of superiority. After all, Shell had made its name there. The California company had been the first of the Shell companies to develop a successful, integrated business. California had given the company a 'springboard to prominence', in the words of historian Kendall Beaton, with a bonanza of low-cost crude from legendary fields like Coalinga, Signal Hill, and Ventura. Gasoline sales in California, especially during the 'Golden Era' of the 1920s, outpaced every other state. During the depression, West Coast earnings helped offset large losses in the mid-continent (Beaton 1957: 171–91).

The West Coast may have been the company's moneymaker in years past, but by 1940 crude oil production east of the Rockies had almost doubled West Coast production. At the end of World War II, the West Coast no longer loomed as large in Shell's national organization. Although Shell continued to earn high profits in the region, it had lost market share and run up exorbitant marketing costs. Shell's 'cracker box' service stations, old metal constructions that sold relatively small volumes of gasoline, were scattered across the landscape. The few stations owned by the company were expensive to operate, as were the leased stations, whose dealers had received generous 1.5 to 2-cent-per-gallon concessions during a period of intense competition. Too many bulk plants existed in too many small towns. Despite the consolidation of some marketing divisions in the 1930s, the West Coast still had an extensive divisional organization that included money-losing territories in parts of the northwest. In 1945, sales in the east exceeded sales in the west by two-to-one. By 1948, that ratio was three-to-one (Beaton 1957: 782).

With increasing frequency, refineries along the Gulf Coast resupplied the West Coast with fuel oil. West Coast refineries had built catalytic cracking facilities to increase the yield of gasoline, which diminished the production of fuel oil. This was just one sign that the three largely separate energy markets (East Coast, Midwest, and West Coast) were evolving into a single national market. Given these considerations, the West Coast could not remain independent within the Shell family very long. Alexander Fraser, president of Shell Union and long-time president of the east-of-the-Rockies companies (1933–47), and Sir George Legh-Jones, Shell Union chairman of the board and former president of the west-of-the-Rockies organization (1924–33), seized the opportunity to finish Shell's 'long-range plan of corporate simplification' when a number of executives born in the 1890s, including the head of Shell Oil's Pacific Coast operations, announced their intention to retire at the end of 1948 (Beaton 1957: 692).

Vice presidents from both east and west started moving to New York to take charge of nationwide operations. The least profitable stations in the West Coast's retail network were eliminated and Shell pulled out of sparsely populated territories in Western Montana and Utah. On 1 January, 1949, the formal centralization in New York went into effect. Under the new structure, the San Francisco office declined in relative importance to Head Office. The final step came in September 1949 with termination of the holding-company arrangement between the Shell Union Oil Corporation and its chief operating subsidiary, Shell Oil Company, Inc. Shell Union was renamed Shell Oil Company, acquiring all assets and assuming liabilities of the chief subsidiary, which was dissolved.

Shell Oil no longer consisted of a collection of small companies largely managed and coordinated from abroad. Now it was a single entity, financed through US earnings, with US managers taking more initiative in decision-making. In the late 1940s and 1950s, Shell expanded all phases of its operations on a nation-wide scale. It also bought out the Group's separate interest in its US research organization, the Shell Development Company, bringing it under direct control and making it more responsive to commercial considerations in the US market. The geographic and organizational rationalization of the Shell Oil Company was facilitated by the shift in management style from European paternalism to the kind of legalistic supervision common to American corporations, with growing teams of lawyers, lobbyists, and media specialists.

American citizenship

The simplification of Shell's corporate structure hinted at profound changes in the company. The number of Group managing directors on the Shell Oil board declined from five to two. The wave of retirements cleared the way for Americans to move into both higher management positions, giving Shell new character and a sense of autonomy from the Group. Officers of the US Shell companies had always been Group men, British or Dutch citizens sent over for a time before leaving for other assignments with the Group. When they came to the United States, many remained largely external to Shell US. The War, however, disrupted the replenishment of Shell managers with Group men and slowed the entry of new people, foreign or American, into Shell ranks. In the late 1940s, a new influx of Americans filled a great need for engineers all across the company. Like other US corporations at that time, Shell hired a generation of young Americans who grew up in the Depression, many of them having served in the armed forces during the War.

The 1950s witnessed the evolution of Shell Oil from a medium-sized, foreign-controlled company, to a major industrial concern that few Americans regarded as anything other than American. By 1952, the company employed a stable workforce of 31,000, with twenty-seven vice presidents, most of whom were US citizens. As former president Monroe Spaght recalled, before the War 'one was forever apologizing and going out of his way to be sure that it was understood that we were American. With some of the senior people being non-Americans, that was a bit of a chore. This all changed after World War II'.

The naturalization of Shell Oil's Scottish-born president, H.S.M. 'Max' Burns (president from 1949 to1961) exemplified the gradual Americanization of Shell. All subsequent presidents of Shell, except one, would be American-born. Although Burns had risen to a high position within the Group, he nevertheless asserted increasing autonomy for Shell Oil within it ('H.S.M. Burns' 1951: 124). Under Burns, the company worked diligently to promote its image as a corporate 'citizen' of the United States. Managers strove to improve public relations across the country through philanthropy, fellowships and grants, and its popular traffic safety campaign. Burns made himself available to security analysts – unusual for a president whose corporation was only 35 per cent public. They discovered a very profitably run business that did not depend on its parent for capital. Shell had financed its tremendous postwar expansion with US dollars, largely from retained earnings and write offs (depreciation, depletion, and amortization) ('Oil – Shell's Game' 1952: 18, 25). The first-time listing of Royal Dutch Petroleum shares on the New York Stock Exchange in 1954, meanwhile, solidified ties to the US financial community and thus aided Shell's public relations push. Few within US financial circles challenged Shell Oil's reputation as US enterprise ('Full Circle' 1956: 25). The same went for the US oil industry. Max Burns was the first representative from Shell Oil to be named chairman of the American Petroleum Institute, the US oil industry's most prominent trade association ('Portraits' 1960: 2). For a company once branded as the yellow peril, this event was rich in symbolism.

The Americanization of Shell Oil involved a reorientation of the US affiliate towards the Royal Dutch/Shell Group. By 1950, Shell Oil had matured into an adult member of the Royal Dutch/Shell family. It became a more autonomous and vital part of the Group's worldwide activities, representing 25–33 per cent of the Group's profits. The Group began to view its 65 per cent interest in Shell Oil as a sound investment that need not, and indeed should not, be micromanaged. When, in 1958, the Group set up its 'service companies' to mediate the relationship between the Group parent companies and affiliates around the world, Shell Oil was the only operating company not required to report to these new companies. As an outside observer once commented:

> There is no imported management at Shell. The Group does not call the signals from London or The Hague. The American managers don't carry chips on their shoulders against the Group's managing directors. They just provide healthy dividend checks every quarter.
>
> (Golden 1967)

The internationalism of Royal Dutch/Shell

From one perspective, the Americanization of Shell Oil revealed a greatly weakened and traumatized Royal Dutch/Shell organization. The Group had been devastated by World War II and the dismemberment of the European colonial empires. The maturation of Shell Oil within the Group corresponded to the new superpower status attained by the United States and the emergence of the US economy as the most dynamic in the world. During World War II, Shell Oil became the centre of innovation, a pioneer in the development of 100-octane aviation fuel and butadiene synthetic rubber. After the War, the US company helped the Group raise valuable dollars in the United States to pay for the expansion of oil production in Venezuela, Columbia, Ecuador, and Canada ('Shell Oil Turns' 1948). Shell engineers travelled abroad to retrain Group engineers in the latest advances and to assist the rebuilding of Group refineries with technologies developed in the United States, such as catalytic cracking. Shell salesmen helped the Group adjust to new competitive conditions around the world created by decolonization and the collapse of the famous 'As Is' cartel. In 1957, for instance, a German sales manager at Deutsche Shell boasted that his company had increased its market share in fuel oil thanks to 220 young salesmen trained in 'American style aggressive selling', whose 'prime aim in life is to beat their targets' ('Royal Dutch/Shell' 1957: 142).

On the other hand, the Americanization of Shell Oil was not something forced upon the Group by an upstart affiliate. Rather, it reflected a reorientation of Royal Dutch/Shell's global strategy. The western hemisphere played a pivotal role in this strategy, as an increasingly important source of crude (Venezuela), the largest market and source of capital (the United States), and the most secure base of operations in the event of another world war. Americanization also reflected the organizational agility and adaptability of the Group. It had always been a decentralized organization, 'not a corporation, not a legal entity, but a condition', wrote one US observer. 'This condition is international business in its most highly developed sense' (Howarth 1997: 262). Royal Dutch/Shell was simply a name used to designate nearly 500 companies owned (wholly, jointly, and indirectly) and coordinated by the British and Dutch holding companies.

Despite the decentralized and cooperative principles underlying the arrangement, control over the entire realm was based in The Hague and London, and Europeans made the big decisions. Prior to World War II, the Group hired only a few foreigners and nationals to run its affiliates, and then chiefly on the basis of 'how closely they resembled Europeans'. A classic Shell story tells of an urgent cable once sent from an affiliate to London: 'Lubrication oil sales dropped 5 per cent. Send two more cricket blues' ('Diplomats' 1960: 98). Sir Henri Deterding, moreover, retained a large amount power. His retirement in 1936 and death in 1939, however, followed by 5 years of global war, signalled the end of an era for Royal Dutch/Shell.

Out of the urgent necessity to recover from the devastation of the War, when the Dutch headquarters had to be relocated to Curação, the RD/S directors redistributed many functions and powers down through the organization. Contact and decision-making between the two parent companies became less distinctly clarified or formalized. To the extent they were, the seven directors – 'of a far different stripe than the rough and ready tycoons of the past', wrote *Time* magazine in 1960 ('Diplomats' 1960: 94) – formed the policy-making Executive Committee, which in 1958 was designated as the Committee of Managing Directors (CMD). Each director assumed a specific area of responsibility. 'Our job here', explained Felix A.C. Guépin, a managing director responsible for marketing and chemicals, 'is one of trying to unravel knots – but only to get the knot loosened up a little so you can look at it and see how it is going to come out. Then we hand it over to the operational managers' (Burck 1957: 140). Of course, top management retained final authority, especially on questions involving major capital expenditures. Wherever possible, though, Group executives refrained from getting bogged down in managing the day-to-day operations of its subsidiaries.

This was easier in some cases than in others. Group companies concerned with only one phase of operations required close coordination. Shell Italiana, for example, depended on the rest of the Group for oil, while Brunei Shell in Borneo looked to other Group companies to market its oil. Shell Oil, on the other hand, could function relatively autonomously. It had built up fully integrated operations that were, for the most part, independent of the rest of the Group (Burck 1957). The versatility that the Royal Dutch/Shell people acquired through their experience with the Group's far-flung operations instilled in the organization a cosmopolitan outlook receptive to the Americanization of Shell Oil. Royal Dutch/Shell's Executive Committee or CMD consisted of 'inside' directors, all of whom had worked their way up through the Group, mostly on long-term assignments overseas. Their experiences trained them to 'think globally, act locally', to borrow a popular American dictum. It is fair to say that they recognized earlier than most other multinational firms the social and political appeal of employing qualified nationals in positions of authority, and not just as hired hands.

The young managing director, John Hugo Loudon, who by the mid-1950s was acting as *primus inter pares* among the seven managing directors, was one of the first to anticipate nationalistic trends and urge the hiring of more locals in executive positions. Once described as 'a handsome man whose casual movements seem under strict control and whose most deliberate movements seem strictly casual', Loudon exhibited the refinement bred by a cosmopolitan background (Burck 1957: 136). He had held positions around the world, spoke five languages fluently, and came from a distinguished lineage within the organization. His grandfather was a Governor General of the Dutch East Indies, his uncle was Holland's Foreign Minister, and his father, Hugo Loudon, was one of the founders of Royal Dutch Petroleum and later a managing director and chairman ('Diplomats' 1960). John Loudon and Sir Francis Hopwood, Shell Oil's chairman from 1951 to 1956, had the vision to recognize that the best way for Shell Oil to grow and develop in the United States was by making it a truly American venture.

The United States as host country

In addition to the organizational changes at Shell Oil and within the Royal Dutch/Shell Group, the domestic political context in the United States was also important to the Americanization of the US affiliate. Scholars who study multinational enterprise in the early postwar period typically focus on the political conditions or terms of entry that other countries, mostly developing ones, imposed on US overseas investment (Bergsten, Horst and Moran 1978). Less appreciated are the political risks faced by foreign investors in the United States, which was undergoing a revival of nationalism, isolationism, and xenophobia during the early Cold War.

Although no longer viewed as the yellow peril, Shell encountered obstacles at the state level that included laws and constitutions that forbade 'alien' landholding. At the Federal level, there were prohibitions against foreign ownership of coastwise shipping and restrictions on the leasing of Federal lands by foreign interests. Further, the Federal Trade

Commission's anti-trust investigation into monopolistic practices in the international oil business during the 1950s heightened fears that Shell might be singled out because of its foreign majority ownership (see below).

The perception of Shell as an independent company with significant American shareholders shielded it from the kind of scrutiny it received after World War I and helped it receive special consideration in cases where Shell's operations might otherwise have been restricted due to its foreign ownership. In the early 1950s, for example, the company successfully lobbied for an amendment to the state constitution of Washington that dropped a prohibition against alien landholding and paved the way for the construction of a new Shell refinery on Puget Sound ('Aliens Welcome' 1953). It is somehow appropriate that a company once branded 'the yellow peril' would be instrumental in overturning alien landholding restrictions originally directed against Asian immigrants. Revision of a commercial treaty between the United States and The Netherlands also gave Shell access to oil reserves in Federal offshore waters, which were largely prohibited to companies from foreign countries not offering reciprocal access to American companies.

Political and legal conditions in the United States significantly shaped the way the Group managed its interest in Shell Oil. The 30–35 per cent minority ownership of Shell Oil by US citizens no doubt substantiated Shell Oil's claims of American 'citizenship', but it also generated a 'complete phobia' on the part of the Group's managing directors about minority shareholder lawsuits, according to one Royal Dutch/Shell official ('Why Royal/Dutch Shell' 1984: 100). As Bamberg describes in Chapter 9, the relationship between a partly-owned US subsidiary and its parent was fraught with legal complications stemming from the rights of minority shareholders and US anti-trust law, which prohibited combinations and conspiracies in 'restraint of trade'. Minority shareholders could sue the majority shareholders on behalf of the company if they felt that a particular transaction or decision was prejudicial to their interests. But if the minority and majority interests were so distinct, could they be prosecuted as separate entities for anti-trust violations? The law was not clear on this question.

Legal questions, therefore, kept Group officials from issuing direct orders to the American affiliate. Shell Oil and the Group took great pains to insure that the pricing of transfers and the sharing of technology between the two were done at arm's length and according to very formalized procedures so that it did not appear that profits were being moved out of the United States or that the US firm was being placed at a competitive disadvantage. To emphasize Shell Oil's distinctiveness, the American company even had its own trademark 'pecten' with a different design from Royal Dutch/Shell's.

Despite Shell Oil's managerial autonomy and special status within the worldwide Group, Royal Dutch/Shell still had a dominant presence on

Shell's board of directors. One could question just how separate and autonomous from the Group the company was. Every top Shell executive worked abroad in some capacity for Group companies on his way up the ranks, vetted by Group leaders. Moreover, there were discernible limits placed on the autonomy of Shell Oil. Most significantly, the majority shareholders discouraged Shell Oil from operating outside the United States, where the US firm might have stepped on the toes of other Group companies. For example, Shell Oil only explored for oil in the United States, and oil and chemical products were only sold to US customers. Although not a formal edict – the minority shareholding interest prevented Royal Dutch from issuing direct commands to Shell Oil management – this geographic constraint was understood.

This constraint also had an interesting and unintended effect. It bred a unique commitment to technology that actually reinforced the proud autonomy of Shell Oil. Confined to the domestic oil province, Shell placed a premium on technological innovation. That was the only way it could compete with its larger rivals in finding and producing more oil. The Group had long been committed to technological research, in the United States and Europe, especially on the Dutch side. But after World War II, Shell Oil's technological orientation took on a life of its own. The company organized one of the most respected exploration and production research laboratories in the industry, which made a name for Shell in geophysics, secondary recovery, and offshore development (Shell Development Company 1986). Shell also developed an organization committed to upgrading petroleum into as many profitable products as possible for the US market. By the late 1960s, Shell Oil's push into premium gasoline and aviation fuel made the company the second largest gasoline marketer in the country (Shell Oil, *Annual Report* 1964). Research into petroleum chemistry established Shell (through the Shell Chemical Corporation) by 1968 as the third-largest petroleum company in the US chemical business and the thirteenth largest overall (ranked by sales) (Backman 1970: 25, 74). Some Shell executives claimed that the company was simply too busy technically with developments in the United States during the postwar period to even think about taking Shell Oil into foreign countries.

Family tension

The ambiguity of divided sovereignty at Shell Oil, however, produced increasing friction in the company's relationship with Royal Dutch. In 1961–2, Shell's determination to break a bitter strike in its three major refineries put Royal Dutch in an uncomfortable position. The strike evoked support from the International Federation of Petroleum Workers, on whom the Group depended to keep communist unions out of its refineries in other countries ('Oil Strikers, 1963; 'OCAW' 1963). The research-sharing agreement between Shell Oil and the Group was revised several times, requiring the Group to pay more for access to Shell Oil's research and allowing Shell to keep some of its proprietary developments to itself. Because Royal Dutch/Shell participated in joint ventures abroad with oil companies who were competitors of Shell Oil in the United States, Shell had a legal obligation to keep strategic technologies from reaching other oil companies through their associations with the Group. At the same time, Shell Oil's push into the new technological frontiers of exploration and production diverged from the belief of some Group managers that trading and buying crude oil was more profitable than searching for new reserves. In 1969–70, the movement of Shell's head office from New York City to Houston, the US oil capital, literally and symbolically increased the company's distance from the Group. And as oil shortages loomed in the late 1960s, minority shareholders pressed Shell Oil to engage in overseas exploration and production.

In June 1969, on behalf of Shell Oil, stockholder Robert Halpern and other plaintiffs entered in the Supreme Court of New York and the Court of Chancery in Delaware parallel shareholder derivative actions against the Royal Dutch/Shell shareholders in Shell Oil. The Halpern plaintiffs alleged that between 1959 and 1969 the Group 'violated its fiduciary duties' in transactions with Shell Oil by requiring the American affiliate to purchase crude oil and other hydrocarbons amounting to 200,000 to 300,000 barrels/day from Group companies at prices substantially exceeding those prevailing in the free market (*Halpern v. Barran* 1970; *Halpern v. Barran* 1973; Shell Oil Company, Form 10-K 1977). Beginning in the late 1950s, the international glut of crude oil had produced an increasing disparity between the 'posted' or official price, which was held constant, and the actual market price at which crude was sold, which was dropping. In other words, companies offered bigger and bigger price discounts for oil sold on the spot market, while the posted price could not be lowered, largely for the political reason that it served as the basis for the revenues of the producing countries. That affiliates could be charged higher prices for crude oil than those paid by independent refiners was so widely acknowledged, it gave rise to the expression 'only fools or affiliates pay posted prices'.

The Royal Dutch/Shell defendants denied the allegations and moved to strike the complaint as a sham. The main evidence for the charges cited by the plaintiffs were speeches and articles published between 1962 and 1964 by oil analysts unconnected to the Group. The articles only referred to crude oil transactions, and not natural gas, petroleum products, and other services mentioned in the complaint. In May 1970, the Delaware judge found that the 'articles do not provide good ground for charges of self-dealing, mismanagement and the like during a ten-year period, half of it after the last of the articles was published, in transactions involving many subjects other than crude oil' (*Halpern v. Barran* 1970). Yet the plaintiffs kept the case alive with an amended complaint. A decision by the Delaware court in November 1973 granted the motion of the defendants to dismiss claims accrued prior to June 1966, on the grounds that such action was barred by the statute of limitations, but ordered further discovery of information for the period January 1966 to June 1969.

This case and two other minority shareholder suits submitted by the same plaintiffs in March 1974 dragged on for another 7 years. The implicit allegation of the Halpern suit was that Royal Dutch/Shell had prevented Shell Oil from operating in more profitable oil producing areas abroad and kept it dependent on Group companies for supplies. Although the Group continued to dispute the charges, the minority shareholder pressure was too strong to ignore. 'This anti-trust action was always a worry to the directors in London and The Hague', recalled Harry Bridges, president of Shell Oil (1971–6). 'Much less of a worry to people in the United States because we realized it was a part of living'. Royal Dutch/Shell finally gave in to this pressure, allowing Shell Oil to explore for oil in selected foreign countries after the OPEC embargo and price shock of 1973–4. In 1980, the Group settled its long-standing US minority shareholder suits out of court by turning over all its producing interests in the West African nation of Cameroon to the Shell Oil subsidiary, Pecten Cameroon. In return, the plaintiffs withdrew all their complaints, ending a bitter chapter in shareholder politics at Shell (Shell Oil Company, Form 10-K 1980).

Shell Oil's limited foreign ventures found only marginal success and never satisfied either side. The company had entered the international oil game much too late, trying to establish overseas positions during a period of international crisis, intense Third World nationalism, and anti-Americanism. Host governments commonly kept large shares of the profits from foreign oil investments, and the only available prospects for Shell Oil tended to be in volatile and corrupt countries. Because of the minority shareholder issue, Shell Oil could not discuss its international business – bidding, concessions, financing, etc. – with the Group. Needless to say, Royal Dutch E&P (Explorational Production) managers resented this arrangement and did not appreciate competition from another member of the Royal Dutch/Shell family.

The buyout[2]

Growing tensions finally came to a head in 1984–5, when the Group engineered a highly controversial buyout of its minority shareholders in Shell Oil and assumed full ownership of the company. Annoyed not only with Shell's new international presence, Group managers had chafed for years at the restrictions on the flows of technology and capital between Royal Dutch and Shell Oil. It was one of the longest-lived rumours in the oil industry: that Royal Dutch/Shell was going to buy up the stock in Shell Oil it did not already own. But for years, the rumours reappeared again and again, and it never happened. Finally, in January 1984, the Group announced it was making a tender offer for the minority stake in the company.

Why did the Group make this offer when it did? The conventional interpretation emphasizes falling oil prices and declining investment opportunities elsewhere. The Group had an estimated $8 billion in cash on hand and, in a glutted world oil market with sinking prices, was looking for some place to put it. The remaining interests were a natural corporate fit, matching Shell Oil's strengths in exploration and production with the Group's strengths downstream. An increased stake in the highly profitable and technologically sophisticated Shell Oil Company was an investment too attractive for the Group to pass up. With the public shareholders out of the way, as Sir Peter Baxendell, chairman of Royal Dutch/Shell pointed out at the time, integrated decision-making could 'take place without inhibitions' ('Why Royal Dutch/Shell is Betting' 1984: 99).

The changing US political and regulatory climate of the mid-1980s, however, must also be taken into consideration a crucial factor in the merger. The deregulation of oil in 1981 lifted protection and increased competition, leading to pressures for consolidations, mergers, and break-ups. The Reagan Administration's emasculation of the Justice Department's anti-trust division and its unwillingness to challenge other big oil mergers (Texaco-Getty, Socal-Gulf, Mobil-Superior) signalled a green light for takeovers, even by foreign companies. 'Royal Dutch would have done this years ago, except for its fear of anti-trust problems', said a former chief of strategic analysis for the Group in 1984. 'This was always a closed continent' for foreign ownership of energy assets. Now, he added, 'you can buy without criticism' ('Royal Dutch is Set' 1984: 32).

Royal Dutch/Shell's purchase of its minority shares was interpreted in some quarters as a hostile takeover. The buyout became a bitterly contested 'family feud', centred around conflicting valuations of Shell Oil's outstanding stock. The Group's initial tender offer for the public shares was $55 per share, significantly higher than the $44 per share at which Shell's stock sold before the offer, but not high enough to match the $80–85 per share estimated value of Shell's crude reserves as determined by a Goldman Sachs study commissioned by Shell's outside directors. Other estimates ranged even higher (Court of Chancery of the state of Delaware 1991). How could the estimates have been so far apart? The Group's share-value estimate, based on an appraisal by Morgan Stanley, was based on a $3.80 a barrel price for Shell's reserves, which is roughly what Texaco had paid for Getty, and Socal for Gulf. But Getty's and Gulf's reserves had been shrinking for years. Meanwhile, during 1978–85, Shell Oil had trailed only Amoco in US reserve replacement and led the industry exploration efficiency (Mack 1986: 128). The varying estimates also reflected disagreement over the net present value of Shell's 'proven' reserves and the extent of its 'probable' reserves. However, it was difficult to place an accurate market value on something which had only one buyer. No other company or investor was about to come forward as a 'white knight' with a competing bid against Shell Oil's majority shareholder.

The tender offer raised objections from Shell's public shareholders. From their perspective, Royal Dutch was not only buying Shell's reserves but the company's talent for replacing them. At stake was the self-worth of Shell's executives and engineers, and their fierce pride in the independent American operation that they had built up over several decades. The Group sweetened its bid to $58 per share, which only seemed to insult the minority shareholders, many of whom were Shell employees (who owned roughly 9 per cent of all Shell stock). T. Boone Pickens, chairman of Mesa Petroleum and Shell shareholder, probably spoke for most of them when he said: '$58 is a rotten price. I'm getting screwed' (Nulty 1984: 184).

However, it was about the best they were going to get without a long and costly court battle. The Group controlled nearly 70 per cent of Shell Oil's shares, and was prepared to enter into private deals for large blocks of stock to achieve the 90 per cent needed to initiate a short-form merger. Led by the top Shell executives, most shareholders accepted the tender offer. Some held out, however, bringing class action suits against Shell charging unfairness of price, unfair dealings, and inadequate proxy disclosure of relevant information. In early 1985, a settlement was reached providing cash payments to class members of $190 million, allegedly the largest class-action settlement ever at the time (Court of Chancery of the state of Delaware 1991). But the Group still achieved full ownership of Shell Oil at a desirable price. The proud autonomy that had characterized Shell Oil since the 1940s began to dissolve. 'We always felt cheated', said George Costa, who worked in Shell's Martinez refinery in California. He grudgingly sold his 2,600 Shell Oil shares to the parent company, but lost enthusiasm for his job afterward, calling the stock deal 'a stab in the back' ('Shell, A Fallen Champ' 1991).

The buyout, on the other hand, did allow Royal Dutch/Shell to gain internalization advantages from its American interests. At first, these advantages were largely financial and technological. In the late 1980s, the Group increased the dividend it took from the wholly-owned US subsidiary from about $700 million to $750 million a year, in effect pulling money out of Shell Oil to finance developments elsewhere (Norman 1992). Flows of technical and scientific information also proceeded more freely than before; the Group benefited from greater access to Shell Oil's seismic technology in pursuing offshore exploration in other parts of the world, especially West Africa.

Organizational and administrative integration did not immediately follow the buyout. In 1985, Shell Oil's strong-willed president John Bookout negotiated a deal that allowed Shell Oil to conduct its affairs post-buyout in very much the same manner as before, in accordance with the Group's decentralized corporate structure. Houston still ran the capital budgets and determined staffing and development strategies for Shell in the United States, and Shell Oil continued to report its corporate earnings separately. By the early 1990s, unfortunately for the US company, those reports began to diverge sharply from the Group's. While fortunes of Royal Dutch/Shell soared (due to the weakening dollar and high margins in refining and marketing, where the Group was strongest), those of Shell Oil plummeted. The mid-1980s price collapse and prolonged industry slump seriously undermined the performance of the company, which was committed to expensive technologies (heavy oil production/refining and offshore exploration and production) in a declining oil-producing country. In the early 1990s, Shell was forced to cut its workforce and sell off major upstream and downstream assets.

By the early 1990s, as the globalization of trade and investment intensified, Royal Dutch/Shell leaders recognized the cross-border internalization advantages of integrating Shell Oil more closely into its world-wide operations. Technological and managerial expertise, service and supply arrangements, and procurement and sales, could be more efficiently and profitably organized on a global basis. Although the Group was several years behind British Petroleum in implementing such a change, both enterprises faced the same imperative in the 1990s of reshaping an international organization of national operations into a single international operation. Like BP, Royal Dutch/Shell borrowed American management theories to help rethink its world-wide management structure. It hired American consulting firms such as McKinsey and Coopers & Lybrand, as well as University of Michigan professor Noel Tichy, who had advised Shell Oil on ways to become more decentralized and entrepreneurial in making its cutbacks and reforms of the early 1990s. In January 1996, based on a McKinsey plan, Royal Dutch/Shell reduced its central bureaucracy by 30 per cent and established five committees to run Shell's major businesses (exploration and production; oil products; gas and coal; chemicals; and central staff functions) on a global basis (Guyon 1997).

Despite the reduction in Shell's central bureaucracy, the reorganization actually centralized decision-making. The Group had long operated with a decentralized and internationalized management structure, based on strong, national-level CEOs who reported to regional coordinators and managing directors. In the 1996 reorganization, Group headquarters asserted more direct control over Shell's world-wide businesses. For Shell Oil, this meant the virtual elimination of its long-cherished managerial autonomy. Step by step, first in chemicals, then in services, then in exploration and production, the Group reduced Shell Oil's authority to act on its own. Managers in Houston increasingly found that their immediate superiors resided in Europe. The history of Shell in the United

States has now come full circle. The company is once again a collection of companies or businesses directly managed and coordinated from abroad. American managers are forced to compete with other Group entities for a finite global budget, and returns to US operations do not necessarily stay in the United States. In 1999, Shell Oil stopped publishing its own annual report, symbolizing the death of the old American Shell.

One could argue that this newly reconstituted relationship is the culmination of a long campaign, possibly going back to the 1960s, by Royal Dutch/Shell to gain greater financial and administrative control over its largest subsidiary operation. The gradual but steady decline of the United States as a major oil-producing country, and the globalization of oil and product markets, eroded justification for a nationally organized and autonomously managed Shell Oil Company. Internalization advantages increasingly outweighed the locational advantages in the management of the Group's US interests. Carrying out internalization meant first gaining complete financial control over Shell Oil, thus eliminating legal barriers to integration, and then folding parts of the company into the global structure of the Group. While integration was traumatic for many Shell Oil employees and shareholders, it proceeded within an increasingly permissive political and legal climate in the United States. Maintaining an American minority shareholding interest for political cover and cultural legitimacy was not as imperative as it had been during the nationalistic decades following World Wars I and II. As Wilkins points out in Chapter 2, the 1970s and 1980s witnessed greater public and political acceptance of foreign enterprises in the United States (despite temporary anxieties about rising Japanese investments), and the 1990s were marked by growing acknowledgement of the extent and depth of the internationalization of the American economy.

National and cultural identities are not as hard and fixed in the new global economy as they once were, but they still shape the business environment. Globalization is not a transhistorical, state-less process, but a political and economic system managed and orchestrated by governments. Foreign investors must still consider distinct local and national conditions. As the heart of the global economy, the United States, in particular, cannot be run as a branch office. It is still as important, perhaps increasingly important, for foreign entities to retain 'American' characteristics, to maintain a national profile and be part of the local fabric – not so much for legal and political reasons, as in the past, but to engage customers and 'stakeholders' who inherently trust American enterprises more than foreign ones, or who are uncomfortable with the consequences of globalization. For this reason among others, the Group in 1999 appointed an American, Steve Miller, as president of Shell Oil. To preserve some degree of American identity, Miller has made special efforts to emphasize its history and heritage in the United States. As long as the United States retains its political and economic dominance in the world, and remains the largest consumer of oil and a formidable producer, Shell will have to keep wearing its American face.

Notes

1 This article benefits from interviews with retired Shell Oil personnel, but the views and interpretations expressed in it are solely those of the author and do not reflect those of Shell Oil or Royal Dutch/Shell.

2 The settlement sum gave an additional $2 per share for all members of a subclass of Shell shareholders who had accepted the $58 tender offer, and the same additional $2 per share for members of another subclass consisting of non-tendering stockholders if they waived their right to a court appraisal of their shares in the short-form merger at the $58 per share merger price. In 1991, however, a Delaware chancery court judge ruled that about 1,000 shareholders who rejected the settlement offer and sued for more should be paid $71.20 a share plus interest.

References

'Aliens welcome' (1953) *Business Week* 170, 21 February.

Backman, J. (1970) *The Economics of the Chemical Industry*, Washington: Manufacturing Chemists' Association.

Beaton, K. (1957) *Enterprise in Oil: A History of Shell in the United States*, New York: Appleton-Century-Crofts.

Bergsten, C., Horst, T. and Moran, T. (1978) *American Multinationals and American Interests*, Washington: Brookings Institution.

Burck, G. (1957) 'The bountiful world of Royal Dutch/Shell', *Fortune* 56, 3: 135–41, 174–6, 182.

Court of Chancery of the State of Delaware (1991) *Smith v. Shell Petroleum, Inc.*, No. 8395, *Delaware Journal of Corporate Law* 16 Del. J. Corp. L. 870.

'The diplomats of oil' (1960) *Time* 9 May: 92–102.

Dunning, J. (2000) 'The eclectic paradigm as an envelope for economic and business theories of MNE activity', *International Business Review* 9: 163–90.

'Full circle' (1956) *Forbes* 1 June: 25–6.

Gienow-Hecht, J. (2000) 'Shame on *us*?', *Diplomatic History* 24, 3: 465–94.

Golden, L. (1967) *Saturday Review* 9 December: 3.

Guyon, J. (1997) 'Why is the world's most profitable company turning itself inside out?' *Fortune* 4 August: 121–5.

Halpern et al. v. *Barran et al.* (15 December 1970) Court of Chancery of Delaware, New Castle, 272 A.2d 118; 1970 Del. Ch. Lexis 93.

—— (25 May 1973) Court of Chancery of Delaware, 313 A.2d 139; 1973 Del. Ch. Lexis 124.

Howarth, S. (1997) *A Century in Oil: The 'Shell' Transport and Trading Company, 1897–1997*, London: Weidenfeld & Nicolson.

'H.S.M. Burns of Shell Oil' (1951) *Fortune* September: 124–5.

Kipping, M. and Bjarnar O. (eds) (1998) *The Americanization of European Business: The Marshall Plan and the Transfer of US Management Models*, London: Routledge.

Mack, T. (1986) 'It's time to take risks', *Forbes* 6 October: 125–33.

Norman, J.R. (1992) 'The opportunities are enormous', *Forbes* 9 November: 92–4.

'OCAW carries shell fight to foreign brass' (1963) *Union News* 19 May, 2: 1.

'Oil – Shell's game' (1952) *Forbes* 1 April, 69, 7: 18–27.

'Oil strikers get global support' (1963) *Business Week* 25 May: 60–2.

'Portraits of two presidents' (1960) *Shell News* 18 December, 12: 2.

'Royal Dutch is set to swallow Shell Oil' (1984) *Business Week* 6 February: 31–2.

'Royal Dutch/Shell and its new competition' (1957) *Fortune* October, 55, 4: 139–44, 174, 176, 178.

'Shell, a fallen champ of oil industry, tries to regain its footing' (1991) *Wall Street Journal* 30 August: 1.

Shell Development Company (1986) *Bellaire Research Cêter: The First Fifty Years, 1936–1986*; Houston Shell Development.

Shell Oil Company, *Annual Report*, various years.

Shell Oil Company (1977) Form 10-K, *Annual Report to the Securities and Exchange Commission.*

Shell Oil Company (1980) Form 10-K, *Annual Report to the Securities and Exchange Commission.*

Shell Oil Company (1999) *Annual Review.*

'Shell Oil turns to Caribbean' (1948) *Business Week* 30 October.

'Why Royal Dutch/Shell is betting on the US' (1984) *Business Week* 20 February: 98–100.

11 What do affiliate exits tell us about the challenges faced by foreign investors in the United States?

Jean-François Hennart, Thomas Roehl and Ming Zeng

Introduction

There are many ways to study the challenges foreign investors face when managing in the United States. Business historians can study the archives of a given business firm and document the problems they faced in the US. Another possible strategy is to look at the survival of the US affiliates of foreign investors. If managing in the United States poses major challenges for foreign investors, then their US affiliates should make losses, and should eventually be sold or liquidated. We could collect systematic data on exits of affiliates of a given investing country in a given host country. We could estimate the relative difficulty that investors of a given investing country have in managing in a given target country by the proportion of their affiliates that exit within a given period of time. We would, for example, infer that managing in the United States is more challenging for French firms than managing in Spain, if we observed that their American affiliates have shorter lives than their Spanish affiliates. Similarly, we could infer the influence of cultural distance on the management of foreign affiliates in a given host country by the relative longevity of affiliates in that host country. For example, we could find out by looking at the comparative longevity of British versus French affiliates in the United States whether the greater cultural similarity between the United Kingdom and the United States makes it easier for British than for French firms to tackle the American market. Comparing relative rates of exit would also tell managers in which markets they are likely to experience difficulties. Lastly, one could run regressions attempting to measure the relative impact on exits of a number of variables that are likely to cause management problems. For example, one could test whether the choice of the appropriate mode of entry (joint venture versus wholly-owned affiliate and greenfield versus acquisitions) may alleviate the problems encountered by investors entering culturally distant countries, and how this appropriate mode of entry should vary according to the cultural distance to the target country and perhaps the industry of the investor.

Such an approach would nicely complement the work of business historians which is detailed, but sometimes hard to generalize. While we would be losing some of the insight and richness that come from detailed studies of individual firms, we would be able to reach more general conclusions. We might, for example, obtain answers to questions such as these:

- Is managing in the United States significantly more challenging for European firms than managing in other countries?
- Is managing in the United States more challenging for Latin than for Anglo-Saxon or Germanic investors?
- Can one systematically identify the type of firms that are likely to have particular difficulties in managing their US operations?

Unfortunately, things are not so simple. There are three basic difficulties in using the longevity of foreign affiliates in a foreign country as an index of the management challenges faced by their parents. The first one is conceptual, and has to do with the less than perfect equation between exit and failure. The second relates to potential differences between firms and between countries in the causal link between failures and exits. The third one is the great difficulty of setting up databases that allow us to compare exit rates across countries.

Exits as symptoms of management difficulties

In 1975, Sumitomo Chemicals decided it wanted to sell in the United States its Sumithion brand of forest insecticide which was selling well in Japan. It therefore set up a joint venture, Mount Pleasant Chemical, with an American partner, Stauffer Chemical. Sumitomo had, however, underestimated the competitive strength of a similar brand of organic phosphate insecticide called Parathion that was sold on the American market. The joint venture never made money and was liquidated in 1984.

Oki Electric's unsuccessful foray into the US market for private branch exchanges (PBX) seems also to have suffered from poor marketing. The firm was set up in 1973 in Oakland Park, Florida, as a wholly-owned affiliate to manufacture and sell PBXs. But the sales were never sufficient to support the operation, and the plant was closed in the mid-1980s.

Production and labour management problems seem also to have plagued some Japanese affiliates. In 1979 Asahi Glass Company purchased from Hordis Glass Co. 80 per cent of West Virginia Flat Glass in Clarksburg, West Virginia. The plant making thick glass sheets had just been shut down by its owner. Asahi attempted to convert the plant's production lines from thick to thin glass, but was unsuccessful, and the affiliate was shut down in 1981 for repairs and refurbishment, and finally sold in 1986 due to poor productivity.

The exits of Everett Piano and New England Drawn Steel seem also to have been caused by labour difficulties, although further investigations would seem to be needed before a definitive assessment can be made. New England Drawn Steel, a plant making cold drawn steel bars, was acquired in 1973 by a consortium made up of Azuma Steel, Oshima Seisen and Nippon Steel Trading. According to its former president, the business was sold to a Canadian firm in 1981 because of labour problems. The demise of Everett Piano, a medium-calibre piano maker acquired by Yamaha in 1973, seems also to have been precipitated, in part, by union troubles, although the official reason for the closing was 'declining piano sales'. Immediately after its purchase by Yamaha, employees of the South Haven, Michigan, factory went on strike. The house of the American president was reportedly shot at, and threatening calls were made to those of the Japanese expatriate managers. While things seem to have later calmed down, it is significant that when, in 1967, Yamaha closed the plant, it moved the manufacturing of the Yamaha line of pianos to its Georgia organ manufacturing plant, and contracted with Baldwin to continue the production of the Everett piano line. This suggests that demand for pianos was not a problem.

While cases such as these show some link between poor management on the one hand (poor market intelligence, poor technological assessment, difficulties with managing American workers), and poor profitability and exit, on the other, our database of Japanese exits from the United States, as well as the literature on exits of business units, shows that the link between management difficulties and exits is not always as strong as usually thought.

The fortunes of foreign affiliates, like those of their purely domestic competitors in the target market, are partly due to luck. Unpredictable factors like the weather affect demand for ice cream and canned soup. To the extent that these factors are purely random, they make up statistical noise in large sample research. Care must be taken in individual case studies not to seek a management failure explanation for what are to a large extent random events. In some cases, however, it is difficult to know whether the demise of a firm is due to unforeseen difficulties, or to failure to anticipate problems and to deal with them in time.

Consider the case of Alaska Pulp and Paper. In the early 1950s, the US government, concerned about the full utilization of the forests of Alaska, decided to provide incentives for the harvesting of trees in isolated areas. It offered long-term cutting contracts at reasonable rates. In addition to a US company, a consortium of two Japanese man-made textile manufacturers (Teijin and Toray) and of three trading companies (Marubeni, Mitsui and Mitsubishi) decided to accept the contracts and to make the large investments necessary to harvest the trees, chip them to pulp, and ship it to Japan. The textile firms used the pulp for their own synthetic fibre production, while the trading companies sold them to Japanese paper companies. The consortium established two pulp mills in Ketchikan and Sitka.

As the price of lumber increased, a major sawmill operation was added in Wrangell.

With the successful development of the North Slope petroleum field and the rise of environmental consciousness, the public started to question the wisdom of cutting old growth forests to make pulp for Japanese consumers. In the 1990s, the environmental movement successfully persuaded the US Congress to abolish the favourable terms under which the consortium obtained lumber from Alaska's national forests; the pulp and lumber mills, now denied access to trees, had to close. By 1997 all three plants had been liquidated. To a large extent, it is difficult to attribute their closure to the difficulties of managing in the United States. It is possible, in fact, that the operations were quite profitable as long as they lasted.

The misfortune of Mitsubishi aircraft seems also another example of bad luck. The firm entered the United States hoping to sell business jets. As it was seeking FAA certification, a door fell off a DC10 aircraft at the Paris Air Show, leading to a tightening of regulations. This change in regulations – but also perhaps Mitsubishi's lack of knowledge of FAA procedures – delayed the launch long enough to make the plane uncompetitive. Mitsubishi finally sold the business to Beech Aircraft.

A third example of how it is difficult for an outsider to separate bad luck from bad management is Southern Metal Service. Kanematsu Gosho established this steel service centre (with a 20 per cent stake) in 1973 in Gulfport, Mississippi. The affiliate was set up for hot bands and related products that used hot-rolled steel imported from Mexico, Brazil, South Africa and other sources. When these supplies dried up after the US imposed so-called 'voluntary restraint agreements' on these countries, Kanematsu chose to close its (by then fully-owned) subsidiary. While the imposition of restraints was clearly a major setback, the survival, and indeed the expansion, of other Japanese steel service centres in the United States during the same period suggests that the choice of products and/or location made by Kanematsu seems to have made its affiliate particularly vulnerable. Other Japanese steel service centres seem to have been better able to replace imported steel with US steel or with that produced by Japanese-US joint ventures.

Not all exits are failures

For exits to be a clear index of management difficulties faced in a given host market, there must also be a clear link between these difficulties (or excessive time spent solving them) and exits. In fact, not all exits are due to management difficulties, and the link between management difficulties and exits may be mediated by the parents' cultural characteristics.

First, it is important to recognize that affiliates of multinational firms may exit from a given host country for reasons that have little to do with the difficulties they experience in managing in the target country. Besides poor profitability of the affiliate, the following are other reasons why an affiliate may be closed by its parents:

- a the parent of the affiliate may experience financial difficulties in its other operations that force it to sell off some or all of its foreign affiliates;
- b the parent may decide that it no longer wants to be in the line of business where the affiliate is active;
- c the parent may decide that the target market is better served from other locations (for example, by exports from the home country);
- d the parent may decide that it still wants to serve the market from plants inside the target market location, but that it wants to do this through contracts as opposed to through equity; it may therefore sell or liquidate its investment and replace it with a long-term contract from a local supplier (for an example, see Appendix 11.1);
- e the parent may decide that an offer to buy its affiliate is too good to resist;
- f the parent may have invested to obtain knowledge of the US, and may decide to sell off when its goals are met (for an example, see Appendix 11.2);
- g the parent may be contractually obligated to sell its share to its joint venture partner (Appendix 11.3);
- h the parent may want to dissolve an existing arrangement in order to move into a new one (Appendix 11.4);
- i there is also the special case of investments made to guarantee trade flows (Appendices 11.1 and 11.5).

That these reasons are important in the aggregate is suggested by three empirical studies of exits of domestic subsidiaries. Duhaime and Grant (1984) asked the managers of forty large American firms for the reasons for the divestment of 59 of their affiliates. Hamilton and Chow (1993) asked the CEOs of New Zealand's 98 largest companies why they sold or liquidated 208 of their units (three-fourths of them were sold). Kaplan and Weisbach (1992) studied the characteristics of units sold off by US firms.

These three studies yielded findings that were basically consistent, and that can be summarized as follows: first, not all divestments were failures; instead, decisions to sell or liquidate affiliates resulted from two sets of factors, those affecting the affiliate and those affecting parents. While divested affiliates were typically poorly performing, a significant number were in fact profitable. Duhaime and Grant found that 16 per cent of the affiliates that were divested had, according to their parents, acceptable profitability. Hamilton and Chow's respondents, when asked to rank from 1 (unimportant) to 5 (very important) the reasons why they closed their domestic affiliates, ranked 'low return of units' at 4.2, but 'focus on core activities' and the need to 'meet corporate liquidity requirements' were not far behind with 3.8. Poor profitability was cited by parents in Kaplan and Weisbach's sample as the cause of the sell-off of only 22 per cent of the affiliates, while accounting measures showed that only half of the divested units were making losses when divested. Profitable affiliates were in fact divested because divestment was also a function of factors affecting the parents. All three studies showed the financial situation of the parent and changes in its strategy to be important (these two factors were the reason for 31 and 42 per cent of Kaplan and Weisbach's sell-offs). Divested units tended to be those less dependent on the rest of the firm (Duhaime and Grant 1984) and less central to its business (Hamilton and Chow 1993).

The idea that exits are not all due to poor profitability is suggested by other studies of exits. Exits can take the form of liquidations/bankruptcies, or that of sell-offs. An affiliate that is liquidated or goes bankrupt ceases to exist as an entity. In contrast, when a foreign parent sells its affiliate, the affiliate continues to exist, but under different ownership. Because the affiliate continues to operate, one would think that its performance was good enough to attract interest from another firm. Hence, while one would expect affiliates that are liquidated or go bankrupt to have had low profitability, one could expect a higher proportion of those that are sold to be profitable. And indeed, Kaplan and Weisbach found that half of the affiliates sold by the US firms they studied were profitable.

Recent studies highlight two important characteristics of exits that suggest caution in interpreting them as failures: first, most exits are not bankruptcies and liquidations, but instead sell-offs; furthermore, econometric studies of the determinants of exits show that these two types of exits are not explained by the same factors. The important role played by sell-offs in total exits was first stressed by Gomes-Casseres (1987), who found that more than three-fourths of the exits in his sample of close to 6,000 foreign subsidiaries established abroad by US parents between 1900 and 1975 were in fact sell-offs. In our research, reported below, on the survival of the US manufacturing affiliates of Japanese corporations between 1980 and 1998, sell-offs made up more than half of all exits (exits include stopping manufacturing, liquidating, and selling the affiliate).

Second, Hennart, Kim, and Zeng (1998) and Mata and Portugal (1998) found that the fit of their models explaining exits were improved by separately analyzing liquidations and sell-offs. Hennart, Kim, and Zeng used event history analysis to identify the reasons why 288 Japanese affiliates established in the US in 1980 had exited by 1991. They analyzed sell-offs and liquidations separately and found that this improved their ability to predict exits. Paradoxically, their model could explain sell-offs better than liquidations/bankruptcies. Sell-offs were explained by economic conditions in the industry entered (Japanese affiliates in US industries benefiting from fast demand growth had a lower probability of being sold off), by the characteristics of the parents (large parents were more likely to sell their US affiliates), and by those of the affiliate (affiliates that were joint ventured and those that manufacture products not manufactured by their parents had shorter lives). Mata and Portugal (1998) analyzed exits of 1033 foreign affiliates that entered Portugal between 1983 and 1989 and also found that exits through liquidations and exits through sell-offs had separate determinants. Minority joint ventures, for example, had a higher probability of being sold, but not liquidated. The reverse was true for affiliates that had been established through acquisitions.

To sum up, a significant proportion of exits are sell-offs. Poor profitability is only one of the factors explaining why these affiliates are sold, and the likely difference in motives between exits through sales and exits through liquidations/bankruptcies shows up when trying to explain them through econometric models.

All parents do not react similarly to failures

We have seen that exits of foreign affiliates from a target foreign market are not an exact measure of the difficulties of managing them because poor profitability is only one of the reasons why affiliates exit. Another problem of inferring management difficulties from exits is that the reaction of parents to poor profitability (or excessive management time spent to prevent poor profitability) may systematically vary across parents depending on their nationality. This makes it more difficult to compare the exit rate of parents based in different countries.

This point is raised by Hennart *et al.* (1999). Hennart and his co-authors compared the survival rates of a sample of north European (Danish, Dutch, Norwegian and Finnish) and Japanese affiliates manufacturing in the US in 1980. Because northern Europe is culturally closer to the United States than Japan, we were expecting to see Japanese affiliates to have a shorter life than their north European counterparts. By 1991, one-third of the affiliates had exited, 22 per cent through sell-offs and 10 per cent through liquidations, but there were significant differences between the two subsamples, with 52 per cent of the north European affiliates having exited (32 per cent through sell-offs and 21 per cent through liquidations) compared to only 27 per cent of the Japanese affiliates (19 per cent through sell-offs, and only 8 per cent through liquidations). Hennart and his co-authors attempted to see whether these differences were statistically significant after controlling for all the other factors that might affect survival, such as the entry mode of the affiliate (joint venture versus wholly-owned, acquisition versus greenfield), the conditions in the US industry entered (such as its rate of growth), those in the parent's home country (proxied by its rate of GNP growth), the exchange rate between the home country and the US, and the size, international experience, and nationality of the parent. Exits were separated into sell-offs and liquidations.

As in the studies cited above, the model explained sell-offs better than acquisitions. Compared to wholly-owned affiliates, joint ventures were more likely to be sold and to be liquidated. Acquired affiliates were more likely to be sold (but not liquidated) than those set up from scratch. Affiliates in fast growing US sectors were less likely to be sold, but this had no impact on their probability of liquidations. Favourable economic conditions in the parent's home country decreased the probability an affiliate would be sold or liquidated. Larger parents had a greater propensity to sell off affiliates, but not to liquidate them. A depreciation of the home currency vis-à-vis the dollar led to more sell-offs, but not to more liquidations.

Interestingly, when all these variables were entered into the regression, the rate of exit of Japanese affiliates became statistically indistinguishable from that of their culturally closer north European rivals. One possible explanation, supported by an analysis of the timing of exits, is that, while Japanese affiliates perform more poorly than their north European counterparts, Japanese parents are more reluctant to pull the plug on them. This can be explained either by their longer time horizon or by their greater reluctance to publicly acknowledge failure (Kim and Nam 1998). Hence the cultural traits shared by parents may also affect exit rates.

What can we conclude from this brief survey of the literature on exits? First, one must distinguish between two types of exits, sell-offs and liquidation/bankruptcies. These two types of exit seem determined by different factors. While it would seem reasonable to assume that poorly performing affiliates cannot easily be sold, and hence will be liquidated, the same is not necessarily true for sell-offs. Hence one should not equate exit with failure. Some parents exit the US because they have decided to change their product portfolio, concentrating on a smaller number of core products. Their affiliates may be doing quite well, and can, in some cases, be sold at great profit.

The second point to keep in mind is that exits occur when the costs of staying put are higher than those of exiting. There may be circumstances where exiting is financially or psychologically costly. The financial cost of exit may be linked to the affiliate's mode of entry. Greenfield affiliates are, to a large extent, customized to the parent – otherwise the foreign investor would have bought an 'off the shelf' firm through an acquisition. It is easier to sell a unit that has been acquired because such units have already been carved off from their former parents, hence they can usually be severed again by their new owners. The transaction costs involved in a sale of an acquisition should therefore be lower than those of selling a greenfield operation. Likewise, joint venture contracts sometimes have clauses which oblige one partner to buy the other partner's stake. This facilitates exit through sale (Nanda and Williamson 1995). The psychological cost of exit may also vary with the home base of the parent. Parents located in countries where major decisions do not require consensus and where managers are comfortable acknowledging their mistakes should have a higher propensity to sell or to liquidate affiliates.

A third important point is that the rate of exit is affected by factors that impact both the parents and the affiliate. Among the factors that affect exits at the affiliate level are:

- a the competitiveness and the growth of the product market entered by the affiliate;
- b unexpected changes in macro or microeconomic conditions, such as changes in exchange rates;
- c political risk, such as the imposition of new regulations or the cancellation of government contracts or, conversely, an unexpected improvement in the regulatory climate;
- d the way the affiliate entered the target country, which often affects the ease of exit.

Parent level factors include:

- a changes in the parent's home country environment, such as growth;
- b the firm's product and geographic strategy;
- c parent size: larger parents may be less sentimental about any given affiliate; and hence more ready to sell or liquidate it;
- d parent experience;
- e parent profitability, since profitable parents have the ability to sustain the losses incurred by their progeny, while parents in difficult financial position may need to sell off profitable affiliates to obtain cash.

Empirical difficulties

Besides the conceptual difficulties noted above, research on exits is also hampered by empirical problems. Evaluating the survival of foreign affiliates means following them over time until a given cut-off date. One must, however, ascertain survival by looking at a cohort of subsidiaries of approximately the same age, since survival does vary with age (although that relationship is not well known in the case of business units). It is therefore important to obtain or build up a list of all the affiliates that were born at a particular point of time. That list must be as complete as possible and have no systematic bias. One must be careful about survival bias, i.e. building a list that excludes affiliates that died before the end of the observation period. Because capital invested in services and trade is typically smaller than in manufacturing, barriers to exit are also lower in the former than in the latter, and one would expect the exit rate to be higher in trade and services than in manufacturing. Hence cohorts should not mix up manufacturing and non-manufacturing affiliates.

Unfortunately, national statistical agencies do not generally publish lists of foreign affiliates active in their countries. The few lists which are available (US Department of Commerce; Toyo Keizai), and which have been used by authors researching exits (for example, Li 1995 and Kogut 1991) are generally inadequate.

There are two main problems that face researchers trying to compile their own list. The first one is that foreign direct investors are not required to make public the list of their plants in a given country, the value of their assets, and the level of production and sales. Foreign investors may provide information on their foreign units in their annual reports or on their web home pages, but the address given may be that of an administrative unit to which plants and sales office report, not that of the plants themselves. This information does not provide any feel for the depth of the investor's presence and may lead to double counting. The administrative offices of Japanese fish processors are typically in Washington State, but their plants are often in Alaska. (For example, Nippon Suisan has a US subsidiary called Unisea that in turns owns Dutch Harbor Seafood, a packing plant in Dutch Harbor, Alaska.) A researcher who does not build his database at the plant level is likely either to double count or to miss the closure of the plant if the firm does not close its administrative offices. It is also very important to separate manufacturing plants from sales or administrative offices, since the barriers to exit are much greater for manufacturing plants than for sales offices. In practice, it is sometimes difficult to ascertain whether the so-called manufacturing affiliates are repackaging units (screwdriver plants) or genuine manufacturing operations.

The next step in ascertaining exit and survival rates is to follow up the affiliate to the end of the observation period and to ascertain whether the affiliate has survived or not, and if not, how and when it exited. One easy (but dangerous) way to do so is to look at published lists, and to assume that absence from the list means exit (the method followed by Li (1995) among others). This is a dangerous assumption to make, because there are many reasons besides exit why an affiliate may no longer be on the list. The name of the affiliate may be missing because of omission by the list maker, or because it has been changed. Such changes are rather common following the integration of acquired affiliates or a change in the parent name. For example, between 1980 and 1998 Kohkoku changed its name to Achilles Corporation, Tofle to Omega Flex, Exar Integrated Systems to Rohm Device USA, Izumi to IDEC-Izumi, Nippondenso to Denso, and Taiyo Fishery to Maruha. Administrative reorganization may also result in the elimination of old administrative units (or the creation of new ones) without any corresponding changes to manufacturing operations. Lastly, a company that outgrows a plant and moves it a few miles to another city might be coded as having exited if matching is done on name and location.

A better way is to positively identify all cases of exits, and to find out whether the exit took the form of a sale or of a liquidation/bankruptcy. This can be ascertained through secondary sources (such as databases of newspaper and journal articles, for example Lexis-Nexis) and through written or verbal contact with the firms involved, or with their parents. Two factors make this time consuming. First, companies are reluctant to talk about exits and corporate memory of these events seems to be extremely short. Furthermore, there is, as far as we know, no centralized statistical record of bankruptcies and liquidations in the United States. Databases of mergers and acquisitions are often limited to large acquisitions made by large firms. Second, an affiliate which is liquidated leaves no trace, and it is generally difficult to contact its former managers. One often has to call the Chamber of Commerce, the City Hall, the Post Office or the newspaper of the city where the affiliate was previously located. We use this approach in the research project described below.

Goal and scope of the project

The research project reported here follows to the end of 1998 a cohort of Japanese manufacturing affiliates active in the United States in 1980. Through cross-listing of many sources, we are confident we have a nearly complete list of all Japanese-owned manufacturing plants that were operating in the United States in 1980. Our goal is to determine the extent and the time pattern of exits, both by sale and by liquidation/bankruptcy. The observation period of 18 years allows for many changes in the environment and in the parent firms. This database will establish, for each ownership link between a Japanese parent and a US manufacturing affiliate, whether, when and how the link was broken.

Among others, we are interested in the following research questions:

1 What determines exit through sale and exit through liquidations? Are unprofitable affiliates liquidated, and profitable affiliates sold? Or are things more complicated?
2 What is the relative influence of parent and subsidiary conditions on exits? In other words, do profitable parents sustain unprofitable affiliates, or inversely, do unprofitable parents sacrifice profitable affiliates. Or do parents decide to sacrifice or to support their US affiliates based uniquely on the affiliate's performance (which may not necessarily be the same as its financial results)?
3 At a later date we want to use this database to extend the work of Hennart *et al.* (1999) that compares the extent and pattern of exits of firms based in different countries entering the United States.

Table 11.1 Industrial composition of 1980 sample

SIC	*Industry*	*Number of links between Japanese firms and US affiliates*
20	Food	47
22	Textiles	15
23	Apparel	6
24	Lumber/wood	17
25	Furniture	2
26	Paper	12
27	Printing	10
28	Chemicals	18
29	Petroleum refining	2
30	Rubber and plastics	25
32	Stone, clay, glass	7
33	Primary metals	47
34	Fabricated metals	28
35	Industrial machinery	49
36	Electrical and electronic equipment	64
37	Transportation equipment	8
38	Instruments	28
39	Miscellaneous manufacturing	14
	Unknown	6
Total		405

Our unit of observation is the manufacturing plant. An ownership link between a Japanese firm and a US affiliate counts as one observation (hence there are, for example, two observations for a plant jointly owned by Mitsui & Co. and Canon). We distinguish between exits due to sell-offs and exits due to liquidations.

There were 405 ownership links between Japanese firms and their US manufacturing subsidiaries in 1980. Table 11.1 provides their industry breakdown. As can be seen, our population is dominated by electronic equipment, machinery, primary metals, and food.

Ownership links are dissolved (exits take place) when (1) the affiliate is liquidated or declared bankrupt; (2) the parent's stake in an affiliate is sold to another firm, American, Japanese, or third country; (3) the plant discontinues manufacturing.

How many of these links were surviving at the end of 1998? We have data on 385 of our 405 links (95 per cent of our population). Two hundred and fifteen (or 55.8 per cent of the 385 links for which we have information) were still in existence in 1998. One hundred and sixty-nine links had been dissolved: in 12 cases (7 per cent of the exits), the affiliates were still in business, but had ceased manufacturing; in 67 cases (or 39.4 per cent of the exits) the affiliates had been closed or liquidated, and in 90 cases (53 per cent of the exits) the affiliates had been sold. Of these 90, 63 had been sold to their joint venture partners and 27 to third

Table 11.2 Number of exits (links) per year of Japanese affiliates manufacturing in the US in 1980

1981	5
1982	4
1983	11
1984	6
1985	8
1986	42
1987	11
1988	1
1989	10
1990	2
1991	2
1992	5
1993	2
1994	9
1995	1
1996	7
1997	6
1998	3
Exited but date unknown:	37
Survived to end 1998:	209

parties. As in the case of US firms, the sale of joint venture stakes to joint venture partners was an important source of exits. This supports the general view that joint ventures are transitory forms, although whether they are intentionally transitory (i.e. they serve as options) or unintentionally transitory (as put forth by the proponents of joint ventures as learning races) is still unclear. In our case, however, all sales to partners are *Japanese sales* to their joint venture partners, i.e. the reverse of Reich and Mankin's (1986) 'Trojan Horse' scenario.

Table 11.2 gives the number of exits per year for the 347 exits for which we have exit dates (there are 37 further exits with unknown dates). We would have liked to know if the end of the Japanese bubble had triggered an acceleration of exits, but little can be said about the pattern of exits until the exact timing of these 37 exits is known. The large number of exits in 1986 is due to the sale by Nippon Steel and Mitsui of their stakes in Alumax to their partner Amax (see Appendix 11.1). Figure 11.1 shows how many links survived the end of each year.

One important point to keep in mind is that our 1980 cohort of Japanese manufacturing affiliates in the United States is characteristic of the early phase of Japanese investment in the US (Wilkins 1990), with a higher proportion of trading-company investments and (consequently) a higher percentage of ventures in food and metals than in subsequent years. We chose the earliest year for which comprehensive data could be obtained in order to have as long an observation window as possible.

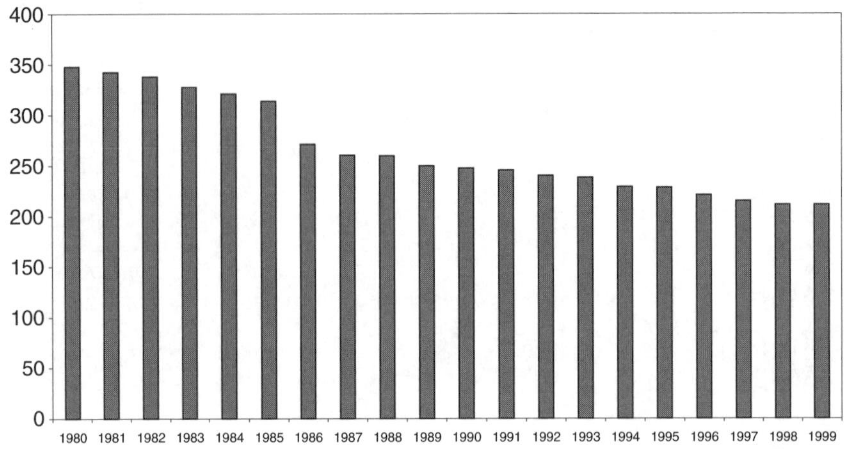

Figure 11.1 Number of surviving links between Japanese firms and US affiliates at year-end, 1980–99.

Conclusions

For both Japanese and Europeans, the US market has represented a remarkable challenge (Rosenzweig 1994). As shown elsewhere in this volume, the large size, peculiar characteristics, and litigious propensities of the US marketplace have put fear in the hearts of European and Japanese managers. Are those fears exaggerated? Beyond the well publicized encounters of Mitsubishi Motors and Astra with the US Equal Employment Opportunity Commission, is there hard evidence that managing in the United States is particularly difficult for foreign multinationals? One possible way to find out is to calculate the survival rate of their affiliates in the United States over a given period and to compare it with survival rates of their affiliates located in other countries.

Unfortunately, such comparisons run into two types of difficulties. The first one is conceptual. There are many reasons besides management problems and subsequent poor profitability why affiliates might be sold or liquidated by their parents. We need to know more about the variety of reasons why affiliates exit, and the extent to which exits are aligned with poor profitability. Estimating the challenge of managing in a country by the exit rate of foreign affiliates in that country is also beset with practical difficulties. Building longitudinal data sets is always time consuming, but building a longitudinal record of the life of foreign affiliates is particularly so.

In spite of all these difficulties, research on how long foreign affiliates survive and why they exit is likely to provide fascinating glimpses into the problems of managing in foreign environments. This chapter has presented some preliminary results of the survival over an 18-year period of a cohort of Japanese affiliates manufacturing in the United States in 1980. But much more remains to be done before we get a more comprehensive picture of the performance of foreign investors, Japanese and European, in the world's largest economy.

Appendix 11.1 Alumax Joint Venture (Nippon Steel, Mitsui Trading and Amax)

The case of Nippon Steel's and Mitsui Trading investments in Alumax provides a good example of the difficulty of attributing all exits to management failures. The Mitsui Group found itself in 1945 without an aluminium plant. As a result, Mitsui & Co., the Group's trading arm, was at a disadvantage in an important product area. Mitsui saw its chance when AMAX was looking for an outside investor to help finance an expansion in capacity. By taking a 50 per cent stake in Amax's aluminium business (renamed Alumax), the Group secured access to low-cost ingot at a time when the Japanese aluminium industry use of oil-based electricity made it uncompetitive. Mitsui provided a secure outlet for Alumax's aluminium, and Alumax a secure source of supply for Mitsui. By 1986 the market for aluminium had developed considerably, and Mitsui sold its Alumax share to Amax and replaced its investment by a series of long-term contracts that assured supply to Mitsui and outlets for Amax. There is some indication that Mitsui's divestment did not involve hard feeling, since 2 years later Mitsui was back into partnership with Amax after buying Pechiney's share in the Intalco and Eastalco smelters.

Appendix 11.2 Key Pharmaceuticals

In 1979, Mitsubishi Kasei bought a 10 per cent stake in Key Pharmaceuticals as a way to get a foothold in the American market. Mitsubishi argues that by 1986 they had achieved their objectives and this was the reason they sold back their share when Key Pharmaceuticals was acquired by Schering-Plough.

Appendix 11.3 Firestone Vineyards

In the early 1970s the Firestone family owned some land they thought suitable for grapes in the Santa Ynex valley, an area not previously used for wine quality grapes. The younger family member wanted to start the vineyard, but could not get financing. The family had good personal relations with the president of Suntory, a Japanese spirits company. The Firestone family asked Suntory to do a feasibility study for the project. The Japanese firm not only found the project to be attractive, they set up a joint venture to carry it out. The vineyard prospered, helping to establish this valley as another prime growing region. The Firestone family still felt the vineyard was a family operation, and put into the contract an option to buy the percentage share that Suntory owned. The Firestones exercised the option in 1994, and Suntory withdrew, apparently without putting any resistance.

Appendix 11.4 Nachi Bearing

In 1974, Nachi Fujikoshi, a bearing manufacturer, together with the Japanese general trading firms of Kanematsu-Gosho and Nissho-Iwai, jointly established a manufacturing subsidiary in South Portland, Maine, to manufacture bearings. In 1987 the plant was closed down when Nachi moved into a new facility in Greenwood, Indiana, closer to Japanese car assembly plants.

Appendix 11.5 Investments to guarantee trade flows

Some equity stakes are taken to secure trade. This is the case, for example, of many stakes taken by Japanese general trading companies (*sogo shosha*). These trading firms tend to take minority stakes in their US suppliers or customers. These stakes may be taken to encourage suppliers or customers to make investments which are specific to the product, or they may be given by manufacturing firms in payment for help received. They are generally temporary (Hennart and Kryda 1998). They are typically sold when the market has matured enough to make financial support and vertical integration unnecessary (as in the Alumax case described above), or inversely when the supplier does not live up to expectations. This later scenario is that of Fletcher Oil and Refining and Dorchester Fabrics. In 1979 Mitsubishi took a 20 per cent stake in Fletcher Oil and Refining, a small Carson, California, oil refinery. In exchange for its 20 per cent investment, Mitsubishi had obtained the right to market 70 per cent of the output of the refinery. Mitsubishi sold its stake in 1987, the main reason being the worsening economics of oil refining in California. Similarly, in 1985 Tomen sold the 80 per cent interest it had taken in 1980 in Dorchester Fabrics because Dorchester could not keep up with market trends.

References

Allison, P. (1995) *Survival Analysis Using the SAS System: A Practical Guide*, Gary, NC: SAS Institute Inc.

Barkema, H., Bell, J. and Pennings, J. (1996) 'Foreign entry, cultural barriers, and learning', *Strategic Management Journal* 17: 151–66.

Barkema, H., Shenkar, O., Vermeulen, F. and Bell, J. (1997) 'Working abroad, working with others: How firms learn to operate international joint ventures', *Academy of Management Journal* 40: 436–42.

Benito, G.R.G. (1997a) 'Why are foreign subsidiaries divested? A conceptual framework', in I. Bjorkman and M. Forsgren (eds) *The Nature of the International Firm: Nordic Contributions to International Business Research*, Copenhagen: Copenhagen Business School Press.

Benito, G.R.G. (1997b) 'Divestment of foreign production operations', *Applied Economics* 29: 1365–77.

Benito, G.R.G. and Larimo, J. (1995) 'Divestment of foreign production operations: The case of foreign direct investment from two Nordic countries', paper presented at the 21st annual conference of the European International Business Academy, Urbino, Italy.

Boddewyn, J. (1983) 'Foreign and domestic divestment and investment decisions: Like or unlike', *Journal of International Business Studies* 14: 23–35.

Caves, R. (1996) *Multinational Enterprise and Economic Analysis*, 2nd Edn, Cambridge: Cambridge University Press.

Chow, Y.K. and Hamilton, R.T. (1993) 'Corporate divestment: An overview', *Journal of Managerial Psychology* 8: 9–13.

Delacroix, J. (1993) 'The European subsidiaries of American multinationals: An exercise in ecological analysis', in S. Ghoshal and E. Westney (eds) *Organizational Theory and the Multinational Enterprise*, New York, NY: St Martin's Press.

Duhaime, I. and Grant, J. (1984) 'Factors influencing divestment decision-making: Evidence from a field study', *Strategic Management Journal* 5: 301–18.

Gomes-Casseres, B. (1987) 'Joint venture instability: Is it a problem?', *Columbia Journal of World Business* Summer: 97–102.

Hamilton, R.T. and Chow, Y.K. (1993) 'Why managers divest: Evidence from New Zealand's largest companies', *Strategic Management Journal* 14: 479–84.

Hannan, M.T. and Freeman, J. (1989) *Organizational Ecology*, Cambridge, Mass: Harvard University Press.

Hennart, J.-F., Barkema, H., Bell, J., Benito, G., Larimo, J., Pedersen, T. and Zeng, M. (1999) 'The survival of foreign affiliates: A comparative study of North American and Japanese investors in the United States', unpublished manuscript.

Hennart, J.-F., Kim, D.-J. and Zeng, M. (1998) 'The impact of joint venture status on the longevity of Japanese stakes in U.S. manufacturing affiliates', *Organization Science* 9: 382–95.

Hennart, J.-F. and Kryda, G. (1998) 'Why do traders invest in manufacturing?', in G. Jones (ed.) *The Multinational Traders*, London: Routledge: 212–27.

Hennart, J.-F. and Larimo, J. (1998) 'The impact of culture on the strategy of multinational enterprises: Does national origin affect ownership decisions by foreign direct investors into the United States?', *Journal of International Business Studies* 29: 515–38.

Hennart, J.-F., Roehl, T. and Zietlow, D. (1999) 'Trojan horse or work horse? The evolution of U.S.-Japanese joint ventures in the United States', *Strategic Management Journal* 20: 15–29.

Kaplan, S. and Weisbach, M. (1992) 'The success of acquisitions: Evidence from divestitures', *Journal of Finance* 47: 107–38.

Kim, J.Y. and Nam, S.H. (1998) 'The concept and dynamics of face: Implications for organizational behavior in Asia', *Organization Science* 9, 4: 522–34.

Kogut, B. (1991) 'Joint ventures and the option to expand and acquire', *Management Science* 37: 19–32.

Kogut, B. and Singh, H. (1988) 'The effect of national culture on the choice of entry mode', *Journal of International Business Studies* 19: 411–32.

Larimo, J. (1998) 'Determinants of divestments in foreign production operations made by Finnish firms in OECD countries', Discussion Paper 233, University of Vaasa.

Levinthal, D. and Fichman, M. (1988) 'Dynamics of interorganizational attachments: Auditor–client relationships', *Administrative Science Quarterly* 33: 345–69.

Li, J. (1995) 'Foreign entry and survival: Effects of strategic choices on performance in international markets', *Strategic Management Journal* 16: 333–51.

Mata, J. and Portugal, P. (1998) 'The exit mode of foreign entrants: The impact of entry and post-entry strategies', unpublished manuscript.

Mitchell, W. (1994) 'The dynamics of evolving markets: The effect of business sales and age on dissolutions and divestitures', *Administrative Science Quarterly* 39: 575–602.

Nanda, A. and Williamson, P. (1995) 'Use joint ventures to ease the pain of restructuring', *Harvard Business Review* November/December.

Park, S.H. and Ungson, G. (1997) 'The effect of national culture, organizational complementarity, and economic motivation on joint venture dissolution', *Academy of Management Journal* 40: 279–307.

Pennings, J., Barkema, H. and Douma, S. (1994) 'Organizational learning and diversification', *Academy of Management Journal* 37: 608–40.

Reich, R. and Mankin, E. (1986) 'Joint ventures with Japan give away our future', *Harvard Business Review* March/April: 23–37.

Rosenzweig, P. (1994) 'The new American challenge: Foreign multinationals in the United States', *California Management Review* 36: 107–23.

Wilkins, M. (1990) 'Japanese multinationals in the United States: Continuity and change', *Business History Review* 64: 585–629.

Yamawaki, H. (1997) 'Exit of Japanese multinationals in U.S. and European manufacturing industries', in P. Buckley and J.L. Mucchielli (eds) *Multinational Firms and International Relocation*, Cheltenham, England: Edward Elgar.

Zaheer, S. and Mosakowski, E. (1997) 'The dynamics of the liability of foreigness: A global study of survival in financial services', *Strategic Management Journal* 18, 6: 439–64.

12 The location strategies of Japanese multinationals in the US

Kenichi Yasumuro

Introduction

This chapter takes a new approach to understanding the geographical location of Japanese multinational enterprises in the United States. It is argued that choice of location must be seen in the context of the distinctive type of management strategy pursued by different Japanese firms. These different strategies reflect differences in the priorities given by firms to acquiring and absorbing local knowledge in the United States, rather than transferring knowledge there from Japan.

The growth of foreign direct investment (FDI) from Japanese multinationals in the United States from the 1970s has been described many times. The first major wave of firms came from the home electrical appliance sector. Subsequently, as Voluntary Export Restraints and other protective devices threatened to restrict access to the world's largest market, Japanese automobile, semiconductor, electronics and precision instruments firms followed. During the 1990s high-tech appliance and auto parts firms followed the large-scale assembly companies. Especially in the automobile industry, Japanese parts makers in co-operation with American supporting industries formed new industrial accumulations in the particular locations.[1] While US-owned parts manufacturers invested outside the United States during the 1980s (Kenney and Florida 1992: 25), hundreds of Japanese suppliers established factories in the United States in the same period, transferring production technology and managerial know-how, and also contributing to the prevention of the de-industrialization of US economy.

The impact of Japanese firms on the United States was important also because of their locational decisions. Japanese multinationals contributed to the economic reactivation of rural economies whose agricultural and manufacturing industries had been in decline (Óhuallacháin and Reid 1996; Shannon, Zeile and Johnson 1999; Ulgado 1996). Japanese FDI had concentrated initially on the Pacific coast, especially California (Friedman, Gerlowski and Silberman 1992; Head, Reis and Swensôn 1995; JETRO 1985). This reflected the fact that imports of Japanese products had largely entered the country through the major harbours of the Pacific coast, such as Los Angeles port. In contrast, European multinationals, especially German companies, imported through the East Coast and concentrated their FDI in the same area (Ulgado 1996).

However, from the middle of the 1980s new locational patterns emerged for Japanese firms. Japanese FDI flowed into the Midwest and the Southern states, a trend symbolized by the automobile industry and the creation of the so-called automobile corridor along National Highways 75 and 65 (Abo 1994; Kenney and Florida 1992, 1993; Mair, Florida and Kenney 1988; Okamoto 2000; Reid 1990, 1991; Rubenstain 1991). Moreover, in the 1990s, Japanese high-tech industries, such as semiconductors, precision equipment, fine chemicals, medicinal and medical appliances preferred the locations where research and development resources had accumulated. They established R&D centres and manufacturing facilities in the knowledge intensive districts of the Pacific coast, the Southern high-tech cities, and the East Coast high-tech corridors.

Conventional industrial location studies on foreign companies in the United States performed by economic geographers have paid little attention to the strategic decision-making of firms choosing sites. Traditionally, economic geographers identify variables such as 'access to the markets', 'labour market conditions', 'state promotion efforts to attract foreign investment', 'state and local personal taxes' (Friedman, Gerlowski and Silberman 1992; Ulgado 1996), 'states with higher per capita incomes', 'higher densities of manufacturing activities', 'wage levels', 'unemployment rate', 'unionization rate', 'transportation infrastructures' (Coughlin, Terza and Arromdee 1991), 'customer's location', 'greenfield or acquired' (Óhuallacháin and Reid 1996). Even if the location selection by US companies, and Japanese and European multinationals in the US are compared, they merely point out the differences, rather than explain why these differences have emerged between them (Coughlin, Terza and Arromdee 1991; Friedman, Gerlowski and Silberman 1992; Head, Ries and Swensŏn 1995; Óhuallacháin and Reid 1996; Shannon, Zeile and Johnson 1999; Ulgado 1996).

In this chapter, the relationship between the management archetype of Japanese firms and their location selection in the United States will be explored. Foreign companies do not select locations in a haphazard way, and thus it is possible to discern the strategic intent of companies from their locations. The common view of Japanese manufacture multinationals in the US is that they prefer 'countryside' locations for factory sites and tend to avoid traditional industrial city sites (Kenney and Florida 1992, 1993; Óhuallacháin and Reid 1996; Shannon, Zeile and Johnson 1999). Although our analysis below supports the existence of such a rural area preference by Japanese manufacturers, it shows that other types of location choice exist. This chapter will seek to explain these different choices by exploring the dynamics between corporate knowledge and the socially embedded knowledge networks of locations (Wilkins 1988). We argue that the interaction between the proprietary knowledge a company holds – the so-called core competence (Hamel and Prahalad 1994) – and the socially embedded network of knowledge of a location is of key importance in the formation of global competitiveness.

The role of location has not received great attention in theories of international business. The major exception is the eclectic paradigm of international production developed by John H. Dunning (1983, 1988, 1991). However, even in the eclectic paradigm, location is mainly considered narrowly in economic terms such as factor costs and availability of resources (Yasumuro 2000). In reality, a more critical contribution of location relates to a knowledge creation infrastructure. Physical locations have a cause and effect on successful knowledge management of companies (Davenport and Prusak 1998). Even if people can manage *knowledge* through the Internet, face-to-face communication retains its importance. Judged from the viewpoint of knowledge management, information and knowledge supplied from external sources is overwhelmingly more important than information and knowledge developed inside a firm (Brown and Duguid 1991). Organizations take in and absorb considerable flows of knowledge from external sources.

Even in a 'virtual economy', therefore, personal knowledge exchange in a physical location is indispensable as means of knowledge acquisition. Even if information technology is advanced and offices are distributed in remote places, knowledge intensive companies may prefer specific locations and shape particular industrial clusters (Porter 1998). The social places composed of knowledge workers and specialists function as knowledge markets (Davenport and Prusk 1998) and we may call these socially embedded networks of knowledge or knowledge infrastructure (Amin 1993; Amin and Thrift 1994; Granovetter 1985).

The following sections introduce some key concepts which are necessary to explore the relationship between firm strategies and locational decisions.

New perspectives on the eclectic paradigm

In the theory of multinational firms, Dunning's eclectic paradigm explains the international production of a company by applying three concepts: ownership advantage (O), internalization advantage (I), and location advantage (L). Each advantage is theoretically based on a different paradigm, and opposed to each other. Although Dunning often accounted those three variables as interrelated (Dunning 1983, Dunning, Kogut and Blomstrom 1990), in the context of economic theories, those variables must be treated as independent.

We intend to transpose the three variables into business management terms. Ownership advantage (O) can be regarded as the proprietary

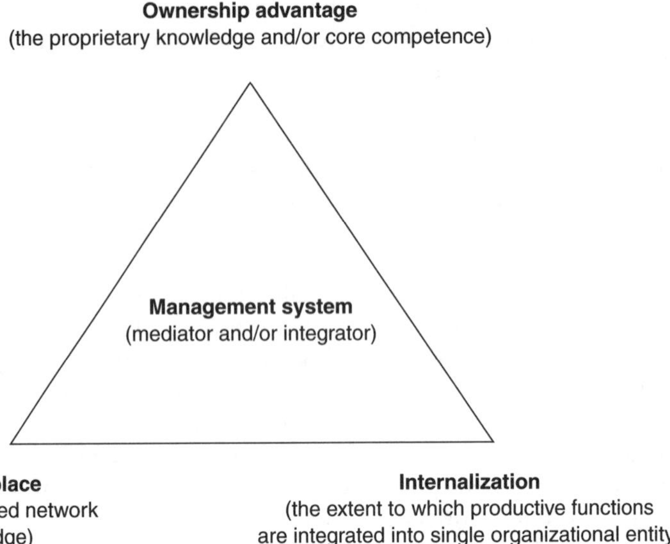

Figure 12.1 Dunning's eclectic triangle.

knowledge of the company that provides its core competence. Location advantage (L) can be taken as referring to the socially embedded network of knowledge which an industrial district holds. We will define internalization advantage (I) as the extent to which management and production functions are integrated into a single organization and/or group of enterprises. For instance, a focal firm within a Japanese *keiretsu* group internalizes research and development, physical distribution system, sale department, assembly lines, parts and components production, financial services, industrial relations, public relations, etc. and integrates those functions into the particular system of the value chain.

When the three variables of the eclectic paradigm are transposed in business management terms, it turns out that they constitute a dynamic network. The management system combines the three variables into a value creating process. We call the relationship of the three variables Dunning's Eclectic Triangle. Figure 12.1 shows the basic model.

Management archetypes: differential and integral

The following analysis distinguishes between two management archetypes based on different architectures of production strategy. The first can be termed *differential* – most typically associated with American firms – and the second is termed *integral* – most typically associated with Japanese firms (Fujimoto 1997; Kokuryo 1999; Takeda 2000). Each archetype has advantages and disadvantages in the product technology and production process.

First, the core competence of *differential* producers can be examined. In the differential archetype, management functions are standardized and integrated in a mechanical way, the interface of each function being designed under open architecture. Simultaneously, in the production process, each production unit is planned using standardized design and connected by common interface architecture. Consequently, parts, components and modules are designed as an open module, and appear on commodity markets in large quantities. A company can easily buy management services, parts and modules from outsourcers.

The advantages and disadvantages of the differential archetype are clear. Since products and services are made from standardized management functions and the combination of standardized modules, it is difficult to attribute a unique feature to products or services. Therefore, product differentiation is a difficult task and the company survives as a low price producer. However, since the product and service are fundamentally designed using an open architecture, it allows for combination with any systems that share the common architecture. Therefore, the differential type can purchase a suitable quality of modules at the lowest price from commodity markets, and is suitable for e-commerce, especially business to business procurement. This archetype requires redundancy in product design. In order to enable the connection of various managerial functions and modules by sharing common interfaces, considerable redundancy in the capacity of each function and module has to be pre-arranged. Without such redundancy the whole system is not able to function smoothly.

Consequently, the ability of new product development by a focal company is limited by the strategic partner's arbitrariness to collaborate in the design development process of specific modules. To design considerable redundant capacity of the module means that the cost burden has to be borne by suppliers. As a lowest cost seeker, suppliers do not welcome such a surplus request. However, if the order of a particular module is sufficiently large, the trade-off to the supplier can still be favourable. Consequently open-architect production is best fitted to supply chain management, such as the one applied by the Dell Computer.

On the other hand, *integral* producers intend to create outstanding quality and service for patronized customers. They aim to give prominent features to their product and service in world markets. Integral production can be defined as a strategic archetype which specifies prominent producers of elaborated goods and services, integrates productive functions inside the focal company and series of company groups (*keiretsu*), and co-ordinates functions through close human relations which are usually not defined on an organization chart. Very often co-operation and co-ordination are achieved through spontaneous work teams across organizational boundaries (Womack and Jones 1996; Womack, Jones and Roos

1990). Each unit of the production process is not subdivided functionally and each interface is not standardized in a common manner. The production systems of small and medium-sized enterprises (SME) are intricately integrated into a large assembly mechanism of a focal company (the so-called *fish bone* structure). As a whole they form a functionally integrated entity. As a result of specifically designed interfaces within the company group, the protocol and form of database for e-commerce is basically for in-house use only, and not standardized formally. Parts and components are fundamentally designed based on *closed-module thinking*, and the potential to connect with other groups modules is intentionally avoided (Takeda 2000). To ensure excellent quality and service, the integral firm encourages their customers to use *house-made* (original) parts and components and may not welcome the adoption of parts and components from the markets. Therefore, for the integral archetype, the potentiality to participate in open-market procurement through e-commerce (B to B) is limited.

The merits of the integral are clear: waste-less production and efficient design of products and service. Since the integral producers hate redundancy in the product design and production process, the involvement of SME suppliers in the collaborative design development is requested. New blueprints for every part and component are drawn up from scratch and sometimes the interface of each module is different. As a result, parts and components for new products lack interchangeability with the old models; achievement of scale economy is hopeless. Although artistic, lightweight, and miniaturized products are developed by this method, almost without exception, it takes time and requires effort for new product development, in addition to the enormous expansion of production costs.

The strategic intention of each type is clear. The differential producer reduces production cost and expands networking potential at the expense of excellence of design and quality reputation. On the other hand, the integral pays dearly for costs and connection-ability instead of its reputation for quality and services.

Matching firm competencies and location

In order to achieve the greatest performance from company-specific knowledge, the synergistic interaction with a specific location has great strategic importance (Porter 1998; Yasumuro 2000). The knowledge creation of a company is influenced not only by the internal ability of an organization, but also by the knowledge introduced from external sources. When a knowledge intensive company decides the location of FDI, it will carefully choose a place where the density of 'intellectuals' is high and the socially embedded network of knowledge is highly developed. This network might include major universities that supply both scientific knowledge and college-graduates; high-level research and development centres supported by government budgets and/or private funds; applied technology development centre management by local governments; technology transfer centres for small and medium-sized enterprises; technical high schools and junior colleges; chambers of commerce; flexible production networks of SMEs; active venture capitalists that support SME and investment banks for medium and large-sized companies; state-owned industrial development corporations that support for SME business, and so on – all connected by close human networks in the local socio-economic milieu (Cook and Morgan 1994; Granovetter 1985; Herrigel 1993).

The opportunity to benefit from locally embedded knowledge networks will be limited for the *integral* type firms because of their closed system orientation. On the other hand, *differential* types can easily adapt to an environment where mass-production thinking has penetrated in the society. The management of differential type firms will not be disturbed by the American business culture. A supply of raw materials, parts and components, standardized modules, and professional management services (consultants) are available in the old industrial regions. The availability of local outsourcers can reduce internalization investment for the investing company. On the other hand, the integral type firm may not actively search for the availability of local outsourcers, even if the level of knowledge accumulation of the old economy in the region is highly developed. This is because these firms have an extremely negative image of the old American economy, and regard the mass-production orientation of the local economy as an obstacle to closed module production.

In the thinking of integral firms, the differentiation of the product is the core competence of the company. Standardized and less quality-oriented modules, easily purchased in a commodity market, are inadequate for the highest quality and excellent design of products, guaranteed by the corporate brands of the integral (for example, Sony's *Vaio* brand computer). However, when the inward investor has a differential orientation, the availability of American mass production accumulation may be considerable, and procurement from local suppliers may be easy. On the other hand, integral firms can seldom utilize the industrial accumulation of the old American economy because of their 'not invented here' syndrome. Consequently, integral firms seek to avoid the old American economy. The integral rather chooses a virgin territory, where mass production culture has not yet penetrated, and/or districts where other Japanese companies are concentrated.

Acceptability of different management cultures

When the production process of a focal company is designed using integral architecture, and the core competence of the company is embedded in manufacturing technologies using tacit expert knowledge (operation skills), it becomes very difficult to transfer technology to different locations. In such a case, technology can only be transferred through on-the-job training. By sharing the workplace with local unskilled employees, experts (skilled Japanese expatriates) can teach production know-how to them. Investment in education and training of local employees has strategic importance. When Toyota Motors transplanted its lean factory system to the Kentucky site, foremen and team leaders were invited to Japanese factories and trained on-the-job for more than 6 months, while middle managers spent less than 2 months in training. For the *integral manufacturer*, the core competence resides in the skilled workers in the workshop rather than in white-collars in the headquarters.[2]

Consequently integral firms tend to choose as location sites areas which are easy to transfer their special architecture, and have high potential to accept a different management culture. Consequently, the integral tends to avoid the old industrial area of the Eastern states, and prefers 'new' industrial areas such as California, Texas, Kentucky, and Georgia. As Japanese management needs labour union co-operation, old industrial areas in the Eastern and Midwestern states where the militant labour unions exist (at least according to the beliefs of Japanese executives) are carefully eliminated as candidates for industrial sites.[3] When the location of customers and the efficiency of delivery have to be first priorities, the location of an old industrial area will be chosen. In such instances, they try to avoid the heart of the industrial district where the labour movement is active, and instead choose the suburbs of cities (Abo 1994; Kenney and Florida 1992, 1993; Okamoto 2000).

Testing the model

The concepts discussed above were explored in a questionnaire survey conducted between December 1999 and March 2000 jointly with Arimura (2000). Using 1999 data on Japanese FDI (*Kaigai Kigyo Shinshutu Soran*), 3,733 Japanese companies' affiliates located in the US were selected. From this group, a sample of 1,168 affiliates employing more than 50 persons were selected. A total of 109 subsidiary companies responded to the questionnaire giving a rate of effective reply of 9.4 per cent. Tables 12.1 to 12.5 provide a profile of the respondents.[4]

Table 12.1 Size of Japanese companies in the US in 1999 sample (by number of employees)

Number of employees	*Number of companies*	*Ratio (%)*
Less than 100	25	22.8
100–499	58	53.3
500–999	14	12.9
More than 1,000	12	11.0
Total	109	100

Table 12.2 Industrial classification of parent companies in 1999 sample

Industry	*Number of companies*	*Ratio (%)*
Agricultural and fishery	1	0.9
Construction	1	0.9
Manufacturing	86	78.9
Transportation and communication	2	1.8
Finance, insurance, and real estate	2	1.8
Wholesale and retail	12	11.2
Other services	5	4.5
Total	109	100

Table 12.3 Date of establishment of Japanese subsidiaries in 1999 sample

Establishment date	*Number of companies*	*Ratio (%)*
1969 or before	5	4.5
1970–9	13	12.0
1980–9	55	50.5
1990–9	36	33.0
Total	109	100

Table 12.4 Ownership policies of Japanese subsidiaries in 1999 sample

Ownership policy (%)	*Number of companies*	*Ratio (%)*
100	75	66.8
50–99	31	28.4
Less than 49	3	2.8
Total	109	100

Table 12.5 Establishment method of Japanese subsidiaries in 1999 sample

Establishment method	*Number of companies*	*Ratio (%)*
Greenfield	86	78.9
Merger and acquisition	17	15.6
Capital participation	6	5.5
Total	109	100

Table 12.6 Motives of location choice in US companies in 1999 sample

Motives of location selection	*Number of respondent company*	*Average importance*	*Standard deviation*
1 Convenience of physical distribution and traffic	100	3.94	1.12
2 Cheaper labour cost	100	2.98	1.11
3 Ease of obtaining raw material	100	3.03	1.27
4 Ease of obtaining components that meet company quality standards	100	3.01	1.27
5 Many Japanese companies are established in the area	100	2.26	1.11
6 Your company's customer in Japan	99	2.19	1.31
7 Close proximity to the consumer market	100	3.38	1.35
8 High level of technology in the area	100	2.92	1.17
9 Absence of militant labour unions, and stable labour-management relations	100	2.99	1.27
10 Low likelihood of forming labour unions	100	3.06	1.29
11 Proximity of universities	100	2.60	1.04
12 Availability of professional employees	100	3.37	1.13
13 Possibilities of recruitment of researchers and engineers from research institutes	100	2.65	1.22
14 A low-crime area and safety of foreign residents	100	3.03	1.17
15 Low-cost plant site	100	3.27	1.18
16 Secure physical infrastructure	100	3.36	1.01
17 Secure information infrastructure	100	3.16	1.05
18 Accessibility to financial markets	100	2.59	1.07
19 American companies, which are parents of joint-ventures and/or alliances, operating in the area	100	2.29	1.23
20 Presence of Japanese competitors in the area	100	2.02	1.05
21 Presence of European and American competitors in the area	100	2.04	1.00

The motives for location choice in the United States by the responding Japanese companies are shown in Table 12.6. The measurement of importance of motives is estimated using a five-point Likert scale method (1: not at all, 2: very little, 3: neutral, 4: considerable, and 5: very important). The table shows that 'convenience of a physical distribution and traffic' (3.94) and 'secure physical infrastructure' (3.36) are regarded as most important. 'Close proximity to the consumer market' (3.38) and 'availability of professional employee' (3.37) are estimated as highly important. In general, Japanese companies gave priority to the logistic advantages and availability of human resources.[5]

On the other hand, according to the average estimation of importance, 'low likelihood of forming unions' (3.06) and 'absence of militant labour unions' (2.99) are estimated, if anything, close to being 'neutral'. 'Company's customer in Japan located here' (2.19), 'presence of Japanese competitors in the area' (2.02), and 'presence of European and American competitors in the area' (2.04) are less important.

These results, although interesting, merit further investigation. The calculations of standard deviations reveals that considerable variation exists among the respondents and a simple analysis of descriptive statistics does not provide a complete image of respondents. In order to explore the data further, therefore, factor and cluster analysis were employed to investigate 'the real image' of the location dynamics, and provide the answer to the question: 'For what reason has a Japanese multinational identified its particular location'?

Motives for location choice

The motives for the location choices of the twenty-one items were applied to factor analysis. Table 12.7 shows the result of the calculation and Table 12.8 lists the representative naming of the five factors. Five factors were extracted. These were, as shown in Table 12.8, knowledge-based location, labour union avoidance and low-cost location, relation-based location, procurement-based location and finally physical infrastructure. The total explanatory ability of the five factors amounted to 63.52 per cent, or almost two-thirds of the location choice behaviour of this sample of Japanese multinationals in the United States.

As a next step, the respondent companies were classified by applying cluster analysis. As a result of the cluster analysis, four company clusters were extracted.[6] To identify each cluster's distinctive feature, we examined

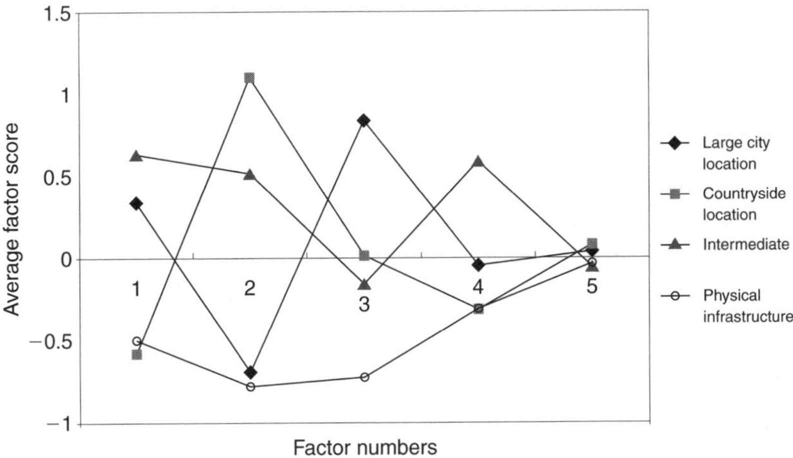

Figure 12.2 The relationship between management styles and location in 1999 sample of Japanese firms in the United States.

Table 12.7 Analysis of 1999 sample of Japanese firms in the US by factor loadings (five-factor solution)

Motives	*Component (factors)*				
Factor numbers	Factor 1	Factor 2	Factor 3	Factor 4	Factor 5
Eigenvalues	5.149	3.557	2.082	1.5	1.109
Percentages of variables	24.5	16.9	9.9	7.1	5.3
Cumulative percentages	24.5	41.5	51.4	58.5	63.8
Possibilities of recruitment of researchers and engineers from research institute	0.759	0.078	0.066	0.109	−0.056
High level of technology in the area	0.733	0.108	0.162	0.012	−0.033
Availability of professional employees	0.712	−0.108	−0.004	−0.031	0.276
Proximity of universities	0.678	0.238	0.002	0.067	−0.008
Secure information infrastructure	0.668	0.079	0.105	0.055	0.416
Accessibility to financial markets	0.573	−0.002	0.270	−0.039	0.155
Low likelihood of forming labour unions	0.131	0.928	−0.013	0.070	−0.008
Absence of militant labour unions, and stable labour-management relations	0.162	0.883	0.017	0.122	−0.024
Cheap labour cost	−0.036	0.712	−0.128	0.218	0.136
Low-cost plant site	0.093	0.575	0.000	0.173	0.354
Presence of Japanese competitors in the area	0.172	−0.063	0.823	−0.150	−0.017
Presence of European and American competitors in the area	0.154	−0.123	0.752	0.038	−0.024
Your company's customers in Japan	−0.029	0.007	0.617	0.070	0.093
Many Japanese companies are established in the area	0.171	0.222	0.612	−0.101	0.020
Ease of obtaining raw materials	0.042	0.052	0.000	0.844	0.004
Convenience of physical distribution and traffic	−0.028	0.205	−0.128	0.533	0.177
Ease of obtaining components that meet company quality standards	0.185	0.326	−0.029	0.516	0.138
Secure physical infrastructure	0.340	0.142	−0.017	0.246	0.645
Low-crime area and safety for foreign residents	0.482	0.259	0.100	0.173	0.327
Close proximity to the consumer market	−0.033	−0.114	0.214	−0.106	−0.160
American companies, which are partners of joint ventures and/or alliances, operate in the area	0.305	−0.123	0.343	−0.034	−0.175

Notes
1. Extraction method: Principal component analysis. 2. Rotation method: Varimax and Kaiser normalization. 3. Rotation converged in 6 iterations. 4. Shaded columns represent varimax factor loadings of more than 0.5.

Table 12.8 Factors affecting location choice of 1999 sample of Japanese firms in the US

Factor number	*Variable name*	*Constituent motives*	*Explanation ability (%)*
Factor 1	Knowledge-based location	Recruitment of researchers/ engineers High level technology area Availability of professionals Proximity of universities Information infrastructure Accessibility to financial markets	24.426
Factor 2	Labour union avoid and low-cost location	Low likelihood of forming unions Absence of militant unions Cheap labour cost Low-cost plant site	16.949
Factor 3	Relation-based location	Japanese competitors in the area European and American competitors Japanese customers located Many Japanese companies located	9.964
Factor 4	Procurement-based location	Obtaining raw materials Physical distribution/traffic Obtaining components that meet company quality standards	7.026
Factor 5	Physical infrastructure	Secure physical infrastructure	5.155

the cross-section analysis with five factors derived from factor analysis. Figure 12.2 shows the relation between five factors and four company clusters.

Cluster 1 can be named a 'large city' location. Twenty-three of the 88 responding companies which disclosed details about their management policies are included in this cluster. Seven subsidiaries (30.4 per cent of the cluster) were established by M&A and equity participation. Compared to the other clusters, the ratio of M&A and equity participation is the highest. When we look at the factor score of Cluster 1, 'knowledge-based,' 'relation-based,' and 'physical infrastructure' are regarded as important, while 'threat of militant labour unions' and 'labour cost' look unimportant. The states the respondent companies are located in are New York (8 companies, including one from New Jersey), California (4 companies), and Indiana (2 companies). The remaining residual 9 companies are located in various other states. Figure 12.3 shows the mapping of the subsidiary companies in Cluster 1.

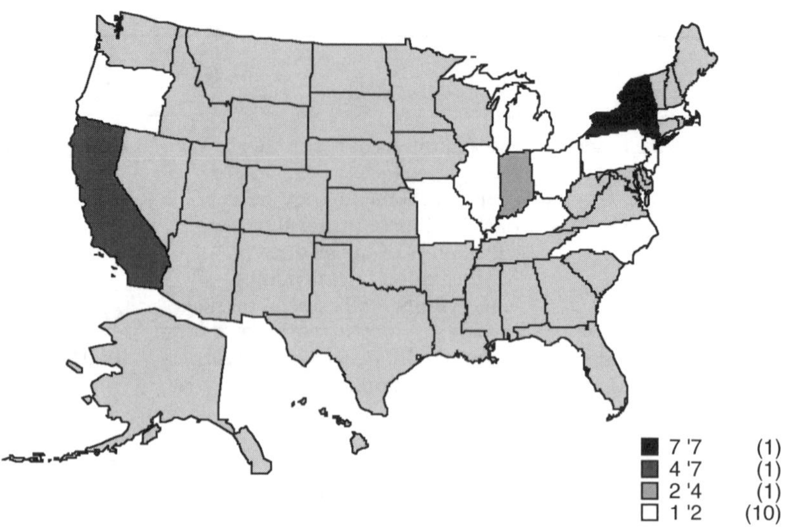

Figure 12.3 Mapping Japanese subsidiaries: large city location type.

Five of the eight companies currently located in New York state are classified in the service industry (communication, finance and insurance, other services). Ten of the sixteen manufacturing companies have research and development (R&D) functions and various management functions, such as production, sale, distribution, and public relations, etc., linked together in an elaborated value chain.

Cluster 2 can be named 'countryside' location. This cluster consists of nineteen companies. The feature of this cluster, by factor score, is the high concern for the evasion of militant labour union areas and the inclination towards a low labour cost site, although relation to other companies and convenience for supply are treated as 'important'. However, the importance and the concerns for knowledge infrastructure are very low. The ratio of M&A is also the lowest (15.8 per cent, 3 out of 19 companies) compared to other clusters. Location classification by states shows 3 companies located in Georgia, 3 in Ohio, 2 in Indiana, 2 in Kentucky, 2 in Texas, 2 in Virginia, and the residual 5 are located in various other states. The state distribution figure means that the Cluster 2 companies choose locations where 'low labour cost' and 'low unionization rate' is secured because 'right-to-work law' is implemented.[7] Figure 12.4 shows the distribution of the respondent companies in Cluster 2.

When we look at the location distribution, it is easy to comprehend the behaviour of Cluster 2 companies. They inhabit places where labour union activity is moderate and labour unions co-operate with the management, average labour cost is relatively cheap, and the acceptability of Japanese style management is expected to be better than in the Eastern

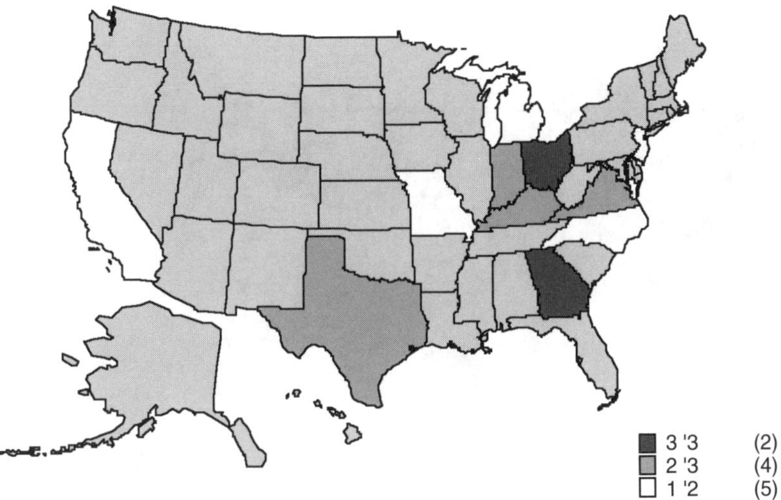

Figure 12.4 Mapping Japanese subsidiaries: countryside location type.

industrial districts. In Cluster 2, 18 of 19 companies belong to the manufacturing industry, but only 6 companies possess a research and development unit. Although 6 companies have a public relations function, but only one company has a financial unit. This cluster represents a typical 'transplant' that seeks a cheap labour cost site and submissive workers.[8]

Cluster 3 is positioned in-between Cluster 1 and Cluster 2 and can be called 'Intermediate' type. Twenty-three companies constitute this cluster. Cluster 3 represents a typical Japanese multinational's preferences: the knowledge infrastructure of the district is regarded as important, the availability of high quality parts and components from local suppliers is thought important, the tendency for avoidance of militant labour unions is clear, as is the preference for a low labour cost site. However, in Cluster 3, relations to other companies and physical infrastructure are seldom thought as important. The ratio of M&A is 17.4 per cent (4 among 23 respondents). Classifying the location by states, 5 companies are located respectively in California and Ohio, 4 in Texas, 2 in Illinois, and the residual 7 companies are located in various other states. Figure 12.5 shows the distribution pattern of Cluster 3. Twenty-one of the 23 companies in Cluster 3 are in the manufacturing industry and 13 companies have a research and development function. All but two of these firms have integrated R&D with other managerial functions such as production, sale, distribution, finance, and public relations.

Cluster 4 can be called 'physical infrastructure' orientation. It includes 23 companies. The features of this cluster by factor score are that the concerns for the knowledge infrastructure of the district, labour union's threat and

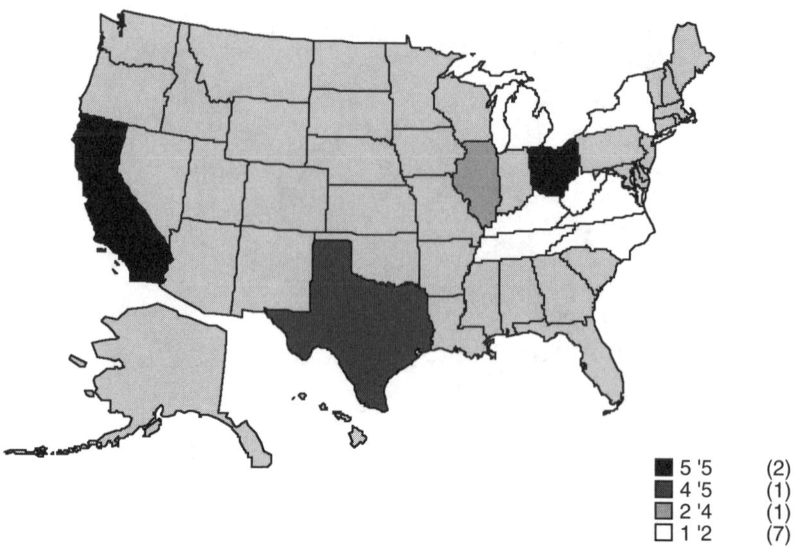

Figure 12.5 Mapping Japanese subsidiaries: intermediate type.

labour cost, and relations with other companies are very low. Only the merits of physical infrastructure are highly valued. The method of establishment by M&A is 18.2 per cent (4 among 23). When looking at the location by states, California is the preferred state locating 6 companies. The next preferred states are Illinois (3), Michigan (3), and Texas (2). The remaining companies are located in various other states. Figure 12.6 shows the distribution of Cluster 4 companies. Among the 23 companies, 15 belong to manufacturing. Of those 15 companies, 11 have R&D function and 9 of those 11 companies have integrated the R&D unit with other managerial functions, such as production, sales, distribution, finance, and public relations.

Location choice and management typology

Based on interview investigation with managers and executives of Japanese parent companies, and by using published data, a typology of the management features of the US subsidiaries of Japanese firms can be established.

Knowledge seekers: large city location

Many of the large city location type settled their management headquarters and/or sales office in the centre of large cities, such as New York. Those offices perform various services, such as sales agency for large-scale transport machinery, qualification and ranking evaluation for credit loans, entrusted trade-related business, advertising agency, sales representative for

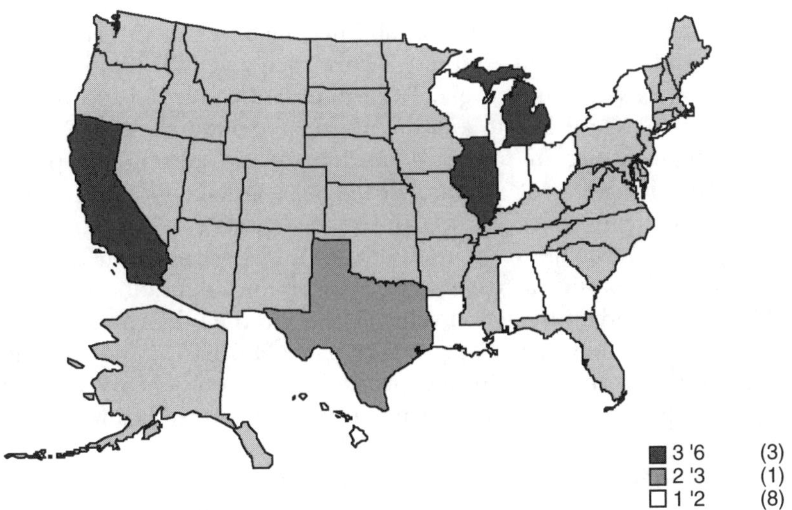

Figure 12.6 Mapping Japanese subsidiaries: physical infrastructure type.

high-tech apparatus, global end user service centre, and import business of special vehicles. Although such offices are relatively small in scale (ranging from 50 to 145 employees), they are mainly constituted with knowledge workers having high educational levels, and limited blue-collar employment. Accordingly, the concern for labour union activities and cheaper labour cost considerations are less important. Of the ten companies having a R&D function, 9 companies integrate the R&D unit with other managerial functions such as production, sales, distribution, finance and public relations. The size of manufacturing subsidiaries is broadly distributed from a maximum of 9,400 to a minimum 57 employees (average 667).

The companies classified as large city location usually belong to high-tech industries. They produce, for example, environmental hygiene apparatus, cellular phones, carbon shafts for golf clubs, precision measurement apparatus, electron beam irradiation equipment, special lamps, photo-sensitizers for copy machines, floppy disks and cartridges, and semiconductors. Moreover, in the genre of heavy and chemical industries, companies such as steel plate, special steel, large-sized engine, synthetic rubber, and paint, are included. In addition to the high-tech companies, there are two companies considered to be low-tech. One is a small-scale food oil maker (New York State, 125 employees), and the other is an automobile sheet making company (Michigan State, 600 employees).

The feature of large city location is that there are various kinds of service offices and high-tech industries, together with a small portion of low-tech industries. This profile is distinctive when compared with other types, especially the countryside location.

Introversion: countryside location

Many companies of this type have established factories in the rural districts in the Midwestern and Southern states, such as Ohio, Illinois, Kentucky, Virginia, Texas, and Georgia. The prominent feature of this type is that the companies are in the automobile related industries: 14 of the total 19 companies are in transport machinery and automobile parts. These include importers of automobile tyres (1 company), production and sales of joint pins (1), fork lifts and related parts (1), car parts (3), lubricating oil (1), switches for automobiles (1), wire-harnesses (1), safety glass for cars (1), plastic car parts (1), parts for car air-conditioners (1), wiper blades (1), and construction vehicles (1). On the other hand, other companies are in chemicals (3), printing plate (1), hard vinyl-chloride sheet (1), and silicone (1). In the processing industry, heavy electric apparatus machinery (1), copying machine (1), and laser beam printer company (1) are also included.

The managerial feature of this cluster is strong production orientation. Only 33 per cent (6 of 18, with the exception of one import trading company) are equipped with an R&D function, and even fewer companies integrate R&D with other managerial functions. This cluster represents a typical transplant company. The number of employees varies greatly, ranging from the maximum of 6500 to the minimum of 50, with the average as 695 employees.

It may safely be said that behind those automobile related industries, huge Japanese automobile companies will exist in the region. These Japanese automobile parts companies are locating in the neighbourhood of large assembly makers in accordance to demands for *lean production* and Just-In-Time (JIT) delivery schedules as applied in the United States (Abo 1994: 112–13). The Japanese automobile companies (assemblers) have a strong tendency to avoid the traditional industrial areas in the United States where old mass production culture is permeated with active and militant labour unions (Abo 1994: 121). In order to transfer the Japanese style production system and management of human resources, Japanese automobile companies choose rural sites for their assembly factories. Therefore, the Japanese parts industry will also have the same tendency as shown by the Japanese assemblers (Abo 1994; Shua 9 2000). The choice of countryside location is not a Japanese company's common characteristic, but the distinctive feature of Japanese automobile industry. We can easily understand this peculiarity when comparing the countryside location type to the intermediate type.

Typical Japanese reaction: intermediate type

It can be said that the feature of the intermediate type in a sense represents the average behaviour of the Japanese multinationals in the United

States. First, 21 of the 23 companies of this cluster are in the manufacturing industry, and only two companies are in the service sector. Fourteen companies of the 23 are concentrated in three major states: California (5), Ohio (5), and Texas (4). Various types of industries are currently located in California: clothes (1), audio equipment (1), electric devices (2), medical supplies and others (2). The companies located in Ohio belong to automobile industry; heat exchanger for cars (1), lighting apparatus for cars (1), sheet making (1), vibration protector rubber for cars (1), and automatic transmission (1). Half of the companies located in Texas are in automobile related industries: car air conditioners (1), the parts for car air conditioners (1), steel pipes for oil wells (1), and films (1). Two companies located in Illinois are also automobile related; transmission belts and steel codes for tyres. The companies currently located in other states are in various types of industries ranging from plastic parts to steel pipes.

This cluster is a mixture of two different characteristics: the automobile industry located in Ohio, Texas and Illinois and the other industries located in various states. In a sense, this cluster is a representative of the average Japanese company.

Logistics: physical infrastructure

Some of companies included in this cluster reflect the former import strategy of Japanese firms. Their central preoccupations are the availability of raw materials and the efficiency of physical infrastructure. When looking at the states where companies in this cluster are located, there are 6 in California, 3 in Illinois, 3 in Michigan, 2 in Texas, with the residual 8 companies located in various other states. California has various companies, ranging from a physical investigation machinery and pathology medical inspection equipment company to a fast food restaurant. Grain harvest machines, toiletries and kitchenware are located in Illinois. The three companies in Michigan are all automobile parts makers. Other companies located in various states belong to diverse industries, from chemical materials to aluminium alloys. In terms of the industry composition, the physical infrastructure is similar to the intermediate type.

Changing environment and strategic choices

The Japanese automobile industry carefully selected the location where unique Japanese production technologies and management know-how which constitute the core competence of the companies, could be accepted and transferred. Because of fear of militant labour unions, Japanese automobile companies kept away from traditional industrial districts and chose rural areas where local governments welcomed Japanese direct investment (Kenney and Florida 1992, 1993).

In the case of Kentucky, before Toyota opened its assembly line in 1986, only a small number of Japanese had lived in the state. However, Toyota's arrival was followed by a large number of Japanese parts makers (*keiretsu* subcontractors). The number of Japanese residents in Kentucky had reached nearly 10,000 by 1999. Especially the Midwest and Southern milieu were relatively flexible in co-operation with Japanese management and the local labour union leaders agreed to the single union system. As a result of this preference, many Japanese automobile related companies are located in the countryside.

Since Japanese automobile assemblers transplanted the technology of the lean production system, based on the closed-module architect, a number of Japanese *keiretsu* subcontractors were invited to the neighbourhood of the assembly sites. Consequently, the production networks by SMEs surrounding the Japanese assembly factories were organized. Since all of the technology and management know-how was introduced from the parent companies, they did not expect much from the local knowledge infrastructure and accumulation. They rather preferred virgin territories, which had not been influenced by mass production culture.[9] Other industries showed different patterns. For example, operating headquarters, sales representatives, corporate services, and high-tech industries preferred sites in or near large cities, where the accumulated knowledge and stock of professionals can be utilized. They show completely different behaviour when compared to those located in the countryside.

Moreover, in the intermediate type, which can be positioned as in-between the large city type and countryside type, the local knowledge infrastructure and the relationship with other companies is considered important. This type also places considerable attention on labour union activities and labour cost. In short, it is thought that the intermediate type represents the behaviour of the average Japanese multinational.

Finally, physical infrastructure types only consider the efficiency of a physical infrastructure as important and hardly show concern for other variables. This is the result of giving top priority to the convenience of a physical distribution when selecting a location.

Why do Japanese companies other than those in the automobile industry select various locations? In general, Japanese manufacturing companies had been oriented to the integral production in US markets in the 1980s. The North American Free Trade Agreement (NAFTA), signed in August 1992, required Japanese manufacturers to raise the ratio of local procurement of parts and materials in order to meet the requirements of the *local content* rules. To achieve more than 70 per cent of local content requests, Japanese manufacturing companies in the US redesigned their products quickly. However, it did not end only with changing centimetres to inches on product design drawings. To meet US standards, all product designs must be carried out in inches from the beginning. Consequently, many Japanese manufacturing firms organized design departments in the

United States, then parts and components were replaced with standard items that could be purchased in the US markets.[10] From such experience, electrical machinery and electronics progressed in the direction of open-architecture and utilized US standards, although they kept the integral feature of product design to an extent. Consequently, the management of those companies evolved to utilize the local network of knowledge and open-modules made in the United States.

Of course, Japanese companies other than in the assembly type industry, such as chemicals, medical supplies, food, and various services, opted for large city locations that utilized local knowledge networks from the beginning. In contrast, to meet local content requests in the early 1990s, the Japanese automobile industry chose instead to transplant the *keiretsu* system to the United States.

Conclusions

This chapter has examined the locational choices of Japanese multinationals in the United States. Following much recent research, it is argued that physical location remains a major essential for knowledge acquisition by firms. However, not all firms want to acquire knowledge from their locations. If a distinction is made between differential and integral management achetypes, it is suggested that the latter primarily sought to transfer its knowledge to sites in the United States which lacked a developed industrial infrastrucure and would accept their specific cultures and working practices.

The argument is developed on the basis of a questionnaire from four different types of firm identified on the basis of their locations. Those located in the countryside are inclined to regard technology transfers from the parent company as important, and they seldom consider utilizing local resources, especially knowledge networks and outsourcing.[11] This strategy has some negative outcomes. First, no advanced industries existed in their locations, and they had no chance to learn the technologies and management of competitors. Human resource management policies, such as application of the Equal Employment Opportunity rules, that had spread in urban areas of the United States by the mid-1980s, had not yet penetrated the Mid and Southern states at the time. Some of the local American managers, who were born and lived in the countryside, were not sympathetic to such affirmative action policies. When located in the countryside, employing conservative local managers and workers, Japanese companies learned slowly and partially about their operating environment.

Those located in large cities had an advantage since urban society provided the latest information and knowledge, and possessed abundant human networks of professionals and specialists. The North American headquarters located in a large city always monitored competitor strategies and benchmarked their latest management. Accordingly, the amount of information and accumulated knowledge between the headquarters and local factory site is significantly different.

Japanese companies located in the American countryside could not learn effectively about contemporary American management and society. This problem was compounded because conservative Japanese multinationals often applied idiosyncratic personnel policies. When expatriate managers returned from foreign assignments, they were sometimes rotated to domestic local factories or sales branches in order to dilute Western management habits and practices. As a result of the separation from international business activities, the knowledge and expertise of such former expatriates was not effectively utilized, and the parent company's executives were doomed to repeat the same mistakes.

In contrast, since large city and intermediate types make the maximum use of local knowledge accumulation and utilized networks of professionals, they had various study opportunities in the United States. They used American consultants in their US offices and subsidiaries. In order to appoint American managers and specialists, they had to adjust their Japanese personnel policies to the American style. They often learned from, and were supported by, consultants, legal, and accounting firms. When the Japanese chief executives from the US headquarters returned home, they used the same consulting firms to advise their Japanese parents. Large city dwellers and intermediate type firms engage in two-way communication systems: technology transfer from the Japanese parent organization, and channels of knowledge from American consulting firms. The latter are especially important for knowledge acquisition as the knowledge base of American management is formalized and depends heavily on explicit knowledge. Consequently, the most effective way to learn from American management is not through the learning-by-doing approach, but rather by learning from American consultant firms. As a result of double-loop learning, large companies in the city and intermediate types utilized American consultants and redesigned Japanese management in the late 1990s, then transformed themselves into global companies.[12]

The Japanese automobile companies and other companies in the countryside faithfully and eagerly transferred their core competencies into the United States, and avoided old industrial districts, but at the cost of learning from their host country. Unlike many foreign multinationals in the United States, they did not invest to acquire knowledge. Initially they appeared as the winners of Japanese management, as the huge new industrial complexes they built in the United States transformed the industrial landscape of that country. However, in the era of globalization they may yet be losers, as they have missed the opportunity to learn from the world's largest market and the centre of world innovation.

Notes

1 For instance, the composition of direct vendors of car parts and materials for Toyota Motor Manufacturing (Georgetown at Kentucky) in 1994 was as follows: local (US) suppliers were largest 65 per cent (153 firms), wholly-owned Japanese vendors were 17 per cent (41 firms), joint venture with US companies were 16 per cent (37 firms), and Toyota group companies were only 2 per cent (6 firms) (TMM US. Information Kit, 1995: 17; see also Kumagaya 1996: 150).

2 Interview with Toyota executive, 31 July 2000.

3 According to Kenney and Florida (1992: 26), engineers from a major Japanese automobile assembler came on-site to help set up production operation at 82 per cent of suppliers, and continue to visit to help with quality control or production problems at 86 per cent suppliers.

4 This response rate is similar to the previously reported effective reply percentage done by *Fortune Diversity Management Research* (*Fortune* 1999) of 11.4 per cent (137 companies).

5 According to Ulgado (1996: 12), Japanese multinationals significantly considered 'attitudes of local government', 'attitudes of local citizens', 'transportation service availability', and 'employee training incentives' to be more important when compared with American and German counterparts. German multinationals significantly considered 'level of unionization', 'labour turnover rates', and 'transportation service availability'.

6 There is no statistically significant difference (T test) in size (number of employees), and the establishment year between four clusters.

7 According to the Kenney and Florida's investigation (1992: 25), less than one-third of the production workers of Japanese car parts transplants have previous manufacturing experience, and only 19 per cent have ever been union members. Most workers, 83 per cent, live within a 30-mile commuting radius of the plant.

8 According to the investigation done by Kenney and Florida (1992: 25), of 232 Japanese transplant suppliers, 37 per cent are located in rural areas, 28 per cent are in small metropolitan communities with population under 25,000; 11.2 per cent in communities with populations between 25,000 and 50,000; and 7.3 per cent in communities with populations between 50,000 and 100,000. Moreover, a large majority of suppliers – 96 per cent – are non-unionized.

9 To supplement the weakness of the local knowledge-base, major Japanese automobile companies had organized the regional headquarters and R&D centre located in the metropolitan area, and soaked up information concerning competitors and advanced technologies. The knowledge management mechanisms of Japanese automobile firms in the North American region has still to be investigated.

10 By my interview records (from 30 September to 11 October 1992) on 'NAFTA and the Strategic Response by Japanese Multinational Corporations', (Kansai Productivity Centre, 1993). The corporations interviewed were: Import and Export Bank of Mexico, Nissan-Mexico, Sanyo Electric, Matsushita Electric Industry (North American Headquarters), WV-Canada, and Toyota Motor Manufacturing Canada (TMMC).

11 The typical case is Kikkoman's Wisconsin soy sauce factory located in the middle of farmland.

12 The successful Japanese CEOs who arrived at their position after 1997 tend to have a common character; they had assigned the top executive position in the foreign operation, mainly North American subsidiary and/or headquarters. They had experiences to appoint American consultants to build systems such

as human resources management, accounting and auditing, advertising and marketing, knowledge management by using information technologies (IT). When they were appointed to the top executive of Japanese parent organisations, they did not hesitate to appoint consultants from American consulting firms' Japanese branches.

References

Abo, T. (ed.) (1988) *Nippon Kigyo no America Genchi Seisan* (Local Production of Japanese Firms in the United States of America), Tokyo: Toyo Keizai Shinpou Sha.

Abo T. *et al.* (1991) *America ni Ikiru Nipponteki Seisan System* (Japanese Production System Applied in the United States), Tokyo: Toyo Keizai Shinpou Sha.

Abo, T. (1994) *Hybrid Factory: Japanese Production System in the United States,* Oxford: Oxford University Press.

Amin, A. (1993) 'The globalization of the economy: An erosion of regional network?', in G. Grabhar (ed.) *The Embedded Firms: On the Socioeconomics of Industrial Networks,* London: Routledge.

Amin, A. and Thrift, N. (1994) 'Living in the global', in A. Amin and N. Thrift (eds) *Globalization, Institution, and Regional Development in Europe,* Oxford: Oxford University Press.

Arimura, S. (2000) 'Diversity management and Japanese companies in the United States of America', Yamaguchi University, mimeo.

Brown, J.S. and Duguid, P. (1991) 'Organizational learning and communities-of-practice: Toward a unified view of working, learning and information', *Organization Science* 1: 40–57.

Cook, P. and Morgan, K. (1994) 'Growth region under duress: Renewal strategies in Baden Würtemberg and Emillia-Romagna', in A. Amin and N. Thrifts (eds) *Globalization, Institutions, and Regional Development in Europe,* Oxford: Oxford University Press.

Coughlin, C.C., Terza, V.J. and Arromdee, V. (1991) 'State characteristics and the location of foreign direct investment within the United States', *The Review of Economics and Statistics* 73, 4: 675–84.

Davenport, T.H. and Prusak, L. (1998) *Working Knowledge,* Boston, Mass: Harvard Business School Press.

Dunning, J.H. (1983) 'Changes in the level and structure of international production: The last one hundred years', in M. Casson (ed.) *The Growth of International Business,* London: George Allen and Unwin.

Dunning, J.H. (1988) *Explaining International Production,* London: Routledge.

—— (1991) 'The eclectic paradigm of international production: A personal perspective', in C.N. Pitelies and R. Sugden (eds) *The Nature of the Transnational Firm,* London: Routledge.

Dunning, J.H., Kogut, B. and Blomstrom, M. (1990) *Globalization of Firms and the Competitiveness of Nations,* Institution of Economic Research, Lund: Lund University Press.

Florida, R. and Kenney, M. (1991) 'Japanese foreign direct investment in the United States: the case of automotive transplants', in J. Morris (ed.) *Japanese and the Global Economy: Issue and Trends in the 1990s,* London: Routledge.

Friedman, J., Gerlowski, D.A. and Silberman, J. (1992) 'What attracts foreign multinationals corporations? Evidence from branch plant locations in the United States', *Journal of Regional Science* 32, 4: 403–19.

Fujimoto, T. (1997) *Seisan System no Sinkaron* (Evolutionary Theory of Production System), Tokyo: Yuhikaku.

—— (2000) 'Architecture to Nouryoku Kouchiku Kyousou' (Architecture and capability building competition), *Management Trend* 5, 2: 51–75.

Grabhar, G. (1993) 'The weakness of strong ties: the lock-in of regional development in the Ruhr area', in G. Grabhar (ed.) *The Embedded Firm: On the Socioeconomics of Industrial Networks*, London: Routledge.

Granovetter, M. (1985) 'Economic action and social structure: The problem of embeddedness', *American Journal of Sociology* 91, 3: 481–510.

Hamel, G. and Prahalad, C.K. (1994) *Competing For The Future*, Boston, Mass: Harvard Business School Press.

Head, K., Ries, J. and Swensǒn, D. (1995) 'Agglomeration benefits and location choice: Evidence from Japanese manufacturing investment in the United States', *Journal of International Economics* 38, 3–4: 223–38.

Herrigel, G.B. (1993) 'Power and the redefinition of industrial districts: Case of Baden Würtemberg', in G. Grabher (ed.) *The Embedded Firm*, London: Routledge.

JETRO (ed.) (1985) *Zaibei Nikkei Seizougyo Keiei no Jittai* (The Research for Japanese Manufacturing Industries in the United States), Tokyo: Nihon Boeki Shinko Kai.

Kenney, M. and Florida, R. (1992) 'The Japanese transplants: Production organization and regional development', *Journal of the American Planning Association* 58: 21–38.

—— (1993) *Beyond Mass Production – Japanese System and its Transfer to the US*, New York: Oxford University Press.

Klier, T.H. (1994) 'The impact of lean manufacturing on sourcing relationships', *Economic Perspectives* 18, 4: 8–19.

Kokuryo, J. (1999) *Open Architecture Senryaku* (Open Architecture Strategy), Tokyo: Diamond.

Kumagaya, F. (1996) *Nipponteki Seisan System in US* (Japanese Production System in the United States), JETRO.

Kumon, H., Kamiyama, K., Itagaki, H. and Kawamura, T. (1994) 'Industrial analysis by industry types', in T. Abo (ed.) *Hybrid Factory*, Oxford: Oxford University Press.

Mair, A.R., Florida, R. and Kenney, M. (1988) 'The new geography of automobile production: Japanese transplants in North America', *Economic Geography* 64: 352–85.

Moulaert, F. and Gallouj, C. (1993) 'The locational geography of advanced producer service firms', *The Service Industries Journal* 13, 2: 91–103.

Óhuallacháin, B. and Reid, N. (1996) 'Acquisition versus greenfield investment: The location and growth of Japanese manufactures in the United States', *Regional Studies* 31, 4: 403–16.

Okamoto, Y. (ed.) (2000) *Hokubei Nikkei Kigyou no Keiei* (Management of Japanese Multinationals in the US), Tokyo: Dobuncan.

Porter. M.E. (1998) *On Competition*, Boston, Mass: Harvard Business School Press.

Reid, N. (1990) 'Spatial patterns of Japanese investment in the US automobile industry', *Industrial Regional Journal* 21: 49–59.

Reid, N. (1991) 'Japanese direct investment in the United States manufacturing sector', in J. Morris (ed.) *Japanese and the Global Economy: Issues and Trends in the 1990s*, London: Routledge.

Rubenstain, J.M. (1991) 'The impact of Japanese investment in the United States', in C. Law (ed.) *Restructuring the Global Automobile Industry*, London: Routledge.

Shannon, D.P., Zeile, W.J. and Johnson, K.P. (1999) 'Regional patterns in the location of foreign-owned US manufacturing establishments', *Survey of Current Business* May: 8–25.

Shua, Y. (2000) 'Hokubei Chiiki ni okeru Sozai? Buhin Kyoukyu Gyousha tono Kankei' (Relationship with raw material and parts suppliers in North America), in Y. Okamoto (ed.) *Hokubei Nikkei Kigyou no Keiei* (Management of Japanese Multinationals in the US), Tokyo: Dobunian.

Takeda, Y. (2000) 'Kigyokan Torihiki Jyohoka no Hensen' (Transition of information-oriented inter-company transaction), mimeo.

Toyo, K. (ed.) (1999) 'Kaigai Kigyo shinshuta Soran (Fact and Figure of Japan's FDI) Toyo Keiza Shinpo Sha.

Ulgado, F.M. (1996) 'Location characteristics of manufacturing investments in the US: A comparison of American and foreign-based firms', *Management International Review* 36, 1: 7–26.

Ulrich, K. (1995) 'The role of product architecture in the manufacturing firms', *Research Policy* 24, 3: 419–40.

Wilkins, M. (1988) 'European and North American multinationals, 1870–1914: Comparisons and contracts', *Business History* 30, 1: 8–45.

Womack, J. and Jones, D. (1996) *Lean Thinking*, London: Simon & Schuster.

Womack, J., Jones, D. and Roos, D. (1990) *The Machine that Changed the World*, London: Macmillan.

Yasumuro, K. (2000) 'Transnational enterprises and the global linkages between local economies: A new perspective of eclectic paradigm', in *The Kobe University of Commerce 70th Anniversary Memorial Collection of Articles*, Kobe: Kobe University.

Index